Critical Theory

On (De)Coloniality: Curriculum Within and Beyond the West

Series Editor

João M. Paraskeva (*School of Education, University of Massachusetts Dartmouth, USA*)

VOLUME 4

The titles published in this series are listed at *brill.com/cwbw*

Critical Theory

Rituals, Pedagogies and Resistance

By

Peter McLaren

BRILL

LEIDEN | BOSTON

The Library of Congress Cataloging-in-Publication Data is available online at https://catalog.loc.gov

Typeface for the Latin, Greek, and Cyrillic scripts: "Brill". See and download: brill.com/brill-typeface.

ISSN 2666-3775
ISBN 978-90-04-50766-1 (paperback)
ISBN 978-90-04-50767-8 (hardback)
ISBN 978-90-04-50768-5 (e-book)

Copyright 2022 by Koninklijke Brill NV, Leiden, The Netherlands, except where stated otherwise. Koninklijke Brill NV incorporates the imprints Brill, Brill Nijhoff, Brill Hotei, Brill Schöningh, Brill Fink, Brill mentis, Vandenhoeck & Ruprecht, Böhlau and V&R unipress.
All rights reserved. No part of this publication may be reproduced, translated, stored in a retrieval system, or transmitted in any form or by any means, electronic, mechanical, photocopying, recording or otherwise, without prior written permission from the publisher. Requests for re-use and/or translations must be addressed to Koninklijke Brill NV via brill.com or copyright.com.

This book is printed on acid-free paper and produced in a sustainable manner.

To Wang Yan

Peter McLaren (photograph by Mia Funk, www.miafunk.com)

Contents

Notes on Original Publications XI

Series Editor's Introduction: 'At the Beginning It Was the Commodity': What Happened to Critical Theory? 1
   João M. Paraskeva
1   The Current Social Havoc 2
2   The Jouissance of a Highly Cultivated Neo-Gramscian 8
3   Critical Theory and the Struggle against Epistemological Fascism 12
4   Itinerant Curriculum Theory: The Decolonial Turn 18

1   Introduction: Challenges to a Post-Democracy America 35

2   The Ritual Dimensions of Resistance: Clowning and Symbolic Inversion 40
   1   Ritual 40
   2   Theories of Resistance 41
   3   Resistances as Rites of Transgression 43
   4   The Class Clown: Arbiter of Passive Resistance, Inversion, and Meta-Discourse 46
   5   Toward a New Conception of Resistance 48

3   On Ideology and Education: Critical Pedagogy and the Politics of Empowerment 54
   1   Sifting through the Remains 54
   2   Ideology and the Correspondence Theory of Truth: The Case for Multiple Subjectivities 55
   3   Ideology Essentialism, and the Contingency of the Social 59
   4   Science, Ideology and Context 61
   5   Ideology and the Reflex of Capital 64
   6   Radical Education and the Production of Meaning 68
   7   Ideology as Ritual Performance 72
   8   The Schooled Body: The Ritualized Regimentation of Desire and the Domestication of Subjectivity 75
   9   Ideology: A Matter of Truth or Praxis? 78
   10   Conclusion 79

4 Multiculturalism and the Postmodern Critique: Towards a Pedagogy of Resistance and Transformation 88

1. Social Justice under Siege 88
2. The Dilemma of Postmodern Critique and the Debate over Multiculturalism 90
3. Subaltern and Feminist Challenges to the Postmodern Critique 91
4. Ludic and Resistance Postmodernism 94
5. Multiculturalism and the Postmodern Critique 97
6. The Subject without Properties 98
7. Difference and the Politics of Signification 101
8. Always Totalize! 103
9. Critical Pedagogy: Teaching for a Hybrid Citizenry and Multicultural Solidarity 110
10. Resistance as 'la conciencia de la mestiza' 115

5 The Anthropological Roots of Pedagogy: The Teacher as Liminal Servant 121

1. Summary 121
2. Teacher, Theatres, and Rituals 123
3. The Resisting Body 126
4. The Liminal Servant 132

6 No Light, But Rather Darkness Visible: Language and the Politics of Criticism 142

7 Collisions with Otherness: "Traveling" Theory, Post-colonial Criticism, and the Politics of Ethnographic Practice – The Mission of the Wounded Ethnographer 150

1. Qualitative Research as a Discourse of Power 150
2. Shipwrecked against Infinity: Field Relations as Competing Discourses 154
3. Knowledge and the Body 155
4. Knowledge and Truth 157
5. Research as Advocacy 158
6. Conversations with Silence: The Discourse of the Other 160

8   On Dialectics and Human Decency: Education in the Dock   171
    1   A New Epistemological Alternative   187
    2   Comrade Jesus: Christian Communism Reborn?   193

9   Rethinking Critical Pedagogy and the Gramscian and Freirean
    Legacies: From Organic to Committed Intellectuals or Critical
    Pedagogy, Commitment, and Praxis   202
        Gustavo E. Fischman and Peter McLaren
    1   Points of Departure   202
    2   Points of Departure I: Ideology and Hegemony   203
    3   Points of Departure II: Resistance, Agency, and the Organic
        Intellectual   209
    4   Points of Departure III: From Organic to Committed
        Intellectuals   211
    5   Points of Departure IV: Critical Pedagogy, Commitment, and
        Praxis   214
    6   Points of Departure V: Committed Intellectuals and Critical
        Pedagogies   219

10 From Liberation to Salvation: Revolutionary Critical Pedagogy Meets
    Liberation Theology   227
        Peter McLaren and Petar Jandrić
    1   Introduction   227
    2   The Path to Liberation Theology   229
    3   Pedagogy of Insurrection   232
    4   The Idolatry of Money   236
    5   Jesus Was a Communist   240
    6   To Endure without Losing Tenderness   243
    7   The First Religious War of the 21st Century   247
    8   Towards a Global Ethics of Solidarity   252
    9   Between the Material and the Spiritual   255
    10 The Socialist Kingdom of God   259
    11 The God of the Rich and the God of the Poor   264

11 The Abode of Educational Production: An Interview with
    Peter McLaren   271
        Jordy Cummings

12 **Karl Marx, Digital Technology, and Liberation Theology** 291
   Peter McLaren and Petar Jandrić
   1 Karl Marx and Digital Technology 291
   2 Karl Marx and Liberation Theology 295
   3 Karl Marx and Christian Spirituality 301
   4 The Christian Morality of Dialectical Materialism 308

13 **Conclusion: The Future of Critical Pedagogy** 316

Notes on Original Publications

The following chapters in this book are reprinted:

Chapter 2: McLaren, P. L. (1985). The ritual dimensions of resistance: Clowning and symbolic inversion. *Journal of Education, 167*(2), 84–97. https://doi.org/10.1177/002205748516700208

Chapter 3: McLaren, P. L. (1988). On ideology and education: Critical pedagogy and the politics of empowerment. *Social Text, 19/20*, 153–185. https://doi.org/10.2307/466183

Chapter 4: McLaren, P. (1993). Multiculturalism and the postmodern critique: Towards a pedagogy of resistance and transformation. *Cultural Studies, 7*(1), 118–146. doi: 10.1080/09502389300490101

Chapter 5: McLaren, P. L. (1987). The anthropological roots of pedagogy: The teacher as liminal servant. *Anthropology and Humanism Quarterly, 12*(3–4), 75–85. https://doi.org/10.1525/ahu.1987.12.3-4.75

Chapter 6: McLaren, P. (1988). No light, but rather darkness visible: Language and the politics of criticism. *Curriculum Inquiry, 18*(3), 313–320. doi: 10.1080/03626784.1988.11076043

Chapter 7: McLaren, P. (1992). Collisions with otherness: "Travelling" theory, post-colonial criticism and the politics of ethnographic practice – the mission of the wounded ethnographer. *International Journal of Qualitative Studies in Education, 5*(1), 77–92. http://dx.doi.org/10.1080/0951839920050109

Chapter 8: McLaren, P. (2015). On dialectics and human decency: Education in the dock. *Open Review of Educational Research, 2*(1), 1–25. doi: 10.1080/23265507.2014.986187

Chapter 9: Fischman, G. E., & McLaren, P. (2005). Rethinking critical pedagogy and the Gramscian and Freirean legacies: From organic to committed intellectuals or critical pedagogy, commitment, and praxis. *Cultural Studies ↔ Critical Methodologies, 5*(4), 425–446. doi: 10.1177/1532708605279701

Chapter 10: McLaren, P., & Jandrić, P. (2017). From liberation to salvation: Revolutionary critical pedagogy meets liberation theology. *Policy Futures in Education*, *15*(5), 620–652. doi: 10.1177/1478210317695713

Chapter 11: Cummings, J. (2015). The abode of educational production: An interview with Peter McLaren. *Alternate Routes* [Special issue: *Neoliberalism and the degradation of education*], *26*, 354–375. http://www.alternateroutes.ca/index.php/ar/article/view/22326

Chapter 12: McLaren, P., & Jandrić, P. (2019). Karl Marx, digital technology, and liberation theology. *Beijing International Review of Education*, *1*(2–3), 544–569. https://doi.org/10.1163/25902539-00102013

Chapter 13: McLaren, P. (2019). The future of critical pedagogy. *Education Philosophy and Theory*, *52*(12), 1243–1248. https://doi.org/10.1080/00131857.2019.1686963

SERIES EDITOR'S INTRODUCTION

'At the Beginning It Was the Commodity'
What Happened to Critical Theory?

João M. Paraskeva

> I am a Marxist Catholic and that is how I would like to be remembered.
> PETER MCLAREN (2021)[1]

∴

This is not another book to add to the booty pile of critical theory and pedagogy. Its importance and uniqueness are related to a myriad of interweaved reasons, a few of which I would like to underline. To begin with, it is a volume that comprehensively grasps the rich intellectual journey of Peter McLaren – one of the most important figures swimming in what I have elsewhere called the 'radical critical educational curriculum river' (Paraskeva, 2021, 2014, 2011). While it is quite impossible to reduce his prolific and powerful matrix to a book, I would argue that this volume translates truthfully McLaren's – quasi-anarchist – unique intellectual jouissance.

Mining from a solid humanist Marxist grid – as this volume demonstrates – McLaren did not hesitate in roaming toward postmodern and poststructural rivers, exploring their potential, and experiencing their limitations. The epistemological silences within the 'post rivers' helped speed 'his return' to the Marxist riverbed. Quite disheartened with his foray into the 'post armada,' McLaren refines his Marxist humanist ark and didn't hesitate to excavate alternative ways to 'understand and transform' the capitalist phenomena realized though the need to pay attention to the world's endless epistemological diversity. In doing so, he reaches out to the anti-colonial and decolonial theoretical weapons to unpack the 'colonial power matrix' (Quijano, 1992; Mignolo, 2012), an exhausted eugenic matrix, as I was able to argue in another context (Paraskeva, 2021) and quite responsible for the current havoc we face as humanity.

1   The Current Social Havoc

> Capitalism is more than the sheet anchor of institutionalized avarice and greed, more than excrement splattered on the coat-tails of perfumed bankers and well-heeled speculators – it is a 'world-eater' with an insatiable appetite. (Peter McLaren, Chapter 8)

The second reason is precisely related to the context in which the volume is published. As I have observed elsewhere (Paraskeva, 2021), we live in a cruel era of the absurd. We are not just trivial readers and spectators of – but the real characters in – a meta play of the type so well penciled in Esslin's 'Theatre of the Absurd,' Artaud's 'Theatre of Cruelty,' or Camus's 'The Myth of Sisyphus.' We are not the readers of Camus's *The Plague*; we are enacting surrealistically and realistically 'the plague.' 'We' are 'the plague.' We are personages in the banality of a cruel absurdity, as Hannah Arendt (1963) would have probably framed it. Absurdism pervades our age. We have no shortage of examples.

Between 1900 and 1999, the United States used 4.5 million tons of cement. Between 2011 and 2013, China consumed 6.5 million tons of cement. That is, in just three years China spent 50% more on cement than United States consumed in the preceding century (Harvey, 2016). In summer 2017, in different states in the United States, for the first time in the history, a significant number of commercial planes were prevented from taking off due to high temperatures (between 123 and 125 degrees Fahrenheit), at a time when President Trump had walked away from the Paris Agreement. By August 2017 and 2018, humanity had already exhausted Earth's natural resources (Revesz, 2017). 'Extractivism' is driving the planet to an unsustainable limit (Walsh, 2018; De La Cadena & Blaser, 2018). We are about to experience an ecological bomb (Virilio, 2012).

In the United States last year, the figure related to the national debt was over $25 trillion. By September 2021 the figure is close to $29 trillion, yet poverty numbers are persistently skyrocketing – with over 16 million children living below the poverty line and only 14% of children born in poverty graduating from college within eight years of graduating high school. Also in the United States, historically racialized pedagogical forms (Selden, 1999) pave the way for the normalization of the 'school to prison pipeline' – quite responsible for the nation's high percentage of people incarcerated. A kid is 'forced out' of school every 41 seconds (Loury, 2008), most of them people of color and from oppressed communities. As Lois Wacquant (2009, p. XI) states, the neoliberal incarceration system in the United States is one of 'penal pornography punishing the poor.'

In 2007, the world sank in a great financial and economic crisis trashing many of the pillars of the capitalist economic matrix and unpacking the fallacy of one of its greatest assets, financial speculation (Paraskeva, 2021; Marazzi, 2011, p. 9). Student debt went out of control with figures beyond $1.3 trillion. Despite such an obscene reality, during the last two elections, the social-democratic independent Bernie Sanders, who was running under the Democratic Party ticket, and the only candidate who vocally and ferociously advocated for free college tuition, was mercilessly toasted within his very own liberal ranks. What is shocking is that, under a much smaller debt obligation, 'the European Union and IMF promptly tore Greece apart and impose[d] austerity measures on the millions of citizens of indebt[ed] countries' (Lazzarato, 2015, p. 65).

In Texas, one school district reinstated corporal punishment (Smith, 2017). Betsy DeVos, Donald Trump's secretary of education, sponsored federal funds to arm school employees and teachers. As we draft this piece, Texas governor Gregg Abbott has signed permit-free gun carrying legislation, as well as new legislation prohibiting abortions in Texas to only six weeks after conception.

Needless to mention that the havoc is not just related to the United States. In China, Deng Xiaoping and Xi Jinping's 'Beijing consensus' pumped a new socialist political economy with Chinese characteristics (Hung, 2011; Hui, 2011; Cheng & Ding, 2017), a 'new political management of the economy' (Touraine (1995, p. 10), which replicates a coloniality model of 'human nature and development' (Walsh & Mignolo, 2018). Dissent has been crushed as the recent violence in Hong Kong, and against religious and cultural minorities testifies. In Brazil, it looks like the masses have no memory. The country did not choose a right turn, but a U-turn. It seems that Jair Bolsonaro was elected president not despite of but precisely because of his overt attacks on minorities, LGBT communities, and people of color (Paraskeva, 2020).

In India, Modi's right turn unleashed 'a belligerent nationalism of the Hindu *rashtra* [nation]' (Vanaik, 2018, p. 45; Patnaik, 1993). Rightist and far-rightist groups understood accurately that the need was 'to listen to those voices without agreeing with them; those issues should be articulated without legitimizing them, and recognized without institutionalizing them' (Gudavarthy, 2018, p. 10). Modi's wave epitomizes how caste constitutes the lethal device in particular parts of the Global South and Global North as well. In Israel things are not that different; it remains probably the only nation in the world without fixed borders.

In Hungary and Poland, the scenario is also frightening. In the former, with Orbán's far-right democratic rise to power, 'cultural classifications have been increasingly biologized and moralized' (Tamás, 2013, p. 26); in the latter,

Duda's conservative-nationalist party re-escalated tribal nationalist impulses, unleashing authoritarian populist policies (Koczanowicz, 2016).

In Venezuela, Chávez's leadership and conquests (interrupted by his premature death) are collapsing with Maduro under constant attack both internally and externally. Venezuela looks like 'a toothless nation that beheads chickens' (Borgo, 2019, p. 27). In Madiba's South Africa xenophobia, inequality, and poverty are reaching alarming figures. South Africa's new political bourgeoisie suspended Mandela's promised revolution (Habib, 2013). Of all of the people in the world without access to safe water, almost 40% live in Africa; 589 million sub-Saharan Africans live without electricity and cook by burning whatever they can find (Paraskeva, 2020). While inequality is a social construction that was well in place before the empire (Muthu, 2003), under the yoke of neoliberal globalization inequality is much greater than inequality within any individual country (Bauman, 1997).

The United Kingdom 'bravely' decided on exiting the European Union. They are done with the 'other' and they have the privilege to 'Brexit.' Brexit uncovers racial impulses (Appadurai, 2018, p. 25). To add more ashes to the Western fire, in Catalonia, people clearly voted for independence from Spain, and, in Andalusia, the far-right party Vox, for the first time, grabbed twelve seats in parliament. Paris faced the Yellow Vests revolt, an inorganic movement that demands quasi everything, yet somehow in contradictory ways (Žižek, 2018). In Scotland, the referendum for independence is at the table with First Minister Nicola Sturgeon tenaciously constructing the right hour to hear the voice of the people.

One is witnessing the balkanization of the world (Rupnik, 2019), a 'good illustration of the impasse created by globalization through market mechanisms' (Amin, 2014, p. 7). It seems that both the right and the left of the political realm failed miserably. Chaos has been determined by a eugenic master desire (Mbembe, 2019), as we are witnessing the overt sordid open hunting season on 'the Other'; a fear that has been pushed beyond the infinite of reason, a 'fear of fear removing the subject from reality' (Badiou, 2008, p. 31). Yesterday 'Negro' and 'Jew' were the favored names of such 'Other.' The criminalization of immigrants, Mayo and Vittoria (2021, p. 13) argue,

> serves to fan the flames of racism and xenophobia. The marginalization of immigrants with no access to citizenship rights and social benefits, especially rejected asylum seekers, leads them to eke out a living at the very margins of society, in the 'underworld' if need be. There is a thriving crime organization among immigrant groups. This furthers the construction of irregular migrants as given to criminality, promiscuity and so forth

rather than being victims of a systemic oppressive and ultimately racist structure that encourages abuse of their vulnerability.

Today, 'Negroes and Jews are known by other names: Islam, the Muslim, the Arab, the foreigner, the immigrant, the refugee, the intruder, to mention only a few' (Mbembe, 2019, pp. 42–43). The 'evil new Other' has to be defeated by whatever means necessary. Such a hunting season unleashes not only a permanent political economy of war and fear but, also, awakens ferocious white supremacist nationalisms, 'stoking anti-immigrant sentiment [with a] fake-populist plutocratic agenda with a toxic brew of hyper-militarism, immigrant-bashing nativism, law-and-order racism, sexism, and anti-intellectualism' (Street, 2017, p. 3).

Fascism 'is becoming respectable,' as Max Horkheimer (1999, p. VI) would certainly put it. The fear of the 'Other' saturated the common view and fertilized the topology of the identic(al) (Han, 2018). The administration of fear has been naturally institutionalized, pushing '[s]tates to create policies for the orchestration and management of fear' (Virilio, 2012, p. 15). The massive waves of immigration, to escape war, poverty, and hunger, only demonstrate the failure of both Western-dominant and counter-dominant human rights (Santos, 2015) and force the reconfiguration of a concrete utopia. A multitude of human beings is announcing ahead of time that they have no intention of just knocking at the empire's door – they want in. They are done with modern Western Eurocentric neoliberal solidarity based on the eugenicism of 'how can I help you to help us?' (Han, 2018, p. 17). Their misery speaks volumes to the reality that, with the advent of globalization, the 'elimination of the distance did not generate more proximity, but destroy[ed] it' (Han, 2018, p. 15). Thus, immigration exposed 'the conditions faced by workers from other countries, which constitute a living proof that – in human terms – the "unified world" of globalization is a sham' (Badiou, 2008, p. 38). With the advent of right-wing impulses within neoliberal globalization's tenure, one witnesses the expulsion of the Other, as Han (2018) would put it. It looks like our time is a time out of joint (Derrida, 1994).

Gradually, absurdism and abnormality become domesticated. Today, we inhabit a 'theater of cruelty,' and a terrorist attack may still make the headlines of major newspapers but, sadly, barely constitutes a surprise. One faces an Areopagus of violence, that is, the return of the war machine as the riverbed of a meaningless social machine (Clastres, 2010). There 'is no innocence in a system which has no meaning' (Baudrillard, 2001, p. 52). Such theater blurred the borders between the spectacle and the symbolic, prompting a 'paralysis of meaning' (Baudrillard, 2001, p. 52). The force of such theater of cruelty comes precisely from its lack of logic, and that is why it is a winning theater (Baudrillard, 2001).

Democracy is thus being used to kill democracy (Wolf, 2007). The state of affairs is so chaotic that 'if the heart could think, it would have stopped' (Pessoa, 2002, p. 31). Dictatorships 'rely on the social neurotic' (Gil, 2009, p. 17). Welcome to the real colors of the epistemicide, which 'depends on the perpetuation of injustice, in a society that is incapable of fighting poverty, thus it fights the poor' (Galeano, 1997, p. 216). One is facing a 'profound historical crisis, a structural crisis of capital, which is a much more serious problem than the crisis of capitalism' (Mészáros, 1996, p. 57).

To worsen the chaotic state in which one is already in, in the fall of 2019, the world sees the emergence of COVID-19 in Wuhan, China. In early 2020, the World Health Organization declares urbe et orbi that the world is facing a pandemic of unimaginable proportions. We are, indeed, facing a paradoxical time. On the one hand,

> our current time is marked by huge developments and thespian changes, an era that is referred to as the electronic revolution of communications, information, genetics and the biotechnological. On the other hand, it is a time of disquieting regressions, a return of the social evils that appeared to have been or about to be overcome. (Santos, 2005, p. VII)

McLaren makes no euphemisms when he unpacks capitalism as the matrix underpinning such a paradox. He deserves to be quoted in length:

> Capitalism is more than the sheet anchor of institutionalized avarice and greed, more than excrement splattered on the coat-tails of perfumed bankers and well-heeled speculators – it is a 'world-eater' with an insatiable appetite. Capital has strapped us to the slaughter bench of history, from which we must pry ourselves free to continue our work of class and cultural struggle, creating working-class solidarity, an integral value system and internal class logic capable of countering the hegemony of the bourgeoisie, while at the same time increasing class consensus and popular support. Inherent in capitalist societies marked by perpetual class warfare and the capitalist mode of production is structural violence of a scale so staggering that it can only be conceived as structural genocide. [...] The hyperbolic rhetoric of the fascist imaginary spawned by the recent 2008 recession is likely to be especially acute in the churches and communities affiliated with conservative groups who want a return to the economic practices that were responsible for the very crisis they are now railing against, but who are now, of course, blaming it on bank bailouts, immigration and the deficit. Fascist ideology is not something

that burrows its way deep inside the structural unconscious of the United States from the outside, past the gatekeepers of our everyday psyche; it is a constitutive outgrowth of the logic of capital in crisis that can be symptomatically read through a neoliberal individualism enabled by a normative, value-free absolutism and a neofeudal/authoritarian pattern of social interaction. The United States has managed to conjure for itself – mainly through its military might and the broad spectacle of human slaughter made possible by powerful media apparatuses whose stock-in-trade includes portraying the United States as a democracy under siege by evil forces that are 'jealous' of its freedoms – a way to justify and sanctify their frustrations and hatreds, and reconstitute American exceptionalism amidst the rampant violence, prolonged social instability, drug abuse and breakdown of the US family. Of course, all of this works in concert with the thunderous call of Christian evangelicals to repent and heed God's prophets, and to welcome the fact that the United States has been anointed as the apotheosis of divine violence. Plain-spoken declarations abound, dripping with apocalyptic grandiosity, for dismantling the barriers of church and state, and creating a global Christian empire. This should not sound unusual for a country in which rule by violence was the inaugurating law, and which has, through the century, marked its citizenry indelibly in their interactions with others. (McLaren, Chapter 8)

If public education was already crumbling from the impact of more than five decades of aggressive neo-liberal conservative policies – so insightfully dissected in this volume – the pandemic came to deeply shake the entire architecture of public education, both in its form and in its content. Capitalism and democracy are blunt oxymorons and 'when democracy concludes that it is not compatible with this type of capitalism and decides to resist it, it may be too late. However, capitalism may have already concluded that democracy is not compatible with it' (Santos, 2018, p. 367). We are witnessing an era of 'random regression symptoms' (Geilselberger, 2017, p. 10). We are facing a collapse, which is not simply related with economic and cultural factors, but also shows 'a crisis of social imagination about the future' (Berardi, 2012, 2012, p. 8).

It is in this *quasi-Agamemnon* that emerges in Peter McLaren's *Critical Theory: Rituals, Pedagogy and Resistance* – which makes the volume timely; the volume speaks to the current challenges we face as humanity, not only situating them historically, but also securitizing the role that our educational institutions, curriculum matrixes and teacher education programs have played in such social havoc.

2   The Jouissance of a Highly Cultivated Neo-Gramscian

> Hegemony is not a form of unidirectional domination; it is not simply a system of ideological constraints imposed from above. [...] [It]gives birth to itself somewhere 'between' the contradictory axes of structural domination and the self-production of subordinate and oppositional groups.
> (Peter McLaren, Chapter 2)

A third reason related to the uniqueness and importance of *Critical Theory: Rituals, Pedagogy and Resistance* is that the volume talks directly to major critical works within and beyond the field of education and within and beyond the so-called critical orthodoxy. That is, the way McLaren unpacks the sagas triggered by a eugenic 'political economy' framing capitalist society and its 'ideological and repressive apparatuses,' the way he places our educational institutions at the very core of the consequences of the wild capitalist 'mode of production,' establishes powerful and permanent intertextuality, to rely on Julia Kristeva's approach, with seminal critical pieces – from Karl Marx's *Das Kapital* and Antonio Gramsci's *Prison Notebooks*, to more contemporary works such as, for example, Giovanni Arrighi's *The Long Twentieth Century* (2005), E. P. Thompson's *The Poverty of Theory* (1971), and Paulo Freire's *Pedagogy of the Oppressed* (1970).

Going through the various chapters of this carefully prepared volume about the prolific work of Peter McLaren – the most prominent Western Marxist pedagogue today – the reader will feel invited and encouraged to engage in a permanent dialogue within and beyond the rich critical intellectual platform. For example, how Giovanni Arrighi dissects the three great twentieth-century hegemonies and justifies such moments historically constitutes a truthful backdrop for the educational battles so well examined by McLaren throughout his rich theoretical journey – accurately exemplified in this volume. McLaren situates his critical analysis within what we might call Arrighi's (2005) third great hegemonic epoch, and in so doing helps a better understanding of the historical metamorphoses that precede such hegemonic period and how the hegemonic blocks are built and deconstructed historically.

Moreover, McLaren's gallantly glorified humanistic streak – quite visible in the chapters of this volume – somehow echoes the sharp altercation between E. P. Thompson and Louis Althusser. In *The Poverty of Theory*, Thompson noneuphemistically charges on Althusser and his followers, criticizing the structural reductionism framing Althusser's matrix; in doing so he advocates the need to embrace a more humanist Marxist tradition, seeking alternative paths on the left that definitively distance themselves from the barbarism perpetrated by Stalinist madness. As McLaren argues, within the Marxist orthodox views, 'the individual subject becomes simply a bearer of social roles (in an Althusserian sense) as they are mediated by economic structures or relations of production' (Chapter 3).

Exfoliating – as José Gil (1998) would say – McLaren's rich intellectual path and triangulating it with the above works helps us to understand even better, for example, not only why Marx choose the 'commodity' as a starting point for his brilliant analysis of the capitalist system – instead of 'exploitation,' 'inequality,' and 'oppression,' among others. Exploitation, he argues, not only alienates, but it also destroys:

> It forces people to work and live in dangerous workplace environments; pollutes the earth with toxic, life-threatening chemicals; and teaches people that indignity and poverty are natural and unchangeable situations. It naturalizes wage labor and the private accumulation of profit and legitimizes the social division of labor within capitalist societies. It subjects workers to the selling of their only commodity, their labor power, to survive. (Chapter 9)

McLaren helps one to understand not only why and how education, as an institutionalized republic of 'exploitation,' 'inequality,' 'segregation,' and 'oppression,' becomes a 'powerful commodity' – within an endless 'immense accumulation of commodities, an object outside us, a thing that by its properties satisfies human wants of some sort or another' (Marx, 1990) – under the third hegemonic phase of capitalism (Arrighi, 2005) and crucial for the current metamorphoses facing the capitalist mode of production, but also the importance of Gramsci's revolutionary matrix of power. In his words,

> Gramsci's theory of hegemony, which conceptualizes ideologies as more than the effluxes of the prevailing economic infrastructure, but rather as entities possessing a logic of their own [...] is often used by Marxist theorists to counter the insularity of the base/superstructural model. (Chapter 3)

Marxists decanted the 'commodity' historically, dissecting it in the light of historical materialism. In doing this, Marxists try to understand how and why the exchanges processes involving any given commodity provokes simultaneously wealth (from a minority) and poverty (from a majority), thus solidifying the division of labor and multiplying class disparity.

Echoing the works of close allies such as Henry A. Giroux (1981), Stanley Aronowitz (1973), Michael Apple (1979), Angela Davis (1971), bell hooks (1981),

Antonia Darder (2012) among others, McLaren opens up the 'base-superstructure' canon, placing ideology, hegemony, and power at the very core of class and cultural struggles for the US curriculum.

> The examination of resistance as a ritual process uncovers untapped possibilities for understanding how hegemony does its 'work' both through dominant structural (e.g. socio-economic) arrangements and through human agency. Hegemony is not a form of unidirectional domination; it is not simply a system of ideological constraints imposed from above. Rather, it partakes of the many outcomes resulting from (often antagonistic) negotiations between symbolic meanings – meanings which are continuously mediated by structural conditions, relationships of power, and the multifarious ways in which we rhythmically and gesturally engage the world.
>
> Hegemony gives birth to itself somewhere 'between' the contradictory axes of structural domination and the self-production of subordinate and oppositional groups. At the ideological level, it is embedded in a welter of contradictions.
>
> At the level of human agency, hegemony is both sustained and contested through our 'style' of engaging the world and the ways in which we ritualize our daily lives: our gestural embodiments, our rhythmical practices, and our lived forms of resistance.
>
> While hegemony is embedded in structural relations and the mediation of class and culture, it is sustained through the contradictions embodied not just in the way we think but in the way we attend to the world through our lived engagement with it. (Chapter 2)

Together with Fischman (Chapter 9), McLaren acknowledges the importance of Gramsci in the critical terrain. As they argue,

> Gramsci's [...] work can help us in understanding the class contradictions that structure the subjectivities and self-activity (agency) of oppressed classes with the understanding that hegemony does not take place in an indeterminate terrain. [...] In light of Gramsci's work, there is a need to understand the overdetermination of self-activity and subjective agency by larger structures of capitalist social relations within the global division of labor (especially in the context of a restructured labor demand). The concept of hegemony that is articulated by many post-Marxists is often recognized as a type of *trompe l'oeil* whereby forces of domination are willfully under-recognized as the structured equanimity of inevitability,

chance, or irreversible fate. Historically, variable structural determinants of action are either detached from cultural formations and social practices or flatly ignored. Built into a number of theories of hegemony is the notion of the reversibility of cultural formations within specified conjunctures, as if such articulatory practices were asocial or ahistorical or otherwise severed from the chains of class determination. (Chapter 9)

Antonio Gramsci's notion of 'hegemony' – 'transversal' in McLaren's rich intellectual journey – which irremediably destroys the concept of 'dual power' advanced by Trotsky, constitutes one of the powerful interfaces which McLaren's intellectuality establishes with one of his mentors, Paulo Freire. Freire's (1970) matrix of banking education – education as an 'act of depositing, in which the students are the depositories, and the teacher is the depositor. Instead of communicating, the teacher issues communiques and makes deposits which the students patiently receive, memorize, and repeat' – unpacks rather well education as a site of permanent battles over the power control – an issue so well examined in this volume.

Working within the Gramscian-Freirean powerful ranks, McLaren – who was closer to the ideas of Freire than many European Marxists – overtly unpacks education and pedagogy as sites of endless diffused forms of power – thus distancing himself from a reductive *Althusserian* approach. His encounters with Freire helped him to refine an oppositional, counterhegemonic project that was thoroughly humanistic. Echoing Freire, he dissects the pedagogical praxis as a permanent cultural battle to gain hegemonic control over common sense.

> Cognizant of the shamanic mission, the teacher as liminal servant seeks to free the body and the mind from the hegemony of the everyday and to transform pedagogy into holy praxis in which both teacher and students are united in the sacred communitas of knowing.
>
> Classroom culture is not a disembodied homogeneous entity but is discontinuous, murky, and provocative of contestation and conflict. It is a collectivity composed of contests between class, cultural, and symbolic relations. It is, furthermore, a symbolic arena where students and teachers both resist and accommodate various ritual performances and symbolic meanings, and where symbols have both centripetal and centrifugal pulls. Classrooms are therefore more than instructional sites; they constitute cultural arenas in which a heterogeneity of ideological and social forms struggle for dominance. As a contested terrain of competing discourses, classrooms often repeat on cultural levels the fundamental conflicts within the larger society. (McLaren, Chapter 5)

The Gramscian-Freirean axis constitutes McLaren's powerful resource to challenge education as a commodity and the responsibility of our higher education institutions in perpetuating such a saga. He states:

> Impecunious students are taught to be dedicated to the hive (as indentured servants as a result of soaring tuition fees), which is conditioned by the pathogenic pressures of profit-making. Within the hive, the capitalist unconscious turns murderously upon what is left of the Enlightenment as the irresolutely corporate conditions under which knowledge is produced reduce the products of the intellect to inert commodities. Higher education offers mainly on-the-cheap analyses of how capitalism impacts the production of knowledge and fails, in the main, to survey ways of creating an alternative social universe unburdened by value formation, and, in the end, offers us little more than a vision of a discount-store democracy. In making capitalism aprioristic to civilized societies, corporate education has replaced stakeholders with shareholders and has become the unthinkable extremity towards which education is propelled under the auspices of the cash nexus – propelled by a hunger for profit as unfillable as a black hole that would extinguish use value if allowed to run its course. (Chapter 8)

While the concepts of ideology, hegemony, and power were also profoundly explored by critical scholars such as Henry A. Giroux, Roger Simon, Stanley Aronowitz, and Michael Apple, I would underline that Peter McLaren's intellectual journey – between the critical and the post – helps one unpack differently and uniquely the hegemonic and counterhegemonic wrangles within the struggle for US education and its curriculum, and the various socially eugenic constructed needs to transform education into a commodity. McLaren's gravitation toward the post platform, with clear incursions in postmodernism and postmodern territories, before resituating himself within the powerful humanistic Marxist platform, makes his approach unique. Justifiably, he is considered in many constituencies as one of the most prominent male neo-Gramscian Western pedagogues.

3 Critical Theory and the Struggle against Epistemological Fascism

> This ego cogito [I think therefore I am] […] arose out of the historical and epistemic conditions of possibility developed through the ego conquiro ('I conquer, therefore I am'), and the link between the two is the ego extermino ('I exterminate you, therefore I am'). (Peter McLaren, Chapter 8)

A fourth reason is related to the state of the critical hemisphere. McLaren's volume constitutes a healthy coercion to question what happened with the critical path. For the vast majority, it seems that the golden age of critical theory, as Eagleton (2003) would put it, is passing. Today, Honneth (2009) states, there is an 'atmosphere of an outdated and antiquated, of the irretrivably lost, which surrounds the grand historical and philosophical ideas of critical theory, ideas for which there no longer seems to be any kind of resonance within the experience of the accelarating present' (p. 19). The younger generation 'carries on the work of social criticism without having much more than a nostalgic memory of the heroic years of Western Marxism' (Honneth, 2009, p. 19). Why?

How come a supradisciplinary 'theory of society against domination in all of its forms' (Held, 1980, p. 35) that challenges the false notion of detached science and runs 'counter to prevailing habits of thought' (Horkheimer, 1999, p. 218) not only has been incapable of assuming a hegemonic position but also in so many parts of the world has been struggling to make a significant footprint or any footprint at all? Santos's (1999) approach challenges the field with another powerful question: *Why is it so difficult to build a critical theory?* In his words, 'in a world where there is so much to criticize, why has it become so difficult to produce a critical theory?' (Santos, 1999, p. 197). To complexify the argument, 'is another politics of the world possible, a politics that no longer necessarily rests upon difference or alterity but instead on a certain idea of kindred and the in-common?' (Mbembe, 2019, p. 40). If so, what would be the role of critical theory? Is it possible that critical approaches faces the same healthy plague of philosophy, that is, being fundamentally and irremediably a praxis of criticism without creation, as Deleuze and Guattari (1994) would put it? I argue that most of the crucial reasons that the critical theoretical movement felt and continues to experience difficulties in imposing itself as dominant – a stark paradox, especially on a planet that raises a white flag against human irrationality – lies also in the critical theoretical terrain itself and not just in the neoconservative, neoliberal triumphalist bestride.

Critical theory, among several issues, erroneously, perceived 'society as a totality and, as such, proposes a total alternative to the society that exists' (Santos, 1999, p. 201). Futhermore, 'there is no single principle of social transformation, and even those who continue to believe in a socialist future see it as a possible future in competition with alternative futures' (Santos, 1999, p. 202). In Santos (1999, p. 202) terms,

> there are no unique historical agents or a unique form of domination; there are multiple faces of domination and oppression and many of them have been irresponsibly neglected by modern critical theory, such as patriarchal domination. Since the faces of domination are manifold, the resistances and the agents that lead it are manifold.

In this context, in the absence of a single principle, Santos (1999, p. 203) argues, 'it is not possible to bring together all resistances and agencies under a common grand theory.' Thus, and echoing Santos's (1999, p. 203) reasoning is 'more than a common theory, what we need is a translation theory that makes the different struggles mutually intelligible and allows collective actors to talk about the oppressions they resist and the aspirations they animate' (Santos, 1999, p. 203).

Such translation theory will help address a crucial weakness within the critical platform propelled by the first generation of *das Institut* intellectuals, one that errouneously 'remained constantly closed in the face of all attempts to consider the historical process other than from the point of view of the development of social labor' (Honneth, 1987, p. 357). This is a fundamental theoretical deficit within the interdisciplinary theory of society advocated by the critical armada. In fact, 'because no other type of social action is conceded along side of social labour, intellectuals such as Horkheimer can only take the instrumental forms of social practice systematically into account on the level of their theory of society' (Honneth, 1987, p. 357); hence, they 'lose sight of that dimension of everyday practice in which socialized subjects generate and creatively develop common action-orientations in a communicative manner' (Honneth, 1987, p. 357).

The need for just respect for epistemological diversity is not minimized by McLaren at all. Walking Freire's chessboard, McLaren reaches out to anticolonial and decolonial intellectuals advocating that 'that dialogue necessarily brings forth the epistemologies grounded in particular social positions' (Chapter 8). He is quite sentient of the abyssal nature (Santos, 2014) of modern Western thinking in which critical theories operate thus, subscribing to Grosfoguel's (2013) claim that 'the historical conditions that have brought us to a place of Western domination are linked to "undialogic" social relations' (Chapter 8).

That reality, the crude mundane everyday practice, is flooded with examples 'that would push us to critically question ourselves about the moral nature and quality of our societies, and to seek for theoretical alternatives based on the answers that we urgently need to face such sagas' (Santos, 1999, p. 199). In this context, that decolonial thinkers have strongly and forcefully denounced Western Eurocentric modernity in its dominant and specific counterdominant forms – such as critial theory – as tout court inconsequential to address global and local needs (Santos, 1999, 2014; Paraskeva, 2014, 2016a, 2016b; Grosfoguel, 2010, 2011; Maldonado-Torres, 2003, 2008; Walsh, 2018).

Despite such a paradoxical alley, and after a concise description of our current social sagas, such a reality should 'cause us enough discomfort or indignation to compel us to question ourselves critically about the nature and moral quality of our society and to seek alternatives that are theoretically based on the answers we give to such interrogations' (Santos, 1999, p. 199). Odd as it might be, Santos (1999) states, it is not easy to edify such theoretical alternatives (p. 200). Marxist and neo-Marxist critical approaches have multiplied in theoretical attempts to better analyze the most crucial social issues. Today, the impact of 'structuralist, existentialist, psychoanalytical, phenomenological approaches that attempt to offer the best analyses of dynamics such as class, conflict, elite, alienation, domination, exploration, racism, sexism, dependence, world system, liberation theology' (Santos, 1999, p. 200) are undeniable and constitute powerful terrains in which social theorists work quite hard to understand and transform reality.

> The move towards the post-critical, poststructural, and postmodern terrain – one that McLaren obstinately and insightfully led is the past – which led to irreparable fractures within the most orthodox critical crux, is the unmistakable sign of a critical crisis within the critical terrain, given the absence of responses to the social problems, a critical framework that has become bogged down in the swamp of a Eurocentric modernity of which it is part of, and, from which, despite its achievements – and there were and are many – it has dangerously built up false promises, generating expectations. (Paraskeva, 2021, p. x)

The towering failed promises of modernity (Eagleton, 2013; Jameson, 2016) – i.e. ,'equality, freedom, peace and domination of nature' (Santos, 1999, pp. 198–199) – triggered the great regeession current societies are facing. Adding to this, Santos (1999) claims, that hunger and poverty have reached alarming figures compared with any preceding centuries. In fact, he adds, the 'violations of human rights in countries living formally in peace and democracy take on overwhelming proportions' (Santos, 1999, p. 199). To make things even worse,

> after the fall of the Berlin Wall and the end of the Cold War, the peace that many thought ultimately possible became a cruel mirage. The promise of the domination of nature was fulfilled in a perverse way in the form of destruction of nature and ecological crisis. (Santos, 1999, p. 199)

Irrespective of palpable noteworthy efforts and accomplishments, it is erroneous to think that 'after all it remains as easy or as possible to produce critical social theory as it has been before' (Santos, 1999, p. 200). Furthermore, firstly, 'many of these concepts no longer have the centrality they once enjoyed or were internally so reworked and nuanced that they lost much of their critical strength' (Santos, 1999, p. 200). Secondly, he (1999, p. 200) adds that 'conventional sociology, both in its positivist and antipolitical aspects, managed to pass as a remedy for the crisis of sociology the critique of critical sociology.' While in the case of positivist sociology, such a critique was based 'on the idea that the methodological rigor and social utility of sociology presuppose that it concentrates on the analysis of what exists and not on the alternatives to what exists' (Santos, 1999, p. 200). The truth of the matter is that such criticism in the case of antipositivist sociology was based 'on the idea that the social scientist cannot impose his normative preferences for lacking a privileged point of view to do so' (Santos, 1999, p. 200).

Sentient of the limitations and contradictions within the very core of the critical platform, McLaren is open to a 'nonderivative' approach (Santos, 2018) that challenges, among other aspects, postcelebratory multicultural forms and places such limitations and contradictions right at the eugenic genesis of the 'colonial power matrix' (Quijano, 1992; Mignolo, 2012) – the agora of the 'ego cogito.' The 'ego cogito' (I think therefore I am), he states, 'did not suddenly drop from the sky; it arose out of the historical and epistemic conditions of possibility developed through the *ego conquiro* ("I conquer, therefore I am"), and the link between the two is the *ego extermino* ("I exterminate you, therefore I am")' (Chapter 8). In doing so, and along with Aníbal Quijano, Enrique Dussel, Ramón Grosfoguel, and other decolonial intellectuals, McLaren frames modernity and 'el padrón colonial del poder' (the colonial pattern of power) (Quijano, 1992) as epistemicidal and the historical maternity of a eugenic imperial being, thus echoing the epistemicidal nature of our education and curriculum structure and the importance of Itinerant Curriculum Theory (ICT).

> Grosfoguel and Dussel maintain that the *ego conquiro* is the foundation of the 'Imperial Being', which began with European colonial expansion in 1492, when white men began to think of themselves as the center of the world because they had conquered the world. The *ego extermino* is the logic of genocide/epistemicide that mediates the 'I conquer' with the epistemic racism/sexism of the 'I think' as the new foundation of knowledge in the modern/colonial world. More specifically, the *ego extermino* can be situated in the four genocides/epistemicides of the sixteenth century, which were carried out.

Without following in maniqueistic temptations – everything Eurocentric is bad by definition – McLaren (Chapter 8) pays attention to the need for alternative ways to think and do critical theory alternatively (Santos, 2014) toward a world we all wish to see (Amin, 2008), a world with *buen viver* as unconditional right, that requires that individuals, communities, peoples and nations are in actual possession of their rights and exercise their responsibilities in the context of interculturalism, respect for diversity and of harmonious coexistence with nature.

> *Buen Vivir* is not geared toward 'having more' and does not see accumulation and growth, but rather a state of equilibrium as its goal. Its reference to the indigenous world view is also central: its starting point is not progress or growth as a linear model of thinking, but the attainment and reproduction of the equilibrium state of *Sumak Kausay*. (Fatheuer, 2011, p. 16, quoted in McLaren, Chapter 8)

Exhibiting, in this particular, a refined *Althusserian* take visible in 'Pour Marx,' McLaren adamantly situates the future of the radical critical river at the very core of the capitalist system – thus placing capitalism as the 'conduit.' The future of the radical critical river, he argues,

> can be seen on the streets, on the picket lines, among young and old alike working to save communities assaulted by corruption and neglect and striving amidst great odds to create sanctuary cities for immigrants under assault by the Trump administration's group of fanatical and ruthless aides-de-camp and adjutants, and his Freikorps group of U.S. Immigration and Customs Enforcement agents. And lest we forget, the future of critical pedagogy can also be found in cramped university offices jammed with metal desks and cheap Office Depot swivel chairs, where lecturers, sometimes working as adjuncts and forced to survive on food stamps, write their articles and books and heat up the conversations in seminar rooms, which in turn get reinvented, reappropriated and repurposed by teacher educators, and then teachers, in classrooms across the country and this helps to fuel the process of *conscientização* (conscientization) among students. (Chapter 13)

Following Althusser's (2005) impulses, McLaren, perceives *Das Kapital* as 'an ethical theory' that unpacks the root of a classed, raced and gendered social system – i.e., capitalism – pillared in segregation, inequality, and slavery dynamics. At the core of such roots relies on the capitalist modes and conditions of production.

McLaren's humanistic Marxist dialogue with anticolonial and decolonial perspectives shows also the possibility of the critical platform to coengage in a just epistemological platform that reflects accurately the world epistemological diversity and difference. In doing so, McLaren shows that an alternative way – within a plurality of alternative ways – to edify an alternative radical critical river is possible, one that dismantles the abyssal nature that germinates from the 'ego-conquer' coloniality matrix toward a nonabyssal platform. This volume thus echoes Kellner's (1989, p. 2) statement. The reader is not confronted with 'just another book on critical theory. It is in fact a volume that constitutes a powerful attempt to do critical theory,' although from a nonderivative river through a radical copresence (Santos, 2019). Such an attempt takes us to a final reason related to the uniqueness and importance of this volume for the current state of the curriculum field, and it is related to the need to deterritorialized curriculum theory. In this sense, McLaren's critical intellectual matrix – accurately exhibited in this volume – constitutes a vivid testimonial of the importance of ICT as the best 'radical co-presence approach' (Santos, 2019), a powerful 'non-derivative platform' (Santos, 2019), one that respects and foster epistemological diversity and difference.

4   Itinerant Curriculum Theory: The Decolonial Turn

> [W]e must cease to attribute to certain groups 'mythical consciousness' while we reserve 'historical consciousness' for ourselves. (Peter McLaren, Chapter 7)

The field of curriculum studies is theoretically shattered and profoundly disputed to such an extent that disputes have become an endemic part of the field's DNA. Such quarrels, on some occasions, have been intellectually sanguinary. Sometimes the field appears to be an estuary of ideological debris upon which new cultural battles will be fought. What/whose knowledge is of most worth, for whom, as well as the way such knowledge has been produced, packaged, legitimized, taught, and evaluated have all always been sites of open ideological carnage among different groups – dominant and counterdominant – aiming to conceptualize and perpetuate a specific power matrix. The struggle for curriculum in the United States was always a struggle for the ideological foundation of its society. As a social construct, curriculum was always both a starting and arriving point of acute political battles, imposing itself as one of the most refined mechanisms of economic, cultural, and political segregation in capitalist societies. The nexus, or the lack thereof, of curriculum and society colonizes the field's theory and development.

The curriculum field, as we know it, is a eugenic 'agora' perpetrated by a Western Eurocentric power matrix that takes no prisoners. Blinded by the cult of positivism as the 'only' pedagogical scientific power, curriculum was always a beacon of epistemological cleansing and witnessed countless crucial critical transformative projects championed by counterdominant groups and individuals, only to succumb, despite certain noteworthy achievements, in the face of the ever-demanding challenges of a threatening capitalist society. As such, curriculum is epistemicide. An epistemological field of blindness supported by a specific growth pattern of knowledge and science that simultaneously fertilizes noisy silences and shameful absences framed by traditional power and interest groups. Such groups have been facing severe challenges from a myriad of counterdominant movements and intellectuals fighting for a more just, equal, relevant curriculum, one that could promote a more democratic society. However, while counterdominant groups – especially those working from and within radical and critical platforms – were able to score some major victories by challenging some conservative curriculum reforms, the truth of the matter is that such counterhegemonic perspectives ended up being as functionalist as the functionalism they criticized, and thus attempted to smash the hegemonic curriculum from traditional dominant positions. To be more precise, counterhegemonic traditions with radical and critical impulses fail to understand the need to expand their epistemological latitude within and beyond the Western Eurocentric epistemological terrain. The results of such distraction were and are devastating: 'conscientized' epistemicide and the production of more and more invisibilities in the richness and diversity of knowledges.

The Brill book series *On (De)Coloniality: Curriculum Within and Beyond the West* is a beacon in the struggle against epistemicide and the colonialities of being, power, and knowledge. It attempts to bring to the fore an analysis that focuses on non-Western/-Eurocentric epistemological frameworks. In a world that still struggles to see its own overt epistemological diversity, *On (De)Coloniality Curriculum Within and Beyond the West* is an open space in which to challenge epistemological fascism. It encourages curriculum scholars to engage in dialogues about non-Western/-Eurocentric epistemologies within and beyond the Western Eurocentric platform. We invite 'complicated conversations' that dig into new avenues such as those of Itinerant Curriculum Theory (ICT), and, in so doing, introduce a new language that will take us to alternative levels of articulation and rearticulation of meanings, through endless and spaceless processes of coding, decoding, recoding, and 'encoding.'

As I have explained elsewhere (Paraskeva, 2011, 2014, 2016a, 2016b), ICT did and does try to say something to the field. It posits new terrains and theoretical situations. ICT participates in a complicated conversation (see Trueit, 2003; Pinar, 2003) – one that cannot bend under the yoke of Western academicism – challenging Western curriculum epistemicides (Paraskeva, 2017) and alerting us to the need to respect and incorporate non-Western epistemes. William Pinar (2012, 2013) acknowledges the influential synopticality of ICT in his recent *Curriculum Studies in the United States*. He states:

> There are other discourses influential now, sustainability perhaps primary among them. Arts-based research is hardly peripheral. [...] One sign is the synoptic text composed by João M. Paraskeva. Hybridity is the order of the day. Pertinent to the discussion is that even Paraskeva's determination to contain in one 'critical river' the multiple currents of understanding curriculum politically floods its banks; he endorses an 'itinerant curriculum theory' that asserts a 'deliberate disrespect of the canon' (2011, p. 184). In Paraskeva's proclamation, this 'river' has gone 'south' (2011, p. 186). That South is Latin America, where we can avoid 'any kind of Eurocentrism' (2011, p. 186) while not 'romanticizing indigenous knowledge' (2011, p. 187). Addressing issues [such as hegemony, ideology, power, social emancipation, class, race, and gender] implies a new thinking, a new theory [...] an itinerant curriculum theory. (Pinar, 2013, p. 64)

Although Pinar's reading of ICT is crucial, I would clarify (maybe complexify) that 'the' South is not just Latin America. Again, Santos is vital here:

> The South is metaphorically conceived as a field of epistemic challenges, which try to address and repair the damages and negative impacts historically created by capitalism in its colonial relation with the world. Such a conception of the South overlaps the geographical South, the group of nations and regions in the world that were subjugated to European colonialism and that, with the exception of Australia and New Zealand, never achieved levels of economic development similar to the Global North (i.e. Europe and the United States of America). (Santos, 2009, pp. 12–13)

Thus, we 'designate the epistemological diversity of the world by South epistemologies' (Santos, 2009, p. 12). In this way, ICT addresses Santos's (2006) claim about the need for a new critical theory, a new emancipatory praxis (p. XI). As he (2006) states, 'contrary to their predecessors, [such] theory and practices must start from the premise that the epistemological diversity of the world is immense, as immense as its cultural diversity and that the recognition of such diversity must be at the core of global resistance against capitalism and of alternative forms of sociability' (p. XI).

ICT is an unblemished claim against dominant multiculturalist forms that are 'Eurocentric, a prime expression of the cultural logic of national or global capitalism, descriptive, apolitical, suppressing power relations, exploitation, inequality and exclusion' (Santos, 2007a, pp. XXIII–XXIV), which have been legitimizing a monoculture of scientific knowledge that needs to be defeated and replaced by an ecology of knowledges (Santos, 2014). ICT challenges the coloniality of power and being (cf. Quijano, 2000; Mignolo, 2012; Grosfoguel, 2007); it is sentient that the 'politics of cultural diversity and mutual intelligibility calls for a complex procedure of reciprocal and horizontal translation rather than a general theory' (Santos, 2007a, p. XXVI). ICT, Süssekind (2016) reinforces, helps one to rethink one's own arrogant ignorance within the curriculum as lived experience toward social and cognitive justice. Formalizing ICT in my mind, through my writing, through dialogues with others, and through the wor(l)d has meant, and still does, considering the intricacies of its conceptions and assertions. Yet, its conceptualization and creation are a natural complex interaction with the wor(l)d, as was perhaps the case for Michelangelo and Picasso with their art.

When one day Michelangelo was asked how a certain picture was painted, i.e., where his idea came from. He answered, 'I had no idea. The figure just stood there, looking at me. I just gave it life/birth.' Picasso had a similar dialogue with a Gestapo officer. In occupied Paris during World War II, a Gestapo officer who had barged into Picasso's apartment pointed at a photo of the mural, *Guernica*, asking: 'Did you do that?' 'No,' Picasso replied, 'you did.' Writing is, Gilles Deleuze (p. 141) argues, 'bringing something to life, to free life from where it's trapped, to trace lines of flight' (p. 141).

These words of Michelangelo and Picasso also highlight the *theory of translation* that works through art. Similarly, ICT is a theory of translation that attempts to prevent the 'reconstruction of emancipatory discourse and practices from falling into the trap of reproducing, in a wider form, Eurocentric concepts and contents' (Santos, 2007a, p. XXVI). Translation is crucial to the processes of coding and decoding between the diverse and specific intellectual and cognitive resources that are expressed through the various modes of producing knowledge about counterhegemonic initiatives and experiences aimed at the redistribution and recognition and the construction of new configurations of knowledge anchored in local, situated forms of experience and struggle (Santos, 2007a, p. XXVI).

In such a context, examples such as Yacouba Sawadogo, an African farmer from Burkina Faso who has been restoring soil damaged by centuries of drought (and desertification) through traditional farming techniques, cannot be arrogantly minimized or eugenically produced as nonexistent or nonscience, just because this work cannot be translated and framed within Western scientificity. Western intellectuals need to consciously acknowledge that the Western epistemological platform – both in its most sophisticated dominant and/or radical critical counterdominant perspectives – is insufficient and inadequate to explain and change its own effects (Seth, 2011). A new system cannot emerge from the ashes of the old. It is pointless to think about the future just with(in) the Cartesian modernity model. It is hopeless to frame the present within such a dated model.

Western counterdominant perspectives are crucial in the struggle for social and cognitive justice, yet not enough. As Sandra Corazza (2002) courageously argues, 'we need to start taking seriously the task of a real theory of curriculum thought' (p. 131), one that opens the Western canon of knowledge and is responsive to the need for a new epistemological configuration. Such a journey of belligerent struggles – against the dominant and within the counterdominant Western epistemological platforms – aims to replace the so-called monoculture of scientific knowledge for an ecology of knowledges. Such an ecology of knowledges is an invitation to the promotion of nonrelativistic dialogues among knowledges, granting equality of opportunities to the different kinds of knowledge engaged in ever broader epistemological disputes aimed both at maximizing their perspective contributions to build a more democratic and just society and at decolonizing knowledge and power (Santos, 2007a, p. xx).

As with any other theoretical exercise intended to understand the educational world in order to transform it (see Pinar, 2004), ICT exhibits a certain latitude and longitude in borderless space to deepen certain claims. For example, among many issues, ICT highlights the linguistic imperialism framed by the English language and culture as an aspect of genocide. Conscious of this linguistic imperialism as a crucial part of genocide, ICT allows one to respectfully understand, for example, how 'camfrenglish' – 'a language used in Cameroon's cities, created daily by Cameroon's urban youth' – deliberately violates the linguistic rules of French and English and, in so doing, desacralizes these imperial languages (Marc Ella, 2013, p. 24). In cities such as Yaounde, camfrenglish is the people's language.

Antonia Darder (2012), in her superb exegesis of the political economy of cultural theory and politics, brings language to the core of the battle against eugenics. As Darder claims, 'the complexity of language and how the students produce knowledge and how language shapes their world represents a major pedagogical concern for all educational settings' (p. 105). Language, Darder argues, is more than a tool that epitomizes a specific learning theory or the cult of a flamboyant method. The language question intersects other social nonepiphenomena such as the question of authority, reframing equality as well as social and cognitive justice. *Any* critical theory that aims at cultural democracy cannot ignore the power of biculturalism as a *poesis* that determines culture and power relations in classrooms (Darder, 2012).

ICT also warns about the need to challenge any form of indigenitude, or the romanticization of indigenous cultures and knowledges, and it is not framed in any dichotic skeleton of West-Rest. In fact, it challenges such functionalist forms. Its itinerant dynamic pushes the theorist to a pluri- (or not necessarily) directional path. That is, ICT and IC T*heorists* are conscious that a significative amount of the anticolonial and decolonial critique on Eurocentrism has been edified with an Eurocentric Cartesian matrix. On this, McLaren's approach toward anticolonial and decolonial parallels Slavoj Žižek's concerns with the anti-Eurocentric armada. Elsewhere, I too have expressed my sympathy – not without reservations – for Žižek's crucial concerns:

> I understand that in criticizing Eurocentrism there have been and there continue to be many exaggerations and misrepresentations. I accept that in many criticisms of Eurocentrism there is a lethal dose of romanticism on non-Eurocentrism. I even understand – that many circuits of intellectual production are scorned to hear, read about coloniality. However, Žižek and others need to come to grips – and I believe they will – that Modern Western Eurocentrism has helped to create the global pandemonium we live in, built a (n)eugenic notion and practice of humanity only possible through a sub-humanity – an issue so eloquently dissected by Žižek. However, we are faced with an 'involution' and the outcome is to re-think how we think about to promote a radical co-presence of epistemological pluriversity. (Paraskeva, 2021, p. 259)

ICT thus confronts the subject with a permanently unstable question: What it is to think? Further, ICT pushes one to think in the light of the future, as well as to question how 'we' can actually claim to really know the things that 'we' claim to know, if 'we' are not ready specifically to think the unthinkable – and to go beyond the unthinkable and master its infinitude. ICT is to be (or not to be) radically unthinkable. ICT is a metamorphosis between what is thought, nonthought, and unthought, but also fundamentally about the temerity of the colonization of the non/un/thought within the thought. ICT attempts to understand and to domesticate the infinity of thought and action. If one challenges infinity, and 'then it is chaos because one is in chaos', that means that the question or questions (whatever they are) are inaccurately deterritorialized and fundamentally sedentary. The focus is to grasp that ICT implies an understanding of chaos as domestic, as public, as a *punctum* within the pure luxury of immanence. In such multitude of terrains, ICT needs to be understood as *poesis*. It plays in the plane of immanence. Being as immanence is 'a life,' ICT is 'a life.' A life paced by a *poesis* or a revolution? 'Yes please,' in a full *Žižekian* way.

ICT is a *poesis* that itinerantly throws the subject against the infinity of representation to grasp the omnitude of the real(ity) and the rational(ity), thus mastering the transcendent. Being more *poesis* than just theory (and not because it is less theory), its itinerant position *epitomizes* a transcendent nomadography which clashes with dominant and counterdominant research Eurocentric traditions. As McLaren (Chapter 7) argues, a 'miasma of smoke often is exhaled by our field research, obscuring the political and ethical ramifications entailed by our analyses, but easily overlooked, absorbed, and displaced by the Eurocentrism and androcentrism found in our research traditions.'

ICT challenges book worship (Mao, 2007, p. 45). In fact, ICT also encourages us to pay attention to the multiplicity of forms to read the wor(l)d. The verbalization of pain and oppression is quite visible in Africa, for example, in art forms such as dance and painting. Dance, Marc Ella (2013) argues, in a country financially and economically moribund, is not just a way to face inequality and oppression. It is, he states, 'the very best way to face discouragement' (2013, p. 26). ICT is an attempt to help us to think in another form of being. Corazza's (2002) insightful framework is crucial here as well. As she claims, and I honestly think ICT addresses her claim, the challenge is to fight against what she coins as *assentado curriculum* toward a *vagamundo curriculum*; that is, 'to create [or cocreate] a *vagamundo* curriculum one needs to question how can one think about the inaddressable, the unthinkable, the non-thinkable of the curriculum thought, the exteriorities, the self-different, the self-other, the other self' (Corazza, 2002, p. 140). Corazza adds that such curriculum thought is meaningless, a real vacuum, without the effective forces acting upon such thought, as well as without the effective indeterminations that force such thought (or forms of thought) to think otherwise, differently, through the creation of new concepts required by real experience and not just by possible experience, thus allowing new life experiences. In fact, the strength of (an)other knowledge, as well as a new philosophy, will be measured by the concepts that it is capable of creating, or its capacity to renew meanings which impose a new framework on things and to *assentados* actions, shuffle their syntax, and organize their thought in a clumsy logic (2002, p. 140).

Corazza's (2002) sharp take equips intellectuals with the necessary extraordinary tools to understand why some African scholars, such as Axelle Kabou (2013), Jean Marc Ella (2013), and others justifiably counter the Western and non-Western hegemonic apparatuses with the following question: What if Africa refuses development? The definition of development must be seen through other lenses beyond its Western monocultural conceptualization as the development needed by the Global South. *Whose* purpose does this development serve? What is the cost to those beneath its grinding wheel of so-called progress? In such a context, ICT is really a matter of human rights as well, due to its commitment to social and cognitive justice. This is a commitment that challenges dominant multicultural forms, creating the conditions for an intercultural reconstruction of human rights and moving toward an intercultural postimperial form of human rights that respects, among other issues: (a) the right to knowledge, (b) the right to bring historical capitalism to trial in a world tribunal, (c) the right to democratic self-determination, and (d) the right to grant rights to entities incapable of bearing duties, namely nature and future generations (Santos, 2007a, 2007b). ICT is a clarion call to challenge curriculum epistemicides (Paraskeva, 2017) by engaging fully in the complex struggle for social and cognitive justice. It is also a call to decolonize the 'decolonized.' This is an intergenerational matter of justice as well.

The struggle against epistemicides and curriculum epistemicides (Santos, 2007b, 2014; Paraskeva, 2011, 2016a, 2016b, 2017) is difficult but necessary. That it is impossible is a fabricated fallacy. Bragança's 'walking and being' is a wake-up call to all of us really committed to the struggle against curriculum epistemicides (Paraskeva, 2017). It allows one to grasp ICT as a political yarn that works within and beyond the capitalist system or against 'world system theory.' ICT is also a human rights issue, a challenge to the dichotomy of ethics and chaos since it is an ethic of [needed] chaos. ICT praises the consistency of inconsistencies and fosters a reckless philosophy of praxis above and beyond the rumble of 'being-nonbeing'; it is a eulogy of 'being.' ICT is, à la Martí, 'an infinite labor of love,' one that perceives that the act of thinking is not just theoretical. ICT works in a never-ending matrix determined by sensations, forces, fluxes, 'happenings,' all of which are linked and reacting against the modes and conditions of production of the capitalist system.

ICT is a curriculum turn. A 'pluri-versal' not 'uni-versal' turn. A decolonial turn. ICT needs to be seen within the cartography of a decolonial being. Mignolo (2011a, 2011b) is of great help here, arguing that the genealogy of decolonial thinking is pluri-versal (not uni-versal). As such, each knot on the web of this genealogy is a point of delinking and opening that reintroduces languages, memories, economies, social organizations, and at least double subjectivities: the splendor and the miseries of the imperial legacy, and the indelible footprint of what existed that has been converted into the colonial wound; in the degradation of humanity, in the inferiority of the pagans, the primitives, the underdeveloped, the nondemocratic (Mignolo, 2011b, p. 63).

Such inquiry implies, as Deleuze and Guattari felicitously unveil, that an itinerant theory is not just a war machine that judiciously collides with ossified truths and fossilized realities. Its itinerant existence is actually only possible in a permanent theater of war. Needless to say, ICT is not cavalier with history. Nor it is just a pale reaction against the way history has been *quasi* suffocated by hegemonic and particular counterhegemonic traditions. While a concept – arguably a geophilosophical one – it goes well beyond an aesthetic wrangle between sedentary theoretical hegemonic and particular counterhegemonic platforms, and toward nomad(ic) approaches free from walls, dams, and institutionally backward bourgeois terrains. ICT implies a nomadic inquiry, but one in which the foci occupy the truly total itinerant capacity of space(less)ness, a permanent smooth itinerant position, a perpetual search that wholeheartedly aims at saturation. The nomadography of such theory is framed in the nonstop itinerant posture in which creators of *poesis* seem to be part of the history of thought but escape from it either in a specific aspect (or in specific aspects) or altogether. ICT attempts to turn curriculum theory against itself as well. It is a philosophy of liberation, which is sentient of the pitfalls of the internationalization of dynamics within the curriculum field. ICT helps us understand how to situate curriculum theory in the project of modernity/colonialism/decolonization.

ICT contends that it is no longer viable to carry on with and in the same epistemological framework. Relying on Habermas, Mignolo (2008) argues that

> [i]t is no longer possible, or at least it is not unproblematic, to 'think' from the canon of Western philosophy, even when part of the canon is critical of modernity. To do so means to reproduce the blind epistemic ethnocentrism that makes difficult, if not impossible, any political philosophy of inclusion. The limit of Western philosophy is the border where the colonial difference emerges, making visible the variety of local histories that Western thought, from Right and Left, hid and suppressed. (p. 234)

Drawing from Marianna Torgovnick's rationale, McLaren (Chapter 7) unpacks 'the damaging effects of the colonial imagination formed out of the sovereign Eurocentric archives of the imperialist West, an imagination that has profound implications for the practice of ethnography undertaken in the spirit of modernism, where certain groups become othered and devoiced through the "male-centred, canonical line of Western primitivism."' In McLaren's mind, the eugenic nature of Eurocentric-based research is unquestionable. As educational researchers, he argues (Chapter 7), 'we must cease to attribute to certain groups "mythical consciousness" while we reserve "historical consciousness" for ourselves; in addition, we should welcome the day when the dominance of modernist dichotomies of literate/non-literate, developed/underdeveloped, and so forth, have substantially ebbed.'

(An)other science is not just really possible; it is real. ICT is a claim for a just theory; a claim for just science. It is possible for ICT – which we argue is the best path for critical progressive curriculum scholars – not only to grasp precious concepts and dynamics, such as hegemony, ideology, power, social emancipation, class, race, and gender in the complex age of globalization (Santos, 2008) or globalisms, but also to better (re)address the towering questions of curriculum, starting with the one asked by Counts in the last century: *Dare the schools build a new social order?* So long as poverty and inequality keep multiplying, this question remains central. The devastating impact of neoliberal policies forces the intemporality of certain challenges. Given these conditions, ICT challenges the critical curriculum project to go beyond its counterdominant and dominant-within-the-counterdominant positions, thus turning the struggle for curriculum relevance into a struggle for social and cognitive justice. As we will see later on in examining Chomsky's (1971) approach, while the transformation of society is crucial, understanding it accurately is no less important.

I am not claiming that ICT is a perfect theory; I've actually claimed that there is no such thing as a perfect theory (see Quantz, 2011). Obviously, there is room for critique; for instance, the clashes within the poststructural positions could be expanded. The ecological domain should not be so silent. ICT questions the linguistic imperialism of English and other Western imperial languages. It also challenges the way science has been defined and legitimized based on the cultural politics of academic writing, which are not only social formulas but also legitimize 'the modern epistemicidium,' and are thus real obstacles to social and cognitive justice. ICT also challenges the momentum of internationalization, as well as in whose language this epoch is occurring. ICT is alert to the fact that the very struggle to internationalize the field of curriculum studies is a relatively recent phenomenon for the United States's academic milieu.

ICT aims precisely at 'a general epistemology of the impossibility of a general epistemology' (Santos, 2014). It is an itinerant posture that is profoundly engaged in its commitment to a radical copresence. It is nonabyssal since not only challenges the modern Western cult of abyssal thinking but also attempts to dilute such fictional vacuums between the lines. ICT is an act of resistance also at the metaphysical level. That is, the struggle against modern Western abyssal thinking is not merely a policy matter. It is also above and beyond that: It is an existential and spiritual question. The struggle against the Western Cartesian model cannot signify the substitution of one Cartesian model for another. Also, the task is not to dominate such a model or to wrap it in a more humanistic impulse. The task is to pronounce its last words, to prepare its remains for a respectful funeral. The task is not to change the language and concepts, although these are key elements. The task is to terminate a particular hegemonic geography of knowledge, one which promotes an epistemological euthanasia.

ICT denounces how internationalization has been, in so many ways, the new apparatus through which modern Western epistemologies have been expanding the very process and significance of 'what it is to think.' It has exposed even more the open wound created by 'the archives of Western knowledge and the question of cultural domination exercised by countries of advanced capital over imperialized countries' (Ahmad, 2008, p. 2). ICT is undeniably a call for a new 'never stable gathering epistemological point.' While it is strongly evident that the struggle against epistemicide is a human rights issue, it is also clear that such a struggle cannot be won with old weapons (Latour, 2005).

(De)Coloniality: Curriculum Within and Beyond the West is about 'curriculum from the South in the Global South and curriculum from the South in the Global North,' as connected with the different metamorphoses of coloniality. It unpacks the Western, Eurocentric, Anglo-Saxon epistemological fascism subsumed in the true colors of policy and reform matters, as well as in daily life within classrooms. It intends to help establish a multifarious corpus of scholarship that will open the curriculum canon to foster social and cognitive justice in itinerant theory and impel movement toward a nonabyssal curriculum; work that fosters such shifts is a crucial part of our collective commitment to the struggle against epistemicide.

While Peter McLaren's *Critical Theory: Rituals, Pedagogy and Resistance* constitutes a major asset in the struggle against the epistemicidal nature of the curriculum field, it is however also an unavoidable tool to map the intricate metamorphoses of what I have called reversive epistemicide (Paraskeva, 2021) – the epistemicide that is committed to challenging the epistemicide. As the volume clear documents, McLaren is a profoundly complex figure, a problem faced by everyone who studies him. While he would like to be remembered as a 'Marxist Catholic,' McLaren is undeniably broader than any label. His work – as this volume documents – needs to be situated within a branch of a particular radical critical (curriculum) river in which the works of Du Bois, George Counts, Harold Rugg, and others should not be minimized. He swims in a powerful critical intellectual river – grasping issues related to ideology, hegemony, power, class, gender, race, resistance, identity, multiculturalism, language, teacher education, curriculum, technology, critical theory and pedagogies, liberatory theologies – providing a solid jouissance peppered with powerful, wrangles between Marxist, neo-Marxist, anarchist, postmodern, poststructural, postcolonial, anticolonial, and spiritual domains. The journey up river necessarily triggered harsh epistemological breaks and fractures, some of them permanent.

Moving from Canada to a nation that is basically in a state of permanent war certainly had a huge impact on McLaren's intellectual matrix. His 'undisciplinary' trajectory placed him, especially in many leftist intellectual constituencies as a 'traveling theorist,' a sharp vagabond in a theoretical trench, a trench from where he blossoms his humanism and his commitment to overcoming the cruel injustices of capitalism. Together with other critical scholars, he championed crucial battles in our field. McLaren's 'return' to the Marxist platform was quite predictable though as he was always unwilling to completely reject Marxism as the fundamental category to understand fascism, white supremacy, oppression, exploitation, segregation in our society and schools, arguing that alienated capitalist relations must be consistently and vigorously countered. As McLaren states in the introduction of this volume, his jouissance reinforced an 'affinity with the humanist tradition of critical pedagogy,' a powerful terrain to smash the dangerous pillars of the capitalist society such as exploitation, oppression, segregation, inequality, poverty – all of that intertwined within class, race, and gender dynamics. Like many critical theorists, McLaren refuses to give up on Marxism; he was always cognizant of one of Marx's fundamental claims which he made in the preface to the first edition of *Das Kapital*. As a crucial card within the political economy of the capitalist system, 'in the analysis of economic forms neither microscopes, nor chemical reagents are of any assistance [and] the power of abstraction must replace both' (Marx, 1990, p. 90).

Needless to say, McLaren's oeuvre should not be seen as 'the grand narrative,' the Magna Carta through which we will accomplish the world we all wish to see (Amin, 2008). While his approach helps us to understand accurately the real eugenic epistemological colors of our society and educational institutions, it also demonstrates very concrete inconsistencies and silences with the critical and postcritical platforms that should make us educators question what is happening with the critical platform as I was able to examine in detail in another context (Paraskeva, 2021, 2022).

The critique of the critical is a sublime way to do critical theory, which, I argue, it needs to be done in order to be responsive to the world's epistemological diversity and to move toward a just theory (Paraskeva, 2021). And while the future of our field, some argue, needs to go beyond Peter McLaren's intellectual thesaurus, it cannot certainly avoid going through him. ICT – and the ICTheorists – are conscious of that.

Note

1 Personal correspondence, 16 April 2021.

References

Ahmad, A. (2008). *In theory*. Verso.

Althusser, L. (2005). *For Marx*. Verso.

Amin, S. (2008). *The world we wish to see: Revolutionary objectives in the twenty-first century*. Monthly Review Press.

Amin, S. (2014). *Capitalism in the age of globalization: The management of contemporary society*. Zed Books.

Appadurai, A. (2018). O Cansaço da Democracia. In H. Ginselberger (Ed.), *O Grande Retrocesso. Um Debate International sobre as Grandes Questões do Nosso Tempo* (pp. 17–31). Objectiva.

Apple, M. (1979). *Ideology and curriculum*. Routledge

Arendt, H. (1963). *Eichmann in Jerusalem: A report on the banality of evil*. Viking Press.

Aronowitz, S. (1973). *False promises*. McGraw Hill.

Arrighi, G. (2005). *The long twentieth century*. Verso.

Artaud, A. (2010). *The theatre and its double*. Alma Classics.

Badiou, A. (2008). The communist hypothesis. *New Left Review, 49*, 29–42.

Baudrillard, J. (2001). Our theatre of cruelty. In C. Kraus & S. Lotringer (Eds.), *Hatred of capitalism: A Semiotext(e) reader* (pp. 51–56). Semiotext(e).

Bauman, Z. (1997). *Globalization: The human consequences*. Blackwell.

Berardi, B. F. (2012). *The uprising: On poetry and finance*. Semiotext(e).

Borgo, K. (2019). *Cai a Noite em Caracas*. Alfaguara.

Camus, A. (1948). *The plague*. Alfred Knopf.

Camus, A. (2005). *The myth of Sisyphus*. Penguin.

Cheng Enfu & Ding Xiaoqin. (2017). A theory of China's "miracle": Eight principles of contemporary Chinese political economy. *Monthly Review, 68*(8), 46–57.

Chomsky, N. (1971). *Problems of knowledge and freedom*. The New Press.

Clastres, P. (2010). *Archeology of violence*. Semiotext(e).

Corazza, S. M. (2002). Noologia do currículo: Vagamundo, o problemático, e assentado, o resolvido. *Educação e Realidade, 27*(2), 131–142.

Darder, A. (2012). *Culture and power in the classrooms: Educational foundations for the schooling of bicultural studies*. Paradigm.

Davis, A. (1971). *If they come in the morning: Voices of resistance*. Third Press.

De La Cadena, M., & Blaser, M. (Eds.). (2018). *A world of many worlds*. Duke University Press.

Deleuze, G. (1995). *Negotiations, 1972–1990*. Columbia University Press.

Deleuze, G., & Guattari, F. (1994). *What is philosophy*? Columbia University Press.

Derrida, J. (1994). *Specters of Marx*. Routledge.

Dussel, E. (1995). *The invention of the Americas: Eclipse of the "other" and the myth of modernity*. Continuum.

Eagleton, T. (2003). *After theory*. Basic Books.

Esslin, M. (1960). The theatre of the absurd. *The Tulane Drama Review, 4*(4), 3–15. https://doi.org/10.2307/1124873

Fatheuer, T. (2011). *Buen Vivir: A brief introduction to Latin America's new concepts for the good life and the rights of nature* (Heinrich Boll Foundation Publication Series on Ecology, vol. 17). Berlin: Heinrich Boll Foundation.

Fraser, N. (2014). Can society be commodities all way down? Post-Polanyian reflections on capitalist crisis. *Economy and Society, 43*(4), 541–558.

Freire, P. (1970). *Pedagogy of the oppressed*. Herder and Herder.

Galeano, E. (1997). *Open veins of Latin America: Five centuries of pillage of a continent*. Monthly Review Press.

Geiselberger, H. (2017). *O Grande Retrocesso. Um Debate International sobre as Grandes Questoes do Nosso Tempo*. Objectiva.

Gil, J. (1998). *Metamorphoses of the body*. University of Minnesota Press.

Gil, J. (2009). Em Busca da Identidade. O Desnorte Relógio D'Água.

Giroux, H. A. (1981). *Ideology, culture, and the process of schooling*. Temple University Press.

Giroux, H. A. (2011). *Education and the crisis of public values: Challenging the assault on teachers, students, & public education*. Peter Lang.

Gramsci, A. (1999). *The prison notebooks*. International Publishers

Grosfoguel, R. (2003). *Colonial subjects: Puerto Ricans in a global perspective*. University of California Press.

Grosfoguel, R. (2007). The epistemic decolonial turn: Beyond political economy paradigms. *Cultural Studies, 21*(2–3), 211–223.

Grosfoguel, R. (2010). Epistemic Islamophobia: Colonial social sciences. *Human Architecture: Journal of the Sociology of Self-Knowledge, 8*(2), 29–39.

Grosfoguel, R. (2011). Decolonizing post-colonial studies and paradigms of political economy: Transmodernity, decolonial thinking, and global coloniality. *Transmodernity. Journal of Peripheral Cultural Production of the Luso-Hispanic World, 1*(1), 1–38.

Gudavarthy, A. (2018). *India after Modi: Populism and the right*. Bloomsbury.

Habib, A. (2013). *Suspended revolution*. Ohio University Press.

Han, B.-C. (2018). *A Expulsão do Outro*. Relógio D'Água.

Harvey, D. (2016). Senior Loeb Scholar Lecture. Harvard University. Graduate School of Design. https://www.youtube.com/watch?v=pm_UgX-ef8&t=927s

Held, D. (1980). *Introduction to critical theory: From Horkheimer to Habermas*. University of California Press.

Honneth, A. (1987). Critical theory. In A. Giddens & J. Turner (Eds.), *Social theory today* (pp. 347–382). Stanford University Press.

Honneth, A. (2009). *Pathologies of reason*. Columbia University Press.

hooks, b. (1981). *Ain't I a woman?* South End Press.

Horkheimer, M. (1999). *Critical theory*. Continuum.

Hui, W. (2011). *The end of the revolution*. Verso.

Hung, H.-F. (2011). Paper-tiger finance? *New Left Review, 72*, 138–144.
Jameson, F. (2016). *American utopia: Dual power and the universal army*. Verso.
Kabou, A. (2013). *E se A Africa se recusar ao desenvolvimento?* Edicoes Pedago.
Kellner, D. (1989). *Critical theory, Marxism and modernity*. Johns Hopkins University Press.
Koczanowicz, L. (2016). The Polish case. Community and democracy under PiS. *New Left Review, 102*, 77–96.
Latour, B. (2005). *O poder da critica discursos*. Edicoes Pedago.
Lazzarato, M. (2015). *Governing by debt*. Semiotext.
Loury, G. (2008). *Race, incarceration, and American values*. MIT Press.
Maldonado-Torres, N. (2003). Imperio y Colonialidad del Ser. Paper presented at the Annual Meeting of the Latin American Studies Association in Dallas, Texas, March 29.
Maldonado-Torres, N. (2008). *Against war: Views from the underside of modernity*. Duke University Press.
Mao Tse Tung. (2007). Oppose book worship. In S. Žižek (Ed.), *Slavoj Žižek presents Mao on practice and contradiction* (pp. 43–51). Verso.
Marazzi, C. (2011). *The violence of finance capitalism*. Semiotext(e).
Mayo, P., & Vittoria, P (2021). *Critical education in international perspective*. Bloomsbury.
Marc Ella, J. (2013). *Restituir a historia as sociedades Africanas*. Edicoes Pedago.
Marcuse, H. (1964). *One-dimensional man*. Beacon Press.
Marx, K. (1990). *Capital*. Penguin.
Mbembe, A. (2019). *Necropolitics*. Duke University Press.
Mészáros, I. (1996). The legacy of Marx. In P. Osborne (Ed.), *A critical sense: Interviews with intellectuals* (pp. 47–62). Routledge.
Mignolo, W. D. (2008). The geopolitics of knowledge and the colonial difference. In M. Moraña, E. Dussel & C. A. Jáuregui (Eds.), *Coloniality at large: Latin America and the postcolonial debate* (pp. 225–258). Duke University Press.
Mignolo, W. D. (2011a). *The darker side of Western modernity: Global futures, decolonial options*. Duke University Press.
Mignolo, W. (2011b). Epistemic disobedience and the decolonial option: A manifesto. *Transmodernity: Journal of Peripheral Cultural Production of the Luso-Hispanic World, 1*(2), 44–66.
Mignolo, W. D. (2012). *Local histories/global designs: Coloniality, subaltern knowledges and border thinking*. Princeton University Press.
Muthu, S. (2003). *Enlightenment against empire*. Princeton University Press.
Paraskeva, J. (2011). *Conflicts in curriculum theory: Challenging hegemonic epistemologies*. Palgrave.
Paraskeva, J. (2014). *Conflicts in curriculum theory: Challenging hegemonic epistemologies* (Updated paperback edition). Palgrave.

Paraskeva, J. (2016a). *Curriculum epistemicides*. Routledge.

Paraskeva, J. (2016b). The curriculum: Whose internationalization? In J. M. Paraskeva (Ed.), *Curriculum: Whose internationalization?* (pp. 1–10). Peter Lang.

Paraskeva, J. (2017). *Towards a just curriculum theory: The epistemicide*. Routledge.

Paraskeva, J. (2021). *Curriculum and the generation of utopia*. Routledge.

Paraskeva J. (2022). The generation of the utopia: Itinerant curriculum theory towards a 'futurable future'. *Discourses – Studies in the Cultural Politics of Education*, 1–20.

Patnaik, P. (1993). The fascism of our times. *Social Scientist*, 21(3/4), 69–77. https://doi.org/10.2307/3517631

Pessoa, F. (2002). *The book of disquiet*. Penguin.

Pinar, W. (2003). Introduction: Toward the internationalization of curriculum studies. In D. Trueit, W. Doll, Jr., H. Wang & W. Pinar (Eds.), *The internationalization of curriculum studies: Selected proceedings from the LSU Conference 2000* (pp. 1–13). Peter Lang.

Pinar, W. (2004). *What is curriculum theory?* Lawrence Erlbaum Associates.

Pinar, W. (2012). *Curriculum studies in the United States*. Palgrave.

Pinar, W. (2013). *Curriculum studies in the United States: Present circumstances, intellectual histories*. Palgrave.

Quantz, R. (2011). *Rituals and student identity in education: Ritual critique for a new pedagogy*. Palgrave.

Quijano, A. (1992). Colonialidad y modernidad/racionalidad. *Perú Indígena*, 13(29), 11–20.

Quijano, A. (2000). Colonialidad del poder y classificacion social. *Journal of World Systems Research*, 6(2), 342–386.

Rupnik, J. (2019, January 20). Hoje temos uma especie the balcanizacao do ocidente. *Jornal Público*. https://www.publico.pt/2019/01/20/mundo/entrevista/hoje-temos-uma-especie-de-balcanizacao-a-ocidente-1858534

Santos, B. (1999). Porque é que é tão difícil construir uma teoria crítica? *Revista Crítica de Ciências Sociais*, 54, 197–215.

Santos, B. (2004). Para uma sociologia das ausências e uma sociologia das emergências. In B. de Sousa Santos (Ed.), *Conhecimento prudente para uma vida decente: Um discurso sobre as ciencias revisitado* (pp. 735–775). Cortez.

Santos, B. (2005). *Democratizing democracy. Beyond the liberal democratic cannon*. Verso.

Santos, B. (2006). *The rise of the global left: The world social forum and beyond*. Verso.

Santos, B. (2007b). Beyond abyssal thinking: From global lines to ecologies of knowledges. *Review*, 30(1), 45–89.

Santos, B. (2008). Globalizations. *Theory, Culture and Society*, 23, 393–399.

Santos, B. (2009). *Epistemologias do sul*. Almedina.

Santos, B. (2014). *Epistemilogies from the South*. Paradigm.

Santos, B. (2015). *If god were a human rights activist: Human rights and the challenge of political theologies*. Stanford University Press.

Santos, B. (2018). *The end of the cognitive empire*. Duke University Press.

Santos, B. (Ed.). (2007a). *Another knowledge is possible: Beyond Northern epistemologies*. Verso.

Santos, B., Arriscado, N. J., & Meneses, M. P. (2007). Opening up the canon of knowledge and recognition of difference. In B. de Sousa Santos (Ed.), *Another knowledge is possible: Beyond Northern epistemologies* (pp. xix–lxii). Verso.

Selden, S. (1999). *The inherited shame*. Teachers College Press.

Seth, S. (2011). Travelling theory: Western knowledge and its Indian object. *International Studies in Sociology of Education, 21*(4), 263–282.

Smith, A. (2017, August 1). School district votes to bring back paddling for disobedient students. Do you support this? American Web Media. http://theoklahomaeagle.net/2017/08/01/school-district-votes-to-bring-back-paddling-for-disobedient-students-do-you-support-this/

Street, P. (2017, April 28). Slandering populism: A chilling media habit. *Counterpunch*. https://www.counterpunch.org/2017/04/28/slandering-populism-a-chilling-media-habit/

Süssekind, M. L. (2016). Currículos-como-experiências-vividas: Um relato de embichamento nos cotidianos de uma escola na cidade do Rio de Janeiro. *Currículo Sem Fronteiras, 15*(3), 614–625.

Tamás, G. M. (2013). Words from Budapest. *New Left Review, 80*, 5–26.

Thompson, E. P. (1971). *The poverty of theory and other essays*. Monthly Review Press.

Todorova, M. (1997). *Imagining the Balkans*. Oxford University Press.

Touraine, A. (1995). *Carta aos Socialistas*. Terramar.

Trueit, D. (2003). Democracy and conversation. In D. Trueit, W. Doll, Jr., H. Wang & W. Pinar (Eds.), *The internationalization of curriculum studies: Selected proceedings from the LSU Conference 2000* (pp. ix–xvii). Peter Lang.

Vanaik, A. (2018). India's two hegemonies. *New Left Review, 112*, 29–59.

Virilio, P. (2012). *The administration of fear*. Semiotext(e).

Wacquant, L. (2009). *Punishing the poor: The neoliberal government of social insecurity*. Duke University Press.

Walsh, C. (2018). Insurgency and decolonila prospect, praxis and project. In C. E. Walsh & W. D. Mignolo (Eds.), *On decoloniality. Concepts, analytics, praxis* (pp. 33–56). Duke University Press.

Walsh, C. E., & Mignolo, W. D. (2018). *On decoloniality: Concepts, analytics, praxis*. Duke University Press.

Wolf, Naomi (2007). *The end of America: Letter of warning to a young patriot*. Chelsea Green Publishing Company.

Žižek, S. (2018). *Slavoj Zizek on yellow vests. How to watch the news* [Short video series]. RT Production. www.you-tube.com/watch?v=TrdPchnAR60

CHAPTER 1

Introduction: Challenges to a Post-Democracy America

For nearly forty years I have watched the democracy of my adopted country disintegrate before my weary and shopworn eyes. America has undergone a dangerous restructuring as the country repurposes its mission from being a refuge of the downtrodden and weary into a Gileadean culture of hatred cloaked in patriotic platitudes and empty paeans. The surge in right-wing extremism, vigilantism and outlawry that has accompanied the growth of fascist-nurturing evangelical communities and goon squads populated by White American ethno-nationalist 'patriots' is a tragedy that has been foreseen for decades. And now these groups, emerging from the furrows of history, are gleefully announcing their puffed-up racism and anti-Semitism with flagrant abandon, even bravado, that signals to others of like mind that they are proudly part of a putrid anti-democratic and state-authoritarian normality. As the son of a veteran of World War II such events are ominous.

As the country reels from the crisis of capitalism, those who a decade ago would be described as bourgeois centrists are now denounced by Republicans as communists and Satanists. What does that make of those of us on the far left? In states like Texas, individuals can buckle on their shiny pearl-handle six-shooters, as it is now legal to openly carry guns without a license or training. Neo-Nazi and White supremacist militias are cheering the Taliban for defeating the United States, and some are advocating that their success warrants the Taliban serving as a strategic military model for overtaking the US government and turning it into a White Christian ethno-state. Texas law has just banned women from getting an abortion. Is not this kind of civil enforcement over a woman's body reminiscent of Mussolini's control over a woman's bodily autonomy when his fascist regime placed major restrictions on access to reproductive health care and outlawed abortion via the Rocco Code? Do women's bodies now belong to the state? We condemn the Taliban for its treatment of women. But how do we treat women's bodies?

The current absurdist attacks on critical race theory (by those same White supremacists who secretly can't wait for an all-out race war to begin) reflects similar attacks on the works of Paulo Freire and Howard Zinn that occurred in Arizona during the storied struggle over ethnic studies – cultural Marxism has invaded our school system and must be ripped from the bowels of colleges of education if the United States is to avoid the impending gulags and massacres of Christians! Or so the narrative goes.

Critical race theory emerged from the field of critical theory (Adorno, Marcuse, Horkheimer, Fromm, Benjamin). While critical race theory specializes in issues of race and the struggle against racialized injustice, critical pedagogy initially concentrated on the struggle for social justice by exploring the intersection of race, class, gender and sexuality. Later, of course, scholars decided to create tributaries of critical pedagogy that focused on feminism, LGBTQ issues, indigenous rights, disability studies and many other important areas. My own contribution to critical pedagogy has been the development of what I called "revolutionary critical pedagogy," which was an approach I felt needed to be exercised since to me the more generic versions of critical pedagogy failed to adhere to the nuanced complexity of Freire's Marxist epistemology as well as his humanist ontology grounded in Catholic social justice imperatives and reflected in liberation theology. In the years to come, I anticipate furious attacks on critical pedagogy by Republicans, neo-Nazis and White supremacists as they attempt to rewrite the narrative of the 6 January 2020 insurrection as a heroic effort to redress the injustice of a stolen election. That Americans are so eager to embrace well-trafficked Orwellian-like conspiracies – Dominion voting machines were programmed to flip the election from Trump to Biden, the election was manipulated by Italian satellites, and Jewish space lasers caused California wildfires – is a topic of much needed research if this country is to prevent itself from becoming an apartheid state headed by a QAnon shaman. And this will greatly depend on what transpires in the schools of this country at a time when states are creating laws attacking mask mandates by school boards, issuing laws prohibiting the teaching of racism or White supremacy as foundational to the creation of the United States, mandating punishments for noncompliant educators, including million-dollar fines for districts in which teachers are found to have willingly violated state laws against discussing racism, White privilege or sexism in class and disciplining teachers who might make White students feel guilty or anguished about historical crimes against people of color. The purpose here is to ramp up the culture wars and White victimhood, frighten parents, create chaos, inspire moral panics, win votes through tactics of "racial erasure" and bolster larger attacks by right-wing forces against multiracial and multiethnic democracy while putting other countries on notice that the United States is an emerging global fascist power. When influential television pundits start calling for teachers to wear body cameras to monitor critical race theory teaching, and when the anti-mask zealots start attacking mask-wearing patrons at airports and supermarkets, then the conditions for intellectual poltroons to prevail on the streets are already set.

The right-wing media has reached a point where it is deliberately spreading fear and violence for the sake of ratings, perpetuating lies about the stolen election, interviewing Trump supporters about their absurd demon-laden conspiracy theories, and elevating whacko fringe groups such as America's Frontline Doctors into the realm of credibility and legitimacy.

There is little or no support for democracy among the members of the current Republican Party. Their banner has been forever tarnished by the blood of Covid victims and their members have been reduced to a cabal of cronies, change-resistant sects foot-weary from battling evidential truth as they amp up White paranoia about the "great replacement" of White America by people of color, preaching the virtues of nationalism and White supremacy and endlessly gaslighting the American public. The right-wing, anti-modern, Latin Mass sectarians, medieval chauvinists and liturgical revanchists of the Catholic Church as well as much of the evangelical Protestant community has chosen to ignore the Jesus of the Gospels in favor of conspiracy-based extremism and feudalistic claims that Pope Francis is in league with the Freemasons. They hold to a sclerotic clericalism and baroque doctrinalism, a narrow-minded cultism and hidebound traditionalism, a hard-core anti-refugee stance and go so far as to support fascist political parties and governments. They entertain a feral association with right-wing populists such as Steve Bannon and defend their intractably reactionary positions on women, gay people, Muslims, immigration, socialism, and climate change. In Poland an activist was detained simply for putting up posters depicting the Virgin Mary with a halo reminiscent of the LGBT rainbow flag.

The country has degenerated to the extent that more dictators, worse than Trump, are poised to emerge from the sidelines and make emotional connections with the aggrieved low-wage and middle-class base and deliberately call for bloodshed. These politicians of hate need to be challenged by a critical pedagogy of everyday life whose Freirean expression is steeped in a self-criticism that merges dialectically with a love of humanity. Every pedagogy needs to be self-critical, otherwise in time it will degenerate into a self-righteous hypocrisy. This is most certainly true for a critical pedagogy which is always evolving. It is my deep hope that the essays contained in this volume speak to such a pedagogy of hope and love.

Before I end this brief introduction, I would like to thank Professor João M. Paraskeva for inviting me to publish this book in his series and for choosing the title. Many of the chapters and articles in this volume were written before my engagement with Marxist theory which, along with liberation theology, has guided my work since 1994. Yet I would contend that the early work presented in this book bears a considerable elective affinity with the humanist tradition of critical pedagogy. As a doctoral student who worked with one of the world's great drama scholars, Richard Courtney (some students seemed to think that he saw me as his successor), I began my undergraduate degree studying Old English, Middle English and Elizabethan drama (I even took a stab at becoming a sculptor) and began my doctoral work studying ritual. It appeared that I had a promising future in dramaturgical studies, possibly working as an educational anthropologist specializing in critical ethnography. That was until I began to read the works of Paulo Freire, Henry A. Giroux, Augusto Boal, Paul Willis, Stuart Hall, Judith Butler, Gloria Anzaldúa, C. Wright Mills, Che Guevara, and the great Jesuit theologian, José Porfirio Miranda. As a newly minted professor, I left Canada to work for eight years alongside the great intellectual and polymath Henry A. Giroux, and I am sure I disappointed my great mentor for not following up on my study of ritual and for moving away from dramaturgy into a field charted by Freire, Giroux, Macedo and others. Yet my work on ritual represents the birth pangs of my engagement with crafting a critical pedagogy of the concrete – a nondualistic pedagogy that addresses flesh and bones and memories as well as ideas. In fact, the field of ritual studies has helped to lay the groundwork for performance studies and other contemporary fields such as arts-based methodology, critical multiculturalism, culturally responsive teaching, and, of course, all of these fields have intersected synergistically with the imperatives of critical pedagogy: To forge a better world from the fetid, truth-obliterating ashes of the present to a transcendent pedagogy of possibility. My goal has been to bring a Marxist critique of political economy and liberation theology into the mix when it came to critical pedagogy. Of course, British educational scholars were far ahead of their North American counterparts on including Marx in their critique of capitalist schooling and I subsequently learned much from visiting comrades in England, including Dave Hill, Mike Cole and Glenn Rikowski. And, of course, when I began regular visits to Latin America and the Caribbean – most importantly, Mexico, Venezuela, Colombia, Brazil, Argentina, Cuba – I was fortunate to meet wonderful scholars and activists who helped me to understand the complex and life-affirming world of political struggle. Visits to Turkey, Greece, Serbia, Croatia, Pakistan, Peru, Costa Rica, Puerto Rico, China, Japan, Thailand, Israel, Palestine, Ireland, Sweden, Finland, Russia, Poland, Hungary, Austria, Germany and South Africa were important for me to understand commonalities and differences in political thinking and the development of social movements.

While the world is turning into ashes, we cannot rest content with our mission of building a future out of the excrement of capitalist social relations. Possibilities do exist, such as the creation of worker co-operatives and creating a social universe that is not dependent upon value production, on monetized wealth. I hope that the essays in this volume will in some fashion assist in such a creation.

CHAPTER 2

The Ritual Dimensions of Resistance

Clowning and Symbolic Inversion

> What is an educational system after all, if not the ritualization of the word!
>
> MICHEL FOUCAULT (cited in Giroux, 1983a, p. 207)

∴

In this chapter I try to establish the primacy of understanding resistance from the perspectives of culture and ritual performance. The major themes which inform my discussion have grown out of an empirical application of the concepts of ritual and resistance to school settings, particularly the events and conditions which provide the context for classroom instruction. In my articulation of ritualized resistance I have drawn heavily upon the work of cultural and symbolic anthropologists.

The idea of bringing the concepts of ritual and resistance into a unified framework grew out of my field work in St. Ryan's (not the real name) Catholic school in downtown Toronto, Canada. The school had been described to me by School Board officials as the "toughest" Catholic junior high school in the city and had a school population which consisted primarily of Portuguese students. My field work was confined to three grade 7 and 8 classrooms.

The cultural terrain of St. Ryan was composed of an intricate ritual system consisting of various symbols, world-views, ethoses, root paradigms, and forms of resistance. I have analyzed classroom instruction as a ritual system and, in so doing, have constructed a typology which includes rituals of revitalization, rituals of intensification, and rituals of resistance (McLaren, 1986). The discussion that follows will be limited to what I have termed "rituals of resistance."

1 Ritual

According to Grimes (1982), a ritual is a form of symbolic action composed primarily of gestures (the enactment of evocative rhythms which constitute dynamic symbolic acts) and postures (a symbolic stilling of action). Gesture is formative. It is related to everyday action and may oscillate between randomness and formality.

Ritualization is a process which involves the incarnation of symbols, symbol clusters, metaphors, and root paradigms through formative bodily gesture. As forms of enacted meaning, rituals enable social actors to frame, negotiate, and articulate their phenomenological existence as social, cultural, moral, and political beings.

Rituals are not ethereal entities distinct from the vagaries of everyday living, somehow perched atop the crust of culture, as a bundle of abstract norms and ordinances to be enacted apart from the concrete constitution of individual roles and relations out of which daily life is built. Rather, rituals are inherently political. They cannot be understood in isolation from how individuals are located biographically and historically in various traditions of mediation (e.g. clan, gender, home environment, classroom, peer group culture). Ensconced in the framework of both private and institutional life, rituals become part of the socially conditioned, historically acquired, and biologically constituted rhythms and metaphors of human agency.

Rituals never communicate in a vacuum or outside history. As carriers of culturally and politically coded meanings, rituals are never neutral. Rather, they channel meaning contextually in ways which rarely escape the historical legacy of sedimented oppression that has become, for the children of the dispossessed, the hallmark of life under capitalism (McLaren, 1984).

2   Theories of Resistance

By the term *resistance*, I refer to oppositional student behavior that has symbolic, historical, and "lived" meaning and which contests the legitimacy, power, and significance of school culture in general and instruction in particular.

Theories surrounding the concept of resistance have been gaining recognition in recent years, largely through the efforts of radical educational theorists such as Willis (1977) and Giroux (1983a, 1983b, 1984). Theories of resistance are generally situated within neo-Marxist social theory and draw upon the ethnographer's understanding of the complexities of culture in order to articulate the relationship between schools and the dominant society. Resistance theorists have challenged the school's ostensible role as a democratic institution which functions to improve the social position of all students – including, if not especially, those groups that are subordinated to the system. Resistance theorists have interrogated the processes by which the school system reflects and sustains the logic of capital as well as dominant social practices and structures which are founded on class, race, and gender divisions.

Resistance theorists have pointed out that schools are more than the ideologically neutral arbiters of the common culture (Giroux, 1984). Furthermore, they have shown that classroom culture does not manifest itself as some pristine unity or disembodied, homogeneous entity but is, rather, discontinuous, murky, and provocative of competition and conflict. Classroom culture is symbolically manipulable and susceptible to change and rupture; it is a collectivity which is composed of "contests" between ideologies and disjunctions between class, cultural, and symbolic conditions. It is, furthermore, a symbolic arena where students and teachers struggle over the interpretation of metaphors, icons, and structures of meaning and where symbols have both centripetal and centrifugal pulls. Similarly, the ideological hegemony of school life is not monolithically impregnable; there is considerable resistance on the part of students to engagement in classroom instruction. The seeming homogeneity and harmony that pervade life in the classroom exist at the imaginary level only. Ritual meaning often lurks in subtle negation, opposition, and resistance as well as in affirmation of the status quo: it is conflictual as well as consensualist.

My own work in resistance theory has been to analyze student resistance as consisting of dynamic cultural forms which I have termed rituals of resistance. I have tried to shift the theoretical terrain of mainstream studies of ritual by addressing the concepts of power and domination and by describing ritual as a cultural production constructed as a collective reference to the symbolic and situated experience of a group's social class. Accordingly, a classroom ritual is considered to be a political event and part of the objectified distribution of school's dominant cultural capital (e.g. systems of meanings, taste, attitudes, and norms which legitimate the existing social order).

Rituals of resistance are often attempts at "purifying" the contaminated and fragmented world of institutionalized social structure. They may be aptly described as a type of ceremonial "destructuring" (cf. Grimes, 1982). Hidden grudges and tensions are mobilized for the purpose of rupturing the culturally axiomatic rules of the school and subverting the grammars of mainstream classroom discourse.

Rituals or resistance partake of two distinct forms: active and passive. Active resistance rituals are intentional or conscious attempts by students to subvert or sabotage teacher instruction or rules and norms established by school authorities. Passive resistance rituals unconsciously or tacitly subvert or sabotage the normative codes of the dominant school order. These rituals are less overt and less demonstrative than active resistance rituals.

3 Resistances as Rites of Transgression

Acts of resistance are, in Turner's (1968) idiom, liminal[1] experiences; they occur among students who have begun to traffic in illegitimate symbols and who attempt to deride authority by flexing, as it were, their countercultural muscles. The provenance of resistance is located in what Turner calls the *antistructure*[2] where contradiction and conflict compete with the continuity of ritual symbols and ritual metaphors. The antistructure is also where students attempt to disrupt, obstruct, and circumvent the incumbent moral demands of the instructional rites. In both subtle and overt ways, recusant students often undermine the consensually validated norms and codes which make up the bric-a-brac of the school's institutional life.

Acts of resistance in inner-city schools comprise a spectrum of modes: from the stirring frenzy of a class "going wild" to the carefree abandonment of students at play or the lugubrious whining of students who feel "cheated" or the orderly resistance of collective struggle. Sometimes present as well are various other ritualized modes of conflict, dramatic confrontational performances, and the release of anarchic behavior – all assaults on the established order.

It is not difficult to understand why working-class students resist schooling through rites of transgression. The norms of how one relates to instruction are drawn from the need of the culture to maintain the status quo – a status quo which many working-class students find overwhelmingly oppressive. Breaching the rules is often a logical response to the oppressive conditions of the classroom and occurs most often when the naked authoritarianism of the teacher becomes too much to bear.

But resistance goes beyond reactions to bureaucrats high on the aphrodisiac of power. It is also a reaction to the gulf between the life-filled informal street culture of the students and the thing-oriented, digital approach of mainstream instruction – an approach in which thinking skills are stressed over political and moral values and individual feelings.

Consisting of a variety of behaviors which are marshaled in opposition to the pro forma curricular declarations of the suite, resistance often takes the form of buffoonery, ribaldry, railler, hoopla, or open disputation. Such general intransigence – a plethora of anti-teacher verbiage (usually in muted or whispered tones), the thwarting of a lesson through brusque remarks, constant carping at the classroom rules, nonnegotiable demands, incessant jabber, insouciant slapstick, marvelously inventive obscenities – these "street corner" characteristics threaten to make hay of established codes of classroom propriety.

Resistance among working-class students at St. Ryan's rarely occurred through legitimate channels of checks and balances. Organized resistance to school policy in the form of student unions or community liaison committees is largely the preserve of the children of the ruling class. Among the disaffected and disenfranchised, resistance was generally tacit, informal, unwitting, and unconscious. These students were resisting more than just a formal corpus of rules and injunctions: they were resisting the distinction between the "lived" informal culture of the streets and the formal, dominant culture of the classroom. The tension between these two cultures, while great, is not inexorable. But the antithesis between them constitutes one of the most important conflicts in urban education (McLaren, 1985).

During my field work at St. Ryan's I discovered that the major cultural "drama" of resistance was an attempt on the part of students to establish informal street-corner culture within the boundaries of classroom instruction. Common instances of resistance included: leaning back on chairs so that students nearly fell over (and often did); knocking one another on the backs of the knees and other forms of "masculine" jostling; leaning over the desks and talking to other students; insurrectionary posing such as thrusting out the chin and scowling at the teacher; being in a restricted space (such as a hallway or washroom) without permission; obeying a teacher's command but performing the required task in slow motion (symbolic stalling); "horsing around" or fighting in class; and wearing "intimidating" clothing.

Possessing a higher status than the students, the teacher attempted to transmit the symbolic reading and writing skills with which the students could create some kind of "rational" order out of the "flux" of working-class existence. What school resisters attempted to do was to disassemble, dismember, and refashion these pedagogical symbols: to turn them into symbols that could be defeated. Resisters challenged the legitimacy of the social pressure which said: "You must do this" or "You must do that." Resistance often forced teachers to abandon their pedagogical role and take on the oppressive guise of the police officer. If teachers wanted to keep control (and ultimately their jobs) they were forced to compel rebellious students to desist, pay recompense and penalty, or make restitution for their profane antics. Redressive measures involved expelling the occasional offender, trying to find a more "appropriate" programme for the student in another school, and administering detentions. There was usually a limit or tolerance level (which the teachers referred to as "drawing the line") beyond which redressive action was taken. Students, for their part, were usually aware when a teachers saturation or tolerance level was reached (it varied with the different teachers) and would often try to keep the teacher at a pitch just below the breaking point.

Classroom rituals possess a collective function beyond simply fostering a sense of organic solidarity. As both organized and spontaneous opposition to instruction, rituals of resistance served both to flush out dead symbols from the clotted cultural conduits of the instructional system – symbols which no longer provided channels for addressing the needs of students – and to replace them with more meaningful symbols. For instance, respect for the picture of the Queen and singing of the national anthem were seen as laughable by the students who preferred to venerate rock groups such as the Clash.

By observing the cramped, defensive posturing of the students and the brusque, authoritative gestures of the teachers, it was possible to see how relationships of power were grafted onto the medium of living flesh and marrow. Power and privilege became "somaticized." The body served both as a mirror of state oppression and an instrument for resisting domination.

Ritualized resistance created a new discourse of student communication, one in which the body provided the metalingual function of inverting and recombining dominant cultural meanings. It is impossible to discuss resistance as a ritual mode without first acknowledging that in addition to being a function of structural domination, hegemony is also carried and expressed within the body.

Every student body carried its own history of subjugation preserved in stratum upon stratum of breathing tissue. Student bodies were pervaded by symbols of oppression which were swollen with meaning and which were enfolded in the musculature, pressed into the tendons, and encased in the meshwork of bones and sinew. Domination, which was inscribed in the physiognomic symbols of student expressiveness, was fundamentally an act of corporeity. Student resistance was a resolve not to be dissimulated in the face of internalized oppression. It was a battle against the erasure of their street-corner "style" and an attempt to reclaim the autonomous rhythms and gestures of the street and playground.

Examining resistance as a ritual mode underscores the differences between the appropriation of cultural knowledge. For example, street-corner knowledge partook of a generic religiosity and involved a visceral *knowing* that was related to bodily knowledge and the rhythms and gestures of informal street-corner culture. This knowing was qualitatively distinct from classroom *knowledge* which was the clinical appropriation of (often unconnected) facts and empirical information.

Participation in rituals of resistance involved enlisting whatever street-corner symbols – or combinations of symbols – were necessary to counter the bland redundancy of classroom instruction. The canopy of predictability created by the sameness and invariance of classroom instructional forms was repeatedly punctured by embodied symbols and gestures which dead time and boredom in school had whittled into oppositional weapons.

4 The Class Clown: Arbiter of Passive Resistance, Inversion, and Meta-Discourse

Situated in the context of more passive ritual resistance to the normative order of the school was the class clown, whom I have identified as embodying some of the characteristics of the ritual fool (McLaren, 1986).

Throughout the course of my field work, I identified several class clowns, one of whom I shall call Vinnie. Vinnie was capricious, vacillating, and frequently obstreperous. His behavior could be described in terms of the way it changed the context of the classroom setting which was shaped by the instructional rituals. Without the benefit of pratfalls, custard pies, or commedia dell'arte masks, class clowns arrogated to themselves – often unconsciously – the function of deconstructing the familiar. They achieved this through sarcastic comments, a Trickster-like prankishness, parody, and burlesque.

Punning, facetious, and irreverent, Vinnie would shift vagariously from farce to satire, and even to mawkishness. Like a character in one of Genet's plays, he was the epitome of pure, stylized action – a performer of wordless skills in the tradition of the *mimus*.

Watching Vinnie act in nonaccordance with the school norms made me aware of just how boring school really was. He revealed the tenuousness and arbitrariness of the codes that prevented possible chaos from breaking out in the suite. Thus, Vinnie's task was not solely buffoonery, but teaching. Structurally marginal and categorically anomalous, Vinnie was stuck in the interface between the street-corner and dominant cultures.

Vinnie nearly always smiled, despite the various degrees of seriousness of the occasion, and despite continued admonishments from the teacher. Although Vinnie was often ignored by his classmates, a large number of students either willfully followed his antics or else were engagingly distracted by him.

Vinnie would do zany things when the teacher's attention was somewhere else: he would roll his eyeballs sarcastically, throw a pen in the air, or joke with his friends. He would frequently make bizarre faces – always incorporating some type of twisted smile. On numerous occasions I watched him gingerly roll a baseball across the floor, between the desks, while others were hard at work or at prayer.

Vinnie's performance as the class clown appeared to be consistent with Bouissac's (1982) observation that the actions of the clown constitute an "acted meta-discourse" on the tacit rules of the social order – that they mirror or express "the basic but unwritten rules" on which our construction of a culturally bound, meaningful universe depends. Along these lines, it could be said that Vinnie trivialized instructional transactions and demonstrated the arbitrariness of the "sacred" cultural axioms and enshrined protocols that held together the symbolic universe of the suite. This profanation of the sacred rules by the clown was more than just the breaking of classroom decorum; it was the blatant exposure before all of the classroom's cultural code. It was not the breaking of the code itself which was important (everybody, at least intuitively, knew what the sacred rules were|, but the knowledge that the clown could communicate through satire and humor what the rules were. He understood the secret of their arbitrariness and the fact that they were not handed down from the heavens.

The antics of the clown became a Damoclean sword continuously poised above the teacher's head; it threatened at any moment to swoop down and cut through the teacher's "bullshit," forcing the teacher to keep "honest."

One of Vinnie's methods of abrogating convention was to silently mock the prayers. With Thespian exaggeration, he would look bored, then crack a smile and cross himself perfunctorily. Sometimes he would prefer to play with a pen or inspect his lapel while the rest of the class stood with bowed heads. He would, on occasion, clasp his hands in front of his face as if in prayer, and then vigorously explore his nostrils with his index finger while licking his lips. This was a signal to the other students that he could slip out of the sacred shackles of the prayer whenever he felt like it; for Vinnie, his performance was invariably a "high" – a demiapotheosis. Another one of Vinnie's tricks was to knock over all the chairs that had been placed on top of the desks at the end of the day. Once, during school mass, I observed several class clowns (including Vinnie) pull each other over the pews during the sign of peace.

As he mocked, scoffed at, lampooned, and parodied the foibles of both teachers and fellow students, the class clown may be said to have "played" with the internal inconsistency and ambiguity of the ritual symbols and metaphors. Possessing a disproportionate zeal for "being an ass," Vinnie symbolically undid or refracted what the instructional rituals work so hard to build up – school culture and its concomitant reification of the cultural order. The clown served to attenuate the rootedness of classroom reality; he diminished the authoritative hold which the master symbols had on the students. Unable to maintain equanimity in the culture of the school, the clown inverted the classroom *lebensraum*. What distinguished the class clown's actions from more typical forms of resistance were his amusing methods of rule profanation, his ingenuous personality, and his often outrageous flouting of the ordinary canons of moral conduct. The resistance of the clown was a reverent violation of the codes of the dominant cultural discourse of the school. In effect, he served to mediate the dualism between the street-corner and school cultures.

In terms of the instructional activity in the suite, the clown offered more than just comic relief. He was threatening in the way that he metaphorically stripped the teachers naked and demythologized the classroom power structure. Every morning the classroom clown symbolically sat in the boardroom of the Ministry of Education and wagged his tongue (at a risk, perhaps, of being streamed into a basic-level programme). Because he was often amusing, the clown was not perceived as a direct threat, yet his antics could not go totally unpunished. He was sometimes described by teachers as "a bit of a nut" – a label which conveniently permitted teachers to place him outside the context of the "normal student" so that the punishment meted out to him need not appear as severe as that which was inflicted upon the rank-and-file "deviant." The clown demanded that the teacher laugh at himself and all that the teacher represented. To a certain extent teachers met this demand (often by engaging in some self-effacing humor) for fear of incurring extended antics from the clown or reprisals from other, more "dangerous" students. The only way a clown could be severely punished was if the teacher was incapable of laughing at himself or herself. If the teacher believed that the clown was actually dangerous in his contravention of the school ordinances, then the teacher would be forced to take whatever measure was necessary to curtail the clown's antics.

5   Toward a New Conception of Resistance

The examination of resistance as a ritual process uncovers untapped possibilities for understanding how hegemony does its "work" both through dominant structural (e.g. socio-economic) arrangements and through human agency. Hegemony is not a form of unidirectional domination; it is not simply a system of ideological constraints imposed from above. Rather, it partakes of the many outcomes resulting from (often antagonistic) negotiations between symbolic meanings – meanings which are continuously mediated by structural conditions, relationships of power, and the multifarious ways in which we rhythmically and gesturally engage the world.

Hegemony gives birth to itself somewhere "between" the contradictory axes of structural domination and the self-production of subordinate and oppositional groups. At the ideological level, it is embedded in a welter of contradictions.

At the level of human agency, hegemony is both sustained and contested through our "style" of engaging the world and the ways in which we ritualize our daily lives: our gestural embodiments, our rhythmical practices, and our lived forms of resistance.

While hegemony is embedded in structural relations and the mediation of class and culture, it is sustained through the contradictions embodied not just in the way we think but in the way we attend to the world through our lived engagement with it. And although it is true that hegemony shrouds the body and shapes the will through an intricate web of symbols mediated by capitalist relations of power and privilege, we must remember that in the process of domination, human agency is always alive, rupturing the unitary pervasiveness of structural, sedimented oppression and allowing for liminal possibilities of emancipation.

The concept of resistance has been a major theoretical advance in understanding how schools are able to reproduce the dominant social order through various cultural "acts" of domination and contestation.

One of the major contributions to resistance theory has been the discovery by Paul Willis (1977) that working-class students who engage in resistance often implicate themselves even further in their own domination. Willis's group of working-class schoolboys resisted the dominant discourse of the school by rejecting mental labor in favor of "masculine" manual labor (which reflected the shop floor culture of their family members). In so doing, they foreclosed any chance that the school could help them escape the shop floor once they left school. Willis's work presented a considerable advance in understanding social and cultural reproduction in the context of student resistance. However, theories of resistance have major advances to make before they achieve the conceptual precision and refinement necessary to help establish a comprehensive critical pedagogy.

According to Giroux (1981, 1983a, 1983b), current discussions of resistance are marked by a number of inadequacies. For example, they overemphasize the promotion of economic and cultural inequality by structural determinants and underemphasize the role of human agency in accommodating, mediating, and resisting the logic of capital (1983a, p. 282); they frequently fail to articulate which forms of oppositional behavior constitute political acts of defiance and which forms simply manifest the worst aspects of capitalist rationality such as racism and sexism (pp. 285–286). And they fail to address less overt acts of rebelliousness in schools or attempt to analyze how domination reaches into the structure of the personality itself (p. 288).

For Giroux, an adequate theory of resistance should celebrate a dialectical notion of human agency and critically use concepts such as intentionality, consciousness, the meaning of common sense, and the nature and value of nondiscursive behavior (p. 290). With emancipation as the dominant or guiding theme, it remains the task of radical educators to give the term "resistance" more conceptual utility by digging into the historical and relational conditions from which oppositional behavior develops while at the same time linking such behavior to interpretations provided by the subjects themselves (p. 291).

Following these recommendations of Giroux, I would suggest, in anthropological terms, that we begin to situate oppositional behavior in a discourse that attends both to emic perspectives (or the native's point of view) and etic perspectives (interpretations from the cultural perspective of the outsider). This must be followed by an analysis of resistance that measures the subjective reasons that students give for resisting in school against their concrete actions and locates these actions within a historical perspective that critically addresses the crucial concepts of ideology, hegemony, and human agency. Only then will we be able to agree upon which behaviors in school settings really constitute legitimate resistance and which behaviors simply constitute an inverted reflection of the dominant capitalist ideology.

A ritual studies approach to understanding schooling has important implications for understanding oppositional student behavior and discourse. At the cynosure of such an approach is the examination of resistance as a liminal cultural formation that is generated in the antistructure.

Important questions come to the fore when we begin to cast resistance in ritual and performative terms. To what extent do resisters become *liminars*[3] in their attempt to escape structural inferiority, low status, and outsiderhood? To what extent does resistance as a ritual process promote changes in consciousness? In what ways do resisters participate in a shared psychic state in which adopted symbols have meaning only to those who are similarly separated from the mainstream society? What is the nature of *communitas*[4] during transgressive acts in the classroom? To what extent is communitas *ad hoc,* normative, and ideological? How, for instance, is resistance functionally adaptive for marginal groups? How do oppositional groups codify their culture of resistance into a sustaining set of symbolic meanings?

While empirical accounts of oppositional student behavior are often discussed in terms of symbolic meaning, few school ethnographers from the reproduction or resistance schools have paid sufficient attention to the morphology of the symbol. Since almost any meaning can be wrenched from an oppositional symbol if interrogated with sufficient indulgence by a school ethnographer, it is time for the resistance theorist to take a serious look at the anthropology of the symbol. Close attention also needs to be paid to advances made in symbolic studies in the areas of liturgical exegesis, semiotics, performance studies, and comparative symbology.

One important way of uncovering the nature of student resistance is to interrogate school culture with its overlaid system of symbols and meanings using methodologies established by symbolic anthropologists such as Victor Turner. We must begin to examine further the correspondence between classroom and oppositional symbols and larger socio-economic structures. We must discover the extent to which symbols of resistance are autonomous and the ways in which they are tied to larger arenas of meaning – such as the domain of popular culture. And we must begin to examine how communitas and classroom ritual both help free students from societal restraints and also reproduce the class location of the students in a way that sustains powerlessness.

To cast resistance in symbolic and ritual terms also has implications for the classroom teacher. It means that attempts must be made to keep our classrooms from becoming empty containers for castaway symbols – symbols that benumb our spirits and which no longer remain linked to the universe of meanings embedded in the codes of contemporary youth culture. This, in turn, emphasizes the need for teachers to critically engage students at the level of their own cultural literacy. The formations of popular youth culture, in all their complexity and potency, must be seen as valuable by the teacher but must not be unqualifiedly endorsed. These cultural formations must also be interrogated for their racist, sexist, and sometimes fascist dimensions (as found in some recent rock video productions, for example).

The reform that I am suggesting is more than the creation of liminal classrooms where students can cavort in an unalloyed, unfettered state of communitas. On the contrary, I am arguing for the creation of an emancipatory politics of schooling which will help to render as problematic the meanings embedded in the ritual forms and content of classroom instruction. Once we understand the classroom as an embattled symbolic arena in which teachers and classroom peer groups struggle over how reality is to be signified, and in what manner and style the cultural terrain is to be engaged, then we, as teachers, can begin to situate classroom reform in both the fight for material equality and the forging of a new symbolic sphere.

The conceptual core of the analyses undertaken by radical scholarship over the last two decades has involved unpacking the relationship between schooling and the economic sphere of capitalist production. Yet all too often this has been done at the expense of understanding the role of symbol and ritual in the colonization of student subjectivities and the proletarianization of teachers. While mainstream studies of ritual (including anthropological and liturgical traditions) often fall prey to a hegemonic instrumental rationality and are imprisoned in a discourse in which positivism becomes the theoretical center of gravity, this must not prevent radical educational researchers from adapting some of the contributions of ritual scholars into their work. These scholars have helped us to understand that rituals are not simply decorative, gesturally superfluous, or forms of corporeal embellishment. They have shown us that ritual symbols are no less than keys to cultural literacy. And once students are able to unlock the doors of cultural literacy, they have taken a major step towards self-improvement.

Teachers must deplore the waning power of classroom symbols to inspire working-class students to take an active role in their own empowerment because in that diminution students' access to political transformation is lost. This calls for both teachers and researchers to incorporate further the concept of ritualized resistance into a pedagogy of liberation, a pedagogy whose heterodoxy is informed by a resolve to scrape through the coagulation of despair and alienation that lies at the heart of the capitalist state.

Acknowledgments

An expanded version of this chapter can be found in Peter L. McLaren, *Schooling as a ritual performance: Toward a political economy of educational symbols and gestures* (Routledge and Kegan Paul, 1986).

This chapter originally appeared as P. L. McLaren, The ritual dimensions of resistance: Clowning and symbolic inversion, *Journal of Education*, 167(2) (1985), 84–97. Reprinted here, with minor edits, with permission from the publisher.

Notes

1 Originally described by Van Gennep (1960) and expanded by Turner (1969), the term liminality refers to a homogeneous social state in which participants are stripped of their usual status and authority. It is a process of mid-transition – sometimes known, as "betwixt and between – in which participants are removed temporarily from a social structure that is maintained and sanctioned by power and force. Comradeship and communion between participants are often liberated in this state.
2 Antistructure is another term to describe the liminal state in which individuals exist outside the structure of roles, statuses, and positions within the society. Rather, the individuals within the antistructure exist in a state of undifferentiated and homogeneous community.
3 A "liminar" is a ritual participant who exists in the second (or liminal) stage of Van Gennep's (1960) ritual process which includes: separation from ordinary, mundane social life; margin or limen [meaning threshold), when the ritual participants enter a limbo of "betwixt and between" (between their past and present modes of daily

existence); and reaggregration (reabsorption), when participants are returned to ordinary life – either at a higher status level or in an altered state of awareness.
4 *Communitas* refers to the temporary camaraderie which occurs when roles or statuses are suspended between fellow liminals. A deep foundational and fundamental bond is established. Victor Turner has defined three types of communitas: (1) spontaneous or existential communitas, (2) normative communitas, and (3) ideological communitas. Spontaneous communitas is the opposite of social structure; it defies the deliberate cognitive and volitional construction. Normative communitas tries to capture and preserve spontaneous communitas in a system of ethical precepts and legal rules. Ideological communitas refers to the formulation of remembered attributes of the communitas experience in the form of a utopian blueprint for the reform of society.

References

Bouissac, R. (1982). *The profanation of the sacred in circus performance?* A paper presented to the Werner-Cren Foundation for Anthropological Research, Symposium No. 89, "Theatre and Ritual," New York.

Giroux, H. A. (1981). *Ideology, culture, and the process of schooling.* Temple University Press.

Giroux, H. A. (1983a). *Theory and resistance in education: A pedagogy for the opposition.* Bergin & Garvey.

Giroux, H. A. (1983b). Theories of reproduction and resistance in the new sociology of education. *Harvard Educational Review, 53*(3), 257–293.

Giroux, H. (1984). Marxism and schooling: The limits of radical discourse. *Educational Theory, 34*(2).

Grimes, R. L. (1976). *Symbol and conquest.* Cornell University Press.

Grimes, R. L. (1982). *Beginnings in ritual studies.* University Press of America.

McLaren, P. (1984). Rethinking ritual. *ETC: A Review of General Semantics, 41*(3), 267–277.

McLaren, P. (1985). A prolegomena towards establishing links between ritology and schooling. In J. Kase-Polisini (Ed.), *Creative drama in a developmental context* (pp. 209–251). University Press of America.

McLaren, P. (1986). *Schooling as a ritual performance: Toward a political economy of educational symbols and gestures.* Routledge and Kegan Paul.

Turner, V. (1969). *The ritual process: Structure and anti-structure.* Aldine.

Van Gennep, A. (1960). *The rites of passage.* Routledge and Kegan Paul.

Willis, P. (1977). *Learning to labour: How working-class kids get working-class jobs.* Gower.

CHAPTER 3

On Ideology and Education
Critical Pedagogy and the Politics of Empowerment

1   Sifting through the Remains

Decades of volatile debates over the term ideology have produced a theoretical residue that continues to fleck the landscape of social theory, creating a conceptual terrain at once murky, distortive, and contradictory. Few concepts in social theory are as pervasive and durable, yet few continue to provoke such a cleavage of opinion among theorists. What makes such an ephemeral concept so tenacious is difficult to ascertain, as it continues to exercise scholars of various theoretical stripe and disciplinary affiliation. Attempts by Marxists and non-Marxists alike to fully delineate a theory of ideology has, over the years, produced a voluminous body of work, the vast sweep of which has so far failed to grasp adequately this often diffuse and impalpable term. The major theoretical traditions have ranged from the work of French rationalists, Anglo-Saxon empiricists to German idealists. The most that scholars have been able to achieve – admittedly no small feat in itself – has been to produce a temporary theoretical truce around contesting definitions of the term.

Over the last decade especially, there has been a steady proliferation of studies attempting to both pry loose some determinate meaning from this historically stubborn concept and to register a new set of analytic claims regarding how it should be defined and employed in critical research (see Hanninen & Paldan, 1983; McLellan, 1986).[1] In the first part of the chapter, I propose to sketch the contours of some of these new analytic claims in order to specify some problems with existing conceptions of ideology and ideology critique and attempt to move beyond them. In the second part I will bring my discussion to bear on a concrete public sphere – that of schooling – in order to illustrate how some of these perspectives on ideology can be rethought in analyzing student resistance and developing a critical pedagogy. A portion of this section will draw from recent ethnographic research which I undertook in a Catholic junior high school in Toronto, Canada.

Analyzing the orthodox Marxian position on ideology means widening the discussion of ideology in order to question some of its underlying theoretical assumptions and premises. While there always exists the possibility of overgeneralizing some of the assumptions of orthodox theorists by addressing issues which they imply but do not directly pose, it nevertheless remains necessary to tap the broader ideological currents of their thought. In a concerted attempt to avoid what Stuart Hall refers to as "epistemological heavy warfare," I shall refrain from taking all the connotations or contextual factors or consequences of this position into consideration. My purpose in drawing attention to this work is to show how the orthodox position on ideology is marred by a number of theoretical shortcomings which characterize its basic assumptions.

The nature of this essay is not so much to challenge the orthodox canon on ideology, at least on a point-by-point basis. To do so would be to give credibility to terms of reference which constitute both a conceptually inadequate epistemology and social theory. It would also be siding with a perniciously narrow view of culture. Instead, the theoretical tension between the orthodox Marxist conception of ideology and alternative radical interpretations will be examined, including what have sometimes been referred to as "post-Marxian" formulations.

2 Ideology and the Correspondence Theory of Truth: The Case for Multiple Subjectivities

Since limitations of space preclude a lengthy sojourn into the volatile and contentious history of ideology, I shall begin by offering a direct rejoinder to one of the mainsprings of the orthodox position, namely its indebtedness to a correspondence theory of truth. Here the question of ideology becomes yoked to the materialist/epistemological question of what can be proven subversive of empirical truth. The correspondence theory of truth presumes an achieved system of equivalence between ideas, beliefs, and reality, and resonates with Popper's criteria that a proposition must be subject to falsifiability, refutation, and empirical test. It is explicitly concerned with the problem of demarcation between science and non-science. From this perspective, the concept of ideology must be defended as something to be logically unveiled according to a defensible criteria rooted in objective reality. This places the individual knower in a complicitous relationship between scientific knowledge and the real world. Such a view asserts that reliable knowledge about the world is objective only when it exists independently of an observer. Here we must ask if one can actually search for knowledge without a knowing subject, or if logic can stand outside of human will or volition or the system of differences we use to semiotically construct the world. Unfortunately, such a position betrays little theoretical acquaintance with the idea that the "real" world within which social construction takes place never stands still but necessarily remains fluid and unfinished.

To adhere to a correspondence theory of truth is to ignore the serious crisis in analytic-referential discourse. Conspicuously absent from this orthodox position is an understanding of ideology as a form of cultural production. Or, in terms we have come to associate with the late Michel Foucault, this position ignores recent post-structuralist formulations which call for the primacy of *discursive formations* in understanding the rudiments of ideological production. In other words, the orthodox position fails to consider the *positivity* of ideology (Foucault, 1980).[2] For all of the theoretical frenzy and epistemic turmoil created by the development of discourse theory, it has at the very least proven an undeniable corrective to simple "action theory" in sociological analysis which assumes the subject as the unproblematic author of choice and agency. Discourses, as any modern scholar of post-structuralism knows, articulate concepts through a system of signs and these signs always signify by means of their relationship to each other rather than to objective entities in the world. The world, in this view, becomes a simulacrum that is itself constructed in language. This post-structuralist perspective dramatically conflicts with the classical realist position on the status of truth, exposing it to be tautological insofar as language always mediates the world by positioning us in particular discursive alignments within distinctive social formations (Belsey, 1980; Lacan, 1977; Henriques et al., 1984; Althusser, 1971).[3] Of significance here is that the ideological codes correlating signifiers and signifieds are never natural, immutable, or unproblematic but are, instead historically and culturally inscribed. From this standpoint, we cannot know the nature of the world or its "truth" in the same way that we can hold up for interrogation the discursive order inscribed in particular truth claims. This is similar to asserting, along with Foucault, that we can discover the "truth effects" of particular discourses and never the "whole truth."

Foucault's understanding of knowledge does not entail a notion of ideas corresponding either to a "reality" independent of knowledge or a notion of truth separate from the conditions of its production (Aronowitz, 1986/1987, p. 11).[4] Foucault understands power as *immanent in the morphology of discourse*, a factor which permits various discursive subject positions to be distributed within a field of asymmetrical relations. In this way, discourses are not simply related to contradictions at the level of production. Notwithstanding Foucault's tendency to essentialize natural history by reducing social relations to discursive formations (Aronowitz, 1986/1987), his approach delivers a formidable blow to the correspondence theory of truth, adding to the growing disillusionment with scientific Marxism (Aronowitz, 1986/1987). Failure of orthodox Marxists to link ideology to a Foucauldian conception of power lets slip an opportunity to analyze the productive aspects of ideology, that is, its positive relation to truth, or the "effects" of truth that it produces. From Foucault's genealogical perspective, ideology does not work to distort and mystify the truth as much as to produce and legitimate a particular regime of truth – a process which in many ways is more dangerous to its victims. The truth, in this view, is not freedom from ideological constraint but rather the result of particular power/knowledge constellations. Power/knowledge regimes of truth govern social relations not by producing coherent subjects with fixed identities but through discursive practices that produce subject positions, which are always potentially contradictory. According to Foucault, the relationship between Marxism's theoretical project and its methodological defense as a science has more to do with the various epistemologies Marxism *unwittingly suppresses* than with the question of truth value (Foucault, 1980; Lacan, 1977; Henriques et al., 1984; Steedman et al., 1985; Althusser, 1971).[5]

The danger, of course, is that Marxism's pursuit of the scientificity of its theory has unwittingly become an exercise in domination because it has become synonymous with an acceptance of the institutions and effects of power that invest scientific discourse with legitimacy and credibility (Smart, 1983). The important idea here is that discursive "rules of formation" – the governing rules under which specific types of statements are consistently produced and distributed within a discursive field – are *not* determined solely or mainly by modes of economic production so much as historical conditions (*some* of which may be economic) which are as various as they are complex. Foucault's position, therefore, necessarily raises some fundamental questions in relation to the orthodox position. Are mental categories, the laws of thought, and criteria of judgment *extra discursive* or are they inscribed in a symbolic order? If they are, indeed, inscribed in the symbolic order, is this order preconstituted by modes of economic production? Are human agents encysted in an ideological matrix that can only reiterate patterns of signification which have been irremediably inscribed according to the logic of capital accumulation and the social relations of production?

Viewed from the orthodox perspective, however, the ideological subject is advanced as being *de facto* constituted by capital; all too cavalierly discredited as the notion that ideologies are not symptomatic of some prior cause but rather constitute both the medium and the outcome of a recursive generation of representations and social practices, all of which coalesce simultaneously in the ideological "event." For post-structuralist theorists, the constitution or "positioning" of the subject constitutes *only one* predetermining element in the functioning of ideological discourses. What is not addressed adequately within the orthodox canon is how individuals can inhabit contradictory ideological positions or how ideologies are often provisionally secured by their contingency upon features other than modes of economic production (such as social ascription according to race, class, and gender) or by their relation to other discourses, institutions, and social formations.

The poverty of the orthodox perspective is revealed most fully in what it ignores. Rarely, if ever, does it take up or even cursorily consider the concept of ideology as the production of multiple subjectivities, a position which permits educators especially to theorize beyond the traditional individual/society dualism when attempting to understand how schools and everyday life locate students within multiple subject positions (Simon, 1986).[6]

A point worth emphasizing is that consciousness, rather than conceived as false, can be better conceived as a "text." In other words, ideologies are best "read" as socially constructed relations which constitute the products of numerous histories, institutions, processes of inscription, and traditions of mediation. Ideology is not, in a word, a domain of pure ideality. In this context, Bakhtin's demolition of the concept of the autonomous self and his theory of language as a kind of ideology-brought-into-speech further exposes the theoretical debility of the classical Marxian approach, helping to put it even further under erasure.

To assert, as many post-structuralists do, that ideologies are inscribed in signifying practices which constitute various representations of reality, is not the same thing as asserting that these representations are false. For example, underlying the work of various theorists such as Raymond Williams, Henry A. Giroux, and Philip Wexler is a common understanding of ideology as forms of representation central to the organization of experiences and subjectivities. Wexler rightly insists that ideology must be studied "not as a collection of entities, ideas, but as itself a production, a set of practices, structures, or methods which make meaning" (Wexler, 1982). Such an understanding of ideology as an imbricated intertextuality constitutes a significant theoretical advance over the vulgar Marxian conception of materialist epistemology based on the concept of false consciousness. The point to consider is that that consciousness is not all of one piece, a seamless web of *either* truth or distortion.

The reluctance of orthodox theorists to appropriate new developments in discourse theory and their failure to theorize adequately on those issues contribute, in part, to their inability to address ideology as a discourse of production. In order to move beyond the strangulated silence of their position, orthodox theorists would have to refute adequately the idea that knowledge does not reflect an objective or pristine ontological reality but instead constitutes a particular ordering and organization of a world constituted by our experience and social relations. Both these positions have a combative history (Von Glasersfeld, 1984).[7]

3   Ideology Essentialism, and the Contingency of the Social

One of the major problems with the orthodox theory of ideology is that it fails to question seriously the idea that perhaps the terms "true" and "false" are themselves theoretically problematic and involve contentious epistemological issues. An assignment of the features of truth and falsity to an empirical status presupposes the very notions of validation, logical consistency, and verifiability. And in an attempt to defend the claims of science to universality, scientificity, and normativity, orthodox theorists unwittingly fall victim to a position dangerously close to a naive essentialism, thus undercutting their argument in two ways: by leaving themselves open to a discursive skepticism regarding their assumption of social totality; and by rendering vulnerable the ontological security that results from taking refuge in a correspondence theory of truth (Shaviro, 1986; Pears, 1977).[8]

By attempting to restore ideology within a correspondence theory of truth, orthodox theorists actually empty ideology of its presumed ability to position subjects within a multiplicity of discursive formations (which I argue are not directly – or mainly – mediated by the reflex of capital).

The question of multiple discursive formations becomes an important focus in the work of Ernesto Laclau. His recent work has attempted to combine post-structuralist discourse theory with a neo-Gramscian non-reductionist concept of hegemony by advancing a politics of signification around the way in which ideologies produce subjects through the articulation and disarticulation of discourses. In his development of Althusser's concept of interpellation and its discursive and ideological function, Laclau has significantly weakened the orthodox position which is predicated upon a base/superstructure model and the concept of false consciousness. Laclau argues that both of these criteria for a restricted conception of ideology are grounded in an *essentialist* conception of society and social agency (Laclau, 1983; Laclau & Mouffe, 1985). The validity of the conception of false consciousness presupposes a concept of human agency which possesses "an ultimate essential homogeneity whose misrecognition was postulated as the source of ideology." (Laclau, 1983, pp. 21–22) Similarly, the validity of the base/superstructure model rests on a conception of society as "an intelligible totality, itself conceived as the structure upon which its partial elements and processes are founded" (Laclau, 1983, p. 21).

Against recognizing the essence of the social order behind the empirical variations at the surface of social life, Laclau argues for accepting "the *infinitude of the social,* that is, the fact that any structural system is always surrounded by an 'excess of meaning' which it is unable to master and that, consequently, 'society' as a unitary and intelligible object which grounds its own partial processes is an impossibility" (Laclau, 1983, p. 22; italics in original). This perspective highlights the relational character of identity and at the same time clearly renounces the fixation of these identities in a system. Instead, Laclau links the social with *an infinite play of discursive differences*. Thus, the meaning of the social becomes impossible to fix as it no longer takes the form of an underlying essence. The order – or structure – which we call society is really an attempt to *hegemonize* the social. The "totality" does not establish the limits of the social by transforming it into a determinate object (e.g. society). Laclau argues that:

> Each social formation has its own forms of determination and relative autonomy, which are always instituted through a complex process of overdetermination and therefore cannot be established *a priori*. With this insight, the base/superstructure distinction falls and, along with it, the conception of ideology as a necessary level of every social formation. (Laclau, 1983, p. 23)

Along the same line of attack, the concept of ideology as "false consciousness" also proves exceedingly vulnerable to Laclau's criticisms. The notion of class consciousness only makes sense if the identity of the social agent (in our case, the student) is fixed. This means, according to Laclau, that identity must be positive and non-contradictory. Only on the basis of recognizing true identity can it be asserted that the consciousness of the subject is indeed false.

Against the position put forward by Laclau, orthodox Marxists are often propelled by a dubious will to totality which is conceptually limiting precisely because it fails to credit sufficiently the concept of shifting discourses, the multiple play of differences, and the precarious discursive nature of any positivity. It also assumes a monolithic concept of ideology and of the ruling class which articulates class interests in a non-contradictory and unambiguous way. Laclau's position is that particular ideological elements do not have a pre-given class location. Of course, we must be careful not to endorse without qualification Laclau's position by detotalizing the social order in such a fashion that we effectively lose the concept of the social formation as centrally directed by relations of oppression (a predicament which constitutes some of the self-contradictions of post-Marxian theorists). Whereas arguments put forward by orthodox theorists do little to free social relations from the burden of scientific Marxism and the scientism of the Second International, contemporary post-structuralists such as Laclau tend to essentialize and eliminate political economy and natural history from their revolutionary text by effectively reducing social relations solely to discursive formations (Aronowitz,

1986/1987; Geras, 1987). To break free from both these extremes means recognizing Laclau's concept of the contingency of the social while keeping in mind that determinate forces of various stripe do exert a hegemonizing influence – *but only within historically specific moments and on the basis of particular cultural configurations.*

It is difficult to see where in the orthodox canon on ideology there is room for a politics of signification. We require a post-structuralist theory of subjectivity where ideology is not conceptualized as false consciousness but as an effort to make sense in a world of contradictory information and indeterminacies, "a way of holding at bay a randomness incongruent with consciousness" (Spivak, 1987). Ideology becomes, within such a perspective, a strategy of containment for beings who cannot "stop making sense" (Lather, 1987).

4 Science, Ideology and Context

Capital-logicians within the classical Marxist tradition demand an empirical science that works within a prescribed rationality whose range of possibilities is narrowly tied to formal criteria of prediction, linear causality (the effect is proportional to the cause) and lineal (straight line) causality. The work of Stanley Aronowitz is worth noting as a worthy rejoinder to the failure of many orthodox theorists to problematize the cohabitation of science and ideology. Aronowitz's position on the relationship between ideology and science can be summarized in remarks he made during a critical reading of Kurt Hubner's classic work, *Critique of Scientific Reason:*

> Every historical period produces precepts that govern what counts as a scientific fact. Facts [...] are generated, not merely discovered; they cannot be understood separately from the theoretical framework that gives them meaning. (Aronowitz, 1983, p. 60)

What Hubner and Aronowitz appear to be saying is that empirical verification is in some sense meaningless because raw data only begin to function when they have already entered theory. That is, there exists no facts-in-the-world which are positioned outside of theory from which a refutation can appeal. From this perspective, science relinquishes the immediate privilege to discover sovereign truth (Aronowitz, 1983).

Drawing upon early attempts by Frankfurt School theorists to collapse natural and social science, Aronowitz has demonstrated the essentially metaphoric nature of science. This position is understandably difficult for classical Marxists who consider scientific observations to be isomorphic to reality and who hold to the nineteenth-century version of science as the natural arbiter of social questions. But it is a position which makes sense whether or not reality is understood in the "picture sense" described by Wittgenstein or in Lenin's "approximate" connotation model. Aronowitz argues (rightly, in my opinion) that the problem is not that of a materialist world that is historically and epistemologically prior to and independent of human cognition, but whether the external world is independent of the social character of knowing (Aronowitz, 1980).

In Aronowitz's view, knowledge gathered in the cool sanctuaries of science cannot be objectively "true" insofar as it can never exist independently of the social processes which generate it. Thus, "doing science" (e.g. the procedures and conditions of scientific inquiry itself) necessarily alters the world by constituting an intervention (Aronowitz, 1980, pp. 75–101). This position is close to that espoused by Gregory Bateson in his critique of classical inductive methods. "Data," according to Bateson, "are *not* events or objects but [are] always records or descriptions or memories of events or objects" (Bateson, 1972, p. XVIII). This leads to the conclusion that the kinds of data required for a purely empirical study simply don't exist. Decisions about facts are always derived from "qualitative evaluations of the subject matter – evaluations that are often largely unconscious" (Wilden, 1980, p. 104). Moreover, as Bateson argues, there is always a transcoding or recoding of the raw event which intervenes between the scientist and his object. However, in the reductionist approach of classical Marxian educators, there is often a denial of context and a reliance on objectivity. The very notion of scientific neutrality that celebrated by orthodox theorists is, from Aronowitz's perspective, blatantly ideological. In actuality, there exists no sovereign referent – no uncontaminated or interpretationless backcloth – from which to assess the validity of scientific observation that isn't subject to an infinite regress of decentering, as poststructuralists and deconstructionists have taken great pains to show. Aronowitz actually claims that there is no longer a normal science, only normal technological research (Aronowitz, 1980). A normal science which presupposes a neutral science contradicts itself since all science is configured by social relations and is in itself a form of social knowledge (and therefore ideological). This position does not imply that there is no reality outside of the "text" or that the external world is somehow a relativistic projection of our collective mentality. But it does deny the existence of some "pristine other," a privileged referent which scientific law is supposed to have as its backcloth.

Aronowitz (1980) goes so far as to argue that the very notion of the material object is itself a metaphor which can be historically situated inside a specific problematic within the capitalist mode of production. While he does concede that the realist theory of truth is in some sense tenable as a kind of article of faith, comparable to Althusser's economic determination in the last instance, he nevertheless claims that this perspective has no practical significance with respect to understanding the nature of scientific inquiry itself. How to escape the relativistic notion of the socially constituted nature of scientific discovery remains a problem, but simply to recycle the myth of the neutrality of science and the separation of science and ideology certainly constitutes a step backwards, especially in this post-Gramscian era of bourgeois late capitalism, when we are compelled to pay close attention to the social relations of signification and to the corporate marketing battle over the sign.

In order to escape the conceptual conundrum of their own position, exponents of the classical Marxian theory of ideology must demonstrate pre-existing concepts which constitute a neutral nomenclature existing independently of the contingency of social practices. To fail to do so precludes the opportunity of challenging with sufficient credibility the impossibility of securing aseptic grounds – beyond the social practice of "doing science" – with which to judge the truth and falsity of theoretical propositions. In short, the orthodox position appears to assert that science occupies the privileged sphere of the *transhistorical*. It is to insist wrongly on the transparency of normative practices such as establishing criteria for empirical validity and an ontological guarantee of truth. Science, in this view, becomes self-justifying. That is, it becomes a self-referential simulacrum.

Foucault, like Aronowitz, rejects the distinction between scientific truth and ideological distortion. Instead of trying to discern the epistemological basis of the "really" real, Foucault undertakes an historical analysis of how the "effects of truth" are produced within discourses that are neither true nor false. He wishes to prevent the history of knowledge from being colonized by epistemological categories. In other words, Foucault never forgets that knowledges are social practices. As Veronica Beechey and James Donald (1986, p. XVI) point out, Foucault refuses to engage with epistemological questions, being more concerned with how truth is produced in discourse and how "regimes of truth" are empowered and deployed in everyday social practices. To explore the various factors which constitute truth's regulating gaze appears to me to be an eminently more worthwhile challenge for radical theorists to undertake than the impossible task of arguing how the ideological superstructure "corresponds to" the economic base or how a particular ideology distorts the real truth of the world.

Nevertheless, there is a danger lurking in current attempts to deconstruct Marxian science which abandon the categories of history and class altogether. In such cases, we can find ourselves saddled with little more than a new empiricism. Therefore, it is important that the concept of truth be defended *within a specific system of rationality*; and not as "discovered laws" that somehow correspond with the "really real." Speaking to this issue, Aronowitz provides us with an excellent definition of truth as "the critical exposition of the relations of humans to nature within a developing, historically mediated, context" (Aronowitz, 1980, p. 100). Truth, in other words, *must always be understood in its historical and discursive specificity.*

Anthony Giddens has taken up similar questions to those posed by Aronowitz. According to Giddens, both Popper and Althusser attempted to demarcate clearly what should fall within the framework of true science, and what should not. Giddens argues that neither scholar was correct and that the concept of ideology must be disconnected from the philosophy of science altogether. In fact, Giddens refers dryly to the differing views of Popper and Althusser as a rather "comic opposition" since Popper considers Marxism and psychoanalysis to be prime examples of ideologies or pseudo-sciences whereas Althusser regards these disciplines as the only forms of knowledge which have truly escaped the fetters of ideology (Giddens, 1983, p. 19). Such opposing views cannot be explained in their own terms but can be resolved only when it is understood that they both represent false starting points (Giddens, 1983). Believing that ideology cannot be defined with reference to truth claims at all, Giddens argues, and I believe correctly, that ideology should be reformulated *in relation to a theory of power and domination;* that is, in relation "to the models in which systems of signification enter into the existence of sectional forms of domination" (Giddens, 1983, p. 19). It was Marx, after all, who connected the concept of ideology to that of domination when in *The German Ideology* he asserted that the ideas in any given epoch are those held by the dominant class. For this and other reasons, Giddens chooses to define ideology as "the mode in which forms of signification are incorporated within systems of domination so as to sanction their continuance" (Giddens, 1983, p. 19). In this way, Giddens is able to assert that the analysis of ideology must take into account recent perspectives and developments in the philosophy of language and action.

While Giddens is essentially correct in removing ideology from a concern with scientific verifiability, he effectively allows the question of the metaphorical nature of science to remain unaddressed. This could unfortunately be read as a denial of the ideological laboratory in which "doing science" is always accomplished. In the end, science still remains sacrosanct.

5 Ideology and the Reflex of Capital

Giving pride of place to the productive moment, orthodox theorists privilege the vaunted mechanistic base/superstructure model. From this vantage point, the signified (or that which is represented) is relegated to a derivative status while correspondence and identity are posited as central axioms of epistemology. There is no inherent problem with a loose application of the base/superstructure model so long as it is not followed by a blithe exclamation that all forms of human practice can be explained in the last instance by reference to an economic "base." As Terry Eagleton (1985, pp. 10–11) points out, the term superstructure "does not designate an ontological 'realm' a fixed determinate, and unequivocal set of functions or structures; it invites us instead to contextualize a certain piece of practice or discourse in a particular way, without the slightest guarantee that this is always and everywhere the most appropriate context for it."

It is highly questionable whether the traditional base/superstructural model is capable of dealing with Eagleton's interdependence of shifting discursive formations or not. It is also doubtful that such a quasi-physicalist model can allow for the relatively autonomous nature of the social relations of signification. Gramsci's theory of hegemony, which conceptualizes ideologies as more than the effluxes of the prevailing economic infrastructure, but rather as entities possessing a logic of their own (Aronowitz, 1986/1987), is often used by Marxist theorists to counter the insularity of the base/superstructure model. In the orthodox view, the individual subject becomes simply a bearer of social roles (in an *Althusserian* sense) as they are mediated by economic structures or relations of production. Here we must be cautious of mechanistic formulations. Ideology does not simply constitute the linear arrangement of ideas, domino-fashion, with the economic as an unalloyed *primum mobile* at one end, presumably acting as a generator of history. Neither can ideology be adequately explained by theories of expressive causality, homology, or overdetermination although Fredric Jameson's (1981) development of the idea of structural causality constitutes a major advance over most Marxian theories of causality[9]. Orthodox theories of ideology have difficulty accounting for the development of interpretive communities within society, with their often antagonistic goals and strategies. In the final instance, it becomes a futile exercise to argue that the economic sphere alone is capable of explaining how men and women are ideologically positioned within asymmetrical relations of power. It is equally as difficult from this position to render intelligible the variety of subject positions and wide range of discourses in which we are all constructed. As Paul Hirst reminds us: "Conducts are *constructed*. They are not mere 'subjective registers' of economic relations – which are somehow more 'real' or 'objective'" (Hirst, 1983, p. 129)

It is not surprising that claims of economic determinism such as those made within the orthodox tradition have been found lacking even among scholars who appropriate many of the theoretical categories of traditional Marxism. If we have difficulty tracing a causal link from the economic base to ideologies in the superstructure it is possibly because, as Ernst Bloch informs us, the superstructure *is not dualistically separate from the base* (Hudson, 1983, p. 113); hence, ideologies can be seen in the details and forms of the organization of everyday life. Bloch claims that there exists both bad ideology (false consciousness) and good ideology (*true* false consciousness). The latter category cannot simply be reduced to false consciousness. While the primary site of ideology is the superstructure, there always exists a cultural "surplus" which outlasts the society and social strata in which it develops (Hudson, 1983). There exists, for instance, social strata which are not contemporaneous with the dominant mode of production. This cultural surplus, when freed from the negative sense of false consciousness and the illusory reconciliation of contradiction, possesses an incipient utopian dimension (Hudson, 1983). It is precisely this utopian dimension that provides both the freedom from restraint and autonomy of purpose for self and social transformation. Bloch insisted that the individual, the natural world, and history all have the fundamental character of not-yet being. Bloch's work can be summarized in the slogan: "the subject is not yet the predicate" (Hudson, 1983).

The incipient epistemological materialism of the orthodox Marxian view, according to which the objective realm independent of agency constitutes the object of social knowledge, has been refuted by numerous theorists such as Derrida, Laclau, Mouffe, and Hirst. That these theorists have argued so convincingly that all objects are constituted discursively as "language games" (as Wittgenstein so precisely put it) undermines, to say the least, the orthodox Marxian distinction between the base and superstructure which implies hierarchy of both determination and historical priority (Aronowitz, 1986/1987, p. 9).

While particular discourses considered in isolation may indeed be structured in dominance within capitalist productive relations, nevertheless through particular intersections, forms of reversal, and combinations with other discourses, they may also be mutually-informing, self-constituting, and capable of generating forms of knowledge which effectively escape assimilation into the dominated contents of capital accumulation. In other words, ideology considered as the production of meaning, the positioning of the subject, and the investment of affectivity, can exist relatively independent of the logic of the economy. Addressing the problem of economic determination, Stuart Hall offers a different conception of determinacy from that generated by the usual "causal determinism" or "expressive totality" ways of conceiving relations between practices within social formations. From Hall's standpoint, relations between different levels are seen as *mutually determining* rather than flowing unidirectionally from the base upward; consequently, the economy cannot effect a final closure on the domain of ideology (Hall, 1983, pp. 82–83).

One innovative critique and reconstitution of the base/superstructure model which has managed to pry loose the vice grip of economism and essentialism has been developed by Stephen Resnick and Richard Wolff. These theorists have substantially reformulated the traditional Marxian perspective on economic determinism by developing a non-essentialist ontological notion of dialectical materialism. In fact, their reconstructed commentary allows their analysis to include many of the objections from post-structuralist criticisms of Marxism, while still remaining loyal to Marxian epistemology. Essentially, Resnick and Wolff argue that empiricism and rationalism are antagonistic to the epistemology of dialectical materialism as originally articulated by Marx (Resnick & Wolff, 1982, 1986, 1987).[10] They argue that "empiricist and rationalist formulations and the essentialism which they support are key blocks to the necessary resolution of the Marxist debates" (Resnick & Wolff, 1982, pp. 44–45). Their distinction between empiricism and rationalism is worth noting because it offers a vital criticism of the orthodox Marxian position.

Empiricists are concerned with ranking theories according to their approximation to the truth. Their own object of knowledge becomes the validity measure of their true science. Like their "empiricist twins," the rationalists seek an absolute truth which is understood as cause, origin, or telos, which can be rationally captured or expressed (Resnick & Wolff, 1982, pp. 44–45). While it is obviously not possible within either an empiricist or rationalist framework to assert that Marxism captures the truth or reality (since every claim to truth by a theory is only as convincing as the theory that produces it), Resnick and Wolff nevertheless see fit to defend Marxist theory as "a necessary constituent element of social change toward socialism" (Resnick & Wolff, 1982, pp. 44–45). In their view, Marxian criticism remains unique and important because it seeks to establish how, why, and with what social consequences various theories differently produce their different knowledges of social life. For Resnick and Wolff, Marxian theory "refuses to entertain the illusion that the 'realism' of one or another theory, its 'proofs' for its supposed 'correspondence' to the 'real,' determine its truth also for other theories – in that sense its absolute truth" (ibid.; see also Wolff & Cullenberg, 1986).

In conclusion, Resnick and Wolff claim that a reconstituted Marxian theory must be anti-essentialist in nature and dissuaded from asserting that any one aspect of the social totality has the capacity to exercise more determinant influence than the others. Marxism's emphasis on economism should, therefore, only be a matter of its particular focus on approaching the social totality.

6   Radical Education and the Production of Meaning

Now I intend to link the concept of ideology more directly to the issue of how it has been theorized by radical educators in their various analyses of schooling. Radical pedagogy has certainly not remained immune to the profusion of debates surrounding theories of ideology. But here, as elsewhere, orthodox Marxists engage in theoretical combat with structuralists and their heirs and successors. The disagreement over how to define ideology has grown increasingly more fierce in recent years through attempts by some Marxian educational theorists to promote – perhaps "resuscitate" is more appropriate – a restricted definition of ideology. Radical theorists who assail such measures contend that an orthodox "straightjacketing" of the term can only impede the progress of radical pedagogy towards developing a programmatic discourse of hope and social transformation. In other words, it is felt that the creeping orthodoxy surrounding the term harbors its own unrecognized ideological assumptions which strips the term of its heuristic and critical potential (Liston, 1985; Giroux, 1985).[11]

A recent attempt by Marxist educator Michael Dale to develop a conception of ideology for employment in educational research offers a fitting example of the orthodox position. Dale argues that ideology should be restricted only to those beliefs and ideas that:

1. are false
2. contribute to the reproduction of production relations and class domination and
3. are determined and explained by the production relations. (Dale, 1986, p. 267)

Clearly, Dale's materialist/realist reading of ideology advances the general but important claim that ideas, beliefs, and values which are duplicitous and distortive can be explained by comprehending the material forces that remain hidden from consciousness (Liston, 1984, 1986; also Sarup, 1978).[12] Dale's conception of ideology covers roughly the same ground as the classical Marxist theory of ideology which argues that specific forms of consciousness produced by signifying practices – music, art, literature, religion, and so on – are at least partially determined by the social relations that inform the organization of economic production in any given social order. Yet while this praiseworthy position serves as an effective counterweight to the idealist who regards consciousness as primarily self-determining, Dale unwittingly sides with a theory of ideology that contributes to its own devaluation.

In its attempt to examine schooling as a state-regulated *social form* as against the process of knowledge transmission, the work of Henry A. Giroux sets forth an approach to ideology that differs significantly from those articulated by orthodox theorists. In Giroux's view, a failure to understand classroom pedagogy as a form of ideological production prevents both teachers and students from recognizing the centrality of their own epistemological claims for truth. Giroux's conception of ideology is *fundamentally grounded in a theory of interest*. That is, Giroux takes seriously which particular interests are embodied in various discursive formations and power/knowledge relations both in schools and the wider society.

While I do not have enough space to do justice to the range and scope of Giroux's work, I will attempt to summarize why Giroux's approach to ideology bodes well for the development of an emancipatory politics of education. In Giroux's terms, not only does ideology work "on and through individuals to secure their consent to the basic ethos and practices of the dominant society" (Giroux, 1983, p. 145; Aronowitz & Giroux, 1985) but it also functions "in the interest of social transformation" (Giroux, 1983, p. 145).

The view of ideology as a double-sided process has been articulated by Douglas Kellner who writes that "the concept [of ideology] commonly refers both to those ideas, images, and theories that mystify social reality and block social change, and to those programs of social reconstruction that mobilize people for social activism" (Kellner, 1978, p. 38). In a similar vein, Gibson Winter writes that

> Ideology [...] faces in two directions. It is a Januslike phenomenon. Ideology may be primarily oriented to preserving and legitimating the established powers in a society. It may also face primarily toward the future and project a utopian model for a more just society. In either case, ideology draws upon the symbolic powers that generate a people's identity whether to legitimate powers that be or to authorize proposals for transformation. (Winter, 1981, p. 97)

The view of ideology expressed by Stuart Hall and James Donald bears a striking similarity to that of Giroux. They define ideology as "the frameworks of thought which are used in society to explain, figure out, make sense of or give meaning to the social and political world. [...] Without these frameworks, we could not make sense of the world at all. But with them, our perceptions are inevitably structured in a particular direction by the very concepts we are using" (Donald & Hall, 1986, pp. IX–X). Ideology in this view possesses both positive and negative functions co-existing at any one moment. For instance, the *positive function* of ideology is to "provide the concepts, categories, images, and ideas by means of which people make sense of their social and political world, form projects, come to a certain consciousness of their place in the world and act in it" (Donald & Hall, 1986, pp. IX–X).

The *negative function* of ideology "refers to the fact that all such perspectives are inevitably selective. This perspective positively organizes the 'facts of the case' in *this* and makes sense because it inevitably excludes *that* way of putting things" (Donald & Hall, 1986, pp. IX–X). According to John Thompson (1987), ideology as a negative function works through four different modes: legitimation, dissimulation, fragmentation, and reification. Legitimation occurs when a system of domination is sustained by being represented as legitimate or as eminently just and worthy of respect. Dissimulation results when relations of domination are concealed, denied, or obscured in various ways; that is, when social processes are described in such a way that they conceal the interests and practices which inform them. Fragmentation occurs when relations of domination are sustained by the production of meanings in a way which fragments groups and places them in opposition with one another, such as in the classic case of "divide and rule." Reification results when transitory historical states of affairs are presented as permanent, natural, and commonsensical, as if they existed outside of time. From the perspectives just sketched, the question of understanding ideology becomes one of investigating *which* concepts, values, and meanings mystify our understanding of the social world and our place within the networks of power/knowledge relations, and which clarify such an understanding. The self and socially transformative aspect of ideology involves the issue of "how ideology creates the terrain for self-reflection and transformative action" (Giroux, 1983, p. 145). For Giroux, ideology is conceptualized both as "a set of representations produced and inscribed in human consciousness and behavior, in discourse, and in lived experiences" (Giroux, 1983, p. 143) and as "concretized in [...] various 'texts', material practices, and material forms" (Giroux, 1983, p. 143).

More specifically, Giroux defines ideology as generic with

> the production, consumption, and representation of ideas and behavior, which can either distort or illuminate the nature of reality. As a set of meanings and ideas, ideologies can be either coherent or contradictory; they can function within the spheres of both consciousness and unconsciousness; and, finally, they can exist at the level of critical discourse as well as within the sphere of taken-for-granted lived experience and practical behavior. (Giroux, 1983, p. 143)

When linked to the concepts of struggle and critique, the notion of ideology can be employed to address critical relationships among discursivity, meaning, and interest. For instance, when the concept of ideology is linked to that of social struggle, it also illuminates the inseparability of knowledge as power. Therefore, when viewed in its historical specificity, ideology can be linked not only to the discursive formations and the social relations they structure, but also to the interests that they further (Giroux, 1983, p. 144). In this way it is important to understand ideology as both *the medium and outcome of human experiences*, including the discourses and institutions which anchor and legitimate them. In this way, ideology functions not only to limit human action but also to enable it. Given Giroux's conception, the term ideology (being a noun which we take to have a single referent) could be more fruitfully appropriated if it were employed as a verb. That is, it's usefulness for critical pedagogy resides in its *operational field*.

Considered as such, ideology is involved in the production of multiple subjectivities; it operates with individual experience in the sphere of the unconscious and through the structure of needs, the realm of common sense, and the sphere of critical consciousness (Giroux, 1983, p. 146). Individuals inhabit an "ideological universe" in which contradictions exist within and between dominant and subordinate cultures. Meaning must not therefore be reduced simply to the domain of the individual but "has to be understood in its articulation with ideological and material forces as they circulate and constitute the wider society" (Giroux, 1983, p. 156).

Giroux maintains that in their attempt to grasp the relations between agency and structure, educators working within the critical tradition should support a theory of ideology that is "also capable of comprehending the way in which meaning is constructed and materialized within 'texts,' or cultural forms such as films, books, curriculum packages, fashion styles, etc." (Giroux, 1983, p. 156). In short, Giroux considers ideology critique to consist of the material manipulation of signs as well as the hidden manifestations of subjectivity and behavior.

By clearly embracing a fully-fledged dialectic approach to ideology, Giroux is able to reveal how individuals are more than just the reflexes of capital and social texts, in that they mediate representations and material practices through their own histories and class- or gender-related subjectivities. These relations are distinct, if not disparate, in their specificity and concrete historicity. In addition, it is to Giroux's credit that he takes seriously both the affective power of ideological production, which is organized around the body, and the individual's affective investment in systems of signification and discursive practices. It is precisely Giroux's uncompromisingly dialectical approach to ideology that permits conceptual access to the relations that characterize the interface among ideology, culture, and schooling. By emphasizing ideology as the production and mobilization of meaning, Giroux is able to uncover those aspects of the dominating culture that shape student subjectivities within asymmetrical relations of power. Consequently, Giroux is able to uncover moments of *self-production* for the purposes of both critique and the construction of emancipatory pedagogical practices. In this way, an understanding of the productive aspects of ideology *can help radical teachers to link more effectively school practices to student experiences.*

Turning briefly to the topic of resistance, it is clear that opposition to the dominant sociocultural order exists not only because language cannot fully formulate unconscious desire, as Kristeva, Lacan, and others have pointed out, but because people actively suffer the materiality of the pain of oppression.

Ideology can never "fix" us as dependent, coherent, and stable subjects, fully positioned in an iron-clad, pre-given relationship to the productive relations of capital. Consequently resistances to domination can never be manifested as merely "attendant" features of ideologies, as some Marxists would argue, but rather serve as *mutually constitutive aspects* of the very process of ideology itself. With this formulation, theorists such as Aronowitz and Giroux have managed in their discussion of resistance to restore some conceptual halftones to the depressingly dark picture of total domination (Newton & Rosenfelt, 1985).[13]

7   Ideology as Ritual Performance

In my ethnographic study of resistant student populations, I have adopted a perspective of ritual which attempts to take seriously the concepts of ideology and power and which addresses ritual as a cultural production constructed as a collective reference to the symbolic and situated experience of a group's social class. Following Aronowitz's (1981) critique of historical materialism. I would argue that the categories of ritual and the symbolic must compete with those of the economic sphere and class in order to understand present-day domination and resistance. Such a position is reinforced by MacCannell's pronouncement that in modern societies cultural productions supersede economic productions as a basis of shared values, lifestyles, and world views (MacCannell, 1976). Not only do social forces give rise to symbolic expressions (as Durkheim has shown us) but symbols and rituals are now in the process of creating social groups (MacCannell, 1976).

My emphasis on analyzing ideology and schooling from the standpoint of ritual performance attempts to uncover the importance of the sundry and the ordinary in social life – the liturgy of the everyday, so to speak – from the full range of symbolic acts running from ritualization behavior in animals, through interaction ritual, to highly differentiated religious liturgies and civil ceremonies. My specific interest lies with the practical and the mundane and how these domains become sanctified inside schools.

The roots of ritual in any society are the distilled meanings embodied in rhythms and gestures. Rituals suffuse our biogenetic, political, economic, artistic, and educational life. To engage in ritual is to "achieve [...] historico-cultural existence" (Sullivan, 1975). Our entire social structure has a pre-emptive dependence on ritual for transmitting the symbolic codes of the dominant culture. Rituals are not ethereal entities distinct from the vagaries of everyday living, as though they are somehow perched atop the crust of culture as a bundle of abstract norms and ordinances to be enacted apart from the concrete constitution of individual roles relations out of which daily life is built. Rather, rituals are inherently social and political; they cannot be understood in isolation from how individuals are located biographically and historically in various traditions of mediation (e.g., clan, gender, home environment, peer group culture). To a great degree, rituals constitute the major symbolic networks, cultural contexts, and ideational domains through which attempts are made to regulate social life and keep it from slipping into "a flux of indeterminacy" (Moore and Myerhoff, 1977, p. 19). Rituals are the generative forces by which social actors adjudicate conflicts within the surrounding culture – with both public and private symbols providing the mise-en-scène; at the same time they are the articulating mechanisms of social control which literally "put us in our place." The cultural forms which constitute our industrial life are tacitly shaped in terms of, and therefore dominated by, the parabolic and discursive contexts provided by ritual symbols and metaphors.

The essence of this position lies in the ineluctable fact that culture is fundamentally formed by interrelated rituals and ritual systems. Culture does not manifest itself as some pristine unity or disembodied, homogeneous entity but is, rather, discontinuous, murky, and provocative of competition and conflict; it is a collectivity which is composed of "contests" between ideologies and disjunctions between class, cultural, and symbolic conditions. It is, furthermore, a symbolic arena where groups struggle within a complex of structural oppositions over the interpretations of metaphors, icons, and structures of meanings, and where symbols have both centripetal and centrifugal pulls. Accordingly, ritual may be considered an ideological event and part of the objectified distributions of a group's dominant cultural capital (e.g., systems of meanings, taste, attitudes, and norms which legitimate the existing social order).

One of the crucial categories often overlooked by theorists of ideology is that of the body and the manner in which it becomes inscribed in the geography of desire through ritual. Related to this is how our affective or visceral investments in the world provide a sense of unity and totality to the "ritualized" creation of multiple subject positions within discursive formations. Ideology has to be seen not simply as the property of the text, in which human agency is denied an active role, but rather *as a process of production* in which pleasure and pain is produced by individuals in gestural engagement with their surroundings (Buckingham, 1986). Rarely considered in the debates over ideology is the notion that ideology is *performatively constituted.* It is, in a word, discourse given sentience. The way we ritualize our lives is culture somaticized – culture incarnated in and through our bodily acts and gestures. Ensconced in the framework of both private and institutional life, rituals become part of the social conditioned, historically acquired, and biologically constituted *rhythms and metaphors of human agency.*

I have given the term "ritual knowledge" to that aspect of ideological production which emphasizes affective investment or bodily knowing as distinct from ideational or semantic competency. Ritual, as I have defined the term, is the gestural embodiment of metaphors and symbols; that is, they are symbols or metaphors somaticized or "bodied forth" (McLaren, 1986). Ideology cannot be theorized in purely cognitive terms so that false beliefs constitute inadequate information or distorted communication. Ideology is fundamentally related to the politics of pleasure and the body. Ideology, in this perspective, lies in the motional world; it "thematizes" its milieu through mindful bodily gesture. As a form of ideology, ritual has a tendency to become self-effacing since it often assumes the second nature of habits. That is, it completes its work by disguising its own activity.

According to MacCannell (1981), "ritual codes are the most arbitrary and the most authoritarian areas of social life"; in fact, he claims that empirically, they constitute *political tracts on political lines of action that can be written with the body.* MacCannell (1981) locates ritual within the debates between Derrida and Levi-Strauss, maintaining that ritual is a *forbidden form of writing,* a type of practice that Eco refers to as "rhetorical over coding," one which blocks undesired readings of events while substituting other concerns (MacCannell, 1981). Ritual, as a form of arche-writing with the entire body, does not establish a particular interpretation of social action as much as it establishes a difference between itself and practical behavior (MacCannell, 1981). Rituals, in this sense, are undeniably ideological since

> Each time you gloss your behavior with a ritual overlay, you are re-inforcing a particular structural relationship or suspending it: i.e., somehow rewriting it. Ritual as a form of political arche-writing is [...] performance

aimed at dominating another's thought, of forcing, suppressing particular interpretations of behavior. (MacCannell, 1981)

8 The Schooled Body: The Ritualized Regimentation of Desire and the Domestication of Subjectivity

Within the framework sketched above, the pedagogical encounter between teachers and students can be understood as a ritual performance consisting of ideologically coded gestures. Students react to and often resist pedagogical instruction which is itself a form of ritual knowledge. Ritual knowledge possesses an incarnate character; it is acquired noetically and inheres in the "erotics of knowing" (Dixon, 1976). It is both reflective and pre-reflective (Zuesse, 1975). Students acquire and react to information viscerally, depending upon both the symbols and metaphors available during the pedagogical encounter and the morphology of the instruction itself; that is, *students make affective investments in certain kinds of knowledge.* In so doing, the distinction between the symbols they employ and their actions often becomes nominal: the student becomes both the means and the end of the ritualizing act. Thus, to speak of students creating classroom rituals is somewhat misleading. Rather, it is better to say that rituals create their participants "ideologically" by providing and legitimating the gestural metaphors and rhythms through which they engage the world. Ritual knowledge is not something to be "understood"; it is always, whether understood or not, something which is felt and responded to somatically.

Ritual knowledge is epistemologically disparate from traditional conceptions of school knowledge. It is a type of *mimesis* or visceral/erotic identification. Research which I undertook in a working-class Catholic school revealed a distinction between street-corner knowledge and knowledge acquired in classroom settings. Knowledge acquired in the streets was "lived" and mediated through discursive alignments and affective investments not found in the school. It was mediated by a different symbol and ritual system in which what mattered was always somehow "felt," whereas school knowledge was often sullied by an inflated rationalism. In the streets, students made use of more bodily engagement and organic symbols. In the classroom, knowledge was more symbolically sophisticated, but because such knowledge was discarnate and not a lived engagement, it remained distant, isolated, and abstract. Students chose not to invest affectively in this kind of knowledge. Students whose subjectivities were "decentered" in school could reclaim their sense of subjective continuity through affective investment in street life. Students battled daily to reconcile the disjunction between the lived meaning of the streets and the thing-oriented, digital approach to learning in the classroom. An inordinate emphasis was placed in school on knowledge *about*, on the digital dimension of learning (univocality, precision, logic) as opposed to knowledge *of* or the analogic dimension (equivocation, ambiguity, description) experienced by students in the street (McLaren, 1986). Classroom instruction constituted what Everhart calls "reified knowledge" – knowledge that is given, linear, relatively unproblematic, and which places students in the role of passive recipients (Everhart, 1983, 1987). Resistance to this type of knowledge in the classroom mirrored student behavior in the street, and constituted a ritualized attempt to bring the street into the school. In Everhart's (1983, 1987) terminology, the type of knowledge gathered through resistance of this sort becomes a form of "regenerative knowledge" which asserts creative control over the knowledge production process. This type of knowledge, which I refer to as "ritual knowledge," is interpretive and does not draw upon assumed categories (Everhart, 1983, 1987). Furthermore, it is established to resist the role that students occupy in the labor process of the school (Everhart, 1983, 1987).

Instructional rituals became useful adjuncts in the ideological positioning of students as subjects within various discursive alignments and in the ingraining – both bodily and cognitively – of certain acceptable dispositions and dimensions which were linked to the cultural capital of the dominant culture. Students reacted against the eros-denying quality of school life in which students became manipulate objects, discarnate beings unsullied by the taint of living flesh. Intellectual labor had little affective currency because it was removed from any celebration of the body as a locus of meaning. This brings us to the idea that ideological hegemony is not realized solely through the discursive mediations of the sociocultural order but through the enfleshment of unequal relationships of power. Hegemony is manifest intercorporeally through the actualizations of the flesh and embedded in incarnate experience.

Student gestures had become reified into intercorporeal manifestations of hegemony and could be described, in the words of David Michael Levin (1982, p. 287), as a "hostile, calculative, reductively mechanistic re-presentation of the body." By observing the cramped, defensive posturing of students and the brusque, authoritative gestures of the teachers, one could see how relations of power were grafted on to the medium of living flesh and marrow like a type of second biology. Power and privilege became somaticized. Ritual, in this sense, is the context of the body turned into ideology.

Every body carries a history of oppression, a residue of domination preserved in stratum upon stratum of breathing tissue. The bodies of the students in my study were ideologically swollen with meaning; they were pervaded by symbols which were enfolded in the musculature, pressed into the tendons, and encased in the meshwork of bone and sinew. Symbols, claim Dixon, are part of human physiology (Dixon, 1976). Hegemony, which is inscribed in the physiognomic symbols of the students' bodies and compressed into gesture, is an act of corporiety. In my study of Catholic schooling, hegemony was revealed to be ideologically laminated over the students' skeletal and muscular structures. The structuration of students' subjectivities begins with their subordination to a field of cultural desire born of the symbols and narratives of the street and the classroom and also with the organization of their bodies. That is, subjectivity is produced corporeally as well as discursively, beginning with the regimes of truth governing desire and movement. The positionalities of ideology become the intersections at which symbols and metaphors are inscribed in the body. Resistance to school instruction among the students was a resolve not to be ritually dissimulated in the face of oppression; a fight against the erasure of their street-corner gestures and symbols. It was, furthermore, an attempt to ritually construct a transitional world that could erase the past and deconstruct present psychosocial adaptations in order to forge new self-presentations of greater potency. Accordingly, the bodies of the students became sites of struggle, in which resistance became a way of gaining power, celebrating pleasure, and fighting oppression in the lived historicity of the moment, and the concrete materiality of the classroom. To resist meant to fight against the monitoring of passion and desire and the capitalist symbolization of the flesh. It became a fight against the privatized body correlated with the interpersonal relations of market ideology and the social encasements of an epistemology correlated with the technocratic imperatives of industry. Resistance became a rejection of the human subject reformulated as a docile object where spontaneity is repressed for efficiency and productivity, in compliance with the grammar of capitalist domination. It was a reaction against the purging of the body of its ability to produce pleasure in favor of a disembodied ideal of what constitutes "proper" learning and behaviour.

Given what has been emphasized in the preceding pages, it would appear wrong to limit our understanding of ideology to the production of signs within particular discursive alignments and at specific historical junctures. Rather, we should give consideration to the affective power invested in particular ideologies and the body's sensuous relationship to the popular and everyday. Lawrence Grossberg understands this relationship as the "totalizing power of ideology." He writes that

> In order to understand the relation of this totalized subject to reality it is necessary to recognize that the world is affectively as well as semantically

structured. I am using the term *affect* to refer to the intensity or desire with which we invest the world and our relations to it [...] this process of affective investment (through which the body is inserted into its physical and social environment) results in the very possibility of a totalized sense of reality. (Grossberg, 1986)

Though not unproblematic, Grossberg's work is important since it allows for the recognition that discursive fields are organized affectively (within a "politics of feeling") as well as ideologically. According to Grossberg, affect is a resource that can be mobilized, although he is quick to point out that affective economies ("mattering maps") are not equivalent to discourses of pleasure which function as the alibi for sexual deployment (Grossberg, 1987). Nor are affective formations which deal with structures of feelings and the texture of lived experience confined to cultural activities such as leisure or romance. Rather, all affective relations, according to Grossberg, are shaped by the materiality and negativity of everyday life.

9 Ideology: A Matter of Truth or Praxis?

Rather than adhering to a restricted notion of a definition of ideology as set forth by the orthodox tradition, it makes more pedagogical sense to ascertain the ways in which social relations and social practices represent various degrees of an emancipatory or dominating logic. This should not be undertaken by employing empirical criteria but by advocating a set of core ethical principles. Our central concern should not simply hinge upon whether or not the subjective "moment" of ideological production is subservient to, or dominated by, material and objective forces. What really matters is *the political project around which the concept of ideology can be put into practice.*

At this point I would assert that it matters less that any test for the "truth" of an idea is incontrovertible than that it matters whether or not the idea can be linked to a praxis of emancipation. While political praxis cannot be the criterion for theoretical truth, it is politics, not philosophy or science, which seems the more appropriate site for understanding the rules of justice and social transformation (Barber, 1984). From this perspective, it is wrong to argue that political considerations are generally irrelevant to the issue of correctly conceptualizing ideology within explanatory theories, since the fundamental question that should be put to any theory of ideology must deal with the inherent political project underpinning the theory. Speaking to this issue, Giroux writes:

radical theory in its first instance should be valued for its political project, its socially relevant criticism, its estranging quality. In other words, it should be valued for the extent to which it can provide potentially liberating forms of critique and the theoretical basis for new forms of social relations. The underlying value of radical educational theory cannot be reduced to the deadening and politically harmless issue of consistency and reliability, a peculiar obsession of dominant social theory; on the contrary, its value should be assessed against the ability of forms of radical educational theory to confront the discourse and social practices of oppression with what Benjamin once called "potentially liberating images of freedom." (Giroux, 1986, p. 167)

All theories are privileged around particular interests and theories of ideology are by no means exempt. The choice that orthodox educational theorists offer is not one based on how subjectivities are constructed, but a choice between a realism with its attendant monism and a radical relativism. The real choice to be made, of course, extends well beyond a muffled plea for scientifically verifiable truth claims.

Ideologies can certainly be presented as "fact" and appear already codified in canons or texts, but they can rarely escape the category of judgment (what Richard Bernstein calls phronesis) since all discourse obeys human imperatives. Clearly, the concept of ideology cannot be made scientific, if by this we mean searching for criteria that are at once axiomatic or apodictic. The issue is not so much whether an ideology is true or false, but whether it is persuasive, coherent, and consistent with particular interests, values, and principles that exist in particular social formations. The operative question that must be raised is: To what extent does the irreducible givenness of the view of ideology as "false consciousness" preclude the possibility of resistance and social change?

10 Conclusion

Orthodox theorists generally adopt a position which fails to register an adequate theory of the subject and which remains ensnared in a naively totalizing view of culture and, by extension, in an ideal of shared subjectivity that absolutely expels any politics of difference. Such a position fails to acknowledge the ideological presuppositions contained within its own assertions. A social critique of ideology that does not consider the complex and other conflicting structures of its own discursive premises does little to further the advancement of a critical pedagogy. In fact, just such a position can only reproduce the very strictures it is seeking to displace. The unfortunate heritage of Marxian political economy has, by its unproblematic ascription of fixed ideologies to relations of production, banished the indeterminacy of cultural formations and modes of symbolization and thereby discounted important advances in contemporary theories of ideology. Furthermore, the onesidedness of the orthodox position oversimplifies and fetishizes the concept of ideology, and effectively bankrupts the transformative potential inherent in more revisionist approaches to ideology.

The sectarian attempts of orthodox educational theorists to breathe new life into Marxism's decomposing text has only buried it deeper under further tissues of distortions and mystifications. Their position enshrines the contradictory nature of their own ideological posture and attenuates the capacity for self-reflection. As a result, they must be called upon to specify and to interrogate the system of rationality that undergirds their own perspectives. Somewhere between the essentialism of the orthodox position and the voluntarism of ultra-relativists, a common ground for discussing ideology must be sought by both Marxists and non-Marxists alike.

The importance of understanding ideology as the production of experience cannot be underscored enough since such a viewpoint is fundamental to developing a project of possibility. It is this standpoint that orthodox Marxian accounts of ideology fail to recognize or acknowledge the positivity of ideology which includes forms of representations central to the organization of experiences and subjectivity. This failure only emphasizes the politically strategic need to enlist ideological struggles in the development of a public language rooted in the traditions, histories, and experiences of the marginalized, displaced, and dispossessed (Giroux, 1983).

Clearly, critical pedagogy must displace questions of ideology from the procrustean bed of economic determination and false consciousness; rather, it must seek other ways of mapping the terrain of ideology. Needed is an approach to ideology in which the emphasis is not simply on capital accumulation or the primary determinates of distortion and false consciousness, but on the means whereby the ruling elite manufactures and mediates the relations between the material and symbolic needs of the dominant culture and the productive, lived and embodied symbols of subordinate groups. That is, a move needs to be made away from criteriologies such as those laid out in orthodox Marxian accounts, which attempt to categorize the formal properties of ideology, in favor of a critical examination of the concrete ideological practices that are constituted and "bodied forth" in the rituals of schooling and everyday life.

In short, needed is a conception of ideology that neither rejects Marxist theory as "false," nor forecloses on the ability to speak to praxis and ideology in a manner that takes the Marxist problematic seriously. At the same time, it is necessary to break through the theoretical limitations of the classical Marxian approach. While the search for a theory of ideology must steer wide of the restricted orthodox position, it must be careful not to abandon the important categories of class and history (or else we run the danger of falling prey to new postmodernist or post-Marxian manifestations of positivism). Instead of dichotomizing ideology into authentic reflections or distortions of reality, a critical pedagogy should conceive of reality – most importantly classroom reality – as a multiplicity of social relations and structures which cohere and contradict, some of them oppressive and some of them liberating.

In the final analysis, the concept of ideology must not be reduced into a brute, intractable articulation, nor allowed to remain so broad that it loses any conceptual utility in a theoretical sense. The more pressing challenge for scholars of ideology is to provide the concept with enough determinate meaning that it works heuristically within a well-defined political project. Especially at a time when the dominant ideologies and social practices are shifting us precariously closer to the Right, where, as Brecht said, "gangsters strut around like statesmen on the stage of history," the Left more than ever must formulate its vision around a language of experience, possibility, and hope. Rather than remain mired in the dead-zone politics of classical Marxist discourse, we need to reinvigorate its roots and reinscribe its vision. To endorse the orthodox Marxist version of ideology as the distortion of consciousness as opposed to its "post-Marxian" conception as the production of meaning displaces critical pedagogy's utopian promise. What is foreclosed in such an endorsement is the possibility of understanding how social systems, including schools, can promote human freedom. In order to help create and guide a liberating praxis, it is necessary for critical pedagogy to seize on a concept of ideology that will allow teachers to construct pedagogical practices that are able to resonate with their students' experiences. Teachers would do well to tap the hidden utopian desire in those experiences in order to develop classroom discourses and practices that provide students with a vision of social change. Of course, the cultural codes and structural constraints that determine how students will generate meaning out of particular experiences must not be unqualifiedly endorsed, but must always remain problematic for the teacher. The point that educators forget at their peril is that ideologies both constrain and enable the project of empowerment. To claim that ideologies merely distort and falsify consciousness can only continue to cause the categories of critique, struggle, and transformative practice to further dissolve under the overbearing weight of a Marxism that lacks a programmatic discourse of hope.

Acknowledgments

An earlier version of some sections of this article may be found in P. McLaren, Ideology, science and the politics of Marxian orthodoxy: A response to Michael Dale, *Educational Theory*, 37(3) (1987), 301–326.

This chapter originally appeared as P. L. McLaren, On ideology and education: Critical pedagogy and the politics of empowerment, *Social Text*, 19/20 (1988), 153–185. Reprinted here, with minor edits, with permission from the publisher.

Notes

1 Hanninen and Paldan (1983) as well as McLellan (1986) provide effort at analyzing theories of ideology.
2 For a good commentary on Foucault's concept of ideology, see Donald, 1986. Foucault would consider the concept of ideology to be somewhat redundant, given that subjectification relies on mechanisms of power within institutions and apparatuses of knowledge and not on the manipulation of ideas and beliefs that constitute consciousness. See Donald, 1986, p. 217.
3 See Belsey, 1980, p. 46. In Belsey's view, language must be recognized as a coding system that constitutes one of many ideological forms. The work of Jacques Lacan is important in understanding the productivity of subjectivity through language, yet his inbuilt phallocentrism is problematic, not to mention the deterministic reductionism implied in the idea that individuals are bound by a timeless, universal language. It is difficult to see how, from this perspective, strategies of resistance can emerge if it is agreed that all ideologies are essentially oppressive since they emerge from the *a priori* patriarchal conditions in which language has been constructed. See Lacan, 1977; Henriques et al. 1984, 1985. The work of Althusser (1971) possesses a similar problem of overdetermination in its reading of ideology as the customs and rituals that operate to position and reconcile individuals to imaginary conceptions of their place and significance in the social order.
4 Aronowitz, 1986/1987. "Foucault's position contravenes the positivistic approach which maintains that truth can best be ascertained by bracketing subjective elements, including political and ethical dimensions, and by paying attention to empirical data alone."
5 Foucault, 1980, pp. 84–85. Here is where Foucault's coupling of "discourse/practice" corrects, as Mark Poster claims, the Western Marxist tendency to separate material life from signification and consciousness, thereby bringing a new perspective to the debate between Hegelian reductionism implied in the idea that individuals are bound by a timeless, universal language. It is difficult to see how, from this perspective, strategies of resistance can emerge if it is agreed that all ideologies are essentially oppressive since they emerge from the *a priori* patriarchal conditions in which language has been constructed. See also Lacan, 1977; Henriques et al., 1984; Steedman et al., 1985. The work of Althusser (1971) possesses a similar problem of overdetermination in its reading of ideology as the customs and rituals

that operate to position and reconcile individuals to imaginary conceptions of their place and significance in the social order.

6   Subjectivity, as I am using the term, is best defined by Simon as follows:

> *Subjectivity* includes both conceptually organized articulated knowledge and elements that move us without being consciously expressed. These elements include both preconscious taken-for-granted knowledge and the radical and sedimented needs and desires that are expressed in our demands on ourselves and others. As an active ongoing construction, subjectivity is always a material and discursive rendering of these forms of knowledge. Subjectivity is not viewed as unitary but is divided by both the repression of that which cannot and refuses to be expressed and the constant processes of reorganization that construct a fragmented, contradictory consciousness. In its manifestation in practice, subjectivity expresses a non-unitary social identity accomplished through the historically produced social forms through which people live. Hence subjectivity reflects both objective conditions and a socially constructed representation of everyday life. (Simon, 1986, p. 157)

7   As early as the sixth century, metaphysical realism was predetermined as the only possible philosophical stance. Since that time, a number of thinkers have challenged the dominant assumption that knowledge must in some fundamental way reflect reality. We do not have time to embark on a philosophical excursion which would take us from the works of Xenophanes, Pyrrho, and Sextus Empiricus to Kant, Giambattista Vico, Bateson, Dewey, and Piaget, right through to George A. Kelley's personal construct theory, so I will limit my remarks here to Vico, whose ideas in many ways prefigure the post-structuralists I mentioned earlier. For Vico, the construction of knowledge is not constrained by the goal of correspondence with an "objective" reality that exists iconically outside the realm of human understanding or experience. Knowledge is, rather, constrained by material conditions which, despite their degree of materiality or abstraction, *always consist of the results of prior construction,* a position on which orthodox Marxists are silent. See Von Glasersfeld, 1984, pp. 30–31. In Vico's view, knowledge cannot lead to a correspondence between reality and truth, but must remain always a conjectural interpretation (ibid.). To extend Vico's thesis somewhat, it has been argued that we can comprehend the world only through *the gaps where our constructions break down* (ibid., p. 39). Yet this hardly gives us a picture of a detailed world which is responsible for the breakdown of our constructions – a world which, in orthodox terms, should appear commensurable to the world of science. Ideologies, therefore, are produced up to and including the point where our constructions break down, and "breakdowns" can only be explained by our own constructions up to the point that they fall apart. This position dovetails with Foucault's thesis that truth is produced by multiple forms of constraint. For Foucault, truth must be removed from the realm of the absolute and be understood as changes in the determination of what can count as true (Foucault, 1980, p. 131). Within this line of reasoning, orthodox explanations of ideology can be interrogated to reveal the archaeological stratifications, "breakdowns," or constraints from which they are constructed. In light of the post-structuralist advances in this area, the persistently empirical stance of orthodox Marxists, which submits to theory virtually on the basis of specifiable and verifiable epistemological criteria, is rendered eminently problematic. That is, their pursuit of objectivity tends to separate knowledge from subjectivity, object from subject, and fact from value.

8   Working within a logic of identity (in the tradition of transcendental philosophy from Descartes through Kant to Husserl), classical Marxists manage to theoretically sidestep

criticisms directed at this tradition by thinkers such as Derrida, Adorno, Kristeva, and others. In fact, the "classical realist" stance was successfully challenged decades ago by Wittgenstein. Sarcastically denouncing the correspondence theory of truth, Wittgenstein once wrote:

> The agreement, the harmony, of thought and reality consists in this: if I say falsely that something is red, then, for all that, it isn't red. And when I want to explain the word "red" to someone, in the sentence "That is not red," I do it by pointing to something red. (Shaviro, 1986, p. 229; see also Pears, 1977, p. 145)

9 Rejecting traditional Marxism's view of ideology as a form of false consciousness, Fredric Jameson subscribes to a view of ideology as a *strategy of containment,* or a way of achieving a unitary positioning of the subject by closing reality to the truth of history and by repressing the contradictions generated by both history and necessity. In so doing, Jameson rejects Althusser's attack on the semi-autonomy of various levels of the social structure (via expressive causality and homology) on the grounds that one cannot discuss differences without recognizing a prior unity. Rejecting mechanical formulations of causality that abound in orthodox perspectives on ideology, Jameson uses the concept of structural causality wherein causation is understood as the structural articulation of its effects. In building a case for an "absent cause" within capitalist relations among elements of the superstructure, Jameson recovers the idea of mediation from orthodox Marxian social analysis in order to reveal the mutual dependency of identity and difference which Jameson refers to as *transcoding.* Within this conceptualization, the economy no longer becomes a hidden essence informing the superstructure but a part of the social totality. See Jameson, 1981.

10 Resnick and Wolff (1982, pp. 44–45) refer to themselves as part of "the anti-reductionist movement" in Marxian theory which has its counterparts in the humanities (e.g., Foucault, Derrida, Jameson, and Rorty), the natural sciences (e.g., Kuhn, Lewontin, and Gould), and the social sciences. See Resnick & Wolff, 1986, 1987. This book attempts to liberate Marxism from "last instance" determinations in epistemology and social theory.

11 An important debate on this issue has occurred between Henry A. Giroux and Daniel P. Liston. See Liston (1985), and Giroux's (1985) trenchant response.

12 The classical orthodox position on ideology is also reflected in the writings of educational theorists Daniel Liston and Madan Sarup. See Liston, 1984, 1986; Sarup, 1978.

13 For a similar position, see Newton & Rosenfelt, 1985, pp. xv–xxxi.

References

Althusser, L. (1971). *Lenin and philosophy.* New Left Books.

Aronowitz, S. (1980). Science and ideology. *Current Perspectives in Social Theory, 1,* 75–101.

Aronowitz, S. (1981). *The crisis in historical materialism: class, politics and culture in Marxist theory.* J. F. Bergins.

Aronowitz, S. (1986/1987). Theory and socialist strategy. *Social Text, 16,* 1–16.

Aronowitz, S., & Giroux, H. A. (1985). *Education under siege.* Bergin & Garvey.

Barber, B. R. (1984). *Strong democracy: Participatory politics for a new age.* University of California Press.

Bateson, G. (1972). *Steps to an ecology of mind*. Ballantine Books.

Beechey, V., & J. Donald (Eds.) (1986). *Subjectivity and social relations*. Open University Press.

Belsey, C. (1980). *Critical practice*. Methuen.

Buckingham, D. (1986). Against demystification: A response to teaching the media. *Screen, 27*(5), 80–95.

Dale, M. (1986). Stalking a conceptual chameleon: Ideology in Marxist studies of education. *Educational Theory, 36*(3), 241–257.

Dixon, J. W. (1976). The physiology of faith. *Anglican Theological Review, 48*(4), 407–431.

Donald, J. (1986). Beacons of the future: Schooling, subjection and subjectification. In V. Beechey & J. Donald (Eds.), *Subjectivity and social relations*. Open University Press.

Donald, J., & Hall, S. (1986). Introduction. In J. Donald & S. Hall (Eds.), *Politics and ideology* (pp. ix–x). Open University Press.

Eagleton, T. (1985). Marxism, structuralism, and post-structuralism. *Diacritics, 15*(4), 2–12.

Everhart, R. B. (1983). *Reading, writing, and resistance: Adolescence and labor in a junior high school*. Routledge and Kegan Paul.

Everhart, R. B. (1987). Understanding student disruption and classroom control. *Harvard Educational Review, 57*(1), 77–83.

Foucault, M. (1980). *Power/knowledge: Selected interviews and other writings 1972–1977* (G. Gordon, Ed.). Pantheon.

Geras, N. (1987, May/June). Post-Marxism? *New Left Review, 1*(163), 40–82.

Giddens, A. (1983). Four theses on ideology. *Canadian Journal of Political and Social Theory, 7*(1/2), 18–21.

Giroux, H. A. (1983). *Theory and resistance in education: A pedagogy for the opposition*. Bergin & Garvey.

Giroux, H. (1985). Toward a critical theory of education: Beyond a Marxism with guarantees. *Educational Theory, 35*(3), 313–319.

Giroux, H. (1986). Solidarity, struggle, and the public sphere: Beyond the politics of anti-utopianism in radical education, part 1. *The Review of Education, 12*(3), 165–171.

Grossberg, L. (1986). Teaching the popular. In C. Nelson (Ed.), *Theory in the classroom*. University of Illinois Press.

Grossberg, L. (1987). The in-difference of television. *Screen, 28*(2), 28–46.

Hall, S. (1983). The problem of ideology – Marxism without guarantees. In B. Matthews (Ed.), *Marx: A hundred tears on*. Humanities Press.

Hanninen, S., & Paldan, L. (Eds.). (1983). *Rethinking ideology: A Marxist debate*. International General.

Henriques, J., et al. (1984). *Changing the subject*. Methuen.

Hirst, P. (1983). Ideology, culture and personality. *Canadian Journal of Political and Social Theory, 7*(1/2).

Hudson, W. (1983). Ernst Bloch: "Ideology" and postmodern philosophy. *Canadian Journal of Political and Social Theory, 7*(1/2).

Jameson, F. (1981). *The political unconscious: Narrative as a socially symbolic act*. Cornell University Press.

Kellner, D. (1978). Ideology, Marxism, and advanced capitalism. *Socialist Review, 8*(6).

Klancher, J. (1987). Review: What critical intellectuals do now. *College English, 49*(2), 202–208. https://doi.org/10.2307/377879

Lacan, J. (1977). *Écrits: A selection*. Tavistock.

Laclau, E. (1983). The impossibility of society. *Canadian Journal of Political and Social Theory, 7*(1/2).

Laclau, E., & Mouffe, C. (1985). *Hegemony and socialist strategy*. Verso.

Lather, P. (1987). *Educational research and practice in a postmodern era*. Paper presented at the Ninth Conference on Curriculum Theory and Classroom Practice, Dayton, Ohio, October.

Levin, D. M. (1982). Moral education: The body's felt sense of value. *Teachers College Record, 84*(2).

Liston, D. (1984). Have we explained the relationship between curriculum and capitalism? An analysis of the selective tradition. *Educational Theory, 34*(3).

Liston, D. (1985). Marxism and schooling: A failed or limited tradition? *Educational Theory, 35*(3).

Liston, D. (1986). On facts and values: An analysis of radical curriculum studies. *Educational Theory, 36*(2), 137–152.

MacCannell, D. (1976). *The tourist: A new theory of the leisure class*. Schocken Books.

MacCannell, D. (1981). Deconstructing ritual. The James A. Becker Alumni Lecture, Cornell University, Ithaca, New York, 23 October.

McLaren, P. (1986). *Schooling as a ritual performance: Toward a political economy of educational symbols and gestures*. Routledge and Kegan Paul.

McLellan, D. (1986). *Ideology*. University of Minnesota Press.

Moore, S. F., & Myerhoff, B. G. (1977). Secular ritual: Forms and meanings. In *Secular ritual*, ed. S. F. Moore & B. G. Myerhoff. Royal Van Gorcum.

Newton, J., & Rosenfelt, D. (1985). Toward a materialist-feminist criticism. In J. Newton and D. Rosenfelt (Eds.), *Feminist criticism and social change* (pp. xv–xxxi). Methuen.

Pears, D. (1977). *Ludwig Wittgenstein*. Penguin.

Rajchman, J. (1986). Ethics after Foucault. *Social Text, 5*(1/2), 165–183.

Resnick, A., & Wolff, R. D. (1982). Marxist epistemology: The critique of economic determinism. *Social Text, 2*(3), 44–45.

Resnick, A., & Wolff, R. D. (1986). Reply to Manza and Takagi. *Socialist Review, 89*, 140–141.

Resnick, A., & Wolff, R. D. (1987). *Knowledge and class: A Marxian critique of political economy.* University of Chicago Press.

Sarup, M. (1978). *Marxism and education.* Routledge and Kegan Paul.

Shaviro, S. (1986). From language to "forms of life": Theory and practice in Wittgenstein. *Social Text, 13/14,* 216–236.

Simon, R. I. (1986). Work experience. In D. Livingstone (Ed.), *Critical pedagogy and cultural power.* Bergin & Garvey.

Smart, B. (1983). *Foucault, Marxism and critique.* Routledge and Kegan Paul.

Spivak, G. C. (1987). *In other worlds: Essays in cultural politics.* Methuen.

Steedman, C., et al. (1985). *Language, gender and childhood.* Routledge and Kegan Paul.

Sullivan, P. (1975). Ritual: Attending to the world. *Anglican Theological Review* (Supplementary series), *5,* 9–43.

Thompson, J. B. (1987). Language and ideology: A framework for analysis. *The Sociological Review, 35*(3), 517–536.

Von Glasersfeld, E. (1984). An introduction to radical constructivism. In P. Watzlawick (Ed.), *The Invented Reality.* W. W. Norton & Company.

Wexler, P. (1982). Structure, text, and subject: A critical sociology of school knowledge. In M. Apple (Ed.), *Cultural and economic reproduction in education: Essays on class, ideology and the state.* Routledge and Kegan Paul.

Wilden, A. (1980). *The imaginary Canadian.* Pulp Press.

Winter, G. (1981). *Liberating creation: Foundations of religious social ethics.* Crossroad.

Wolff, R. D., & Cullenberg, S. (1986). Marxism and post-Marxism. *Social Text, 15*(3), 126–135.

Zuesse, E. M. (1975). Meditation on ritual. *Journal of the American Academy of Religion, 43*(3), 517–530.

CHAPTER 4

Multiculturalism and the Postmodern Critique
Towards a Pedagogy of Resistance and Transformation

> For the proletariat does not need all the thousands of little words by which the bourgeoisie masks class struggles in its own pedagogy. The 'unprejudiced,' 'understanding,' 'empathetic' bourgeoisie practices, the 'child-loving' teachers – these we can do without.
> WALTER BENJAMIN (1973, p. 32)

∴

1   Social Justice under Siege

We inhabit skeptical times; historical moments spawned in a temper of distrust, disillusionment and despair. Social relations of discomfort and diffidence have always pre-existed us but the current historical juncture is particularly invidious in this regard, marked as it is by a rapture of greed, untempered and hypereroticized consumer will, racing currents of narcissism, severe economic and racial injustices and heightened social paranoia. The objective conditions of Western capitalism now appear so completely incompatible with the realization of freedom and liberation that it is no understatement to consider them mutually antagonistic enterprises. Situated beyond the reach of ethically convincing forms of accountability, capitalism has dissolved the meaning of democracy and freedom into glossy aphorisms one finds in election campaign sound bytes or at bargain-basement sales in suburban shopping malls. The American public has been proffered a vision of democracy that is a mixture of Sunday barbecue banality, *American Gladiators* jocksniffery, Amway enterprise consciousness, and the ominous rhetoric of 'New World Order' jingoism.

The heroic cult of modernism which has naturalized the power and privilege of 'dead white men' and accorded the pathology of domination the status of cultural reason has all but enshrined a history of decay, defeat and moral panic. Greed, avarice and cynicism have insinuated themselves into virtually every aspect of cultural life, and have become rationalized and aestheticized as necessary resources that must be fed into a vast technological machine known as Western civilization. It is a history that has installed Willie Horton into our structural unconscious and helped make possible and desirable the legal torture and dehumanization of Rodney King and people of color in general. That the fortified, postmodern *noir* metropolises of this *fin-de-siècle* era have grown more Latinophobic, homophobic, xenophobic, sexist, racist and bureaucratically cruel is not reflective of the self-understanding of the public-at-large but of the way that the public has been constructed through a politics of representation linked to the repressive moralism of the current conservative political regime and current counterattacks on cultural democracy from the right.

The present moral apocalypse, perhaps most vividly represented by the maelstrom of anger and violence under the smoke-filled skies of Los Angeles, has not been brought on simply by the existence of midnight hustlers, the drug trade, skewered ambition, or gang members taking advantage of public outrage over the justice system but by shifting economic, political and cultural relations that have worsened over the last two decades. We have been standing at the crossroads of a disintegrating culture for the last two decades where we have witnessed a steady increase in the disproportionate level of material wealth, economic dislocation and intergenerational poverty suffered by African-Americans, Latinos and other minorities. Such conditions have been brought about by the frenetic and at times savage immorality of the Reagan and Bush administrations as evidenced in their direct attacks on the underclass, the disintegration of social programs and the general retreat from civil rights that occurred during their tenure in office.

Other characteristics of this current juncture include: changes in the structure of the US economy, the declining inner-city job market, growing national unemployment rates, a drastic decline in the number of unskilled positions in traditional blue-collar industries in urban areas, the increasing numbers of youth competing for fewer and fewer entry-level unskilled jobs, the automation of clerical labor, the movement of the African-American middle class out of the once multiclass ghetto, the shifting of service sector employment to the suburbs (Kasinitz, 1988), the destructive competition among nations that results from a free trade policy fuelled by the retrograde notion that other nations can achieve economic growth by unbalanced sales to the US market; increased global competition provoking capitalist manufacturing firms to reduce costs by exploiting immigrant workers in US cities or 'out-sourcing' to Third World countries; and a post-Fordist de-monopolization of economic structures and the deregulation and globalization of markets, trade and labor as well as deregulated local markets 'that makes local capital vulnerable to the strategies of corporate raiders' (Featherstone, 1990, p. 7).

In addition, we are faced with an increasing assault on human intelligence by the architects of mass culture, an increasing dependency on social cues manufactured by the mass media to construct meaning and build consensus on moral issues, and the strengthening of what Piccone (1988, p. 9) has called the 'unholy symbiosis of abstract individualism and managerial bureaucracies.' The white-controlled media (often backed by victim-blaming white social scientists) have ignored the economic and social conditions responsible for bringing about in African-American communities what Cornel West has called a *'walking nihilism* of pervasive drug addiction, pervasive alcoholism, pervasive homicide, and an exponential rise in suicide' (cited in Stephanson, 1988, p. 276).

Furthermore, the white media has generated the racially pornographic term, 'wilding', to account for recent acts of violence in urban centers by groups of young African-Americans (Cooper, 1989). Apparently the term 'wilding', first reported by New York City newspapers in relation to the Central Park rapists, was relevant only to the violence of black male youth since the term was conspicuously absent in press reports of the attack of white male youths on Yusef Hawkins in Bensonhurst (Wallace, 1991). Thus, the postmodern image which many white people now entertain in relation to the African-American underclass is one of a violently hybrid population, spawning mutant Willie Horton-type youths who, in the throes of bloodlust, roam the perimeter of the urban landscape high on angel dust, randomly hunting whites with steel pipes (see Giroux's discussion of *Grand Canyon* in this issue). Latino youth fare no better in the public eye.

2 The Dilemma of Postmodern Critique and the Debate over Multiculturalism

I have foregrounded the social and cultural situatedness of oppression as a background to my discussion of multiculturalism since I share Michele Wallace's conviction that the debates over multiculturalism cannot afford to have their connection to wider material relations occulted by a focus on theoretical issues divorced from the lived experiences of oppressed groups. She is worth quoting on this issue:

> Many individual events on the current cultural landscape conspire to make me obsessed with contemporary debates over 'multiculturalism' in both the art world and the culture at large, but my concern is grounded first and foremost in my observation of the impact of present material conditions on an increasing sector of the population. These material conditions which include widespread homelessness, joblessness, illiteracy, crime, disease (including AIDS), hunger, poverty, drug addiction,

alcoholism, as well as the various habits of ill-health, and the destruction of the environment are (let's face it) the myriad social effects of late multinational capitalism. (1991, p. 6)

A focus on the material and global relations of oppression can help us to avoid reducing the 'problem' of multiculturalism to simply one of attitudes and temperament or, in the case of the academy, to a case of textual disagreement and discourse wars. It also helps to emphasize the fact that, in the United States, the concoction called 'multiculturalism', which has resulted from a forensic search for equality and the political ladling of the long-brewing 'melting pot', has produced an aversion to, rather than a respect for difference. Regrettably, multiculturalism has been too often transformed into a code word in contemporary political jargon that has been fulsomely invoked in order to divert attention from the imperial legacy of racism and social injustice in this country and the ways in which new racist formations are being produced in spaces culturally de-differentiated and demonified by neoconservative platforms that anathematize difference through attacks on the concept of heterogeneous public cultures (see Ravitch, 1990, 1995; Kimball, 1991; Browder, 1992).

In the sections that follow, I want to discuss recent articulations of the postmodern critique in order to examine the limitations of current conservative and liberal formulations of multiculturalism. In doing so, I would like to posit an alternative analysis. I shall argue that, despite its limitations for constructing an emancipatory politics, postmodern criticism can offer educators and cultural workers a means of problematizing the issue of difference and diversity in ways that can deepen and extend existing debates over multiculturalism, pedagogy, and social transformation. Certain new strands of postmodern critique that fall under the rubric of 'political' and 'critical' postmodernism deserve serious attention in this regard.

More specifically, I shall redraw the discussion of multiculturalism from the perspective of new strands of postmodern critique that emphasize the construction of 'a politics of difference'. I will conclude by urging critical educators to reclaim the importance of relational or global critique – in particular the concept of 'totality' – in their efforts to bring history and materiality back into theoretical and pedagogical discourses.

3   Subaltern and Feminist Challenges to the Postmodern Critique

Enlightenment reason mocks us as we allow it to linger in our educational thinking and policies; for some of the most painful lessons of modernity have been that a teleological and totalizing view of scientific progress is antipathetic to liberation; that capitalism has posited an irrecuperable disjunction between ethics and economics; and that, paradoxically, modernity has produced an intractable thralldom to the very logic of domination which it has set out to contest and in doing so has reproduced part of the repression to which it has so disdainfully pointed.

The postmodern critique has set out to challenge these modernist assumptions and rationalities. Broadly speaking, the postmodern critique concerns itself with a rejection or debunking of modernism's epistemic foundations or metanarratives; a dethronement of the authority of positivistic science that essentializes differences between what appear to be self-possessing identities; an attack on the notion of a unified goal of history; and a deconstruction of the magnificent Enlightenment swindle of the autonomous, stable and self-contained ego that is supposed to be able to act independently of its own history, its own cultural and linguistic situatedness, and free from inscriptions in the discourses of, among others, gender, race and class.

Postmodern social theory has rightly claimed that we lack a vocabulary or epistemology that is able to render the world as empirically discoverable or accurately mappable, and that experience and reason cannot be explained outside of the social production of intelligibility. Further, the postmodern critique has been exemplary in revealing the hopelessness of attempts by empiricists to transcend the political, ideological and economic conditions that transform the world into cultural and social formations. While postmodern social theory has advanced our understanding of the politics of representation and identity formation, certain postmodern articulations and inflections of critical social theory have noticeably abandoned the language of social change, emancipatory practice and transformative politics. In fact, many of them carry mordantly pessimistic and distinctively reactionary potential.

Postmodern criticism's shift in the concept of the political through its emphasis on signification and representation, the dispersion of history into the after-image of the text, and in its challenge to logocentric conceptions of truth and experience, have not gone uncontested. For instance, Paul Gilroy has made clear some of the problems with theorizing under the banner of postmodernism – if under such a banner one assumes one has constructed a politics of refusal, redemption, and emancipation. Gilroy writes:

> It is interesting to note that the very moment when celebrated Euro-American cultural theorists have pronounced the collapse of 'grand narratives' the expressive culture of Britain's black poor is dominated by the need to construct them as narratives of redemption and emancipation. This expressive culture, like others elsewhere in the African diaspora,

> produces a potent historical memory and an authoritative analytic and historical account of racial capitalism and its overcoming. (1990, p. 278)

What some prominent cultural critics view as the constituent features of postmodernism – depthlessness, the retreat from the question of history, and the disappearance of affect – do not, in Gilroy's view, take seriously enough what is going on in African-American expressive culture. Blatantly contradicting this supposed 'cultural dominant' of postmodernism is 'the repertoire of "hermeneutic gestures"' emanating from black expressive cultures. Gilroy points out that widely publicized views of the postmodern condition held by such prominent critics as Fredric Jameson may simply constitute another form of Eurocentric master narrative since black expressive cultures use all the new technological means at their disposal 'not to flee from depth but to revel in it, not to abjure public history but to proclaim it' (1990, p. 278). Similarly, Cornel West qualifies black cultural practices in the arts and intellectual life as examples of a 'potentially enabling yet resisting postmodernism' (1989, p. 96) that has grown out of

> an acknowledgement of a reality that [black people] cannot *not know* – the ragged edges of the real, of necessity; a reality historically constructed by white supremacist practices in North America during the age of Europe. These ragged edges – of not being able to eat, not to have shelter, not to have health care – all this is infused into the strategies and styles of black cultural practices. (p. 93)

Important concerns about the postmodern critique have also been posed by feminist theorists. They have questioned why men, in particular, find the new gospel of postmodernism to be so significantly compelling at this current historical moment. Not the least of their objections is related to the fact that a theoretical conversion to the postmodern critique in many instances allows men to retain their privileged status as bearers of the Word precisely because it distracts serious attention from the recent concentration on feminist discourse (Kaplan, 1987, pp. 150–152). Dominant strands of the postmodern critique also tend to delegitimize the recent literature of people of color, black women, Latin Americans and Africans (Christian, 1987, p. 55). In addition, we are reminded that just at a time in history when a great many groups are engaged in 'nationalisms' which involve redefining them as marginalized Others, the academy has begun to legitimize a critical theory of the 'subject' which holds the concept of agency in doubt, and which casts a general skepticism on the possibilities of a general theory which can describe the world and institute a quest for historical progress (Harstock, 1987; Di Stephano, 1990).

It is difficult to argue against these calls to de-capitalize the registers of Patriarchy, Manhood and Truth as they manifest themselves within dominant variants of the postmodern critique. And with such a consideration in mind, I would ask if it is at all possible to recuperate and extend the project of postmodernist critique within the context of a critical pedagogy of multiculturalism in a way that remains attentive to the criticisms posed above. To attempt to answer such a question demands that I establish at the outset both my own convergences with and departures from the discourse genre of postmodernism.

4   Ludic and Resistance Postmodernism

My general sympathy with the postmodern critique does not come without serious qualifications. Postmodernist criticism is not monolithic and for the purposes of this essay I would like to distinguish between two theoretical strands. The first has been astutely described by Teresa Ebert (1991, p. 115) as 'ludic postmodernism' – an approach to social theory that is decidedly limited in its ability to transform oppressive social and political regimes of power. Ludic postmodernism generally occupies itself with a reality that is constituted by the continual playfulness of the signifier and the heterogeneity of differences. As such, ludic postmodernism (e.g., Lyotard, Derrida, Baudrillard) constitutes a moment of self-reflexivity in deconstructing Western meta-narratives, asserting that 'meaning itself is self-divided and undecidable' (Ebert, 1991).

Politics in this view is not an unmediated referent to action that exists outside of representation. Rather, politics becomes a textual practice (e.g., parody, pastiche, fragmentation) that unsettles, decenters and disrupts rather than transforms the totalizing circulation of meaning within grand narratives and dominant discursive apparatuses (Ebert, 1991; Zavarzadeh & Morton, 1991). While ludic postmodernism may be applauded for attempting to deconstruct the way that power is deployed within cultural settings, it ultimately represents a form of detotalizing micropolitics in which the contextual specificity of difference is set up against the totalizing machineries of domination. The contingent in this case determines necessity as ludic postmodernism, sets up as "superstructuralism" that privileges the cultural, discursive and ideological over the materiality of modes and relations of production (Zavarzadeh & Morton, 1991).

I want to argue that educators should assume a cautionary stance towards ludic postmodernism critique because, as Ebert notes, it simply reinscribes the status quo and reduces history to the supplementarity of signification or the free-floating trace of textuality (1991, p. 115). As a mode of critique, it rests its case on interrogating specific and local enunciations of oppression but often fails to analyze such enunciations in relation to larger dominating structures of oppression (McLaren, 1996; Aronowitz & Giroux, 1991).

Ludic postmodernism is akin to what Scott Lash (1990) calls 'spectral postmodernism' – a form of critique that deals with the de-differentiation and blurring of disciplinary knowledge and genres (e.g., literature and criticism) and involves the implosion of the real into representation, the social into the mediascape, and exchange-value into sign value. For the spectral postmodernists, the social is sucked up and dissolved into the world of signs and electronic communication while depth of meaning is imploded into superficiality. Pauline Marie Rosenau (1992) refers to this as 'skeptical postmodernism' – a strand of postmodernism that reflects not only an ontological agnosticism that urges a relinquishing of the primacy of social transformation but also an epistemological relativism that calls for a tolerance of a range of meaning without advocating any one of them.

The kind of postmodern social theory I want to pose as a counterweight to skeptical and spectral postmodernism has been referred to as 'oppositional postmodernism' (Foster, 1983), 'radical critique-al theory' (Zavarzadeh & Morton, 1991), 'postmodern education' (Aronowitz & Giroux, 1991), 'resistance postmodernism' (Ebert, 1991), and 'critical postmodernism' (McLaren, 1996; Giroux, 1992; McLaren & Hammer, 1989). These forms of critique are not alternatives to ludic postmodernism but appropriations and extensions of this critique. Resistance postmodernism brings to ludic critique a form of materialist intervention since it is not solely based on a textual theory of difference but rather on one that is social and historical. In this way, postmodern critique can serve as an interventionist and transformative critique of US culture. Following Ebert, resistance postmodernism attempts to show that 'textualities (significations) are material practices, forms of conflicting social relations' (1991, p. 115). The sign is always an arena of material conflict and competing social relations as well as ideas and we can 'rewrite the sign as an ideological process formed out of a signifier standing in relation to a matrix of historically possible or suspended signifieds' (Ebert, 1991). In other words, difference is politicized by being situated *in* real social and historical conflicts and not simply *over* abstract differences or *between* semiotic contradictions.

Resistance postmodernism does not abandon the undecidability or contingency of the social altogether; rather, the undecidability of history is understood as related to class struggle, the institutionalization of asymmetrical relations of power and privilege, and the way historical accounts are contested by different groups (Zavarzadeh & Morton, 1991; Giroux, 1992; McLaren & Hammer, 1989). On this matter Ebert remarks: 'We need to articulate a theory of difference in which the differing, deferring slippage of signifiers is not taken as the result of the immanent logic of language but as the effect of the social conflicts traversing signification' (1991, p. 118). In other words, to view difference as simply textuality, as a formal, rhetorical space in which representation narrates its own trajectory of signification, is to ignore the social and historical dimensions of difference (Ebert, 1991). Ebert elaborates this point as follows: 'A postmodern analytics of difference would enable us to move beyond the theory of difference as reified experience, and to critique the historical, economic, and ideological production of difference itself as a slipping, sliding series of relations that are struggled over and which produce the significations and subjectivities by which we live and maintain existing social relations' (1991, p. 118). She further describes resistance postmodernism as a politics of difference, as a theory of practice and a practice of theory:

> a resistance postmodern cultural critique – interrogating the political semiosis of culture – would be an oppositional political practice produced through the activity of reading, of making sense of cultural texts. However, opposition does not lie within – in other words it is not inherent in – a text or individual but is produced out of the practice of critique itself. Moreover the critic herself is always already interpellated in the hegemonic subject positions of the culture, and contestation derives not from some will to resist but again is produced through the practice of critique. (p. 129)

Resistance postmodernism takes into account both the macropolitical level of structural organization and the micropolitical level of different and contradictory manifestations of oppression as a means of analyzing global relations of oppression. As such, resistance postmodernism bears a considerable degree of affinity to what Scott Lash has recently termed 'organic postmodernism'. Organic postmodernism tries to move beyond epistemic skepticism and explanatory nihilism to concern itself with issues related not just to the commodification of language but to the commodification of labor and the social relations of production. According to Lash, it attempts to reintegrate the cultural into the natural, material environment. From this perspective, rationality is not pan-historical or universal but is always situated in particular communities of discourse. In addition, organic postmodernism argues that high modernism articulates reality in a way that often serves as a cover for validating a Cartesian universe of discrete parts disconnected from wider economies of power and privilege. In other words, high modernism is accused of collapsing difference into the uneasy harmony we know as white patriarchal privilege – a privilege inextricably bound up with nationalism, imperialism and the state.

5 Multiculturalism and the Postmodern Critique

In this section I want to bring a critical or resistance-postmodernist perspective to bear on the issue of multiculturalism. For me, the key issue for critical educators is to develop a multicultural curriculum and pedagogy that attends to the specificity (in terms of race, class, gender, sexual orientation, etc.) of difference (which is in keeping with ludic postmodernism) yet at the same time addresses the commonality of diverse Others under the law with respect to guiding referents of freedom and liberation (which is in keeping with resistance postmodernism).

Viewed from the perspective of resistance postmodernism, the liberal and conservative attacks on multiculturalism as separatist and ethnocentric carry with them the erroneous assumption that North American society fundamentally constitutes social relations of uninterrupted accord. This view furthermore underscores the idea that North American society is largely a forum of consensus with different minority viewpoints simply accretively added on. This constitutes a politics of pluralism which largely ignores the workings of power and privilege. More specifically, it 'involves a very insidious exclusion as far as any structural politics of change is concerned: it excludes and occludes global or structural relations of power as "ideological" and "totalizing"' (Ebert, 1991). In addition, it presupposes harmony and agreement – an undisturbed space in which differences can coexist. Yet such a presupposition is dangerously problematic. Chandra Mohanty notes that difference cannot be formulated as negotiation among culturally diverse groups against a backdrop of presumed cultural homogeneity. Difference is the recognition that knowledges are forged in histories that are riven with differentially constituted relations of power; that is, knowledges, subjectivities and social practices are forged within 'asymmetrical and incommensurate cultural spheres' (1989/1990, p. 181).

Too often liberal and conservative positions on diversity constitute an attempt to view culture as a soothing balm – the aftermath of historical disagreement – some mythical present where the irrationalities of historical conflict have been smoothed out. This is not only a disingenuous view of culture, it is profoundly dishonest. The liberal and conservative position on culture also assumes that justice already exists and needs only to be evenly apportioned.

However, both teachers and students need to realize that justice does not already exist simply because laws exist. Justice needs to be continually created, constantly struggled for. The question that I want to pose to teachers is this: Do teachers and cultural workers have access to a language that allows them to sufficiently critique and transform existing social and cultural practices that are defended by liberals and conservatives as democratic?

6 The Subject without Properties

The critical postmodernist critique provides us with a way of understanding the limitations of a multiculturalism trapped within a logic of democracy that is under the sway of late capitalism. One of the surreptitious perversions of democracy has been the manner in which citizens have been invited to empty themselves of all racial or ethnic identity so that presumably they will all stand naked before the law. In effect, citizens are invited to become little more than disembodied consumers. As Joan Copjec points out:

> Democracy is the universal quantifier by which America – the 'melting pot', the 'nation of immigrants' – constitutes itself as a nation. If *all* our citizens can be said to be Americans, this is not because we share any positive characteristics, but rather because we have all been given the right to *shed* these characteristics, to present ourselves as disembodied before the law. I divest myself of my positive identity, therefore I am a citizen. This is the peculiar logic of democracy. (1991, p. 30)

Rosaldo (1989) refers to this process as 'cultural stripping' wherein individuals are stripped of their former cultures in order to become 'transparent' American citizens. While the embodied and perspectival location of any citizen's identity has an undeniable effect on what can be said, democracy has nevertheless created formal identities which give the illusion of identity while simultaneously erasing difference. David Lloyd refers to this cultural practice as the formation of the 'Subject without properties' (1991, p. 70). As the dominated are invited to shed their positive identities, the dominators unwittingly serve as the regulating principle of identity itself by virtue of their very indifference.

The universality of the position of dominator is attained through its literal indifference and it 'becomes representative in consequence of being able to take anyone's place, of occupying any place, of a pure exchangeability' (70). Such a subject without properties governs the distribution of humanity into the local (native) and the universal by assuming the 'global ubiquity of the white European' which, in turn, becomes the very 'regulative idea of Culture against which the multiplicity of local cultures is defined' (70). Lloyd notes that the domination of the white universalized subject 'is virtually self-legitimating since the capacity to be everywhere present becomes an historical manifestation of the white man's gradual approximation to the universality he everywhere represents' (70).

Against this peculiar logic of democracy, resistance postmodernism argues that individuals need always to *rethink the relationship between identity and difference*. They need to understand their ethnicity in terms of a politics of location, positionality or enunciation. Stuart Hall argues, rightly in my view, that 'there's no enunciation without positionality. You have to position yourself *somewhere* in order to say anything at all' (1991, p. 18) One's identity, whether as black, white or Latino, has to do with the discovery of one's ethnicity. Hall calls this process of discovery the construction of 'new ethnicities' or 'emergent ethnicities'. Entailed in such a discovery is the

> need to honor the hidden histories from which [...] [people] [...] come. They need to understand the languages which they've been not taught to speak. They need to understand and revalue the traditions and inheritances of cultural expression and creativity. And in that sense, the past is not only a position from which to speak, but it is also an absolutely necessary resource in what one has to say. So the relationship of the kind of ethnicity I'm talking about to the past is not a simple, essential one – it is a constructed one. It is constructed in history, it is constructed politically in part. It is part of narrative. We tell ourselves the stories of the parts of our roots in order to come into contact, creatively, with it. So this new kind of ethnicity – the emergent ethnicities – has a relationship to the past, but it is a relationship that is partly through memory, partly through narrative, one that has to be recovered. It is an act of cultural recovery. (Hall, 1991, pp. 18, 19)

While the discourse of multiculturalism has tended to oppose hierarchical exclusiveness with arguments in favor of unrestricted inclusiveness (Wallace, 1991, p. 6), a resistance-postmodernist critique further problematizes the issue of exclusion and inclusion by articulating a new relationship between identity and difference. Not only can a resistance postmodernist articulation of difference theorize a place where marginalized groups can speak *from* but it can also provide groups a place from which to move *beyond* an essentialized and narrow ethnic identity since they also have a stake in global conditions of equality and social justice (Hall, 1991).

Homi K. Bhabha (1990) has articulated an important distinction between 'difference' and 'diversity'. Working from a poststructuralist perspective, Bhabha breaks from the social democratic version of multiculturalism where race, class and gender is modeled on a consensual conception of difference and locates his work within a radical democratic version of cultural pluralism which recognizes the essentially contested character of the signs and signifying apparatuses that people use in the construction of their identities (Mercer, 1990, p. 8).

Bhabha is critical of the notion of diversity used in liberal discourse to refer to the importance of plural, democratic societies. He argues that with diversity comes a 'transparent norm' constructed and administered by the 'host' society that creates a false consensus. This is because the normative grid that locates cultural diversity at the same time serves to *contain* cultural difference: The 'universalism that paradoxically permits diversity masks ethnocentric norms' (1990, p. 208). Differences, on the other hand, do not always speak of consensus but are often incommensurable. Culture, as a system of difference, as symbol-forming activity, must in Bhabha's view be seen as 'a process of translations' (p. 210). From this follows the observation that while cultures cannot be simply reduced to unregulatable textual play, neither do they exist as undisplaceable forms in the sense that they possess 'a totalized prior moment of being or meaning – an essence' (p. 210).

Otherness in this sense is often internal to the symbol-forming activity of that culture and it is perhaps best to speak of culture as a form of 'hybridity'. Within this hybridity, there exists a 'third space' that enables other discursive positions to emerge – to resist attempts to normalize what Bhabha refers to as 'the time-lagged colonial moment' (1991a, p. 211). This 'third space' opens up possibilities for new structures of authority, and new political vistas and visions. Identity from this perspective is always an arbitrary, contingent and temporary suturing of identification and meaning. Bhabha's distinction makes it clear why people such as Ravitch, Bloom, Hirsch and Bennett are so dangerous when they talk about the importance of building a common culture. Who has the power to exercise meaning, to create the grid from which Otherness is defined, to create the identifications that invite closures on meanings, on interpretations and translations?

This essay has suggested that conservative and liberal multiculturalism is really about the politics of assimilation because both assume that we really do live in a common egalitarian culture. Such an understanding of difference implies, as Iris Marion Young notes, 'coming into the game after the rules and standards have already been set, and having to prove oneself according to those rules and standards' (1990, p. 164). These standards are not seen as culturally and experientially specific among the citizenry-at-large because with a pluralist democracy privileged groups have occluded their own advantage by invoking the ideal of an unsituated, neutral, universal common humanity of self-formation in which all can happily participate without regard to differences in race, gender, class, age or sexual orientation. Resistance postmodernism, in particular, unsettles such a notion of universal common humanity by exploring identity within the context of power, discourse, culture, experience, and historical specificity.

7 Difference and the Politics of Signification

Resistance postmodernism has been especially significant in reformulating the meaning of difference as a form of signification. Differences in this view do not constitute clearly marked zones of auto-intelligible experience or a unity of identity as they do within most conservative and liberal forms of cultural pluralism. Rather, differences are understood through a politics of signification, that is, through signifying practices that are both reflective and constitutive of prevailing economic and political relations (Ebert, 1991). Against the conservative multiculturalist understanding of difference as 'self-evident cultural obviousness', as a 'mark of plurality', or 'the carefully marked off zones of experience – the privileged presence – of one group, one social category against another that we faithfully cultivate and reproduce in our analyses', Teresa Ebert defines difference as

> culturally constituted, made intelligible, through signifying practices. [For postmodern theories] 'difference' is not a clearly marked zone of experience, a unity of identity of one social group against another, taken as cultural pluralism. Rather, postmodern differences are relations of opposing signifiers. (1991, p. 117)

According to Ebert, our current ways of seeing and acting are being disciplined for us through forms of signification, that is, through modes of intelligibility and ideological frames of sense-making. Rejecting the Saussurian semiotics of signifying practices (and its continuing use in contemporary poststructuralism) as 'ahistorical operations of language and tropes', Ebert characterizes signifying practices as 'an ensemble of material operations involved in economic and political relations' (1991, p. 117). She maintains, rightly in my view, that socioeconomic relations of power require distinctions to be made among groups through forms of signification in order to organize subjects according to the unequal distribution of privilege and power.

To illustrate the politics of signification at work in the construction and formation of racist subjects, Ebert offers the example of the way in which the terms 'negro' and 'black' have been employed within the racial politics of the United States. Just as the term 'negro' became an immutable mark of difference and naturalized the political arrangements of racism in the 1960s, so too is the term 'black' being refigured in the white dominant culture to mean criminality, violence and social degeneracy. This was made clear in the Willie Horton campaign ads of George Bush and in the current Bush and David Duke position on hiring quotas. And in my view it was evident in the verdict of the Rodney King case in Los Angeles.

Carlos Muñoz, Jr., has revealed how the term 'Hispanic' in the mid-1970s became a 'politics of white ethnic identity' that de-emphasized and in some cases rejected the Mexican cultural base of Mexican Americans. Muñoz writes that the term 'Hispanic' is derived from 'Hispania' which was the name the Romans gave to the Iberian peninsula, most of which became Spain, and 'implicitly emphasizes the white European culture of Spain at the expense of the nonwhite cultures that have profoundly shaped the experiences of all Latin Americans' (1989, p. 11). Not only is this term blind to the multiracial reality of Mexican Americans through its refusal to acknowledge 'the nonwhite indigenous cultures of the Americas, Africa, and Asia, which historically have produced multicultural and multiracial peoples in Latin America and the United States' (11), it is a term that ignores the complexities within these various cultural groups. Here is another example of the melting pot theory of assimilation fostered through a politics of signification. So that we might ask ourselves what signifieds (meanings) will be attached to certain terms such as 'welfare mothers'? I think we know what government officials mean when they refer derisively to 'welfare mothers'. They mean black and Latino mothers.

The examples discussed above confirm the observation of resistance postmodernism that differences are produced according to the ideological production and reception of cultural signs. As Mas'ud Zavarzadeh and Donald Morton point out, 'Signs are neither eternally predetermined nor pan-historically undecidable: they are rather "decided" or rendered as "undecidable" in the moment of social conflicts' (1990, p. 156). Difference is not 'cultural obviousness' such as black versus white or Latino versus European or Anglo-American; rather, differences are historical and cultural constructions (Ebert, 1991).

Just as we can see the politics of signification at work in instances of police brutality, we can see it at work in special education placement where a greater proportion of Black and Latino students are considered for 'behavioral' placements whereas white, middle-class students are provided for the most part with the more comforting and comfortable label of 'learning disabled' (McLaren, 1989a). Here, a resistance-postmodernist critique can help teachers explore the ways in which students are differentially subjected to ideological inscriptions and multiply organized discourses of desire through a politics of signification. For instance, a resistance-postmodernist critique helps to understand how student identities are produced by a type of discursive ventriloquism in that they are creatures of the languages and knowledges that they have inherited and which unconsciously exert control over their thinking and behavior. As James Donald (1993) points out, social norms often surface as guilt-provoking desires since they have gone through a process that Foucault referred to as *folding*. James Donald points out that the

> norms and prohibitions instituted within social and cultural technologies are folded into the unconscious so that they 'surface' not just as 'personal desires' but in a complex and unpredictable dynamic of desire, guilt, anxiety and displacement. Subjects have desires that they do not want to have; they reject them at the cost of guilt and anxiety.

While subjects are invariably prisoners of a male monopoly on language and knowledge production (Grosz, 1990, p. 332), they are also active agents who are capable of exercising deliberate historical actions in and on the world (Giroux, 1992). The point, of course, is that conscious knowledge is not exhaustive of either identity or agency. We need to acknowledge what is not so obvious about how difference is constitutive of *both identity and agency.*

While abandoning all vestiges of the dominant culture can lead to a futile search for pre-modern roots that, in turn, leads to a narrow nationalism as in the case of what Hall calls the 'old ethnicity', abandoning the search for identity in the midst of the prevailing ideological and cultural hegemony can serve as a capitulation to assimilation and the loss of forms of critical historical agency. Needed is a view of multiculturalism and difference that moves beyond the 'either-or' logic of assimilation and resistance. To make a claim for multiculturalism is not, in the words of Trinh T. Minh-ha, 'to suggest the juxtaposition of several cultures whose frontiers remain intact, nor is it to subscribe to a bland 'melting pot' type of attitude that would level all differences. It lies instead, in the intercultural acceptance of risks, unexpected detours, and complexities of relation between break and closure' (1991, p. 232).

8   Always Totalize!

In this section I want to focus my analysis of multiculturalism on the concept of totality. I would like to emphasize that while educators must center their pedagogies on the affirmation of the 'local' knowledges of students within particular socio-political and ethnic locations, the concept of totality must not be abandoned altogether. Not all forms of totalization are democratically deficit. Not all forms truncate, oppress and destroy pluralism. As Fredric Jameson remarks, 'Local struggles [...] are effective only so long as they remain figures of allegories from some larger systematic transformation. Politics has to operate on the micro and the macro levels simultaneously; a modest restriction to local reforms within the system seems reasonable, but often proves politically demoralizing' (1989, p. 386). George Lipsitz underscores this idea, arguing that while totality can do violence to the specificity of events, a rejection of all totality would likely 'obscure real connections, causes, and relationships – atomizing common experience into accidents and endlessly repeated play. [and that] only by recognizing the collected legacy of accumulated human actions and ideas can we judge the claims to truth and justice of any one story' (1990, p. 214).

Without a shared vision of democratic community, we risk endorsing struggles in which the politics of difference collapses into new forms of separatism. As Steven Best points out, poststructuralists rightly deconstruct essentialist and repressive wholes, yet they often fail to see how crippling the valorizing of difference, fragmentation and agonistics can be. This is especially true of ludic postmodernism. Best writes: 'The flip side of the tyranny of the whole is the dictatorship of the fragment [...] without some positive and normative concept of totality to counter-balance the poststructuralist/postmodern emphasis on difference and discontinuity, we are abandoned to the seriality of pluralist individualism and the supremacy of competitive values over communal life' (1989, p. 361). Best is correct in suggesting that what needs to be abandoned is the reductive use of totality, not the concept of totality itself. Otherwise we risk undermining the very concept of democratic public life.

Teresa Ebert (1991) argues – brilliantly, to my mind – that we need to reassert the concept of totality not in the Hegelian sense of an organic, unified, oppressive unity, but rather 'as both a system of relations and *overdetermined structure of difference.*' Difference needs to be understood as social contradictions, as difference in relation, rather than dislocated, free-floating difference. Systems of differences, notes Ebert, always involve patterns of domination and relations of oppression and exploitation. We need to concern ourselves, therefore, with economies of relations of difference within historically specific totalities that are always open to contestation and transformation. As structures of difference that are always multiple and unstable, the oppressive relations of totalities (social, economic, political, legal, cultural, ideological) can always be challenged within a pedagogy of liberation. Ebert argues that totalities shouldn't be confused with Lyotard's notion of universal meta-narratives.

Only when they are used unjustly and oppressively as all-encompassing and all-embracing global warrants for thought and action in order to secure an oppressive regime of truth, should totality and universality be rejected. We need to retain some kind of moral, ethical and political ground – albeit a provisional one – from which to negotiate among multiple interests. Crucial to this argument is the important distinction between universal metanarratives (master narratives) and meta-critical narratives. The resistance-postmodernist critique that I am suggesting educators consider repudiates the necessity or choice of any one master narrative because master narratives suggest that there is only one public sphere, one value, one conception of justice that triumphs over all others. Resistance postmodernism suggests, on the contrary, that 'different spheres and rival conceptions of justice must be accommodated to each other' (Murphy, 1991, p. 124). In other words, 'the communitarian, the liberal or social democrat, the developmental liberal or humanist, the radical, and the romantic must find ways of living together in the same social space.' This does not mean trying to press them all into a homogenous cultural pulp but to suggest that there must be a multiplication of justices and pluralistic conceptions of justice, politics, ethics and aesthetics.

Again, the crucial question here is one that deals with the notion of *totality*. While I would argue against one grand narrative, I believe that there exists a primary meta-discourse that could, in fact, offer a *provisional* engagement with discourses of the Other in a way that can be unifying without dominating and that can provide for supplementary discourses. This is the meta-critical narrative of rights or freedom. Peter Murphy distinguishes between a master discourse and a meta-discourse, arguing that 'A master discourse wants to impose itself on all the other discourses – it is progressive, they are reactionary; it is right, they are wrong. A metadiscourse, on the other hand, seeks to understand society as a *totality* (1991, p. 126). Murphy, like Ebert, argues against a Lyotardian rejection of the grand narrative of emancipation. Instead, he embraces the idea of totality as set forth by Charles Jencks. This distinction is worth emphasizing.

> Postmodernism, Jencks, following Venturi, argues is concerned with complexity and contradiction, and precisely because it is concerned with complexity and contradiction, it in fact has a special obligation to the whole. This is not the 'harmonious whole' of canonic classicism, but rather the 'difficult whole' of a pluralized and multi-dimensional world. Postmodernism, Jencks argues, is committed to synthesizing a 'difficult whole' out of fragments, references, and approaches. Its truth lies not in any part, but, as Venturi puts it, *in its totality or implication of totality.* (Murphy, 1991, p. 126; italics in original)

Here I am not reclaiming or rewriting totality as a synonym for political economy or suggesting that a critical postmodernism resist narrating the location of the theorist or abandon local struggles. I want to make clear that I am not using the concept of 'totalizing' to mean an act of generalizing from the law of intelligibility of one phenomena to the level of all social or cultural phenomena (Zavarzadeh & Morton, 1991). Nor I am using it to mean some forgotten plenitude, formalized auratic experience, or bygone world that needs to be recovered for the sake of some noble nostalgia. Rather, I am using 'totalizing' in the manner that Zavarzadeh and Morton have described as 'global'. Global understanding is a 'form of explanation that is *relational* and *transdisciplinary* and that produces an account of the "knowledge-effects" of culture by *relating* various cultural series' (1991, p. 155). It is a mode of inquiry that attempts to address how the ludic-postmodernist critique serves as a strategy of political containment by privileging forms of 'local' analysis which center the subject in experience as the archic site of truth and posit technology as the sole 'reader' of experience.

Global or relational knowledge points to the existence of an underlying logic of domination within the signifying practices that constitute the cultural products of late capitalism and for this reason it sets itself against ludic postmodernism's dismissal of knowledge as integrative and political because of the supposed incommensurability of cultural, political and economic phenomena. It moves beyond the cognitivism and empiricism of the dominant knowledge industry by dispossessing individuals of their imaginary sense of the auto-intelligibility of experience. Further, it reveals that *difference* is not an inherent condition of textuality but a socially overdetermined historical effect that acquires its tropicity only within given historical and cultural modes of intelligibility. Zavarzadeh and Morton argue that

> in the ludic space of playfulness, the social relations of production are posited not as historically necessary but as subject to the laws of the alea: chance and contingency. In ludic deconstruction chance and contingency perform the same ideological role that 'native' (i.e., non-logical, random, inscrutable) difference plays in traditional humanistic discourses. Both posit a social field beyond the reach of the logic of necessity and history. (1991, p. 194)

Resistance postmodernism offers teachers working in multicultural education a means of interrogating the locality, positionality and specificity of knowledge (in terms of the race, class and gender locations of students) and the generation of a plurality of truths (rather than one apodictic truth built around the invisible norm of Eurocentrism and white ethnicity) while at the same time situating the construction of meaning in terms of the material interests at work in the production of 'truth effects' – that is, in the production of forms of intelligibility and social practices. Consequently, teachers working within a resistance postmodernism are able to call into question the political assumptions and relations of determination upon which social truths are founded in both the communities in which they work and the larger society of which they are a part. Ludic postmodernism, in contrast, effectively masks the relationship between dominant discourses and the social relations that they justify through an immanent reading of cultural texts (reading texts on their own terms) in which their internal and formal coherence takes priority over the social relations of their production. In fact, Zavarzadeh and Morton go so far as to suggest that ludic postmodernism gained ascendency in the academy just at the time when capitalism became de-territorialized and multinational. In effect, they are arguing that the ludic-postmodern critique has suppressed forms of knowing that 'could explain multi-national capitalism's trans-territoriality and its affiliated phenomena' (1991, p. 163).

Viewed from the perspective of constructing a global or relational understanding, the idea of organizing postmodern critique around the referents of freedom and emancipation is an attempt to avoid a unifying logic that monolithically suppresses or forecloses meaning. Conversely, it is a determined effort to retain and understand the 'difficult whole' of a pluralistic and global society. It is to take up a position against reactionary pluralists such as William Bennett, Diane Ravitch, and Allan Bloom, who embrace and advocate the idea of a harmonious common culture.

I have tried to argue that in order to have a liberating narrative informing our pedagogies, educators need to address the concept of totality. The idea of a master narrative's 'phallic projectory' into the telos of historical destiny needs to be discredited, yet the idea of totality itself must be recuperated. The concepts of totality and infinity need to be dialectically positioned within any pedagogy of liberation. Lévinas (1969, p. 25) notes that the idea of infinity delivers subjectivity from the judgement of history to declare it ready for judgement at every moment' (cited in Chambers, 1990, p. 109). Isn't this precisely what Fanon was trying to describe when he urged us to *totalize infinitely* as a communicative act (Taylor, 1989, p. 26)? For me, spaces for rewriting dominant narratives come into being by the very fact of the patience of infinity, the diachrony of time which, observes Lévinas, is produced by our situatedness as ethical subjects and our responsibility to the Other. The problem, of course, is that the remaking of the social and the reinvention of the self must be understood as dialectically synchronous that is, they cannot be conceived as unrelated or only marginally connected. They are mutually informing and interanimating processes.

According to Patrick Taylor, the essential ingredient of a narrative of liberation is the recognition of freedom in necessity (1989, p. 25). In this sense, the necessity of freedom becomes a *responsible totalization.* Not in the sense of a master narrative but in the sense of a meta-discourse or discourse of possibility (Giroux, 1992). If we talk about totalization in the sense of a master narrative, we are referring to a premature closure on meaning, a false universalism (what Taylor calls an 'ordered totality') that leads to a categorical utopia – that leads, in other words, to fascism. Infinite totalization, on the other hand, refers to a hypothetical or provisional utopia. As Dauenhauer (1989) notes, the hypothetical embrace of utopian representation must be distinguished from the categorical embrace. To embrace ideology or utopia categorically is a form of 'bad infinity' by denying alternatives to the present reality.

Teachers need to stress in their teaching (following Ernst Bloch) the hypothetical or provisional and not the categorical embrace of utopia. Paradoxically, hypothetical utopias based on infinite totalization are the most concrete of all because they offer through their negative content (i.e., the concrete negation of domination) *the end of totalities.* Patrick Taylor, citing Jameson, notes that 'the ultimate interpretive task is the understanding of symbolic works in relation to a demystifying, open-ended narrative of liberation that is grounded in the imperative of human freedom' (1989, p. 19).

Narratives of freedom are ways of transcending those social myths (with their pre-given narrative orders) that reconcile us through the resolution of binary oppositions to lives of lived subordination. Narratives of liberation are those that totalize infinitely, but not by integrating difference into a monolithic identity produced by modernity's colonial or neocolonial situation – by forcing difference into silence precisely when it is asked to speak (Saenz, 1991, p. 158). They do not simply negate the difference produced by identity secreted in a situation of domination, because this simply saps the sustenance of the identity of the dominator (Saenz, 1991). Narratives of liberation do not simply construct an identity that 'runs counter Eurocentric identity; for such would be a mere resurrection of the racist European myth of the 'noble savage' – a millenarianism in reverse, the expression of Eurocentric self-dissatisfaction and self-flagellation over its own disenchantment with the 'modernity' produced by its project of 'possessive individualism'' (Saenz, 1991, p. 159). Rather, narratives of liberation point to the possibility of new, alternative identities contemporaneous with modernity but not simply through inverting its normative truths.

As historical agents, educators are positioned within the tension produced by modernist and postmodernist attempts to resolve the living contradiction of being both the subject and object of meaning. But their mode of critical analysis needs to move beyond the tropological displacement of discursive familiarity or a highjacking of meaning in the back alleys of theory (as is the case with ludic postmodernism). Educators require narratives of liberation that can serve a *metacritical* function – that can meta-conceptualize relations of everyday life – and that do not succumb to the transcendental unity of subject and object or their transfiguring coalescence (Saldivar, 1990, p. 173). In other words, such narratives promote a form of analectic understanding in addition to a dialectical understanding. As Enrique Dussel (1985) has argued, analectics reaches exteriority not through totality (as does dialectics) but rather *beyond* it. But Saenz (1991) remarks that the 'beyond' that Dussel speaks about must not be interpreted as an absolute beyond all criticism (i.e., God) but rather as a 'beyond' that has its roots 'in the midst of domination', that is, in the suffering of the oppressed 'understood within its colonial textuality'. Analectics could be thus described as a form of 'pluritopic' dialectical critique aimed at revealing the monotopic understanding of Eurocentrism as merely contingent to its own cultural traditions (Saenz, 1991).

Through a praxis of infinite totalization educators can provide analectically a new vision of the future that is latent in the present, immanent in this very moment of reading, in the womb of the actual. Such a praxis can help us understand that subjective intentions do not constitute the archic site of truth. Subjectivities and identities of students and teachers are always the artifacts of discursive formations; that is, they are always the products of historical contexts and language games (see Kincheloe, 1991; Carspecken, 1991). Students and teachers are all actors in narrative configurations and emplotments that they did not develop but which are the products of historical and discursive struggles that have been folded back into the unconscious. Teachers need to recognize the discourses that not only inform the ritualization of their teaching practices, but those that organize their vision of the future. They must recall, too, that human agency is not a substratum that props them up like the crutches in a Dali painting, but has *imperative force*. The theatre of agency is *possibility* and *infinity*.

Agency is informed by historical discourses which have been gridded in the subject positions teachers and students take. Yet while there is a logos immanent to the discourses that constitute teachers that make them functionaries within modern technologies of power, this does not mean that educators and cultural workers cannot foster and realize potentialities destined through their language and communities. Educators have a heritage of possibilities from which to work and while these affect the ground of their constitution they do not saturate their will nor do they prevent them from struggling against the constraints that bind freedom and justice. David Trend speaks to this issue when he emphasizes the importance of understanding the productive character of knowledge. While the influence on the process of knowledge production is always partial, cultural workers exert considerable influence on it:

> Acknowledging the role of the 'learning subject' in the construction of culture, we affirm processes of agency, difference and, ultimately, democracy. We suggest to students and audiences that they have a role in the making of their world and that they need not accept positions as passive spectators or consumers. This is a position that recognizes and encourages the atmosphere of diverse and contradictory opinions so dreaded by the conservative proponents of a 'common culture.' It functions on the belief that a healthy democracy is one that is always being scrutinized and tested. (1992, p. 150)

Exerting an influence over cultural production means finding ways of speaking and acting outside the totalizing systems of modernist understanding by creating meta-critical and relational perspectives. Educators need to get outside the admixtures and remnants of languages – the multiplicity of voices that already populate their vocabulary and suffocate all the available linguistic spaces – in order to find different ways of appropriating or mediating the real. Educators and cultural workers need to cross borders into zones of cultural difference rather than construct subjectivities that simply reassert themselves as monadic forms of totality facilitated by a consumerist ethics and market-place logic (Giroux, 1992; McLaren, 1996).

9 Critical Pedagogy: Teaching for a Hybrid Citizenry and Multicultural Solidarity

Resistance postmodernism has figured prominently in the development of new forms of pedagogical praxis concerned with rethinking educational politics in a multicultural society (Giroux, 1992; McLaren & Leonard, 1993; McLaren, 1996; Aronowitz & Giroux, 1991). Of particular significance is Giroux's concept of 'border pedagogy' which enables educators to affirm and legitimate local meanings and constellations of meanings that grow out of particular discursive communities but at the same time interrogate the interests, ideologies and social practices that such knowledges serve when viewed from the perspective of more global economies of power and privilege.

A pedagogy informed significantly by resistance postmodernism suggests that teachers and cultural workers need to take up the issue of 'difference' in ways that don't replay the monocultural essentialism of the 'centrisms' Anglocentrism, Eurocentrism, phallocentrism, androcentrism and the like. They need to foster a politics of alliance-building, of dreaming together, of solidarity that moves beyond the condescension, of say, 'race awareness week' that actually serves to keep forms of institutionalized racism intact. A solidarity has to be struggled for that is not centered around market imperatives but develops out of the imperatives of freedom, liberation, democracy and critical citizenship.

The notion of the citizen has been pluralized and hybridized, as Kobena Mercer notes, by the presence of a diversity of social subjects. Mercer is instructive in pointing out that 'solidarity does not mean that everyone thinks the same way, it begins when people have the confidence to disagree over issues because they "care" about constructing a common ground' (1990, p. 68). Solidarity is not impermeably solid but depends to a certain degree on antagonism and uncertainty. Timothy Maliqualim Simone calls this type of multiracial solidarity 'geared to maximizing points of interaction rather than harmonizing, balancing, or equilibrating the distribution of bodies, resources, and territories' (1989, p. 191).

While guarding against the privileging of a false universalism, a false unity that denies the internal rifts of bodily desire, both teachers and students need to open themselves to the possibility of Otherness so that the particularity of individual being can become visible. Students especially need to be provided with opportunities to devise different assemblages of the self by dismantling and interrogating the different kinds of discursive segmentarity that inform their subjectivities, subverting those stratified and hierarchized forms of subjectivity that code the will, and developing nomadic forms of individual and collective agency that open up new assemblages of desire and modes of being-in-the-world (Grossberg, 1988).

Educators must examine the development of pedagogical discourses and practices that demonize Others who are different (through transforming them into absence or deviance). A resistance postmodernism that takes multiculturalism seriously calls attention to the dominant meaning systems readily available to students – most of which are ideologically stitched into the fabric of Western imperialism and patriarchy. It challenges meaning systems that impose attributes on the Other under the direction of sovereign signifiers and tropes. And this means not directing all our efforts at understanding ethnicity as 'other than white', but by interrogating the culture of whiteness itself. This is crucial because unless we do this – unless we give white students a sense of their own identity as an emergent ethnicity – we naturalize whiteness as a cultural marker against which Otherness is defined. Coco Fusco warns that 'To ignore white ethnicity is to redouble its hegemony by naturalizing it. Without specifically addressing white ethnicity there can be no critical evaluation of the construction of the other' (cited in Wallace, 1991, p. 7). White groups need to examine their ethnic histories so that they are less likely to judge their own cultural norms as neutral and universal. 'Whiteness' does not exist outside of culture but constitutes the prevailing social texts in which social norms are made and remade. As part of a politics of signification that passes unobserved into the rhythms of daily life, and a 'politically constructed category parasitic on "Blackness"' (West, 1990, p. 29), 'Whiteness' has become the invisible norm for how the dominant culture measures its own civility.

With this in mind, a critical pedagogy that embraces a resistance postmodernism needs to construct a politics of refusal that can provide both the conditions for interrogating the institutionalization of formal equality based on the prized imperatives of a white, Anglo male world and for creating spaces to investigate how dominant institutions must be transformed so that they no longer serve simply as conduits for a motivated indifference to victimization, for the production of asymmetrical relations of power and privilege.

Here it is important to contest the charge made by some liberal humanist educators that teachers should only speak for themselves and not for others. Those who claim that teachers can and should only speak for themselves – a claim that is at the very least implied by many critics of critical pedagogy forget that 'When I "speak for myself" I am participating in the creation and reproduction of discourses through which my own and other selves are constituted' (Alcoff, 1991/1992, p. 21). Linda Alcoff notes that we need to promote a *dialogue with* rather than a *speaking for* others (although this does not preclude us from speaking for others under certain restricted circumstances). Drawing upon the work of Gayatri Chakravorty Spivak, Alcoff maintains that we can adopt a 'speaking to' the other that does not essentialize the oppressed as nonideologically constructed subjects. It is important, notes Spivak, that the intellectual 'neither abnegates his or her discursive role nor presumes an authenticity of the oppressed but still allows for the possibility that the oppressed will produce a "countersentence" that can then suggest a new historical narrative' (cited in Alcoff, 1991/1992, p. 23). Educators need to be exceedingly cautious about attempts to speak for others, questioning how their discourses as an *event* position them as authoritative and empowered speakers in ways that unwittingly constitute a reinscription of the discourse of colonization, of patriarchy, of racism, of conquest – 'a reinscription of sexual, national, and other kinds of hierarchies' (Alcoff, 1991/1992, p. 29). Educators also need to avoid a 'tolerance' that appropriates the difference of the Other in the name of the colonizer's own self-knowledge and increased domination.

Critical pedagogy does not work towards some grandiose endpoint of an ideologically perceived world history but rather attempts to make understandable the indefinite and to explore modes of sociality and self-figuration that go beyond dominant language formations and social organizations. In doing so, it has often been accused of being inaccessible to rank-and-file teachers. Trinh T. Minh-ha issues a very telling warning against such calls for accessibility of language. She writes that resistance to the language of complex theory can reinstitute 'common sense' as an alternative to theory – that is, it can usher in a new dictatorship of pre-theoretical nativism in which experience supposedly speaks for itself. To be 'accessible', writes Minh-ha, often suggests

> one can employ neither symbolic and elliptical language, as in Asian, African, or Native American cultures (because Western ears often equate it with obscurantism); nor poetic language (because 'objective' literal thinking is likely to identify it with 'subjective' aestheticism). The use of dialogical language is also discouraged (because the dominant worldview can hardly accept that in the politics of representing marginality and resistance one might have to speak at least two different things at once). (1991, p. 228)

Minh-ha further notes, after Isaac Julien, that resistance to theory is embodied in white people's resistance to the complexity of black experience. Not only does such resistance point to the illusion that there exists a natural, self-evident language but such a call for accessibility can also lead to forms of racism and intolerance and the politics of exclusion. The 'diversely hybrid experiences of heterogeneous contemporary societies are denied' by such a form of binary thinking that would reduce the language of analysis to white, hegemonic forms of clarity (Minh-ha, 1991, p. 229).

A pedagogy that takes resistance postmodernism seriously does not make the nativist assumption that knowledge is pre-ontologically available and that various disciplinary schools of thought may be employed in order to tease out different readings of the same 'common sense' reality in a context of impartiality. Rather, the discourses that inform the educator's problematics are understood as constitutive of the very reality that he or she is attempting to understand. Consequently, the classroom is the site of the teacher's own embodiment in theory/discourse, ethical disposition as moral and political agent, and situatedness as a cultural worker within a larger narrative identity. In recognizing the important role played by 'place' in any critical pedagogy, it should be clear that we are talking not about the physical milieu where knowledge is made visible within preordained and circumscribed limits but rather the textual space that one occupies and the affective space one creates as a teacher. In other words, the discursive practice of 'doing pedagogy' does not simply treat knowledge outside of the way that it is taken up by both teachers and students *as a form of dialogue*. Knowledge can never be treated as a cultural artifact or possession that serves as a pristine, prefigurative source of cultural authenticity inviting unbiased analysis.

The project of critical pedagogy means bringing the laws of cultural representation face-to-face with their founding assumptions, contradictions, and paradoxes. It also means encouraging teachers to participate in the affective as well as intellectual cultures of the oppressed, and to challenge in the spirit of Bloch's 'militant optimism' ethical and political quietism in the face of operating homilies such as 'progress is inevitable' or what might seem like historical inevitability – a perspective that leads to the cult of the mausoleum. Educators can no longer project on to the student-as-Other that part of themselves they rejected or subtracted from their identities in their attempt to become unified subjects – that 'split-off part of themselves which prevents them from becoming whole, that disfiguring surplus that they have cast out in order to become white or live in its thrall, that metaphysical double that guarantees their own self-regarding autonomy. From this point of view, liberation is never an encapsulated fulfillment of some pre-figured end constructed in the temple of memory but a lived tension between the duration of history and the discourse of possibility. It resides in an approach to the '*Aufhebung*' – our passing *into* the 'not-yet', and seeking the immanent utopia in the crisis of meaning and the social relations that inform it. It is found, too, in the proleptic consciousness of liminality – the liberating intention of the reflective will caught in the 'subjunctive' moment of the 'ought' and disabused of metaphysical illusion. It is formed out of an ethical intent commensurate with the love that Paulo Freire and Che Guevara both argue constitutes the ground from which all revolutionary action should take place.

Neither the academy nor the public school system needs to sow future priests of deconstruction in the desacralized horizon of the postmodern scene by turning the college classroom into a pre-war Europe Nietzschean café or Cabaret Voltaire for leftist educators who wish to reap no real political consequences for their semiotic revolution. Rather, the more pressing need is to transform present social practices and institutional relations because history compels us to do so, because the present historical juncture in which we witness so much misery and suffering necessitates it. History compels us because our dreams and our suffering are forged in it; it is what houses the furnace of our will. In the iron womb of history we cast the shape of our longings, and to reclaim history is to be fully present in its making.

Educators need to do more than to help students redescribe or represent themselves in new ways – although the way we seek to imagine ourselves is an important step in the struggle for liberation. As Sander L. Gilman has pointed out in his study of stereotypes of sexuality, race and madness, 'we view our own images, our own mirages, our own stereotypes as embodying qualities that exist in the world. And we act upon them' (1985, p. 242). More specifically, a pedagogy must be made available to teachers that will enable them along with their students to outface the barrenness of postmodern culture by employing a discourse and set of social practices that will not be content with resurrecting a nostalgic past which can never be reclaimed, or with redescribing the present by simply textualizing it, leaving in place its malignant hierarchies of power and privilege, its defining pathologies. For these latter acts only stipulate the lineage of and give sustenance to those social relations responsible for the very injustice critical educators are trying to struggle against. Educators need to stare boldly and unflinchingly into the historical present and assume a narrative space where conditions may be created where students can speak their own stories, listen loudly to the stories of others, and dream the dream of liberation.

A critical pedagogy also demands political and cultural tactics that can fight multiple forms of oppression yet achieve a cohesiveness with divergent social groups working towards liberatory goals. To this end, Chela Sandoval suggests that cultural workers develop 'tactical subjectivities' which she describes as forms of oppositional and differential consciousness and counter-hegemonic praxis (which she discusses in the context of feminism). Tactical subjectivity enables teachers as social agents to recenter their multiple subjectivities with respect to the kinds of oppression that are being confronted and 'permits the practitioner to choose tactical positions, that is, to self-consciously break and reform ties to ideology, activities which are imperative for the psychological and political practices that permit the achievement of coalition across differences' (1991, p. 15).

10   Resistance as 'la conciencia de la mestiza'

The invitation posed by critical pedagogy is to bend reality to the requirements of a just world, to decenter, deform, disorient and ultimately transform modes of authority that domesticate the Other, that lay siege to the power of the margins. Educators would do well to consider Gloria Anzaldúa's (1987) project of fostering *mestizaje* theories that create new categories of identity for those left out or pushed out of existing ones. Critical pedagogy calls for the construction of a praxis where peripheralized peoples such as African Americans and Latinos are no longer induced to fear and obey the White Gaze of Power, where bonds of sentiment and obligation can be formed among diverse groups of oppressed peoples, where resistance can enable schools to become more than instruments of social replication, where contrasting cultural styles and cultural capital among diverse groups cease to remain tokens of estrangement that separate them but rather become the very impetus that brings them together as liminal travelers under an arch of social dreaming. It is a praxis that gives encouragement to those who, instead of being content with visiting history as curators or custodians of memory, choose to live in the furnace of history where memory is molten and can be bent into the contours of a dream and perhaps even acquire the immanent force of a vision.

The sites of our identity within postmodernity are various; as seekers of liberation, we recognize the heterogeneous character of our inscription into colonial texts of history and cultural discourses of empire. New sites of agency are irrupting at the borderlines of cultural instability, in the transgressive act of remembering, and through the disavowal and refashioning of consciousness in the in-between spaces of cultural negotiation and translation. Marcos Sanchez-Tranquilino and John Tagg (1991) refer to this as the borderland, the 'in-between' space that Gloria Anzaldúa calls *la frontera*. It is a space of borders where teachers may be able to recognize

> another narration of identity, another resistance. One that asserts a difference, yet cannot be absorbed into the pleasures of the global marketing culture. One that locates its different voice, yet will not take a stand on the unmoving ground of a defensive fundamentalism. One that speaks its location as more than local, yet makes no claim to universality for its viewpoint or language. One that knows the border and crosses the line. (Sanchez-Tranquilino & Tagg, 1991, p. 105)

The rhythm of the struggle for educational and social transformation can no longer be contained in the undaunted, steady steps of the workers' army marching towards the iron gates of freedom but is being heard in the hybrid tempos of bordertown bands; in the spiralling currents of an Aster Aweke Kabu vocal, in the percussive polyrhythms of prophetic Black rap, in meanings that appear in the folds of cultural life where identities are mapped not merely by diversity but through difference.

Acknowledgment

This chapter originally appeared as P. McLaren, Multiculturalism and the postmodern critique: Towards a pedagogy of resistance and transformation, *Cultural Studies*, 7(1) (1993), 118–146. Reprinted here, with minor edits, with permission from the publisher.

References

Alcoff, L. (1991/1992). The problem of speaking for others. *Cultural Critique, 20,* 5–32.

Aronowitz, S., & Giroux, H. A. (1991). *Postmodern education.* University of Minnesota Press.

Anzaldúa, G. (1987). *Borderlands/La frontera: The new mestiza.* Spinsters/Aunt/Ute.

Benjamin, W. (1973, March-April). Program for a proletarian children's theater. *Performance, 1*(5), 28–32. (Translated by Susan Buck-Morss from Walter Benjamin, Programm eines proletarischen Kindertheaters (1928), in *Ober Kinder, Jugend und Erziehung,* Edition Suhrkamp, no. 391, Suhrkamp Verlag, Frankfurt am Main, 1969.)

Best, S. (1989). Jameson, totality and post structuralist critique. In D. Kellner (Ed.), *Postmodernism/Jameson/critique* (pp. 233–369). Maisonneuve Press.

Bhabha, H. K. (1990). Introduction: Narrating the nation. In H. K. Bhabha (Ed.), *Nation and narration* (pp. 291–322). Routledge.

Bhabha, H. (1991a). The third space: Interview with Homi Bhabha. In J. Rutherford (Ed.), *Identity: Community, culture, difference* (pp. 207–221). Lawrence & Wishart.

Bhabha, H. K. (1991b). 'Race' time, and the revision of modernity. *Oxford Literary Review, 13*(1–2), 193–219.

Browder, L. H. (1992). Which America 2000 will be taught in your class, teacher? *International Journal of Educational Reform, 1*(2), 111–133.

Carspecken, P. F. (1991). *Community Schooling and the nature of power: The battle for Croxteth Comprehensive.* Routledge.

Chambers, I. (1990). *Border dialogues: Journeys in postmodernity.* Routledge.

Christian, B. (1987). The race for theory. *Culture Critique, 6,* 51–63.

Cooper, B. M. (1989). Cruel and the gang: Exposing the Schomburg Posse. *Village Voice, 34*(19), 27–36.

Copjec, J. (1991). The *unvermögende* other: Hysteria and democracy in America. *New Formations, 14,* 27–41.

Dauenhauer, P. B. (1989). Ideology, utopia, and responsible politics. *Man and World, 22,* 25–41.

Di Stephano, C. (1990). Dilemmas of difference: Feminism, modernity and postmodernism. In L. J. Nicholson (Ed.), *Feminism/postmodernism* (pp. 63–82). Routledge.

Donald, J. (1993). The natural man and the virtuous woman: Reproducing citizens. In C. Jenks (Ed.), *Cultural reproduction.* Routledge.

Dussel, E. (1985). *Philosophy of liberation.* Orbis Books.

Ebert, T. (1991). Political semiosis in/of American cultural studies. *American Journal of Semiotics, 8*(1/2), 113–135.

Ebert, T. (1991). Writing in the political: Resistance (post) modernism. *Legal Studies Forum, XV*(4).

Featherstone, M. (1990). Global culture: An introduction. *Theory, Culture & Society, 7*(2-3), 1-14.

Foster, H. (Ed.). (1983). *The anti-aesthetic: Essays on postmodern culture*. Bay Press.

Frank, A. W. (1990). Bringing bodies back in: A decade review. *Theory, Culture and Society, 7*(1), 131-162.

Gilman, S. L. (1985). *Difference and pathology*. Cornell University Press.

Gilroy, P. (1990). One nation under a groove: The cultural politics of 'race' and racism in Britain. In D. T. Goldberg (Ed.), *Anatomy of racism* (pp. 263-282). University of Minnesota Press.

Giroux, H. A. (1992). *Border crossings: Cultural workers and the politics of education*. Routledge.

Grossberg, L. (1988). *It's a sin*. Power Publications.

Grosz, E. (1990). Conclusion: Notes on essentialism and difference. In S. Gunew (Ed.), *Feminist knowledge: Critique and construct* (pp. 332-344). Routledge.

Hall, S. (1991). Ethnicity: Identity and difference. *Radical America, 23*(4), 9-20.

Harstock, N. (1987). Rethinking modernism: Minority vs majority theories. *Culture Critique, 7*, 187-206.

Jameson, F. (1989). Afterword – Marxism and postmodernism. In D. Kellner (Ed.), *Postmodernism/Jameson/critique* (pp. 369-387). Maisonneuve Press.

Kaplan, E. A. (1987). *Rocking around the clock: Music, television, postmodernism and consumer culture*. Methuen.

Kasinitz, P. (1988). Facing up to the underclass. *Telos, 76*, 170-180.

Kimball, R. (1991). Tenured radicals: A postscript. *The New Criterion, 9*(5), 4-13.

Kincheloe, J. (1991). *Teachers as researchers: Qualitative inquiry as a path to empowerment*. Falmer.

Lash, S. (1990). Learning from Leipzig ... or politics in the semiotic society. *Theory, Culture and Society, 7*(4), 145-158.

Larsen, N. (1990). *Modernism and hegemony: A materialist critique of aesthetic agencies*. University of Minnesota Press.

Lévinas, E. (1969). *Totality and infinity*. Duquesne University Press.

Lippard, L. R. (1990). *Mixed blessings: New art in a multicultural America*. Pantheon Books.

Lipsitz, G. (1990). *Time passages*. University of Minnesota Press.

Lloyd, D. (1991). Race under representation. *Oxford Literary Review, 13*(1-2), 62-94.

McLaren, P. (1989a). Schooling the postmodern body: Critical pedagogy and the politics of enfleshment. *Journal of Education, 170*(3), 53-83.

McLaren, P. (1989b). *Life in schools*. Longman Inc.

McLaren, P. (Ed.). (1996). *Postmodernism, postcolonialism and pedagogy*. James Nicholas Publishers Ltd.

McLaren, P., & Hammer, R. (1989). Critical pedagogy and the postmodern challenge. *Educational Foundations, 3*(3), 29–69.

McLaren, P., & Leonard, P. (1993). *Paulo Freire: A critical encounter.* Routledge.

Mercer, K. (1990). Welcome to the jungle: Identity and diversity in postmodern politics. In J. Rutherford (Ed.), *Identity: Community, Culture, Difference* (pp. 43–71). Lawrence & Wishart.

Minh-ha, T. T. (1991). *When the moon waxes red: Representation, gender and cultural politics.* Routledge.

Mohanty, C. T. (1989/1990). On race and voice: Challenges for liberal education in the 1990s. *Cultural Critique, 14,* 179–208.

Muñoz, C., Jr. (1989). *Youth, identity, power: The Chicano movement.* Verso.

Murphy, P. (1991). Postmodern perspectives and justice. *Thesis Eleven, 30,* 11732.

Piccone, P. (1988). Roundtable on communitarianism. *Telos, 76,* 2–32.

Ravitch, D. (1990). Multiculturalism: E pluribus plures. *American Scholar, 59*(3), 337–354.

Ravitch, D. (1991, December). A culture in common. *Educational Leadership,* 8–16.

Rosaldo, R. (1989). *Culture and truth: The remaking of social analysis.* Beacon.

Rosenau, P. M. (1992). *Post-modernism and the social sciences: Insights, inroads, and intrusions,* Princeton University Press.

Saenz, M. (1991). Memory, enchantment and salvation: Latin American philosophies of liberation and the religions of the oppressed. *Philosophy and Social Criticism, 17*(2), 149–173.

Saldivar, R. (1990). *Chicano narrative: The dialectics of difference.* University of Wisconsin Press.

Sanchez-Tranquilino, M., & Tagg, J. (1991). The Pachuco's flayed hide: The museum, identity and Buenas Garvas. In R. Griswold de Castillo, T. McKenna, & Y. Yarbro-Bejarano (Eds.), *Chicano art: Resistance and affirmation* (pp. 97–108). Wright Art Gallery.

Sandoval, C. (1991). U.S. Third World feminism: The theory and method of oppositional consciousness in the postmodern world. *Genders, 10,* 1–24.

Simone, T. M. (1989). *About face: Race in postmodern America.* Autonomedia.

Stephanson, A. (1988). Interview with Cornel West. In A. Ross (Ed.), *Universal abandon? The politics of postmodernism* (pp. 269–286). University of Minnesota Press.

Taylor, P. (1989). *The narrative of liberation: Perspectives on Afro-Caribbean literature, popular culture, and politics.* Cornell University Press.

Trend, D. (1992). *Cultural pedagogy: Art/education/politics.* Bergin & Garvey.

Wallace, M. (1991, October). Multiculturalism and oppositionality. *Afterimage,* 6–9.

West, C. (1989). Black culture and postmodernism. In B. Kruger & P. Mariani (Eds.), *Remaking history* (pp. 87–96). Bay Press.

West, C. (1990). The new cultural politics of difference. In R. Ferguson, M. Gever, T. T. Minh-ha & C. West (Eds.), *Out there: Marginalization and contemporary cultures* (pp. 19–36). MIT Press and the New Museum of Contemporary Art, New York.

Young, I. M. (1990). *Justice and the politics of difference*. Princeton University Press.

Zavarzadeh, M., & Morton, D. (1990). Signs of knowledge in the contemporary academy. *American Journal of Semiotics, 7*(4), 149–160.

Zavarzadeh, M., & Morton, D. (1991). *Theory, (post) modernity, opposition*. Maisonneuve Press.

CHAPTER 5

The Anthropological Roots of Pedagogy
The Teacher as Liminal Servant

1   Summary

Bringing contemporary work in ritual studies into rapprochement with fieldwork in urban classrooms provides the reform-minded educator with a broad construction for decoding obstacles that working-class students face in acquiring an education. A classification of classroom activity developed in the field study of a Canadian junior high school allows me to apply Turner's concepts of liminality and communitas to create a typology of teachers in the context of the classroom as theatre or ritual. Unlike the more conventional types of overlord and entertainer, the teacher as a liminal servant understands that knowledge is perfomatively constituted and consequently calls forth the body. Cognizant of the shamanic mission, the teacher as liminal servant seeks to free the body and the mind from the hegemony of the everyday and to transform pedagogy into holy praxis in which both teacher and students are united in the sacred communitas of knowing.

Classroom culture is not a disembodied homogeneous entity but is discontinuous, murky, and provocative of contestation and conflict. It is a collectivity composed of contests between class, cultural, and symbolic relations. It is, furthermore, a symbolic arena where students and teachers both resist and accommodate various ritual performances and symbolic meanings, and where symbols have both centripetal and centrifugal pulls. Classrooms are therefore more than instructional sites; they constitute cultural arenas in which a heterogeneity of ideological and social forms struggle for dominance. As a contested terrain of competing discourses, classrooms often repeat on cultural levels the fundamental conflicts within the larger society. As cultural sites, classrooms also constitute powerful symbol systems (cf. Geertz, 1973), and to conceive of them as such allows us, in Wilk's view, "to gain greater precision in our attempts to understand the imposition of cultural realities" (1977, p. 13).

St. Ryan, a pseudonym, is a Catholic junior high school in Toronto, Canada, whose students are primarily from working-class families of Portuguese and Italian background. Drawing on recent fieldwork in St. Ryan's, I have analyzed classroom instruction as a ritual system and have presented elsewhere an

© AMERICAN ANTHROPOLOGICAL ASSOCIATION, 1987

extended exegesis of that system (McLaren, 1984b, 1985, 1986b, 1988a, 1988b). Here, I offer a discussion of pedagogical roles, or teacher types, and focus on one of the three types, the liminal servant. These roles are performed in the context of certain rituals of instruction, which constitute the following typology:

1. The micro ritual: The micro ritual consists of the individual lessons that take place on a day-to-day basis in the classroom.
2. The macro ritual: The macro ritual consists of individual classroom lessons, prayers (and occasional school masses) as they appear collectively over a single school day; the macro ritual also encapsulates classroom activity between lessons and immediately before and after lessons.
3. Rituals of revitalization: A ritual of revitalization is a processual event that functions to inject a renewal of commitment into the motivations and values of the ritual participants (Wallace, 1966). Staff meetings serve as revitalization rites during which authority figures such as the principal or vice-principal attempt to boost staff morale and strengthen commitment to the values of Catholic education. Rituals of revitalization in the classroom usually take the form of emotional discussions between teachers and students that revolve around the importance of mastering coursework and school objectives. For some students, the school-wide masses and confessions, which formally link the values of the school and church, serve as rituals of revitalization.
4. Rituals of intensification: Rituals of intensification comprise a subtype of revitalization rituals that emotionally recharge students or teachers and that unify the group without necessarily reinforcing the values or goals of the ritual participants (Wallace, 1966). Rituals of revitalization and intensification may be either micro or macro rituals.
5. Rituals of resistance: Rituals of resistance emerge as a series of both subtle and dramatic cultural forms that partake of symbolic inversion and invariably prove refractory for the dominant authoritative tenets and pre-established codes of conduct established by the teacher (McLaren, 1982, 1985).

As participants in the rituals of instruction, especially in the day-to-day micro-rituals of classroom activity, teachers play a number of pedagogical roles. As an observing anthropologist at St. Ryan's, I identified three ideal types. These are (a) teacher as liminal servant; (b) teacher as entertainer; and (c) teacher as hegemonic overlord. A characterization of these types, and I stress these are ideal typical roles, is now sketched.

2 Teacher, Theatres, and Rituals

Liminality, a term adopted by Turner (1969) from Van Gennep (1960), is a process in which participants are removed temporarily from a social structure maintained and sanctioned by power and force. The participants are stripped of their usual status and authority; consequently they come to enjoy an intense comradeship and communion. Liminal servant is a term I have adopted from Holmes (1978a, 1978b), who applied it to the priest.

When the students respond, verbally or gesturally, with a sense of immediacy to the teacher's performance, when they become the primary actors in the rituals of instruction, then they engage in an authentic rite and the surroundings become sanctified, that is, the classroom assumes a "quality of unquestionableness" (Rappaport, 1980, p. 189). The students are cocelebrants of knowledge with the teacher and the class is transformed into a congregation. As in religious ritual, where the metacongregation is God, the metacongregation of a successful instructional ritual is the Logos. In Christian theology the Logos is equivalent to the second person of the Trinity and its functions are associated with the creative activity of Christ. In this sanctified curriculum moment during which students bear witness to the universal truth claim embodied in the rites of instruction, the teacher's role partakes of liminal dimensions.

When students are actively engaged by the instructor, but – because of various obstacles inherent in the ritual structure and performance – remain isolated viewers of the action, then the students are being entertained. The classroom is transformed into a theatre and the students become an audience. In this instance, the teacher loses his or her shamanic function and functions

through entertainment as a propagandist – or even worse, an evangelist – for the dominant culture.

When, however, the students are not provoked to respond to the teacher's instruction – either verbally, gesturally, or silently in their heads, when they cease to think at all about what went on – then the students no longer figuratively sit in a church or a theatre but in an iron cage. The teacher is reduced to a hegemonic overlord and knowledge is passed on perfunctorily – as though it is a tray of food passed under a cell door. In such a situation, the few feet surrounding the student might as well be a place of solitary confinement in which the student is trapped in a numbing state of spiritual and emotional emptiness.

Rappaport has made an important distinction between ritual and theatre. He suggests that "rituals may [...] be distinguished from drama by the relationship of those present to what is being performed. While an audience is in attendance at a drama, a congregation is present at a ritual. An audience merely watches but a congregation participates, usually in some degree actively. [...] And while those who enact a drama are 'only acting' in a play, those who celebrate rituals are 'not playing' or 'play-acting,' they are taking action, and it is often very serious action" (1976, p. 86).

Similarly, Victor Turner (1982) writes, "Ritual, unlike theatre, does not distinguish between audience and performers. Instead, there is a congregation whose leaders may be priests, party officials, or other religious or secular ritual specialists, but all share formally and substantially the same set of beliefs and accept the same system of practices, the same sets of rituals or liturgical actions" (1982, p. 112).

Richard Schechner articulates the difference between ritual and theatre as, "Theatre comes into existence when a separation occurs between an audience and performers. The paradigmatic theatrical situation is a group of performers soliciting an audience who may or may not respond by attending. The audience is free to stay away – and if they stay away it is the theatre that suffers, not its would-be audience. In ritual, stay-away means rejecting the congregation – or being rejected by it, as in excommunication, ostracism, or exile" (cited in Turner, 1982, p. 112).

Following the distinction between theatre and ritual made by Rappaport, Turner, and Schechner, we may say that the classroom at St. Ryan functions essentially as a theatre. Instruction lacks the participatory ethos of genuine ritual. The pretense that learning is a product of individual student volition – despite an ineffective performance by the teacher – inures students to the absence of active, intersubjective experience. Students are reduced to the role of pure spectators who assimilate knowledge *about* things rather than *of* things in the context of lived cultural experience.

Unfortunately, students often accept theatrical antics from teachers as entertainers as a surrogate for true instructional liminality. They accept as natural and commonsensical the role of teacher as a prison guard or hegemonic overlord and as a consequence fail to appreciate the shamanic dimensions of the pedagogical encounter. Students do, however, resist instruction but resistance in this case manifests itself more as a form of gestural communication than rational argumentation.

Teacher roles too often manifest what Richard Courtney calls an "improper use of impersonation." Courtney tells us that

> under certain conditions identification can degenerate into pseudo-roles: the individual who surrenders to a role acts according to the image he would like to maintain. He is guided by role expectations rather than the demands of the situation and his own Being. He "pretends" to be a teacher or a student; he gestures and postures. The student pretends to pay attention. The teacher pretends to teach. Then schooling becomes an elaborate game and dramatization has got out of hand. Neither must submit to their roles. Their authentic pedagogic relationship is an encounter where they acknowledge each other. That is genuine drama. (1982, p. 151)

Instruction that primarily consisted of the recitation of facts by teachers too often amounts to a pseudo-ritual bereft of organic symbols and gestural metaphors. Teachers distance (Scheff, 1977) their performance to such an extent that what they have to say does not make an impression on the students. There is little tension and therefore little catharsis. The teacher offers no portrayal of events that students recognize as being fundamentally important. As lived bodies of authorized precedent, the micro rituals serve mainly as sacred shields behind which teachers hide from the incessant attempts by students to create their own personalized street-corner culture inside school walls.

> Student: Most of the lessons are boring. Same old thing all the time. Why can't teachers make things interesting? They never ask us what we think is important.

Teachers consciously – even self-consciously – manipulate ritual symbols and gestures both to entertain, in the sense of keeping the students occupied, and to control the students, to keep their behavior within predictable limits. Teachers spend much time "being in one's head" while externally acting the role of the teacher.

> Teacher: Sometimes I can see myself in different roles. Sometimes I'm like a parent. Other times I'm more like a sergeant. But you can't be too friendly or the kids will take advantage of you and you'll lose some respect and suffer the consequences for the rest of the year.

In contrast, many students regard imitating the good student with a certain amount of disdain. Some students are able to collude in search of appropriate decorum to fit the values perceived to be those held by the teachers. These are students who have mastered the art of acting middle-class and reap the rewards of a good evaluation and a chance to remain at a level 5 or 6, the advanced program.

> Student: I hate trying to act like a browner. But you can get away with it. If the teacher thinks you're trying to be a browner before exams, then you'll get better marks. But you might lose your friends if you stay a browner too long.

3   The Resisting Body

The curriculum at St. Ryan is inattentive to the physical body as a vehicle for the acquisition of knowledge or the production of meaning. Either as a focus of theorizing or as a pedagogical strategy, the body carries little epistemological weight. Psychologist Howard Gardner conceptualizes bodily knowledge "as a realm discrete from linguistic, logical, and other so-called higher forms of intellect" (1983, p. 213). Largely as a legacy of Western Cartesian thought, such bodily-kinesthetic intelligence has been perceived as "less privileged, less special, than those problem-solving routines carried out chiefly through the use of language, logic, or some other relatively abstract symbolic system" (1983, p. 208). Other cultures do not draw such a sharp distinction between the active and the reflective. In fact, Hanna writes that "of all possible media of communication the body is the least removed from our associations of personal experience" (1983, p. 7).

Brian Fay argues that learning is not simply a cognitive process but also a somatic one in which "oppression leaves its traces not just in people's minds, but in their muscles and skeletons as well" (1987, p. 146). That is, ideology is not realized solely through the discursive mediations of the sociocultural order but through the enfleshment of unequal relationships of power; it is manifested intercorporeally through the actualization of the flesh and embedded in incarnate experience (McLaren, 1986c, 1989b). Fay puts it thus:

> An important mechanism for transmitting elements of a culture to its newest members is by penetrating their bodies directly, without, as it were, passing through the medium of their minds. In these cases the shaping of the initiates' bodies – their acquiring certain perceptual and behavioural skills and dispositions, their coming to have bodies with certain strengths and rigidities – is not done through their acquiring a set of beliefs or concepts (however unconscious); and their acting in terms of these skills is not the casual result of their having certain beliefs or concepts. The importance of this sort of bodily learning for social theory is that understanding the way it occurs will not involve ferreting out hidden symbolic meanings which their subjects have internalized. It will require instead discovering the material processes through which these bodies are molded through direct behavioural influence and physical environment. (1987, p. 146; see also 1986, p. 152)

Elsewhere (McLaren, 1986c) I have used the term "ritual knowledge" to refer to that aspect of learning that emphasizes bodily knowing as distinct from ideational or semantic competency. Ritual refers to the gestural embodiment of metaphors and symbols; that is, rituals are symbols or metaphors somaticized or "bodied forth." This concept of ritual knowledge follows Grimes (1982) and Merleau-Ponty in maintaining that the body itself "knows" and "comprehends" (cf. Zaner, 1971).

Students at St. Ryan experience an abrupt cleavage between information codified in texts and transmitted by teachers and identification with themselves as active, bodily subjects. Learning is perceived by teachers as a cognitive process while the body is viewed as an object of surveillance or a cluster of behaviors to be policed. This turns the body into a medium for pain. Francis Barker explains that the modern body, having been separated from its previous unmediated carnality through textual representation, has become supplementary to written communication. In effect, desire and meaning are becoming detached as the modern body becomes more "de-realized [...] confined, ignored, exscribed from discourse" (1984, p. 63).

The current postmodern condition has witnessed a reconstitution of the body as a decentered text – a mythical product of enlightenment rationality. The fracturing of the sovereign subject has been a major theme in the writings of a number of postmodern social theorists: Baudrillard, Foucault, Lyotard, and Jameson, to name just a few (McLaren, 1986a). The poststructuralist critique of meaning has left us floundering in a universe of simulacra, of copies without originals, in which texts collapse into readers, messages collapse into meanings, and signs collapse into their referents. Fewer stable structures or finalities exist in which to anchor theory, ethics, or politics (Kellner, 1984); even the literary work "occupies a liminal position, being both inside and outside the epistemic formation, and thus allows us to see the dark processes of discursive practices" (Van den Abbeele, 1987, p. 9). In a growing cyberneticized and rationalized society, identity and humanism are challenged by a hyperreality of media simulations in which the play of signs and the politics of signification have replaced the logic of production and class conflict as key constituents of contemporary societies. The former structuring principles of identity – family, peers, institutional life – now take on a vertiginous flux.

In the postmodern era, the subject is unable to secure itself within a unified identity, but itself becomes a site of struggle. As Grossberg explains, "this 'post-humanistic' subject does not exist with a unified identity [...] that somehow manifests itself in every practice. Rather, it is a subject that is constantly remade, reshaped as a mobilely situated set of relations in a fluid context. The nomadic subject is amoeba-like, struggling to win some space for itself in its local situation. The subject itself has become a site of struggle, an ongoing site of articulation with its own history, determinations and effects" (1986, p. 72). As a primary characteristic of the postmodern condition is a lack of metaphysical referents with which to ground descriptions, values, symbols, or methods of inquiry – "neither transcendental science nor transcendental religion can be at home in it" (Tyler, 1986, p. 135) – it is not surprising that resistant students privilege the body in their struggle against the oppressive features of schooling. The body itself becomes a master symbol – a tablet upon which referentiality is inscribed through feeling and gestures – in a world in which significations are increasingly free-floating and the institutionalized symbology of the school is growing more and more suspect and desacralized. This desacralization is largely because of the intertexuality of the student's world: street-corner life filled with a heteroglossia of cultural forms ranging from video games to break dancing to MTV counterposed with school life and its linear rationality of print and a pedagogy based on traditionalism and conceptual empiricism (Giroux & McLaren, 1987). In fact, the "resisting body" is one of the central symbols of student culture.

How can the religious symbology of St. Ryan, with its emphasis on the crucified body of Christ and the Virgin Mary, hope to compete with the signifiers of popular culture? Situated throughout the school, religious symbols are highly context-bound and take on distinct meanings dependent on the authoritative readings that occurred in the varied contexts of class discussions, school rules, and religion classes. As I have noted elsewhere (McLaren, 1986b), the religious symbols of the school are fused with secular meanings linked to the logic of the capitalist marketplace so that to be a good Catholic means to be a docile, obedient, and industrious worker; whereas, the more free-floating signifiers of music videos and rock 'n' roll created a social space that was based on the politics of pleasure and the physical senses.

Speaking of the effect of MTV's popular culture on youth, John Fiske writes that "MTV is read by the body, experienced through the senses, and resists sense which is always theirs. MTV is experienced as pleasure. [...] The threat of the signifier is its resistance to ideology, its location in the sensations of the body, the physical senses rather than the mental senses. The plurality of meanings on video clips makes us talk of their senses, not of their sense" (1986, p. 75).

Outside of the classroom students engage in popular cultural forms in which affective investment (Grossberg, 1986) outstrips the cognitive meanings transmitted by the traditional curriculum. Student engagement is "popular" in form rather than "public." This contrast Mercer advances in his discussion of Bourdieu:

> "Nothing," argues Pierre Bourdieu, "more radically distinguishes popular spectacles – the football match, Punch and Judy, the circus, wrestling or even in some cases the cinema – from bourgeois spectacles, than the form of the participation of the public." For the former, whistles, shouts, pitch invasions are characteristic, for the latter the gestures are distant, heavily ritualized – applause, obligatory but discontinuous and punctual cries of enthusiasm – "author, author" or "encore." [...] A certain *distance*, Bourdieu argues, has been central in the bourgeois economy of the body: a distance between "reflexion" and corporeal participation. (1986, p. 59)

In the realm of the popular, the body becomes a locus of pleasure; in the realm of schooling public, the body becomes a locus of pain.

The pain of being a student is considerable – manifested in the bland, dreary impotency of instructional rituals and routines, the grinding, drudging familiarity, the deadening, mechanical applications of instructional rites, the unremitting banality of the subject matter, the unemotional, generalized stream of boring events, the bleak inevitability of repetition and invariance, the tedious succession of unrelated episodes, and the wearisome wait for instruction to end. Students "wear" the hegemonic culture of the school in their very beings: in their wrinkled brows, in their tense musculature, in the impulsive way they react to their peers, and in the stoic way they respond to punishment. There is the pain of enduring the hours spent hunched over a desk, and the pain of censure should one request to attend to bodily functions at an inappropriate time – in the middle of a lesson. In fact, sitting through an entire macro ritual may be described as a symbolic cicatrization of the scarification of mind and body. For students enmeshed in classroom ritual, there is the manifestation of a more "abstract" and "existential" pain resulting from the thematization and simplification of emotions that are abstracted from physical conduct and experience, for example, "today's lesson deals with kindness; tomorrow's lesson deals with vandalism."

Students appear as anguished configurations against sterile landscape of formica and concrete. They are transformed into bodies subjugated and fragmented, distilled to spectral shadows, and pushed to the margins of acceptability. Pain is made legible in the body postures and facial expressions of the students; it is inscribed in the tight mouths, clenched jaws, hunched shoulders, and angry glares – typical gestures of institutional embodiment. Student gestures become so highly reflexive that they invert themselves and begin to wither. Brenneman et al. call such gestures "industrial" or "scientific" and compared them to the gestures of a factory worker, assembly line worker, or laboratory technician. They are quick and impulsive (1982, p. 114).

Resistance by students to the pain and oppression of schooling, as I have theorized it (McLaren, 1985, 1986a, 1986b, 1988a, 1988b), is played out as part of a cultural drama consisting of an active refusal to legitimate cultural meanings hostile to the lived experiences of the students. It is also a form of somatic or corporeal *unlearning* in which students struggle against institutional embodiment and the enfleshment of oppression brought on by the policing and regulation of gesture and the containment of desire. It is a form of excorporation into a resting group – a collective body that often partakes of subcultural dimensions. A number of students actively resist the eros-denying quality of school life in which they are turned into discarnate beings, unfettered by the desires that play on the nerve endings of living flesh. Accordingly, the students' bodies become sites of struggle, in which resistance is a way of gaining power, celebrating pleasure, and fighting oppression not in an abstract, discursive sense, but in the lived physicality and historicity of the moment and in the concrete materiality of the classroom.

School resistance is the discipline of "using" pain that is otherwise unendurable and irremediable. Resistance is inextricably linked to the quality of the students' forbearance in the midst of what they consider to be oppressive circumstances. Students adhere to the unwritten rule that stresses the admirable – even heroic – nature of maintaining self-composure under stress and teacher harassment.

Liminality is more than a marginal sanctuary for the creation of warm feelings and creative insight – it also provokes anger and engenders resistance. Student resistances appear to support the notion of Bilmes and Howard (1980) that pain is a cultural drama that is associated with increased liminality and changes in status on the part of the victim or recipient of pain.

The inflictor of pain, the teacher, stands as a representative of the social category to which the victim is either being assimilated, in the case of elevation, or contrasted, in the case of degradation. The inflictor's own status is on the line together with that of the victim.

Teacher: If you decide to punish a student, you'd better know what you're doing. If it's not effective you'll just make the situation worse for yourself.
Peter: Why is that?
Teacher: For one thing, you get a reputation for being too soft and the kids will take you for a ride.

Because pain promotes the perception of the victim's liminality, and hence the victim's marginal – often "heroic" – status, pain is sometimes self-inflicted. Students frequently engage in subversive behavior that is assured to bring them swift and sometimes severe punishment. Punishment takes various forms, graduated in severity from a simple reprimand to a detention or expulsion. By bearing up under punishment – by experiencing the holy pain of resisting – the victim takes on a liminal and quasi-sacerdotal status. Resistance thus becomes a form of crypto-religion. It is significant that Turner compares liminality to the experiential notion of Christian grace (1982, p. 34).

Resistance, in this sense, partakes of the characteristics of antistructure in which individuals exist in a liminal state outside the structure of roles, statuses, and positions within the society (in this case, outside the institutional order of the school). The antistructure of resistance engenders a strong emotional bonding and a temporary state of undifferentiated and homogeneous community.

4 The Liminal Servant

The following is a composite description of what I consider the best attributes of a teacher working within a liberatory pedagogy. These attributes derive from observing teachers both formally and informally for more than a decade. Some of the characteristics of the liminal servant were evident in the teacher performances at St. Ryan.

When a teacher possesses the attributes of a liminal servant, an added vitality is brought to the rites of instruction. Figurative significance is given to the learning process. The context of the lessons is transformed from the indicative, a stress on mere facts, to the subjunctive, a stress on the "as if" quality of learning, from resistance to undifferentiated humankindness, and from the institutional confines of social structure to the seedbeds of creativity located in the communitas of antistructure. Liminal servants can create empowering antistructural elements within their lessons that defeat the need for students to engage in the antistructure of resistance.

The liminal servant is both a convener of customs and a cultural provocateur – yet he or she transcends both roles. The political rights of students are not subordinated to their utility as future members of the labor force. The liminal servant is a social activist and spiritual director as much as a school pedagogue.

The liminal servant does not shy away from the ambiguity and opacity of existence. He or she is androgynous and draws upon both feminine and masculine ways of knowing. Through observation and diagnosis, the liminal servant becomes aware of the strengths and weaknesses of students. Liminal servants view working-class students as members of an oppressed group. Not only do they fight for the equality of students outside the classroom, but they also attempt to educate fellow teachers to the dangers of false consciousness. The terrain upon which the liminal servant often chooses to work is that of popular culture and the liturgy of the everyday. Like the post-modern ethnographer, the liminal servant privileges discourse over text and emphasizes cooperation and collaboration in contrast to transcendental authority (Tyler, 1986, p. 126).

The liminal servant presents an array of symbols that have a high density of meaning for the student; a felt context is established for the subject matter that allows students to internalize both exegetical, normative, and oretic, physical meanings. By thus creating a particular posture toward symbols, the liminal servant ensures that symbols possess a fecundating power and are encountered by students through both cognition and affect.

Ever cognizant of their shamanic roots, liminal servants are questers of knowledge. A mystagogue rather than ideologue, the liminal servant does not eschew theory, which would be a form of pedagogic pietism, nor does he or she avoid intuition that comes with practice, where avoidance would amount to a moribund intellectualism. The métier of the liminal servant is the clearing away of obstacles to the embodiment of knowledge. He or she abjures making excuses for the deficiencies of students; rather, academic equality is proclaimed for all.

Liminal servants recognize the contradictions that exist between the openness of human capacities that we encourage in a democratic society and the cultural forms within which we live our lives. The recognition of these contradictions forms the starting point for a pedagogical project designed to transform the relation between human capacities and cultural forms (Giroux & Simon, 1988). Cultural forms become important for mediating experience and promoting intersubjective dialogue. Ridington notes that "cultural forms exhibit more generally the organizational principle found in neuromotor and linguistic activity. Culture is the central hierarchy of organized information that brings together the experiences of people removed from one another in space and time. It is the symbolic mediator of inter-subjective relationship and the hierarchy to which subjective experience must be related in order to become meaningful. For human beings, meaningful experience is cultural experience" (1979, p. 3).

The liminal servant is aware that to a large extent cultural forms instruct the individual visionary experience. As a consequence, the classroom is treated as a cultural form constructed out of a view of human freedom as the understanding and the transformation of necessity (Giroux & Simon, 1988). The pedagogy required both affirms and legitimates the experiences students bring to the classroom (Giroux & McLaren, 1987): Students are taught to take risks and struggle with on-going relations of power from within a life-affirming moral culture (Giroux & Simon, 1988). The liminal servant is wary of too much ratiocination and leans toward divining myths, metaphors, and rhythms that will have meaning and purpose for students – not as abstractions, but as lived forms of consciousness. Modes of symbolic action are employed that do not betray a cleavage between the passive reception of facts and the active participatory ethos of learning by doing. The liminal servant encourages students to enact metaphors and embody rhythms that bypass the traditional mind/body dualism earlier described.

Liminal servants do not put a high priority on structure and order, although their classes may be highly structured and ordered. They are able to conjure conditions amenable to the eventuation of communitas, the temporary camaraderie that occurs when status differentials are suspended between fellow liminals (Turner, 1969), and of flow, the holistic sensation that engulfs people when they act with total involvement (Csikszentmihalyi, 1975). Thus, they seek to establish between themselves and students a deep, fundamental bond.

Liminal servants understand that what others see as a manifestation of ignorance is often a form of student resistance to a culture that dehumanizes students and engages in an institutional remaking of their bodies, dreams, and desires. They are actually aware that learning is a bodily phenomenon as well as a mental one. They acknowledge that students are necessarily subordinated to a field of cultural desire born of both the free-floating symbols of popular cultural forms and the more context-bound symbols of the classroom. Escaping from a cognitivist conception of social life, liminal servants recognize that knowledge is also *performatively constituted.* The cultural intersections at which symbols and ritual metaphors are inscribed in the body become sedimented as ideologies that students carry in the folds of their flesh. This form of non-discursive bodily knowledge is as significant to the liminal servant as teaching discursive rules and values.

With their awareness of how schooling morally regulates the body, liminal servants recognize physical manipulation to be a necessary feature of human emancipation, a fact understood in Hatha Yoga postures (asanas) associated with Hinduism; the sitting (zazen) techniques of Zen Buddhism; the whirling dances in Sufism; and the meditative postures of Christian monks (cf. Fay, 1987, p. 153). Consequently the liminal servant often uses techniques of improvised drama to literally re-shape students' attitudes and dispositions (McLaren, 1989b).

To understand the sub-text of the student, the liminal servant must become the student as part of the dramatic encounter. While in the thrall of such a drama, the liminal servant knows that the results will be unpredictable; that understanding, like play, has a spirit of its own (cf. Courtney, 1982). Consequently, the ontological status of the liminal servant is intrinsically ambiguous. Whereas the teacher-as-entertainer tries to suppress individuality, the liminal servant fosters individual endowment. The teacher-as-entertainer is intent upon conditioning for sameness; the liminal servant nurtures counter-hegemonic forces through the cultivation among the students of an alter-ideology. Through this alter-ideology, the liminal servant educates for individuality, distinction, and eccentricity. Liminal servants are closer to their students than to their profession.

With the promotion of the common good their goal, liminal servants commit themselves to a pedagogy that is in solidarity with subordinated and marginalized groups. Liminal servants identify with the victims of injustice; they support the poor and the oppressed. Not only do liminal servants give public witness of their solidarity with the dispossessed, they also defend publicly the dignity and human rights of their students. Furthermore, they denounce the historical, ideological, and material forces that inflict oppression and exploitation (Baum, 1987).

Liminal servants make theirs a double commitment to both perspectival and activist dimensions. Both these dimensions "create a circular movement that sharpens the perception of oppression in society and summons forth greater involvement in the transformation of society" (Baum, 1987, p. 8).

The pedagogy of the liminal servant arranges a textual space for the students to have and speak their own voices (Giroux & McLaren, 1987). To accomplish this emancipation, liminal servants not only teach; they practice pedagogy. To practice pedagogy means to organize experience and specify what forms of knowledge are of most worth and what classroom practices are best suited for teaching. The broad aim of pedagogy is the transformation of the relation between human capacities and social forms so as to make possible the development of social imagination and a vision of the future. In other words, pedagogy practiced becomes a deliberative attempt to influence how and what knowledge and social identities are produced within and among particular sets of social relations (Giroux & McLaren, 1987; Giroux & Simon, 1988).

Liminal servants engage in a form of pedagogical surrealism as a prime court of appeal against rational educational practices. They make the strange familiar and the familiar strange. Confronting schools as normalizing agencies, agencies that legitimate existing social relations and practices and thereby rendering them normal and natural, they set out to relativize schools and seek to dismantle and rearrange the artificial rules and codes that constitute classroom reality. Unlike the traditional humanist who begins with the different and renders it comprehensible, the liminal servant engages in what I call a "radical humanism," attacking the ordinary, provoking the eruption of Otherness, and perturbing taken-for-granted assumptions (cf. Clifford, 1981).

Liminal servants decenter the institutional space from which traditional school critics speak by attempting to go beyond answering the conventional question of what knowledge is by answering instead the more important question of *how* schooling has come to mean what it has. Unlike the orthodox Marxist critic, the liminal servant does not view the dominant culture as unbounded oppression but as a terrain of contestation that contains elements of oppositional and potentially emancipatory moments.

Liminal servants engage in a social analysis the Frankfurt School theorists call "immanent critique," in which the values of the dominant culture are turned against current cultural forms and social practices (cf. Kellner, 1984). Even the most oppressive schools exhibit some emancipatory classroom activity that liminal servants articulate into counter-ideological practice (McLaren, 1986a), and the liberal belief in democracy is used to counter state-mandated curricula that offer little choice to students.

Generally eschewing the more cynical forms of ideology critique used by orthodox Marxian educators, liminal servants work within categories of liberation and project visions of what Ernst Bloch (1986) calls "concrete utopia" and what Victor Turner (1969) calls "ideological communitas." The language of hope that liminal servants speak is the discourse of therapeutic anthropology. Their words move beyond shattering the dominant myths to embrace "the mastery of the mythic medium so as to contribute to the realization of humanly enriching concrete events, and the minimization of concrete events that are humanly degrading" (Wilk, 1977, p. 12).

The liminal servant views pedagogical theorizing as a form of praxis. Praxis is more than the mere application of theory; rather, with praxis, theory flows from action and leads to further action. Theory in this case is never abstract but "reflects the social location of the person who theorizes as well as his or her orientation to society. As people change their social identification, they gain a new perspective on society" (Baum, 1987, p. 9).

Liminal servants recognize that only when theory becomes a political act can it realize its socially transformative potential. This perspective is also reflected in current experiments with ethnographic writing in which references are made to the broader world of the ethnographer and embedded in the text (Crapanzano, 1980, 1981) and in which attempts are made to merge the perspective of ethnography and political economy (Willis, 1981; McLaren, 1986c).

All teachers are cultural practitioners who produce, orchestrate, integrate, and distribute cultural meanings; offer their incantations of various educational mythologies; and suffuse the classroom with particular orders of experience. To a far greater extent than the other pedagogical types, the liminal servant helps students crack the prevailing cultural crust and discover alternative meanings. The liminal servant is a vagrant, a "tramp of the obvious" who becomes the "tramp of demystifying conscientization" (Freire, 1985, p. 171). The ordinary thus becomes the object of critical examination and reflection.

The liminal servant is a parashaman (Grimes, 1982); he or she is performance oriented. Liminal servants teach, not because they wish to share available answers, but to discover meanings for themselves. Teaching is a form of holy play that is more akin to the drama of hunting societies than to the theatre of agricultural societies (Grimes, 1982). Liminal servants constitute a "radical transformation of the shamanic spirit into modern terms" (Ridington, 1983, p. 4). They practice pedagogy in the manner of modern shamans who " understand how the human psyche has been damaged by the modern condition" (1983, p. 2). The task of the liminal servant is essentially a therapeutic task (Wilk, 1977), one in which the teacher is called to accept human paradox, to disdain dogma, and to refrain from personal imposition (Golliher, 1978, p. 19).

This shamanic task is not unlike the achievement of the postmodern ethnographer described by Tyler.

> A post-modern ethnography is a cooperatively evolved text consisting of fragments of discourse intended to evoke in the minds of both reader and writer an emergent fantasy of a possible world of commonsense reality, and thus to provoke an aesthetic integration that will have a therapeutic effect [...] it defamiliarizes commonsense reality in a bracketed context of performance, evolves a fantasy whole abducted from fragments, and then returns participants to the world of commonsense – transformed, renewed, and sacralized. (1986, pp. 125–126)

Under the guidance of the liminal servant, classrooms are transformed into critical spaces that truly endanger the obviousness of culture as a collection of unalterable truths and unchangeable social relations. Within these critical spaces, the pedagogy of the liminal servant takes on an anticipatory character rooted in a dialetical logic that makes critique and transformation its central moments. The defining theme for such a project can be described as a preferential option for the poor and oppressed. The pedagogy that accompanies this project is designed to restore human potential and transform the world from the vagaries of what is to what *could be*. The struggle for restoration and transformation is not easy and has no end. Liminal servants are acutely aware that the quest for knowledge is one that can never be won or pedagogy stops (Lewis & Simon, 1986).

The liminal task defined as the dismemberment and reinvention of society through the empowerment of the social imagination often takes place within the interstices of institutional life. Yet the marginal status inflicted on liminal servants must never be an index of their importance for the transformation of unequitable and oppressive social relations. As long as there are educators who are willing to practice pedagogy in the subjunctive mode of "as if," history will not simply continue to make students, but students will be able and willing to make history.

Acknowledgments

I would like to thank Miles Richardson for his comments, criticisms, and editorial efforts in preparing the final draft of this chapter. I would also like to thank Stan Wilk for providing me with some relevant resource material.

This chapter is an expanded treatment of my *Schooling as a ritual performance: Toward a political economy of educational symbols and gestures* (Routledge and Kegan Paul, 1986). It originally appeared as P. L. McLaren, The anthropological roots of pedagogy: The teacher as liminal servant, *Anthropology and Humanism Quarterly*, 12(3–4) (1987), 75–85. Reprinted here, with minor edits, with permission from the publisher.

References

Apple, M. (1979. *Ideology and curriculum.* Routledge and Kegan Paul.
Aronowitz, S., & Giroux, H. A. (1985). *Education under siege.* Bergin & Garvey.
Barker, F. (1984). *Francis Barker, the tremulous private body: Essays on subjection.* Methuen.
Baum, G. (1987). Option for the powerless. *The Ecumenist, 26,* 5–11.
Bilmes, J., & Howard, A. (1980). Pain as cultural drama. *Anthropology and Humanism Quarterly, 5,* 1013.
Bloch, E. (1986). *The principle of hope,* vols. 1–3. MIT Press.
Bourdieu, P. (1980). The aristocracy of culture (R. Nice, Trans.). *Media, Culture & Society, 2*(3), 225–254.
Brenneman, W., Jr., & Yarian, S. O. (in association with A. M. Olson). (1982). *The seeing eye: Hermeneutical phenomenology in the study of religion.* Pennsylvania State University Press.
Courtney, R. (1982). *Re-play: Studies in human drama and education.* OISE Press.
Clifford, J. (1981). On ethnographic surrealism. *Comparative Studies in Society and History, 23*(4), 539–564.
Clifford, J. (1986). On ethnographic allegory. In J. Clifford & G. E. Marcus (Eds.), *Writing culture: The poetics and politics of ethnography.* University of California Press.
Crapanzano, V. (1980). *Tuhami: Portrait of a Moroccan.* University of Chicago Press.
Crapanzano, V. (1981). Text, transference, and indexicality. *Ethos, 9,* 122–148.
Crapanzano, V. (1986). Hermes' dilemma: The masking of subversion in ethnographic description. In J. Clifford & G. E. Marcus (Eds.), *Writing culture: The poetics and politics of ethnography* (pp. 51–77). University of California Press.
Csikszentmihalyi, M. (1975). *Beyond boredom and anxiety.* Jossey-Bass.
Fay, B. (1987). *Critical social science: Liberation and its limits.* Cornell University Press.

Fiske, J. (1986). MTV: Post-structural post-modern. *Journal of Communication Inquiry,* 10(1), 74–79.

Foucault, M. (1980). Truth and power. In M. Foucault, *Power/knowledge: Selected interviews and other writings 1972–1977* (G. Gordon, Ed.; pp. 109–133). Pantheon.

Freire, P. (1985). *The politics of education: Culture, power and liberation.* Bergin & Garvey.

Gardner, H. (1983). *Frames of mind: The theory of multiple intelligences.* Basic Books.

Geertz, C. (1973). *The interpretation of cultures.* Basic Books.

Giroux, H. A., & McLaren, P. (1987). Teacher education as a counterpublic sphere: Radical pedagogy as a form of cultural politics. *Philosophy and Social Criticism,* 12(1), 51–69.

Giroux, H. A., & Simon, R. I. (1988). Schooling, popular culture, and a pedagogy of possibility. *Journal of Education,* 170(1), 9–26.

Golliher, J. M. (1978). The therapeutic function of the anthropological enterprise. *Anthropology and Humanism Quarterly,* 3, 17–20.

Grimes, R. L. (1982). *Beginnings in ritual studies.* University Press of America.

Grossberg, L. (1986). History, politics and postmodernism: Stuart Hall and cultural studies. *Journal of Communication Inquiry,* 10(2), 61–77.

Heidegger, M. (1972). *What is called thinking?* (J. G. Gray, Trans.). Harper Torchbooks.

Holmes, U. T. (1976). *Ministry and imagination.* Seabury Press.

Holmes, U. T. (1977). What has Manchester to do with Jerusalem? *Anglican Theological Review,* 1, 5875.

Holmes, U. T. (1978a). Revivals are un-American: A recalling of America to its pilgrimage. *Anglican Theological Review,* 1, 58–75.

Holmes, U. T. (1978b). *The priest in community: Exploring the roots of ministry.* Seabury Press.

Jameson, F. (1981). *The political unconscious: Narrative as a socially symbolic act.* Cornell University Press.

Kellner, D. (1984). *Herbert Marcuse and the crisis of Marxism.* Macmillan and University of California Press.

Lewis, M., & Simon, R. I. (1986). A discourse not intended for her: Learning and teaching within patriarchy. *Harvard Educational Review,* 56, 457–472.

Lyotard, J. F. (1984). *The postmodern condition: A report on knowledge.* University of Minnesota Press.

McLaren, P. (1980). *Cries from the corridor: The new suburban ghettos.* Methuen.

McLaren, P. (1982). "Bein' tough": Rituals of resistance in the culture of working-class school girls. *Canadian Woman Studies,* 4(1), 20–24.

McLaren, P. (1984a). Victor Turner: In memoriam. *International Semiotic Spectrum,* 1.

McLaren, P. (1984b). Rethinking ritual. *ETC: A Review of General Semantics,* 41(3), 267–277.

McLaren, P. (1985). The ritual dimensions of resistance: Clowning and symbolic inversion. *Journal of Education, 167*(2), 84–97.

McLaren, P. (1986a). Postmodernism and the death of politics: A Brazilian reprieve. *Educational Theory, 36*, 389–401.

McLaren, P. (1986b). Making Catholics: The ritual production of conformity in a Catholic junior high school. *Boston University Journal of Education, 168*, 5577.

McLaren, P. (1986c). *Schooling as a ritual performance: Toward a political economy of educational symbols and gestures.* Routledge and Kegan Paul.

McLaren, P. (1987a). Ideology, science and the politics of Marxian orthodoxy. *Educational Theory, 37*, 301–326.

McLaren, P. (1987b). Schooling for salvation: Christian fundamentalism's ideological weapons of death. *Boston University Journal of Education, 169*(2), 132–139

McLaren, P. (1988a). The liminal servant and the ritual roots of critical pedagogy. *Language Arts, 65*(2), 164–179.

McLaren, P. (1988b). Foreword: Critical theory and the meaning of hope. In H. Giroux, *Teachers as intellectuals* (pp. vii–xix). Bergin & Garvey.

McLaren, P. (1989a). *Life in schools: An introduction to critical pedagogy in the foundations of education.* Longman.

McLaren, P. (1989b). Ideology and critical educational thought. In H. A. Giroux & P. McLaren (Eds.), *Schooling, politics, and cultural struggle.* State University of New York Press.

Mercer, C. (1986). Complied pleasure. In T. Bennett, C. Mercer, & J. Woolacoot (Eds.), *Popular culture and social relations* (pp. 51–69). Open University Press.

Merleau-Ponty, M. (1975). *The primacy of perception* (J. M. Edie, Ed.). Northwestern University Press.

Myerhoff, B., & Metzger, D. (1980). The journal as activity and genre: On listening to the silent laughter of Mozart. *Semiotica, 30*(l/2), 97–114.

Rappaport, R. (1976). Liturgies and lies. *International Yearbook for the Sociology of Knowledge and Religion, 10*, 75–104.

Rappaport, R. (1980). Concluding remarks on ritual and reflexivity. *Semiotica, 30*(1/2), 181–193.

Ridington, R. (1979). Sequence and hierarchy in cultural experience: Phases and the moment of transformation. *Anthropology and Humanism Quarterly, 4*, 2–9.

Ridington, R. (1983). Electronic eyes. *Anthropology and Humanism Quarterly, 8*, 3–7.

Schechner, R. (1982). *The end of humanism: Writings on performance.* Performing Arts Journal Publications.

Scheff, T. J. (1977). The distancing of emotion in ritual. *Current Anthropology, 18*(3), 483–504.

Scheff, T. J. (1979). *Catharsis in healing, ritual and drama.* University of California Press.

Turner, V. (1969). *The ritual process: Structure and anti-structure.* Aldine.

Turner, V. (1982). *From ritual to theatre: The human seriousness of play.* Performing Arts Journal Publications.

Tyler, S. A. (1986). Post-modern ethnography: From document of the occult to occult document. In J. Clifford & G. E. Marcus (Eds.), *Writing culture: The poetics and politics of ethnography* (pp. 122–140). University of California Press.

Van den Abbeele, G. (1987). Sade, Foucault, and the scene of enlightenment lucidity. *Stanford French Review, 1*(1), 7–16.

Van Gennep, A. (1960). *The rites of passage* (M. B. Vizedom & G. L. Caffee, Trans.). University of Chicago Press.

Wallace, A. (1966). *Religion: An anthropological view.* Random House.

Wilk, S. (1977). Therapeutic anthropology and culture consciousness. *Anthropology and Humanism Quarterly, 2,* 12–18.

Wilk, S. (1980). Don Juan on balance. In R. DeMille (Ed.), *The Don Juan papers.* Ross-Erickson.

Wilk, S. (1986). The meaning of "religion as a cultural system." *Anthropology and Humanism Quarterly, 11,* 50–55.

Willis, P. (1981). *Learning to labor: How working-class kids get working-class jobs.* Columbia University Press.

Zaner, R. (1971). *The problem of embodiment: Some contributions to a phenomenology of the body.* Martinus Mijhoff.

CHAPTER 6

No Light, But Rather Darkness Visible
Language and the Politics of Criticism

> You can't depend on your eyes when your imagination is out of focus.
>
> MARK TWAIN (*A Connecticut Yankee in King Arthur's Court*, 1889)

∴

At a time in which most possibilities are unthinkable, and consequently few people want to think too much, there is a natural tendency to avoid engaging in serious criticism. Peter Gronn's review of my book, *Schooling as a Ritual Performance*, is a case in point. On this note, I find myself hesitant in responding to Peter Gronn's critique. It is especially difficult to respond in a reasoned and thoughtful manner to a reviewer who uses such terms as "pretentious apocalyptic socio-babble." But at the risk of tearing open the seventh seal and revealing all, I shall attempt a short rejoinder.

Faced with Gronn's unfortunate disregard for evidence, his fundamental disregard for the basic theoretical issues my text addresses, his vapid deployment of terms, his refusal to proffer any detailed examination of my understanding and use of ritual, and his conceptual and analytical naiveté, it would be easy to dismiss Gronn's review as trivial and silly. Yet what appears as initially embarrassing within the trivial text can provide us with a textual and political space for questioning its position of intelligibility as it relates to larger social and political concerns. This is why the trivial text must sometimes be engaged: assumptions that inform it often reveal tacit, yet important structuring operations linked to larger ideological interests.

Upon first receiving Gronn's review, and confronting its headings, its subheadings, its numbers, and its selected quotations, page after page, I thought I would be reading a thorough review (albeit smelling somewhat pedantic). But upon closer inspection it became clear that the headings, the subheadings, the numbers, the quotations, and the general anatomization in reality do not signal a rigorous engagement with my text, but rather something I will label as "Gronn's ploy." It is *not* a thorough review. It is, however, complete in one account; namely, in its philistine refusal to engage a number of substantive

© TAYLOR & FRANCIS, 1988

issues I raise in my book. In this regard, Gronn's review constitutes a kind of literary antimatter that swallows up the subject under discussion and leaves nothing behind but a Cheshire cat smile.

Sometimes a writer reads a reviewer and wonders what book the reviewer has been reading. This same feeling followed me as I read through every ponderous page of Gronn's lamentable response. Not only does Gronn's myopic, ungenerous, and maundering analysis avoid engaging the substantive issues dealt with in my book, it generally refuses to acknowledge that these issues even exist. We can only be baffled by the fact that he has overlooked – or perfunctorily dismissed – such central issues as the polysemy of the symbol; the sanctification of classroom discourse; the narrative symbolic nature of root paradigms; the liminal nature of resistance; and my appropriation of crucial ideas from information theory, speech-act theory, and cultural Marxism in an attempt to analyze student conformity.

Gronn's review operates by extrapolating material from my book, laundering its theoretical subtlety, and moving it around to fit his own apocalyptic agenda. Such a discursive intervention – bereft of sound argumentation but profuse in fragmented opinion – ignores crucial theoretical features of the book. Ultimately, Gronn's method of analysis is tied more to the logic of bad journalism than to the logic of progressive social theory. Within this rationality, researchers who attempt to be thorough are labeled "name droppers" and those who attempt to appropriate a new theoretical discourse are admonished as being "theoretically top heavy." Such are the tactics of tabloid scholarship.

The nature of my rejoinder is not so much to challenge Gronn on a point-by-point basis. To do so would be tantamount to dignifying what he is attempting to pass off as criticism and accepting terms of reference I consider to be ill-informed. However, I shall address some general issues Gronn has tried to raise in order to situate his review within a larger context that addresses the failure of his particular type of analysis. I should like to begin by responding to Gronn's discussion (or perhaps we should call it "nondiscussion") of ritual.

Gronn indicates that my work is a "battle for the hearts and minds" and that I am attempting to offer a "new altar (ritual studies) at which to worship a new god (critical theories of emancipation)" while at the same time "refusing to arbitrate between claims to theoretical sainthood." Gronn fears that I am "angel-making" and, in the posture of the patriarchal God of Christendom, he attempts to cast me from the academic firmament "hurled headlong flaming from the ethereal sky" (Milton, 1961, p. 38). Throughout my book, Gronn sees Lucifer falling in all his ugliness. His apparent fear that a critical theory of ritual may find its way into the discourse of radical forms of analysis is buttressed by two give-away lines early on in his review. The first line reads as follows: "I eschew any detailed examination of McLaren's understanding and use of ritual except to note, in passing, that the *tenor* of his discussion has a straw man ring to it" (italics mine). In other words, Gronn chooses to forsake any serious engagement with the theoretical underpinnings of my book and decides, instead, to comment on its "tenor." At its best, this represents a form of intellectual passivity, at its worst, a form of intellectual cowardice. Gronn's second give-away line reads: "We don't need the space devoted to discussing the persistence of rituals in a secular, industrial society." He adds that those of us who have lived through the turmoil of the 1960s know enough about the persistence and power of ritual and that Bocock's (1974) study has said it all, anyhow. This, of course, presumes the majority of the readers and potential readers of my book have lived through such turmoil and that somehow they read their own cultural histories in ways that are collectively similar. It also totally ignores the fact that Bocock and I share enormous differences in our understanding of the ritual process. This type of logic is tantamount to suggesting that students of Marx should stop reading Marxist ethnographies once they have read *Learning to Labor*.

For a reviewer of a book dealing with the topic of ritual in a contemporary urban setting to assume such a position raises a fundamental moral issue surrounding the hidden agenda of the reviewer. Gronn's easy, almost willful dismissal of my approach to ritual theory betrays, in my mind, a curious affinity to what Jacques Lacan (1978, p. 110, quoted in Penley, 1986, p. 135) has called "the passion for ignorance." Ignorance, according to Lacan, is not a passive state but an active excluding from consciousness whatever it does not want to know. In Gronn's case there appears to be an active refusal – perhaps fear of – any discourse that attempts to probe social life in ways strange and unfamiliar to him. This is, to say the least, a failure of intellectual nerve. Gronn's position does, however, become even more confusing in light of his own admission that he lacks the requisite anthropological background to "fine grain" my definition of ritual. One can only try to fathom why Gronn chose to review such a book when he is so hopelessly antagonistic and theoretically ill-equipped (by his own admission) to deal with its conceptual underpinnings in a responsible and nuanced way. While I realize some people may consider certain books pernicious within an ongoing academic discourse, and therefore something to stamp out (allowing again for the free-floating paranoia implied by such responses), invoking conceptual closure on my book in the particular manner undertaken by Gronn is both irresponsible and illiberal. It is certainly one way to guard orthodoxy; it is surely not an effective way to advance possibility or promote dialogue.

It is not that Gronn has to *like* ritual theory. But in refusing to engage its theoretical complexity, I don't see how he can criticize it. I find it to be rather ironic that in one breath Gronn pronounces ritual to be decidedly self-evident and as such doesn't need to be examined on its own terms, and in another claims that it is certainly a complex phenomenon. The concept of ritual, with its long history of anthropological and liturgical association, cannot be so easily dismissed as Gronn would like it to be. In this sense, one could apply to the term ritual, Dick Hebdige's (1986, pp. 78–98) summary of a claim made by Raymond Williams: "that the more complexity and contradictorily nuanced a word is, the more likely it is to have formed the focus for historically significant debates, to have occupied a semantic ground in which something precious and important was felt to be embedded."

As far as the charge of Catholic obscurantism is concerned (not in Gronn's text but implied throughout), I am not attempting to create "new altars" or engaging in "making angels" (whatever Gronn really implies by choosing these metaphors) but rather trying to elevate certain concepts as central to an understanding of schooling as a form of cultural production, and I happen to take the concepts of symbol, ritual, root paradigm, performance, liminality, and sanctity to be indispensable to such an understanding. Can a person be engaged in creating a new theoretical deity, as Gronn claims in my case, and then qualify that theory with the following: "I do not foresee ritology as providing insights which will lead to the *new* theoretical elixir, metalanguage or single all-encompassing theory for classroom instruction" (p. 242). These are hardly words by which to consecrate a new religion.

As long as Gronn refuses to give any theoretical currency to the terms that structure my argument, then we are hopelessly at cross purposes. Gronn may reject my "compromising" definition of ritual, but should that be enough to stop him from examining other important themes and concepts that structure my text? These include, among others, the proliferation of classroom symbols, their emotional appeal, and their structural counterpoint between order and disorder and between structure and antistructure. These are hardly tangential to the political project that informs my book.

As for Gronn's remarks about my concept of resistance, it appears as though he fails to appreciate the polysemic nature of resistance, including its liminal or antistructural characteristics. Resistance, as I have theorized it, refers to the power to contest meaning through the corporeal nature of symbols which inscribe subjectivity and which manifest themselves in both discursive and nondiscursive forms. There is a liberating pleasure resulting from the surface of resistance as well as within its condensed, symbolic layering. Certainly, its polysemy is easily co-opted and actively exploited by the guardians of the social structure, but it is theoretically silly to equate my concept of resistance with mere loutishness or brute behavior, as Gronn chooses to do, if one has any understanding of how resistance operates within the realm of meaning and subjectivity as much as in the more overt realms of social and political behavior. Resistance, as I have theorized the term, is played out as part of a cultural politics of the body and geography of desire and as such it deals in the currency of signs, symbols, and gesture. Resistance, as I am presenting it, is a more complex process than Gronn is willing to admit. It is, among other things, an unfixing of signifiers among relatively stable constellations of discourses, an attempt at exploiting the polysemic nature of the symbol in order to prise open a space for articulating one's own lived meaning and thereby creating a subject position that operates from a position of strength rather than weakness, that is, one that is better able to resist a life of lived subordination. It is also a form of somatic or corporeal unlearning in which students struggle against institutional embodiment and the enfleshment of their own oppression brought on by the policing and containment of gesture and the regulation of desire.

Given Gronn's implied respect for Tom Brown, Dr. Arnold, and rugby school, and the empire that was won on the playing fields thereof, it is not surprising that he also likens what I call resistance to "crude mob rule," "plain wanton destruction," "primitive morality, appalling brutality and sheer barbarism," and the atavistic imprecations of uncouth louts. Oddly, I've never thought of myself as an apologist for Flashman.

Gronn laments my "fervent underdog outlook" and my apparent attempt to "ferret out oppression everywhere." Would Gronn have me assume, instead, a ruling class stance, to look the other way? Perhaps he would. He laments, as well, my book's apparent lack of "distinctly Canadian flavor." Here I would remind Gronn that people who have not lived in Canada occasionally harbor strange ideas about lumberjacks, Mounties, trusted Indian guides, and everything else not available in Toronto. What is it, exactly, that Gronn is looking for?

I will agree with Gronn on one point. I could have been more explicit about the methodology I have used in my research. While I do not have space here to describe the enterprise of doing surrealistic ethnography, I will direct Gronn and readers of my book to an essay by James Clifford that might help to shed some light on this matter (see Clifford, 1981; Clifford & Marcus, 1986). I consider the following assertion of Gronn to be particularly telling: "Any writer who strives to depict some aspect of the social world at the same time as he strives to be rid of it places himself in an untenable position in respect of his research evidence unless he is particularly careful. Ramsey manages to get away with it, *despite his neo-Marxist leanings*" (italics mine).

Gronn is obviously at odds with critical research in general, as is apparent from his uneasiness with theorists who have "neo-Marxist leanings." It is not clear whether Gronn's uneasiness is a result of the uncertainty of his own political position or an aversion to those Marxist ethnographers who conduct research nondialectically as a means of providing empirical specificities for *a priori* theory. While he seems to be inferring that social action research itself is fraught with almost insurmountable difficulties, he offers no concrete agenda beyond citing other works.

What Gronn finds so ironic in my observation that schools both constrain and enable social emancipation, or the possibilities for it, is rather baffling. It should be obvious to Gronn after reading my text that schools do more than simply oppress, just as students do more that resist.

Let me conclude my response by examining the issue of language, which Gronn raises on a number of occasions throughout his review. As for using words that are not found in the *Oxford English Dictionary,* I must confess that I'm certainly sympathetic to the average reader who is just out to get the facts. But what are we to make of Gronn, flipping through those ponderous tomes, tediously looking up those unfamiliar words?

It is too bad that my style of writing sets Gronn's teeth on edge. Yet I must admit that I am astonished he could write that McLaren offers his readers "a new altar [...] at which to worship a new god," and then criticize my own use of metaphor. Gronn's criticism of my language and his inability to recognize the ways in which neologisms evolve from generative metaphors within the territory of nascent theory, speaks to an issue that is larger than the question of tasteful prose, the insolvency of words, the baroque play of an esoteric language, or acquiring an economy of style. It typifies a particular ideology that is not uncommon among lecturers in faculties of education, even senior lecturers. In fact, it is an ideology that is not uncommon among individuals working both within the academy and outside in the broader arena of cultural commentary.[1] It is characterized primarily by its preoccupation with technique and the mechanics of expression. Gronn's concern with my language fails to acknowledge the theoretical traditions that provide a referent for the language that I use. More importantly, the central issue that needs to be raised here is not whether language is clear or abstruse, though these are concerns that every writer has to address. Instead, what needs to be examined with respect to any form of language use is the theoretical framework that gives it both meaning and legitimacy. Thus, a more fundamental question than that of style needs to be raised: What is the theoretical perspective that informs such a language?

In Gronn's case, the political nature of language as a contested terrain in which meaning is constructed and legitimated is ignored in favor of a procedural concern that focuses on whether or not a language is clear or recondite. In short, Gronn fails to see the issue of language as part of the present crisis in the legitimation of knowledge and power. This failure of insight has apparently given Gronn a licence for lazy thinking and for presenting readers as too unintelligent to be able to grapple with a discourse that provides new categories for understanding the polydimensional nature of schooling and classroom rituals, and the symbolic and material dimensions of resistance. The prime issue surrounding recondite language is not whether one can find every word in the *Oxford English Dictionary,* but whether such a language adequately grasps and illuminates the political project it identifies and attempts to analyze. In Gronn's case, economy of style becomes the prevailing issue, and canned simplicity becomes the referent by which serious questions of substance and politics can be safely avoided. By separating knowledge and language from the question of power, Gronn's critique ends up reinforcing the dominant ideological practice of ignoring the social construction of meaning. It appears that Gronn would prefer to look to the *Oxford English Dictionary* for meaning rather than attempt to come to terms with the contextual specificity of theory itself. New terms are not dropped from heaven into the lap of a dictionary editor, even if it happens to be the editor of the *Oxford English Dictionary,* but are cobbled from the forces of tradition, present-day theorizing, and research as praxis.

As difficult as complex language may be (outside of the tedium of checking all those big words against the canonical weight of the *Oxford English Dictionary*), the ideas embodied within such a language do not warrant dismissal simply because the language is difficult or recondite. Rather than reinforcing an ideology that structures the discourse of consumer culture, Gronn would have done better to reflect upon his own position on language, which reinforces the dominant educational practice of supporting causal explanations "based on psychological definition."

I will not be so presumptuous as to advise Gronn to read a particular book on writing, as he has suggested in my case. But I would ask that he be more reflective about the theoretical framework that shapes his own language and method of criticism it appears to promote. The attitude that anything worth saying can and should be said in a stark and simple prose represents a dismal, disheartening, and ultimately condescending ideology for educators who are, after all, supposed to take the social power of intelligence seriously.

Acknowledgments

The main title for this rejoinder has been taken from Milton (1961, p. 38).

This chapter originally appeared as P. McLaren, No light, but rather darkness visible: Language and the politics of criticism, *Curriculum Inquiry, 18*(3) (1988), 313–320. Reprinted here, with minor edits, with permission from the publisher.

Note

1 I have drawn liberally from two previous rejoinders. See Giroux & McLaren, 1986. See also my response to Salvatore D'Urso (McLaren, 1987).

References

Bocock, R. (1974). *Ritual in industrial society*. George Allen & Unwin.

Clifford, J. (1981). On ethnographic surrealism. *Comparative Studies in Society and History, 23*(4), 539–564.

Clifford, J., & Marcus, G. E. (Eds.). (1986). *Writing culture: The poetics and politics of ethnography*. University of California Press.

Giroux, H. A., & McLaren, P. (1986, February 1). Rejoinder in which Professors Giroux and McLaren reply to Mr. Lunn's concern about language. *Ontario Public School Teachers Federation News*, p. 10.

Hebdige, D. (1986). Postmodernism and "The Other Side." *Journal of Communication Inquiry, 10*(2), 78–98.

Lacan, J. (1978). Seminar XX. In *Le moi dans la théorie de Freud et dans la technique de la psychoanalyse: 1954–1955*. Éditions du Seuil.

McLaren, P. (1987). A response to Salvatore D'Urso in "Commentary." *Educational Studies, 18*(1), 184–185.

Milton, J. (1961). *Paradise Lost* (annotated by E. Le Comte). New American Library.

Penley, C. (1986). Teaching in your sleep: Feminism and psychoanalysis. In C. Nelson (Ed.), *Theory in the classroom*. University of Illinois Press.

CHAPTER 7

Collisions with Otherness
"Traveling" Theory, Post-colonial Criticism, and the Politics of Ethnographic Practice – The Mission of the Wounded Ethnographer

1   Qualitative Research as a Discourse of Power[1]

This essay will discuss qualitative research in general and critical ethnography in particular from the perspective of new developments within critical social theory over the last several decades, particularly continental and poststructuralist variants of critical postmodernist discourse (see McLaren, 1986, 1989). Those strands of more orthodox anthropological field-work, including both liberal and conservative accents, that continue to enjoy uncontested power in contemporary educational research situate the challenge of field analysis in largely instrumental terms, or in what the Frankfurt School theorists refer to as "instrumental rationality." From the perspective of a defanged and defamed modernism, ethnographic research generally has been normalized to mean those practices in which researchers engage in order to gain entry into the field site, establish an ongoing rapport with subjects through the generation of a reciprocal trust, maintain the confidence of the subjects, and achieve a longevity in the field by remaining as unobtrusive as possible, sometimes effecting an almost bold detachment to the point of self-effacement. In so doing, they attempt to construct representations of social life that both mirror and explain the events that transpired throughout their field-work practices.

The general assumption on which this essay is founded cuts against the grain of this traditional approach to ethnographic research and attempts to stand outside the policing structure of its sovereign discourses. Operating within an anthropological subterrain where subjects of the anthropologist's gaze rarely assume their appointed roles and places, and where unconventional alliances can be made between descriptions and meanings, this essay takes the position that ethnographic research and the production of knowledge never is self-authenticating or self-legitimating. Debate over issues of meaning construction becomes inexorably bound up with questions of language and interpretation, the knowledge/power nexus, and the sovereign "logocentric" discourses of modem scientific rationality. As a form of praxis, ethnographic research neither determines its own effects nor speaks its own truth in a manner that transcends its relation to the metaphors that are constitutive of its meanings. For example, normative definitions of woman, man, colonizer, researcher, and informant, and so on, enforce particular ideological exclusions and promote an insider politics that often freezes and ossifies difference. This is so because within modernist theoretical discourse, binary oppositions enforce a dependent hierarchy where one of the two terms forcefully restricts, undermines, and usurps the meaning of the other and produces ideologically disfiguring effects (Hammer & McLaren, 1991).

In a recent essay in *Out there: marginalization and contemporary cultures,* Cornel West (1990) asserts that "One cannot deconstruct the binary oppositional logic of images of Blackness without extending it to the contrary condition of Blackness/Whiteness itself" (p. 29). He notes further that "social theory is what is needed to examine and *explain* the historically specific ways in which 'Whiteness' is a politically constructed category parasitic on 'Blackness'" (p. 29). Consequently, it is the historical meanings linked to these terms that need to be placed under theoretical stress such that the terms may not be simply reversed but subverted (Hammer & McLaren, 1991).

It is the transparency of whiteness and maleness that makes it possible for white male researchers to arrogate to themselves the exclusive right to "nominate" all other groups while monumentalizing their own. Those groups that do not fall into the category of white or male are positioned irrevocably as *Other-,* and this category of *Other* must be assumed or internalized in order for them to become part of the totality.

Viewed from this poststructuralist and ethnosemiotic vantage point, ethnographic research and the production of qualitative meaning needs to be extended beyond the prevailing logocentric and humanistic *anthropologos* that informs its central axioms and needs to be taken seriously within the context of the following question: Under what conditions and to what ends do we, as educational researchers, enter into relations of cooperation, mutuality, and reciprocity with those whom we research?

Most of the discussion in the remainder of this essay follows an assertion frequently associated with the disciplinary trajectory known as *critical ethnography:* that field research is the creature of cultural limits and theoretical borders and as such is implicated necessarily in particular economies of truth, value, and power (see Kincheloe, 1991; McLaren, 1986; Simon & Dippo, 1988). Correlatively, I want to address the antecedents and implications of recent perspectives in critical social theory in connection with formulating a new conception of ethnographic work.

Specifically in this postmodern era of blurred genres, we are witnessing the "literaturization of the social sciences" (Loriggio, 1990, p. 235) and a "welding of the literary and the sociopolitical" (Manganaro, 1990, p. 35). Intersections between the Anglo-American philosophical tradition and European social theory have yielded creative implications for our understanding of social life. For instance, Manganaro's volume, *Modernist anthropology: from fieldwork to text*, cogently illustrates intellectual affinities and a continuity of ideas among work carried out by surrealist sociologists, poststructuralist semiologists, deconstructionist theorists, and French ethnologists. Similarly, it is not difficult to tease out among these various strands of contemporary theory what Manganaro (1990) calls "new hybridic possibilities for cultural critique" (p. 45).

Examining ethnography in light of this new mapping of anthropological research, I suggest that new understandings that have implications for an emancipatory social practice can develop if researchers are able to situate and analyze field research as textual strategies and discursive practices that ineluctably are entangled within larger structures of power and privilege. In this view, knowledge is understood as a social text made up of competing rhetorical strategies. The current postmodern perspective of knowledge production that emphasizes experience, subjectivity, reflexivity, and holistic understanding can be situated in German romanticism – a movement that grew out of a dissatisfaction with and criticism of the Enlightenment search for general laws and scientific rationality. The crisis of representation in current anthropological discourse can be linked to both strengths and limitations within the romantic tradition in anthropology – a tradition that has been chronicled in recent books such as Michael Jackson's *Paths toward a Clearing: Radical Empiricism and Ethnographic Inquiry* (1985), Renato Rosaldo's *Culture and Truth: The Remaking of Social Analysis* (1989), and George W. Stocking, Jr.'s *Romantic Motives: Essays on Anthropological Sensibility* (1989).[2] My emphasis in this essay is on how the postmodern turn in anthropological theory has effected this crisis of representation and on the implications the crisis holds for the practice of critical ethnography.

A way of pitching the perspective that has resulted from the revolution in critical social theory over the last several decades is to make the claim that field researchers undertake their projects not just *in* a field site, but *within a field of competing discourses that help structure a variegated system of socially constituted human relationships*. The field site no longer can be considered simply the geographical location of the study; it also is the location where geopolitical vectors of power crosscut the cultural terrain under investigation. The field site additionally may be considered *the site of the researcher's own embodiment in theory/discourse and his or her own disposition as a theorist, within a specific politics of location*. Here it should be recognized that discourses do not simply reflect the field site as a seamless repository for transcriptions of a pristine "source" of cultural authenticity, but *are constitutive of such a site*. In other words, field-workers always are cultural workers who engage in not just the analysis of field sites but *in their active production* through the discourses used to analyze field relations. The cultural terrain of the field site is never a monadic site of harmony and control, but is a site of disjuncture, rupture, and contradiction that is better understood from a research perspective as a contested terrain that serves as the loci of multivalent powers. It is within this context of framing our concept of field relations and research that we can situate more critically our role as field researchers.

This perspective shares some of the insights of recent feminist and critical approaches to anthropological research that probe the nature of representation and power relations themselves, a perspective that shifts the emphasis of anthropology from a field-work-based "science" of culture to a form of textual analysis in which knowledge is viewed as an interlaced network of conflictual and arborescent discursive practices, forms of ideological production, and what Giroux (1990) has termed modalities of ethical address (see also Britzman, 1991; Clifford, 1987; Clifford & Marcus, 1986; Mascia-Lees et al., 1989; McLaren, 1986; Van Mannen, 1990).

Discourses, as I am referring to them here, are modalities that, to a significant extent, govern what can be said, by what kinds of speakers, and for what types of imagined audiences (Weedon, 1987). They are social practices that constitute both social subjects and the objects of their investigation. The rules of discourse are normative and derive their meaning from the power relations of which they are a part. That is, discourses *organize a way of thinking into a way of doing*. They actively shape the practices that the discourses serve. But they always are indexical to the context of the researchers and their interpretations. In other words, there exists no single privileged and perdurable set of research practices whose name is "field relations."

Modernist ethnography is preoccupied with locating through description and analyses the identity of research subjects from a position of intelligibility that either refuses to locate the agency of the researcher or falsely assumes that the researcher speaks from a prediscursive and stable site untouched by the very discourses used in the research process. That is, the "onto-epistemological" tradition within ethnography fails to recognize that the identity of the researcher *qua* researcher is both a discursive fiction and a social practice. The discursive tools of analysis used to uncover the authenticity of the studied "other" become the unconscious predicates of the researcher's own identity and subjective disposition (politics of location) in the field. A poststructuralist approach to critical ethnography, on the other hand, refuses the imposition of an epistemological construction of the identity of both the researcher and the researched that the tradition of Western epistemology has produced as a series of established, hierarchical binarisms: the knower and the known, the subject who inquires and the object of inquiry, the researcher and the researched (Butler, 1990, p. 144). The critical poststructuralist ethnographic practice I am both summarizing and advocating calls for a radical reconceptualization of culture as a field of discourse (see Clifford & Marcus, 1986) that is implicated in relations of power and is constituted by normative understandings; such a perspective can enable researchers to understand field relations better as social practices that are not immediately present to themselves. As ethnographic researchers, we actively construct and are constructed by the discourses we embody and the metaphors we enact (McLaren, 1986, 1989). We are, in effect, both the subject and the object of our research. It is within this context that we unconsciously strive as field researchers to create an atmosphere of place and tradition that will act as a lure to the "right" kind of informants – those who largely will be compliant with our research agenda by conforming to our normative understanding of them.

I am suggesting that it is extremely tempting to absolutize or totalize the groups we study, to see them as existing homogeneously, rooted in particular world views, and to ignore the way in which power operates as a regulating force that centralizes and unifies often conflicting and competing discourses and subjectivities (cf. Giroux, 1988; McLaren, 1989). There is, of course, something rather estranging in all of this, something perhaps duplicitous. This is why it is vitally important that we connect empirical data to the discourses that produce them and, at the same time, produce our subjects under study. In so doing, we can attempt to engage in a form of theoretical decolonization; that is, in a critical way of unlearning accepted ways of thinking, of refusing to analyze in the mode of the dominator while at the same time paying attention to the dangers of assuming the sponsorship of a postcolonial elite. Such a task is but a first step to the larger goal of transforming our field relations and research efforts within the context of a politics of difference and vision of social justice.

2 Shipwrecked against Infinity: Field Relations as Competing Discourses

The discourses of ethnographic research consist of rhetorical tropes that both reflect and shape the way in which we consciously and unconsciously identify ourselves with our role in the field and with the subjects of our study. Mainstream research and field relations become, in the context I have set forth, an appeal to a *particular understanding* of reality that is deeply rooted in what moves us to take for "human" what is merely the discursive form of humanity in our society. We often situate ourselves as field researchers by viewing ourselves as a paradigm of humanity and then construct the origins of this universal presence in our selected ethnographic methodologies (cf., Litchman, 1982). The discourses of ethnographic research may, in fact, possess the power of truth, but in reality they are historically contingent rather than inscribed by natural law; they emerge, in other words, out of social conventions, but they always are profoundly implicated in the question of the ethical formation of the self and other.

3 Knowledge and the Body

Consequently, it is important to pursue this question: If discourses are not grounded transcendentally, and if they are not mappable by intellection, how, in fact, are they grounded? Recent research on the body suggests that knowledge is grounded through forms of embodiment. The concept of the body as a site of cultural inscription is growing in prominence as a topic of investigation among contemporary social theorists. Efforts tire being made to uncouple the idea of the feminine body/subject and the Black and Latino body/subject from the negative and unspoken Other and to recognize the body as a site of *enfleshment* – that is, as a site where epistemic codes freeze desire into social norms. In other words, bodies are becoming recognized and explored as socially situated and incarnated social practices that are semiotically alive. However, I should add that the importance of understanding the body is not for researchers to turn it into a textualized semiotic laboratory, but rather to recognize knowledge as a typography of embodiment; that is, to recognize the body as the grounds for all our intersubjective relationships with the subjects of our investigations and for our affective investment in our own research projects. We cannot separate the body from the social formation, since the material density of all forms of subjectivity is achieved through the "micropractices" of power that are socially inscribed into our flesh.

As Allen Feldman reports in his brilliant ethnography of political terror in Northern Ireland, *Formations of Violence* (1991), the body is "the factored product of the unequal and differential effects of intersecting antagonistic forces" (p. 176) that "coheres onto an economy of the body" (p. 177). Although the body is the product of history, it is, through the workings of the subject, also the shaper of history. Ethnography in my estimation should help produce those forms of agency necessary for the transformation of historical forces and structures of oppression. Feldman's formulation of agency is important.

> Exteriority folds the body, but agency, as a self-reflexive framing of force, subjectivates exteriority and refolds the body. It is not only a matter of

what history does to the body but what subjects do with what history has done to the body. (p. 177)

It is important that ethnographers engage the means by which discourses "live" inside of both "us and them" as linguistic and extralinguistic mediations. Our capacity as researchers to understand the body as an effect of power/knowledge relations and also as a site of their articulation can help us to escape the political paralysis that often accompanies the poststructuralist recognition that values, desires, and practices always originate elsewhere in predisclosed structures and in conditions not of our own making. In other words, while it is true that our desires and intentions and those of our subjects never can be completely mapped or made conscious, this should not compel us as researchers to assume a passive, passionless, and politically inert role. Nor should it be an occasion for a voluntaristic denial or abandonment of hope – a sanctioned refusal to upstage despair in the face of the dominant culture's persistent demonization of the Other.

If the objectivist program in the social sciences was grounded in empirical studies, the postmodernist approach to research is grounded in the metaphoricity and tropicity of all discourse. Metaphor and polyseme form the cornerstones of what George Lakoff calls "experiential realism" and what Mark Johnson calls "embodied, nonpropositional, and imaginative meaning" (cited in Frank, 1990). Metaphor and polyseme are constituent not only of speech but also of thought, and we can trace our embodiment in knowledge preverbally to our early experiences of balance, containment, forces, cycles, and so forth, that become our image schemata and which in turn inform our propositional logic (Frank, 1990, p. 158). As Arthur Frank (1990) notes, understanding and knowledge are projections of embodied image schemata that are multivocal, yet can form the basis of mutual understanding, since bodily experience is shared. Cartesian philosophy managed to overlook the fact that validity claims no longer can afford to exclude the body. In fact, I would go so far as to say that theoretical knowledges constitute externalized metaphors of the body; they form the prostheses of the body, artifacts that offer *strategies of desire; they advocate; as embodied metaphors, metonymies, and images based on experience, they solicit; they seduce; they hypnotize; they cannot be considered lifeless nor can they be considered objective.*

This is why our research agendas with their accompanying theoretical formulations must be situated within the borders that constitute their respective projects. A project is more than a subjective disposition, but rather constitutes a political imperative grounded in an ethical discourse (Giroux, 1990). The ethical project known as critical ethnography is one that does not emerge transcendentally in textual forms detached from perception, bodily experience, and the friction of social reality. It is an ethics that emerges *from the body, is situated in the materiality and historicity of discourse, in the call of the flesh, in the folds of desire*. It is an imperative that presupposes an answer, in a response *from the other*. If the way in which metaphors are grounded in bodily experience becomes part of the theoretical structures through which we perceive the world, and if such structures bring about changes in the way we act in the world, then it is important for critical ethnographers to utilize an ethics fully grounded in the body (see Chambers, 1990; McLaren, 1989).

4 Knowledge and Truth

There is another perspective from which knowledge must be analyzed and understood, and that is in the lived relation of knowledge to truth. I am suggesting here, along with Foucault and others, that the constraints of discourse, that the very act of signification, construct an impassable and implacable division posed by alterity; discourse itself creates barriers or constraints at the point at which its own situatedness in social relations becomes apparent. This suggests that Truth cannot be spoken of in the absence of power relations, and each relation necessarily speaks its own truth (Foucault, 1980). Another way that ethnographers and field researchers can begin to think of the "truth" of their work is not to render knowledge as something ultimately to be discovered, but rather as social texts that are relationally produced in a multiplicity of mutually informing contexts. When such truths become official, when they are presented as discourses of sanctioned legitimacy, then they often serve as an impediment to further truth and must therefore be deformed – even perverted – by rhetorizing moves on the part of the researcher that deconstruct their metaphysical bearings. Representation is always re-presentation within particular ideological configurations.

If every signification constitutes a mask (Lévinas, 1981; Patterson, 1990), then the way to truth becomes the absolute pursuit of alterity – to probe the totality of otherness. Patterson (1990, p. 102) writes that "[i]n its alterity, truth belongs to what we shall have been, in the light of what we are in the process of becoming." Truth is "that juncture where the *not yet* of alterity proclaims itself." Further, truth "is not what we try to find out but what we endeavour to become." That is, "truth is not what we know but what we are not yet" (p. 303). It is the process of becoming "other" to one's "I".

Of course, the pursuit of alterity is fraught with danger. As Gayatri Spivak (1990) argues, the postcolonial elite consisting mainly of metropolitan intellectuals must persistently unlearn their privilege in the context of a neo-colonial world in order to engage the truth of otherness.

5 Research as Advocacy

Critical ethnography contests the epistemological closure of the so-called "objectivity" and "scientificity" of mainstream ethnographic research (Lather, 1986; McLaren, 1986). Typically, critical ethnographers do not shrink from the charge of perspectivism; rather, they openly contest those discourses that attempt to occlude the historicity and partisanship characteristic of the analysis of social life (Kincheloe, 1991; McLaren, 1986; Simon & Dippo, 1988). Critical social inquiry situates its project in a non-objectivist view of knowledge that challenges certain ethical standards and imperatives of the dominant culture (Bennett & LeCompte, 1990).

Within the discourse of science, explanation surpasses understanding and empathy (Agger, 1989). Read from the perspective of critical ethnography, such an emphasis is highly problematic, which is not to suggest that questions of validity, verifiability, and explanation are not important (Lather, 1986; Simon & Dippo, 1988). However, critical ethnographers have made their position on knowledge quite clear: they cannot hide the world's inherence in the constitutiveness of and ingress to the world – a position which, rather than vitiating the objectivity of knowledge, underscores its insinuation in human interest and social power (Kincheloe, 1991; McLaren, forthcoming). Consequently, they raise a fundamental question: What social effects do you want your evaluations and understanding to have?

Mainstream social science forswears its own ideological constitutivity, but its discursive underpinnings are clear; the problem is that researchers who work within its limits refuse to acknowledge the interests that such research serves. As Ben Agger (1989) notes, research is never free of presuppositionlessness, but rather must always narrate its own ideological contingency within networks of power relations. Agger rightly objects to analytic cleavage of description and exhortation, the temporal separation of knowledge and desire, the sundering of analysis and social criticism, and the refusal of researchers to examine their textual practices as imaginative fictions.

It is necessary here to assert that all research – qualitative or quantitative – exists as a form of rhetoric, but not as "mere" rhetoric. As Bruce Robbins (1990) maintains, rhetoric involves much more than merely technical or pure instrumentality prostituting itself in the service of any user without a sense of critical oppositionality or narrative anchoring in the common good. Rather, rhetoric's limits belong to the domain of social theory, and its perpetually destabilizing function and indeterminacy should not be linked solely to language and tropes but to "the contingencies of action, of historical audience, and of politics" (p. 110). That is, rhetoric necessarily foregrounds the public issue of value and accountability.

As a defence of the rhetoricity of research, Agger (1989) argues against what he terms "methodological pluralism." According to Agger, methodological pluralism assumes that the world is really all one piece but can be read differently through different sociological approaches. In other words, the same world can be explained differently; it is all simply a question of the researcher's ontological coordinates. This view prevails in so many courses in educational research, especially during instances in which prospective researchers are invited to conceptualize the educational and social milieu according to functionalist, interpretivist, and conflict theories. The problem with explaining the social world through these three somewhat overlapping conceptual lenses is that it "assumes a single, simple world named differently" and therefore "misses the constitutiveness of writing entwining a theory of being and explanation" (p. 315).

What Agger underscores with such sharpened insight is that when the researcher neglects how the relationship between subject and object has been historically produced within a nexus of power relations, the world's own self-understanding then becomes the basis of the researcher's criticism of the social world, and thus critical writings can become dismissed and domesticated and ultimately discarded as weakened versions of other forms of analysis. Critical ethnographic knowledge becomes, in this view, just another "gloss" on reality. And presumably the classroom instructor, who is standing in a site unspoiled by ideology, can invoke "conflict theory" as one item in an entire menu of theoretical perspectives on the world. Structural functionalism, phenomenology, or conflict theory become one of the many "lenses" through which to look at the world, or one of the many "hats" the liberal researcher wears to show that he or she is willing to see the world from all sorts of research perspectives – even radical ones. Epistemological pluralism is really a form of neo-positivism that always is "preontologically available" for the researcher to read the world. Yet the centrist position of slicing up the world into its functionalist, interpretivist, and critical pieces really works to usurp critical research under a liberalism that locates it as an example of the "openness" of the social system. Critical research thus becomes "ironically a genuflection to an *uncritical* discipline" (Agger, 1989, p. 316).

Research practices undertaken in a critical mode necessitate recognizing the complexity of social relations and the researcher's own socially determined position within the reality that one is attempting to describe. A failure of such a recognition can conjure into being the concretely elaborated idea of the researcher/outsider as master of the discourse *on* schooling, on the one hand, and on the other hand, the figure of the hapless teachers and their students who not only are prevented from becoming authorities on the discourse *of* schooling but also are left as vulnerable, unwitting victims of the outsider/ researcher's study.

The status of field researchers as truth-bearers from the culture of maleness and whiteness putatively imbues them with an impartial and rational intelligence, reinforces the idea that the teacher's anecdotal logics and local knowledge are of lesser status, and binds power and truth together in such a way as both to privilege and normalize existing relations of power. This only habituates teachers to the established direction of educational research and the cultural-political regime of truth ascribed to by the dominant culture. This is precisely why it is important to enter field relations collaboratively rather than purge difference through the universal calculus of putatively disinterested objective analysis. The field researcher needs to share with his or her subjects the discourses at work that are shaping the field site analysis and how the researcher's own personal and intellectual biography is contributing to the process of analysis.

6   Conversations with Silence: The Discourse of the Other

Poststructuralists acknowledge explicitly that meaning consists of more than signs operating or being operated in a context. Rather, there is a struggle over signifying practices. This struggle is eminently *political* and must include the relationship between discourse and the contradictions involved in subjective formation/the formation of subjects (Butler, 1990, p. 145). According to poststructuralism, we construct ourselves, our identities, through the availability and character of signs of past and present events as well as possible futures. That is, the parameters of the human subject vary according to the discursive practices, economies of signs, and subjectivities (experiences) engaged by individuals and groups at any historical moment. We need to jettison the outmoded and eminently dangerous idea that we possess as researchers a timeless essence or a consciousness that places us beyond historical and political practices. Rather, we need to understand our "working identities" as an effect of such practices. Our identities as researchers are not fettered to or dependent on some transcendental regime of truth beyond the territory of the profane and the mundane. In other words, our identities are constitutive of the literacies we have at our disposal through which we make sense of our day-to-day politics of living.

Consequently, when considering the characteristics that are constitutive of the researcher or those being researched – the "insiders" and "outsiders" of the research process – it is important not to fall into the trap of essentializing either one. This position emphasizes that those with whom the researcher works cure always necessarily *partners* in the research and are not inert referents abstracted from social history and practice; that is, referents isolated by the research process and problematic from the concreteness of heteroglossia, the socio-economic and the historical. Trinh T. Minh-ha (1988) articulates a view of the subject (as researcher, as researched) that speaks to a refusal to naturalize the *I:*

> The moment the insider steps out from the inside she's no longer a mere insider. She necessarily looks in from the outside while also looking out from the inside. Not quite the same, not quite the other, she stands in that undetermined threshold place where she constantly drifts in and out. Undercutting the inside/outside opposition, her intervention is necessarily that of both not-quite an insider and not-quite an outsider. She is, in other words, this inappropriate other or same who moves about with always at least two gestures: that of affirming "I am like you" while persisting in her difference and that of reminding "I am different" while unsettling every definition of otherness arrived at. (p. 76)

One of the most important tasks in which a field researcher can engage is understanding and transforming the various ways in which his or her own subjective formation privileges certain discourses that unwittingly construct subjects as the Other. Iris Young (1990) argues that the cultural imperialism of the researcher not only provides and insists on only one subject position, that of unified, disembodied reason identified with white bourgeois men, but it promotes members of culturally imperialized groups to devalue themselves and other oppressed groups. Groups who are researched by metropolitan ethnographers often learn to devalue members of their own groups and other oppressed groups by internalizing the cultural knowledge that dominant groups "fear and loathe them." However, oppressed and marginalized groups do not simply assume the dominant subjectivity toward themselves and other members of the groups with which they identify; they also live a subjectivity different from the dominant subject position that they have derived from their positive identification and social networks with others in their group. The dialectical relationship between these two subjectivities – "the point of view of the dominant culture which defines them as ugly and fearsome, and the point of view of the oppressed who experience themselves as ordinary, companionate, and humorous" (p. 148) – represents what Young calls "double consciousness."

Before engaging in fieldwork relations and analysis, researchers need to become aware of how they unwittingly can become complicitous in the hostile displacement of minorities as those who possess a prehistorical surplus of culture that celebrates the distance that middle-class whites have evolved (e.g., have become rational). Educators, like ethnographers, often fall into the mistake of regarding "authentic" culture as something that distinguishes them from those they are studying. The Other therefore becomes a cultural generality that accounts for the ethnographer's "difference." That is, the Other becomes invasive and corrosive of the researcher's self-contained subjectivity. Put another way, the proliferative and meretricious figure of the Other becomes in this case a cultural fiction that allows educators and researchers to ignore the partiality of their own perspectives that assign cultural "otherness" to certain groups in order to render invisible how such a practice often is a form of ideological violence and an exercise of the power to dominate. A miasma of smoke often is exhaled by our field research, obscuring the political and ethical ramifications entailed by our analyses, but easily overlooked, absorbed, and displaced by the Eurocentrism and androcentrism found in our research traditions.

Ethnographic research needs to be so checked in order that it does not fall prey to privatization and self-absorption due to the narcissism of the researcher, a narcissism which, as a form of regenerative barbarism, assumes the researcher's own subjectivity and human agency to be the privileged reference point for judging not only the cultural and social practices under his or her gaze but those who engage in them. Such a form of engagement amounts to little more than a form of ethnographic vampirism, an imperialist and imperious act of ethnographic voyeurism and cultural appropriation. This process is brilliantly spelled out by Marianna Torgovnick (1990) in *Gone primitive: savage intellects, modem lives*. Torgovnick makes a compelling case against the damaging effects of the colonial imagination formed out of the sovereign Eurocentric archives of the imperialist West, an imagination that has profound implications for the practice of ethnography undertaken in the spirit of modernism, where certain groups become othered and devoiced through the "male-centred, canonical line of Western primitivism" (p. 248).

We need to move beyond the perspective that James Clifford (1987, p. 122) has identified as "salvage ethnography" (recording the languages and lore of disappearing peoples) and represented by the works of Boas, Kroeber, and others, studies that attempt to "rescue authenticity out of destructive historical change." Such a perspective, argues Clifford, allows human differences to be "redistributed as separate, functioning cultures." The "ethnographic present" that is constructed by Western researchers, largely white males, as a point of reference for judging the worth of varying degrees of "primitiveness" is what keeps ethnic groups buried in the past and "marginal to the advancing world system." The "lowly' knowledge of the ethnic minority becomes, in this view, helpful to us only in terms of "aesthetic appreciation." As educational researchers, we must cease to attribute to certain groups "mythical consciousness" while we reserve "historical consciousness" for ourselves; in addition, we should welcome the day when the dominance of modernist dichotomies of literate/non-literate, developed/underdeveloped, and so forth, have substantially ebbed. Similarly, it is necessary that we cease to characterize ourselves as "dynamic and oriented towards change," while those from non-Western societies constantly "seek equilibrium and the reproduction of inherited forms" (Clifford, 1987, p. 125).

One way out of this dilemma is suggested by Iris Young (1990), who argues against constructing totalizing and monolithic representations of difference and encouraging representations of subjects as plural, shifting, and heterogeneous, and helping to confront "the very desire to have a unified, orderly identity, and the dependence of such a unified identity on the construction of a border that excludes aspects of subjectivity one refuses to face" (p. 155). This perspective on cultural identity and difference is implicit in the pointed reminder in Minh-ha (1987) that "authenticity" is always produced, never salvaged, any clear-cut opposition between authenticity and inauthenticity is bound to be misleading and reductively dualistic" (p. 140).

We have seen among ethnographers an inordinate emphasis placed on rationality and intellectualization that has provoked them to overlook the specificity of the investments that the so-called "masses" or "primitives" make in everyday social life. Valerie Walkerdine (1986) considers this emphasis on the part of qualitative researchers to be the result of the Cogito "which culminates in the scientific management of populations, the power/knowledge of the modern social world" (p. 196). She writes that

> Rather than seeing the pleasures of "the masses" as perverse, perhaps we should acknowledge that it is the bourgeois "will to truth" that is perverse in its desire for knowledge, certainty and mastery. This is the proper context in which to understand the *desire* to know the masses, the voyeurism of the (social) scientist. (p. 196)

As researchers we must avoid what Renato Rosaldo (1989) calls "imperialist nostalgia," which is a nostalgia for the traditional colonized culture before it was destroyed by agents of colonialism, "where people mourn the passing of what they themselves have transformed" (p. 69). We must not become elegists lamenting the disappearance of our imperial inheritance, which saw pastoral primitives as objects of bourgeois curiosity and pathos. Consequently, when field relations are undertaken, they must be undertaken in such a way *as to narrate their own contingent, their own situatedness in power/knowledge relations*. But I would caution against often fashionable calls for auto-critique through more autobiographical and dialogical writing forms that demand writers acknowledge the biographical and sociological contexts surrounding their modes of analysis. Epistemologically, reflexive writing forms can fall into the trap of assuming that any text is really a description of the author's subjective experience of whatever he or she is writing about. As Larry Grossberg (1988, pp. 66–67) points out, many of the calls for auto-critique make the mistake of assuming that the interpretation of the text must be measured by how "accurately" it represents reality. This assumption too often leads to damaging consequences for ethnographers and their readers. These include the reinscription of the privileged place of the author's experience, the undermining of critical authority and the potential for texts to become forms of strategic intervention and social transformation, and the forcing of authors into an endless production of self-determined interpretations.

The primary referent for the empowerment of those who have been deemed lesser or unredeemed should not be their moral strangeness or displacement outside the boundaries of the familiar, but rather *the establishment of criteria that can distinguish claims of moral superiority which we exercise as outsiders.* That is, the Others have a hermeneutical privilege in naming the issues before them and in developing an analysis of their situation appropriate to their context (cf. Mihevc, 1989). The marginalized have the first right to name reality, to articulate how social reality functions, and to decide how the issues tire to be organized and defined (Mihevc, 1989). Critical ethnography has a tendency to become evangelizing, and to enunciate its call for liberation as if it were the sole theoretical representative of the oppressed. But this warning against metaphysical seduction should not prevent the researcher from giving up all critical authority in interpreting how the reality of the marginalized has been named, voiced, and in analyzing the social consequences that follow.

Ethnographers must accept the responsibility that comes with giving the world meaning and for providing critical spaces for subjects to understand the literalness of the reality in which their subjectivities are inscribed, the contexts through which such a reality is articulated, and how their experiences and those of the researcher are imbricated in contradictory, complex, and changing vectors of power. Of course, as ethnographic researchers it is important to be aware of the controlling cultural mode of our own research and the ways, often multifarious and unwitting, in which our subjects and our relationship to them become artifacts of the epistemes that shape the direction of our theorizing. This occurs by fixing the conceptual world in a specific way through selecting *particular* discourses from a cultural range of possibilities. The invisibility of the dominant ideology in its own privileging norms (made possible by a generally accepted mimetic theory of representation) enables the dominant group to reinvent the group it is studying for its own purposes. This cloaking device is not "merely" rhetoric, but is the way in which language is embedded in social practices and relations of power.

Judith Stacey (1988) warns of the potential for the ethnographer to manipulate and betray the subject. At least some of the manipulation and betrayal of the subject can be avoided by avoiding the romanticism of "yearning to know the 'Other'" (Mascia-Lees et al., 1989) and locating the "other" in oneself through self-reflection (Stacey, 1988, p. 26). These temptations of the field researcher can be potentially subversive of critical anthropology's own political agenda by "turn[ing] ethnographers into the natives to be understood and ethnography into virgin territory to be explored" (Stacey, 1988, p. 26). The ethnographic project needs a "politically reflexive grounding" without which "the 'Other' can too easily [...] be reconstituted as an exotic in danger of being disempowered by that exoticism" (p. 30).

In Benita Parry's (1987) terms, a critical research practice must do more than simply repossess "the signifying function appropriated by colonialist representation" or demystify or deform the rhetorical devices that "organize capitalism's discursive field" (p. 28). Rather, the founding concepts of colonialism's "received narratives" and "monolithic figures and representations" must be refused rather than recoded in another tale of neocolonialism.

Of course, in attempting to dislocate the fixity of Eurocentric, sovereign narratives that structure our practice as theorists, it is impossible to remain totally outside the Western frame of reference, and this certainly is not what I am suggesting. As Spivak (1989, 1990) notes, it is important to speak "from within" emancipatory master narratives while simultaneously taking a distance from them. At the same time, it is important not to fall prey to hegemonic nativist counternarratives that make one complicitous with the forms of oppression one is struggling against. Gloria Anzaldúa (1990) refers to the task ahead as one of trying to formulate marginal theories

> that are partially outside and partially inside the Western frame of reference (if that is possible), theories that overlap many "worlds." We are articulating new positions in these "in-between," Borderland worlds of ethnic

> communities and academies, feminist and job worlds. In our literature, social issues such as race, class and sexual difference are intertwined with the narrative and poetic elements of a text, elements in which theory is embedded. In our *mestizaje* theories we create new categories for those of us left out or pushed out of the existing ones. We recover and examine non-Western aesthetics while critiquing Western aesthetics; recover and examine non-rational modes and "blanked-out" realities while critiquing rational, consensual reality; recover and examine indigenous languages while critiquing the "languages" of the dominant culture. [...] If we have been gagged and disempowered by theories, we can also be loosened and empowered by theories. (p. XXVI)

Critical ethnographers need to develop the will and the competence to reposition their sites of enunciation and narrative authority and to make choices outside the comfort and danger of an a priori standard based on Western, monocultural and universal constructions of identity and difference. It also is essential that ethnographic researchers act *with* the oppressed, not *over them* or *on behalf of* them. Critical ethnography must be *organic to* and not *administered upon* the plight of struggling peoples. Field researchers constantly should place themselves in relations of "risk for knowledge," which means assuming a stance towards field research that is not founded on political deceit or moral absolutism.

It is important in this context that the field researcher not use the field as a site for his or her psychotherapy or a *mise-en-scene* where his or her own politics of difference is reduced to an essentializing confrontation with otherness such that difference remains fetishized and pleasurably infantilized and eroticized for Western consumption. Yet, at the same time, the ethnographer needs to recognize that the techniques of gaining objectivity in the field often serve as rituals to protect researchers from the necessary *wounding* needed to acknowledge and promote interconnections between their lives and the lives of those whom they study. A wounded ethnographer is one who feels the pain and appreciates the joy of the "other," while refusing to disown culpability for the production of the colonizing subject and the mythopoetics of imperialism that marks its discursive inscription. Self-inflicted wounding, however, is the bourgeois stigmata worn by the guilt-ridden liberal ethnographer and has little emancipatory potential in a postcolonial ethnography of resistance.

One of the most significant challenges for critical ethnographic work, and qualitative studies in general, is to begin to rethink the categories we use to shape the problematics of our research. The questions that are being asked, whether posed by centrist liberal researchers or postcolonial metropolitan intellectuals, must be radically decentred and re-examined in light of new critical voices that are being sounded from the margins: feminist voices, Afro-American voices, Latino voices, and other voices that up to the present have been dampened – and in some cases violently subdued – by the discourses and social practices constructed at the cultural and economic centres of global power.

Critical ethnographers need to recognize that too often the notion of "otherness" is a means of marketing "savagery" in the name of research, an attempt to render "otherness" as the recrudescence of archaic barbarism, to culturally annex "them" for the benefit of "us." Why do white, male researchers think that they are less "ethnic" than the darker-skinned populations who are the objects of their research? While it is true that Eurocentric culture is based on a denial of its own violent, racist formation, we cannot really frame "researcher/other" as a binary opposition, since what we are witnessing in the exchange between the researcher and the research subject is a collaborative construction, not absolute differences (MacCannell, 1992). Within this construction, however, ethnographic researchers need to interrogate the repressed "Otherness" contained in their own presuppositions of identity as researchers so that such a collaboration does not work to undermine their emancipatory intentions and practices (cf., hooks, 1992).

In conclusion, I am arguing that ethnographic research must take into consideration its form of analysis sis a narrative practice that is institutionally bound, discursively situated, and geo-politically located. What critical postcolonial ethnography needs at the present historical moment is not simply another means of constructing a knowledge of the partial, the particular, and the contingent, but new forms of theoretical practice that can engage difference without absorbing, accommodating, homogenizing, or integrating it into the totalizing schemes of Western essentialist ethnographic practices. We need to resist facile forms of postmodern detailism and anecdotalism and refuse the appropriation of difference into totalizing identities by ontologizing Otherness and thereby sublating the Other within itself through a violent act of self-possession (R. Young, 1990). One way that ethnographers can avoid the tyranny of cultural imperialism is by fashioning themselves as ethical subjects who both acknowledge and respect the heterogeneity of the Other not by stepping outside Western culture but by using, as Robert Young (1990) suggests, "its own alterity and duplicity to effect its deconstruction" (p. 19). As critical ethnographers, we must take human agency beyond the curator's display case where lost histories are contained, itemized, and made unimpeachable by the colonizer's pen and recover the meaning of identity as a form of cultural struggle, as a site of remapping and remaking historical agency within a praxis of liberation. In this way, ethnography can serve both as a practical ethics and an ethics of practice that is never far removed from the frontiers of hope sought by those who still choose to struggle and to dream.

Acknowledgment

This chapter originally appeared as P. McLaren, Collisions with otherness: "Travelling" theory, post-colonial criticism and the politics of ethnographic practice – the mission of the wounded ethnographer, *International Journal of Qualitative Studies in Education*, 5(1) (1992), 77–92. Reprinted here, with minor edits, with permission from the publisher.

Notes

1 Some sections of this essay are expanded versions of McLaren (1991).
2 See the review essay of these books by Marcus (1990).

References

Agger, B. (1989). *Socio(onto)logy.* University of Illinois Press.
Anzaldúa, G. (1990). Making face, making soul: An introduction. In G. Anzaldúa (Ed.), *Making face, making soul* (pp. xv–xxviii). Aunt Lute Foundation Books.
Bennett, K. P., & LeCompte, M. D. (1990). *How schools work.* Longman.
Britzman, D. P. (1991). *Practice makes practice: A critical study of learning to teach.* State University of New York Press.
Butler, J. (1990). *Gender trouble.* Routledge.
Chambers, I. (1990). *Border dialogues: Journeys in postmodernity.* Routledge.
Clifford, J. (1987). Of other peoples: Beyond the "salvage" paradigm. In H. Foster (Ed.), *Discussions in contemporary culture: Number one* (pp. 121–130). Bay Press.
Clifford, J., & Marcus, G. E. (Eds.). (1986). *Writing culture: The poetics and politics of ethnography.* University of California Press.
Feldman, A. (1991). *Formations of violence: The narrative of the body and political terror in Northern Ireland.* University of Chicago Press.
Foucault, M. (1980). Truth and power. In M. Foucault, *Power/knowledge: Selected interviews and other writings 1972–1977* (G. Gordon, Ed.; pp. 109–133). Pantheon.
Frank, A. W. (1990). Bringing bodies back in: A decade review. *Theory, Culture, and Society, 7*(1), 131–162.

Giroux, H. A. (1988). *Schooling and the struggle for public life: Critical pedagogy in the modern age.* University of Minnesota Press.

Giroux, H. A. (1990). Postmodernism as border pedagogy: Redefining the boundaries of race and ethnicity. In H. A. Giroux (Ed.), *Postmodernism, feminism, and cultural politics: Redrawing educational boundaries* (pp. 217–256). State University of New York Press.

Grossberg, L. (1988). *It's a sin.* Power Publications.

Grossberg, L. (1992). *We gotta get out of this place.* Routledge.

Hammer, R., & McLaren, P. (1991). Rethinking the dialectic: A social semiotic perspective for educators. *Education Theory, 41*(1), 23–46.

Harland, R. (1987). *Superstructuralism: The philosophy of structuralism and poststructuralism.* Methuen.

hooks, b. (1992). bell hooks speaking about Paulo Freire: The man – his work. In P. McLaren & P. Leonard (Eds.), *Paulo Freire: A critical encounter.* Routledge.

Jackson, M. (1985). *Path towards a clearing: Radical empiricism and ethnographic inquiry.* Indiana University Press.

John, M. E. (1989). Postcolonial feminists in the Western intellectual field: Anthropologist and native informants? *Inscriptions, 5,* 49–74.

Kincheloe, J. (1991). *Teachers as researchers: Qualitative inquiry as a path to empowerment.* Falmer.

Lather, P. (1986). Research as praxis. *Harvard Educational Review, 56,* 257–277.

Lévinas, E. (1981). *Otherwise than being or beyond essence* (A. Lingis, Trans.). Martinus Nijhoff.

Litchman, R. (1982). *The production of desire.* Free Press.

Loriggio, F. (1990). Anthropology, literary theory, and the traditions of modernism. In M. Manganaro (Ed.), *Modernist anthropology: From fieldwork to text* (pp. 215–242). Princeton University Press.

MacCannell, D. (1992). *Empty meeting grounds.* Routledge.

Manganaro, M. (1990). Textual play, power, and cultural critique: An orientation to modernist anthropology. In M. Manganaro (Ed.), *Modernist anthropology* (pp. 3–47). Princeton University Press.

Marcus, G. E. (1990). [Review of *Paths toward a clearing: Radical empiricism and ethnographic inquiry, Culture and truth: The remaking of social analysis,* and *Romantic motives: Essays on anthropological sensibility*]. *Anthropologica, 32,* 121–125.

Mascia-Lees, F. E., Sharpe, P., & Cohen, C. B. (1989). The postmodern turn in anthropology: Cautions from a feminist perspective. *Signs, 15,* 7–33.

McLaren, P. (1986). *Schooling as a ritual performance: Toward a political economy of educational symbols and gestures.* Routledge and Kegan Paul.

McLaren, P. (1989). Schooling the postmodern body: Critical pedagogy and the politics of enfleshment. *Journal of Education, 170*(3), 53–83.

McLaren, P. (1991). Field relations and the discourse of the other. In W. B. Shaffir & R. A. Stebbins (Eds.), *Experiencing fieldwork* (pp. 149–163). Sage.

McLaren, P. (forthcoming). Critical literacy and postcolonial praxis: A Freirean perspective. *College Literature*.

Mihevc, J. (1989). Interpreting the debt crisis. *The Ecumenist, 28*, 5–10.

Minh-ha, T. T. (1987). Of other peoples: Beyond the "salvage" paradigm. In H. Foster (Ed.), *Discussions in contemporary culture: Number one* (pp. 138–141). Bay Press.

Minh-ha, T. T. (1988). Not you/like you: Post-colonial women and the interlocking questions of identity and difference. *Inscriptions, 3/4*, 71–77.

Minh-ha, T. T. (1989). *Woman, native, other: Writing postcolonialism and feminism.* Indiana University Press.

Parry, B. (1987). Problems in current theories of colonial discourse. *Oxford Literary Review, 9*, 27–58.

Patterson, D. (1990). Laughter and the alterity of truth in Bakhtin's aesthetics. In R. F. Barsky & M. Holquist (Eds.), *Bakhtin and otherness* [Special issue]. *Social Discourse, 3*, 295–310.

Robbins, B. (1990). Interdisciplinarity in public. *Social Text, 8/9*, 103–118.

Rosaldo, R. (1989). *Culture and truth: The remaking of social analysis.* Beacon.

Simon, R., & Dippo, D. (1988). On critical ethnography. *Anthropology and Education Quarterly, 17*, 195–202.

Spivak, G. C. (1989). Who claims alterity? In B. Kruger & P. Mariani (Eds.), *Remaking history* (pp. 269–292). Bay Press.

Spivak, G. C. (1990). *The post-colonial critic: Interviews, strategies, dialogues.* Routledge.

Stacey, J. (1988). Can there be a feminist ethnography? *Women's Studies International Forum, 11*, 21–27.

Stocking, G. W., Jr. (Ed.). (1989). *Romantic motives: Essays on anthropological sensibility.* University of Wisconsin Press.

Torgovnik, M. (1990). *Gone primitive: Savage intellects, modem lives.* University of Chicago Press.

Van Mannen, M. (1990). *Researching lived experience.* SUNY Press.

Walkerdine, V. (1986). Video replay: Families, films, and fantasy. In V. Burgin, J. Donald & C. Kaplan (Eds.), *Formations of fantasy* (pp. 167–199). Methuen.

Weedon, C. (1987). *Feminist practice and poststructuralist theory.* Basil Blackwell.

West, C. (1990). The new cultural politics of difference. In R. Ferguson, M. Gever, T. T. Minh-ha & C. West (Eds.), *Out there: Marginalization and contemporary culture* (pp. 19–36). MIT Press.

Young, I. M. (1990). *Justice and the politics of difference.* Princeton University Press.

Young, R. (1990). *White mythologies.* Routledge.

CHAPTER 8

On Dialectics and Human Decency
Education in the Dock

As critical educators we take pride in our search for meaning, and our metamorphosis of consciousness has taken us along many different paths, to different places, if not in a quest for truth, then at least to purchase a crisper and more perspicuous reality from which to begin a radical reconstruction of society through educational, political and spiritual transformation. What forces are at work to disable our quest are neither apparent nor easily discerned and critical educators have managed to appropriate many different languages with which to navigate the terrain of current educational reform. This article adopts the language of Marxist humanism, revolutionary critical pedagogy and Christian socialism.

What this article recriminates in official education is not only its puerile understanding of the meaning and purpose of public knowledge but its hypocrisy in advocating critical thinking – as in the case of the recent educational panacea known as 'common core' – but at the same time publicly suturing the goals of education to the imperatives of the capitalist marketplace. The idea of the new global citizen – cobbled together from a production line of critically-minded consumers who have been educated make good purchasing choices – is a squalid concept lost in the quagmire of bad infinity, and will only advance the notion that growth through the expansion of neoliberal capitalism automatically means progress. Critical pedagogy offers an alternative vision and set of goals for the education of humanity. Critical pedagogy is the lucubration of a whole philosophy of praxis that predates Marx and can be found in Biblical texts. If we wish to break from alienated labor then we must break completely with the logic of capitalist accumulation and profit, and this is something to which Marx and Jesus would agree.

It is no exaggeration to say that public education is under threat of extinction. The uneven but inexorable progress of neoliberal economic policies clearly provided the incubus for transferring the magisterium of education in its entirety to the business community. The world-producing power of the corporate media has not only helped to create a privatized, discount store version of democracy that is allied with the arrogance and greed of the ruling class, but it has turned the public against itself in its support of privatizing schools. The chiliasm of gloom surrounding public schooling that has been fostered by

© PETER MCLAREN, 2015

the corporate attack on teachers, teachers unions and those who see the privatization of education as a consolatory fantasy designed to line the pockets of corporate investors by selling hope to aggrieved communities, is not likely to abate anytime soon.

Erudite expositors on why the 'what', 'how' and 'why' of effective teaching understand that it cannot be adequately demonstrated by sets of algorithms spawned in the ideological laboratories of scientific management at the behest of billionaire investors in instrumentalist approaches to test-based accountability. At a time in which exercises in 'test prep' have now supplanted the Pledge of Allegiance as the most generic form of patriotism in our nation's schools, critical pedagogy serves as a sword of Damocles, hanging over the head of the nation's educational tribunals and their adsentatores, ingratiators and sycophants in the business community.

In an age of 'advocacy philanthropy', where the business elite and other financial opportunists sit comfortably at the helm of educational policy-making, where advocates for programs supported by funds from the student loan business to increase access to college for students who must borrow heavily to attend are not judged to be enemies of democracy but rather held up as examples of good citizenship, and where the overall agenda of educational reform is to establish alternatives to public education at public expense, we shudder at just how retrograde public education has become in their hands.

All of us indignantly reject social inequality as a major impediment to our goals of reforming the state through education, but many of us have chosen to follow a path that takes the struggle against inequality further than simply denouncing the peremptory mandates of austerity capitalism. My own goal has to use education to create critically-minded citizens willing and able to consider alternatives to capitalist value production. One of the major obstacles has been imputing to socialism false maxims that we socialists 'hate America' and attributing to us irreformably demonic characteristics – contemporary spin-offs that we are 'reds' hiding under America's 'beds'. One of the key problems here, of course, is the confusion of capitalism with market anarchy and socialism with planned production by a centralized state. The bulk of social wealth is consumed not by people but by capital itself. The answer is not to be found in exchange relations in the market but rather the domination of dead over living labor The inability of capitalism to reproduce its only value-creating substance – labor power – means that capitalism can be defeated. We need a philosophically grounded alternative to capitalism (Hudis, 2012).

The inexorable reprobation to which socialists have been subjected and their execration by the public-at-large has less to do with a willful ignorance than with a learned ignorance created through the decades by the corporate media, an ignorance that Chomsky famously coined as 'manufacturing consent'. This has led over time to an instinctive repugnance toward socialism and a knee-jerk anti-Marxism. The culpable absence of the public in looking beyond capitalism can be ascribed to many factors, but in particular to a motivated amnesia about the history of class struggle in the United States, to an unscrupulous crusade against welfare and social programs carried out by both Republicans and Democrats, and to a celebratory adherence to official doctrinal propaganda that claims that capitalism might be flawed but it is the only viable alternative for economic prosperity and democracy. The idea of a socialist alternative to capitalism is not an idea that needs to be immediately amenable to scientific investigation. Suffice that for the purposes of this article, we view it as moral exhortation – a categorical imperative, if you will – that some other sustainable form of organization has to be adopted in order for the planet to survive and human and non-human life along with it.

Clearly, this is a pivotal moment for humanity, when the meanings, values and norms of everyday life are arching towards oblivion, following in the debris-strewn wake of Benjamin's Angel of History; when human beings are being distributed unevenly across the planet as little more than property relations, as 'surplus populations'; when a culture of slave labor is increasingly defining the workaday world of American cities; when capital's structurally instantiated ability to supervise our labor, control our investments and purchase our labor power has reached new levels of opprobrium; when those who are habitually relegated to subordinate positions within capital's structured hierarchies live in constant fear of joblessness and hunger; and when the masses of humanity are in peril of being crushed by the hobnailed boots of storm trooper Capitalism. The winds of critical consciousness, enervated by outrage at the profligate use of lies and deceptions by the capitalist class – a class that gorgonizes the public through a winner-takes-all market fundamentalism and corporate-driven media spectacles – are stirring up the toxic debris from our austerity-gripped and broken humanity. Wearing the nationalist armor of settler-colonial societies, capitalism subordinates human beings to things, splitting human beings off from themselves, slicing them into pieces of the American Dream with the nonchalant dexterity of the Iron Chef wielding an eight-inch Honbazuka-processed knife.

Greg Palast (2013) has exposed what he calls the 'End Game Memo' which signaled part of the plan created by the top US Treasury officials to conspire 'with a small cabal of banker big-shots to rip apart financial regulation across the planet'. In the late 1990s, the US Treasury Secretary, Robert Rubin, and Deputy Treasury Secretary, Larry Summers, were frenetically pushing to deregulate banks, and they joined forces with some of the most powerful Chief Executive

Officers (CEOs) on the planet to make sure that this was accomplished. The 'end game' was tricky and seemed indomitable because it required the repeal of the Glass-Steagall Act to dismantle the barrier between commercial banks and investment banks. Palast describes it as 'replacing bank vaults with roulette wheels'. The banks wanted to venture into the high-risk game of 'derivatives trading' which allowed banks to carry trillions of dollars of pseudo-securities on their books as 'assets'. But the transformation of US banks into 'derivatives casinos' would be hampered if money fled US shores to nations with safer banking laws.

So this small cabal of banksters decided – and were successful – at eliminating controls on banks in every nation on the planet – in a single cunning stroke by using the Financial Services Agreement (FSA). The FSA was an addendum to the international trade agreements policed by the World Trade Organization that was utilized by the banksters to force countries to deal with trade in 'toxic' assets such as financial derivatives. Every nation was thus pushed to open their markets to Citibank, JP Morgan and their derivatives 'products'. All 156 nations in the World Trade Organization were pressured to remove their own Glass-Steagall divisions between commercial savings banks and the investment banks that gamble with derivatives. All nations were bribed or forced in other ways to comply and only Brazil refused to play the game. Of course, as Palast notes, the game destroyed countries like Greece, Ecuador and Argentina, just to name a few, and contributed catastrophically to the global financial crisis of 2008.

Amidst the turmoil and conflagration of the current historical moment, capitalism keeps a steady hand with the flippant arrogance of the most famous smirking apologist of US imperialism, William F. Buckley, his Yale-educated tongue wagging jauntily from the pillow-feathered cloud of his heavenly perch as he adroitly deploys his clipboard-prop gently upon his succulent lap, otherwise reserved for his King Charles spaniels. There seems to be nothing standing in the way of capitalism's continuation, save a few irritants in the alternative media that are flippantly swatted away from time to time, like flies on the arse of a barnyard goat. Today's unrelenting urgency of redeeming life from the belligerent forces of social reproduction – the internally differentiated expanding whole of value production, inside of which is coiled an incubus – marks a watershed in the history of this planet.

The paradigmatic innovation of anti-colonial analysis in North America has been significantly impacted by what has been taking place since capital began responding to the crisis of the 1970s of Fordist-Keynesian capitalism – which William Robinson (1996, 2000, 2004, 2008, 2011a, 2011b) has characterized as capital's ferocious quest to break free of nation-state constraints to accumulation and twentieth-century regulated capital (labor relations based on some [at least a few] reciprocal commitments and rights) – a move which has seen the development of a new transnational model of accumulation in which transnational fractions of capital have become dominant. New mechanisms of accumulation, as Robinson notes, include a cheapening of labor and the growth of flexible, deregulated and de-unionized labor, where women always experience super-exploitation in relation to men; the dramatic expansion of capital itself; the creation of a global and regulatory structure to facilitate the emerging global circuits of accumulation; and, finally, neoliberal structural adjustment programs which seek to create the conditions for unfettered operations of emerging transnational capital across borders and between countries.

In my work with teachers, education scholars, political activists and revolutionaries worldwide, I have repeatedly visited mean and lonely streets that span numerous counties, countries and continents. Whether I have been visiting the Roma district of Budapest, the barrios on the outskirts of Medellín, the cartel-controlled neighborhoods of Morelia or Juarez, the favelas of Rio or Sao Paulo, the crowded alleys of Delhi, the alleyways of Harbin (near the Siberian border), or the streets of South Central Los Angeles, I have encountered pain and despair among the many as a result of the exploitation by the few. Whether I have been speaking to hitchhikers caught in a snowstorm, Vietnam vets in overflowing homeless shelters, elderly workers in emergency warming centers whose food stamps had just been cut by Republican legislation, jobless men and women resting on pillows of sewer steam wafting through the cast iron grates of litter-strewn streets, a group of teenagers hanging out in strip malls festooned with faded pockmarked signs offering discount malt liquor, or day laborers crowded around hole-in-the-walls offering cheap pizza, I hear the same voices of desperation and resignation. Even in such concrete situations that reek of economic catastrophism, I would like to stress the importance of philosophy. That is, class struggle as cultivating a philosophy of praxis.

Class struggle appears not to be a popular topic in universities today, at least not throughout the United States. A fresh new breed of postmodern rebels festooned with brand-name-theory knock-offs and thrift-shop identity politics now exercise their fashionable apostasy in the new techno-mediated social factories known as universities. They are very much present in our graduate education programs through their postmodern theorizing of identity, which hinges on the linkage of identity-formation and the creation of a discount store version of democracy as a mixture of meritocracy and the American Dream. Rather than challenging the marriage of the university and the capitalist class or fighting for the emancipation of the oppressed worldwide through pedagogies of liberation that have a transnational reach, class antagonisms are universally normalized through the pettifoggery, the sophistry, the pseudo-profundities, the convulsions and casuistries of political disengagement and the vertigo-inducing terminology that has distinguished these disquieting hellions of the lecture hall over the past few decades – not to mention their dismissal of class struggle in favor of questions of ethnicity, race, gender and sexuality. This domestication of the economic and divine activation of the cultural has led to the exfoliation of some of the most verdant contributions of socialist pedagogy during these decades. From this vantage point, postmodernism appears to be an ideology of the prosperous, 'which itself is a product of the type of capitalism that arose in the imperialist core of contemporary capitalism during the "Golden Age of Capitalism" between 1945 and 1973' (Ahmad, 2011, p. 16). If, during these years of prosperity, creating a democracy embracive of economic equality in the United States was about as realistic as Astroland's Burger Man seizing the controls on the rocket ship that sat atop Gregory and Paul's Hamburgers on Coney Island, and orbiting it around the Statue of Liberty, then economic equality through education today is about as realistic as the National Rifle Association calling for a ban on assault weapons, or McDonalds eliminating the Big Mac. Much of the self-styled brigandage exercised by these postmodern outlaws involves turning away from the cultural and claiming to be materialists. But this so-called productive materialism grounded in immanence equates the material with the 'thing-ness' of signs, symbols, discourses, values – part of the cultural 'real' – rather than with how the mode of production of material life and social being determines consciousness. Teresa Ebert (2009) sees this move as a return to 18th century matterism that stipulates experience as the limit of what can be known.

Regrettably, in this milieu Marx's ideas become increasingly domesticated, and not all the blame lies with the postmodern hipsters of the seminar rooms. Marx's ideas have been increasingly ripped out of their revolutionary soil by decades of toxic bombardment by the corporate media and repotted in glass-house megastores where, under hydrofarm compact fluorescent fixtures, they can be deracinated, debarked and made safe for university seminars and condominium living alike, and made palatable for highly committed twenty somethings who like to whistle to ballpark tunes in their faux Victorian bathtubs.

Erstwhile radicals once sympathetic to Marx but who became disillusioned and disgusted by revelations about the Gulag, and traumatized by the failure of 'really existing socialism' worried that they would be condemned as dusty dilettantes still clinging to the paltry spirit of socialism (or worse, traduced as Stalinists). They decided instead to ride the new wave of postmodern social theory that embraced a linguistic turn and managed in turn to find comfortable abodes in literature and cultural studies departments. Positioning themselves thus enabled them both to smite the gross profligacy of the capitalist class and its command structure comprised of greedy corporatists and bankers with self-aggrandizing tirades and at the same time put paid to their academic critics by adopting a more digestible 'deconstruction'. This was a deft academic move that allowed them to assume a political agenda through a stringent labyrinth of explanations yet without dragging research and scholarship away from the compromise of incremental reformism. Here, the institutional framework informed by neoliberal assumptions is already prejudged as the only rational framework for a society bent on justice, and unwittingly supported by a postmodern embrace of playfulness and the undecidability of the sign.

Reveling in the sagacity of cultural criticism and eager to keep their gladiatorial attitude in tact without suffering an unsettling cost for their radicalism, these prodigies of cosmopolitan learning embraced an unutterably reactionary 'anti-foundationalism' that condemns all 'master narratives' of progress. Marx would occasionally find a polemical way into some of the debates but was mostly banished from serious consideration. And while the work of Marx is a bit more fashionable these days, with the current crisis of neoliberal capitalism, the postmodernists have to a large extent fallen into tacit agreement with their modernist adversaries and pushed themselves into self-limiting alliances with liberals. By leaving the challenge to capitalism untouched their politics eventually and unwittingly colludes with those whom they despise.

In the arena of educational reform, these defanged revolutionaries abrade the cause of their more militant colleagues often with self-serving maunderings and sententious commentary about educational reform that are mere coinages of the general currency used in mainstream educational debates, never challenging the primacy of capital. Here we need to recall the storied comment by Benjamin (1936) that those who call for a purely cultural or spiritual revolution without changing asymmetrical relations of power and privilege linked to class antagonisms can only be served by the logic of fascism and authoritarian political movements.

And then there are the Marxists who attempt to descry the positivity ensepulchered within the negativity of Hegel's absolutes but who are shunned for their embrace of a dialectics of transcendence (transcendence could lead to the Gulag again, it is much safer to remain in a politics of immanence). The Marxist-humanist position that emphasizes transcendence, the position to which I ascribe, holds that we are the flesh-and-blood idea of capital, waxed fat from our complicity in advancing class society and in doing so enabling millions to be exiled into Marx's reserve army of workers (the unemployed). Thus we need to break out of the social universe of value production by creating a democratic alternative.

My agnostic relationship to liberal modernity with its emphasis on the apolitical drama of personal development while crucifying class struggle on the altar of culture such that the politics of 'representation' is substituted for a politics of 'revolution', does not mean that I rely on some ghostly psychopomp for advice; rather, I ascribe to the concept of praxis (an ordered chaos or irrational regularity) without retreating into the hinterlands of metaphysics and in doing so express critical pedagogy in germinal form as a philosophy of praxis, steering a path between the Scylla of an intractable rationalism and the Charybdis of metaphysical ravings.

The annihilation of humanity that capitalism prosecutes with such an illustrious savagery is not some ramped-up bit of catastrophism, but the foundation of civilization's unfinished obelisk, against which we can only smash our heads in horror and disbelief. The chilling realization is that eco-apocalypse is not just some fodder for science fiction movie fans who revel in dystopian plots, but the future anterior of world history that is upon us. Under the guise of responsible job-producing growth ('jobs for the jobless'), we have an infestation of eco-fascisms, whose distracting sheen belies the horrors lurking underneath the surface. Preoccupied with the beautiful translucent hues of a soap bubble catching the noonday sun as it floats aimlessly down a seaside boardwalk, courtesy of a bulbous-nosed local clown, we fail to notice the fish floating upside down amidst the rank and stink of the nearby ocean sewage. As our biosphere goes, so goes the public sphere, including public schooling, with its mania for high-stakes testing, accountability, total quality management and a blind passion for privatization (which usually begins with private-public partnerships), effectively dismantling a public education system that it took 200 years to build.

Capitalism is more than the sheet anchor of institutionalized avarice and greed, more than excrement splattered on the coat-tails of perfumed bankers and well-heeled speculators – it is a 'world-eater' with an insatiable appetite. Capital has strapped us to the slaughter bench of history, from which we must pry ourselves free to continue our work of class and cultural struggle, creating working-class solidarity, an integral value system and internal class logic capable of countering the hegemony of the bourgeoisie, while at the same time increasing class consensus and popular support. Inherent in capitalist societies marked by perpetual class warfare and the capitalist mode of production is structural violence of a scale so staggering that it can only be conceived as structural genocide. Garry Leech (2012) has argued convincingly and with a savage aplomb that capitalist-induced violence is structural in nature and, indeed, constitutes genocide.

The hyperbolic rhetoric of the fascist imaginary spawned by the recent 2008 recession is likely to be especially acute in the churches and communities affiliated with conservative groups who want a return to the economic practices that were responsible for the very crisis they are now railing against, but who are now, of course, blaming it on bank bailouts, immigration and the deficit. Fascist ideology is not something that burrows its way deep inside the structural unconscious of the United States from the outside, past the gatekeepers of our everyday psyche; it is a constitutive outgrowth of the logic of capital in crisis that can be symptomatically read through a neoliberal individualism enabled by a normative, value-free absolutism and a neofeudal/authoritarian pattern of social interaction. The United States has managed to conjure for itself – mainly through its military might and the broad spectacle of human slaughter made possible by powerful media apparatuses whose stock-in-trade includes portraying the United States as a democracy under siege by evil forces that are 'jealous' of its freedoms – a way to justify and sanctify their frustrations and hatreds, and reconstitute American exceptionalism amidst the rampant violence, prolonged social instability, drug abuse and breakdown of the US family. Of course, all of this works in concert with the thunderous call of Christian evangelicals to repent and heed God's prophets, and to welcome the fact that the United States has been anointed as the apotheosis of divine violence. Plain-spoken declarations abound, dripping with apocalyptic grandiosity, for dismantling the barriers of church and state, and creating a global Christian empire. This should not sound unusual for a country in which rule by violence was the inaugurating law, and which has, through the century, marked its citizenry indelibly in their interactions with others.

In the midst of the current epochal crisis, the US Department of Education and its spokespersons in the corporate media are diverting us away from the central issues of the crisis of capitalism and the ecological crisis by turning our attention to the failure of public schools (McLaren, 2006, 2012). They propose, as a solution, to smash public schools and the commons by unleashing the hurricane of privatization (the term hurricane is metaphorically appropriate here in a double sense, since New Orleans went from a public school system to a charter school city after Hurricane Katrina [see *Democracy Now*, 2007]), causing unionized teachers to drop from 4700 to 500. Of course, this is not symptomatic only of the United States. We are facing the imperatives of the transnational capitalist class and so the challenge to public education is occurring on a transnational scale.

Yet violence is not simply linked to financial indexes, as frightening as those have been of late. Violence is more than a series of contingencies unleashed by the labor/capital antagonism that drives the engines of capitalism. It is more than a series of historical accidents transformed into a necessity. In fact, it is the very founding act of US civilization. While violence can be traced to worldwide social polarization linked to the phenomenon of capitalist over-accumulation and attempts by the transnational capitalist class to sustain profitmaking by means of militarized accumulation, financial speculation and the plundering of public finance (Robinson, 2008), it can also be traced historically to epistemologies of violence and linked to the genocides brought about by the invasion and colonization of the Americas (Grosfoguel, 2013). Here, violence can be viewed as foundational to the Cartesian logic of Western epistemology, as the universal truth upon which all our understandings of the world must rely. Such violence can be seen across a host of institutional structures, including education, and in particular through 'banking' approaches to teaching that preclude dialogue and thus privilege Western epistemology, omitting and systematically erasing other worldviews. Indeed, Paulo Freire would maintain that dialogue necessarily brings forth the epistemologies grounded in particular social positions. Not surprisingly, the historical conditions that have brought us to a place of Western domination are linked to 'undialogic' social relations (Grosfoguel, 2013).

Ramón Grosfoguel, Enrique Dussel, Aníbal Quijano and other decolonial thinkers have argued convincingly that the *ego cogito* ('I think, therefore I am') which underwrites Descartes's concept of modernity replaced the prior Christian dominant perspective with a secular, but God-like, unsituated and monolithic politics of knowledge, attributed mainly to white European men. The presumed separation and superiorization of mind over body of the *ego cogito* establishes a knowledge system dissociated from the body's positioning in time and space, and achieves a certitude of knowledge – as if inhabiting a solipsistic universe – by means of an internal monologue, isolated from social relations with other human beings (Grosfoguel, 2013). This *ego cogito* did not suddenly drop from the sky; it arose out of the historical and epistemic conditions of possibility developed through the *ego conquiro* ('I conquer, therefore I am'), and the link between the two is the *ego extermino* ('I exterminate you, therefore I am').

Grosfoguel and Dussel maintain that the *ego conquiro* is the foundation of the 'Imperial Being', which began with European colonial expansion in 1492, when white men began to think of themselves as the center of the world because they had conquered the world. The *ego extermino* is the logic of genocide/epistemicide that mediates the 'I conquer' with the epistemic racism/sexism of the 'I think' as the new foundation of knowledge in the modern/colonial world. More specifically, the *ego extermino* can be situated in the four genocides/epistemicides of the sixteenth century, which were carried out

> (1) against Muslims and Jews in the conquest of Al-Andalus in the name of 'purity of blood'; (2) against indigenous peoples first in the Americas and then in Asia; (3) against African people with the captive trade and

their enslavement in the Americas; (4) against women who practiced and transmitted Indo-European knowledge in Europe burned alive accused of being witches. (Grosfoguel, 2013, p. 77)

According to Grosfoguel (2013), these four genocides are interlinked and 'constitutive of the modern/colonial world's epistemic structures' and Western male epistemic privilege, and we can certainly see these genocides reflected in the founding of the United States, in particular the massacre of indigenous peoples, the transatlantic slave trade and the Salem witch trials.

This genocidal history has been repressed in the structural unconscious of the nation (the term 'structural unconscious' is taken from Lichtman, 1982). The assertion here is that the contradiction between the claims of ideology and the actual structure of social power, and the need to defend oneself against socially constructed antagonisms, is the primary challenge that faces the ego. The function of the structural unconscious is therefore to reconcile reality and ideology at the level of the nation state, and this requires conceptual structures to help citizens adjust to its genocidal history (McLaren, 1999; Monzo & McLaren, 2014). These structures comprise the foundations for coping strategies and are provided by the myths of democracy, rugged individualism and White supremacy that lie at the heart of US capitalist society. Racialized violence is the domestic expression of the American structural unconscious, whose function is to provide psychic power to the myth of America's providential history – that as a country it has been ordained by providence to democratize and civilize the heathen world. The structural unconscious is the lifeblood of the national religion of genocide (Monzo & McLaren, 2014). It continues to legitimize genocide, ecocide and epistemicide (the obliteration of indigenous ecosystems of the mind).

Today, we see this totalizing effect on America's structural unconscious as we live out our lives through the whims of the market, seeking happiness in an ever increasing consumption of things we feel we need and justifying our superficial existence as the 'successful' outcome of our 'hard work'. We have stopped questioning, and perhaps even caring as a society, why some people are more deserving than others of the basic necessities of life – food, health and dignity – and simply accepted the myth that some people do not work hard enough to get ahead, and that individual social ascendance based on presumed merits and motivation is just and right – that our existence alone is not sufficient to deserve basic human needs and that these must be 'earned'. Likewise, we have stopped questioning who benefits from the chaos that exists in particular communities, and have accepted that the natural world has been antiseptically cleaved and cordoned off into binary oppositions – wealthy/poor, white/of color – and that it is the providential role of the United States to 'democratize' by means of our mighty arsenal of weapons those populations who threaten our economic interests and geopolitical advantage. We operate, of course, by the divine mandate that mere mortals must simply accept – that accepting our role as the global policeman is 'God's will' and is as 'good' for us as it is for the rest of the world.

I wish to make a few comments about critical pedagogy as a lodestone through which we can consider how to organize the social division of labor and the realm of necessity, so as to enable humans to satisfy their social and individual needs. This is a daunting challenge, given that public education today is all but dead yet refuses to acknowledge its own demise, and its once proud luminaries fail to see how capitalism is one of the key factors that bears much of the responsibility. The terms of the debate over what to do with education's rotting carcass are selectively adduced by blue-chip brokers in the flora-stuffed, starched-linen breakfast rooms of expensive hotels to remind the public in opulently elusive ways that the importance of education today revolves around increasing the range of educational choices available to communities by privatizing education. Consequently, the debate today – which could only be described as death-haunted and excremental – has an uncompromisingly narrow and understocked conceptual vocabulary, consisting of pithy yet comparatively slippery terms such as 'free choice', 'common core', 'competency-based education' and 'accountability', all bound up in a supererogatory embrace of democracy. Competencies, which clearly define what students will accomplish to demonstrate learning for a workforce-related need, are an improvement in some ways – i.e. students can better pace themselves – but ultimately these competencies must be rendered measurable. All of these terms, of course, are endlessly retranscribable depending on what educational crisis happens to be the public's flavor of the month.

The emergence of Massive Open Online Courses, adaptive learning environments, peer-to-peer learning platforms, third-party service providers, and new online learning technology, and increased emphasis on learning outcomes and assessment, obscures the question of why we are educating students in the first place. Standardized testing occupies a world where the humanity of students is enslaved to a particular analytic structure, combining instrumental reason, positivism and one-dimensional objectivity. Its heteronomous dogma is all about increasing control of our external and internal nature, creating a reified consciousness in which the wounds of our youth are hidden behind the armor of instrumentality. Reason has become irrational as the animate is confused with the inanimate; students are turned into objects where the imprint of unbeing is left upon being.

Higher education pundits are propitious for saying that university education creates democratic citizens who are ready to take the hefty helm of government and steer it to glory. Yet the hysterical nucleus of capitalism – in which systems of higher education are inextricably embedded – is one in which the labor of the working class is alienated and in which the surplus value created by workers in the normal functioning of the economic process is appropriated by the capitalist. The workers are paid wages that are less than the price of the force of labor expended in their work. This value beyond the price of labor is surplus labor and is made possible only because the workers themselves do not possess the means of production. All the good works made possible by higher education are calamitously wasted in the pursuit of profit. While cautiously adjusting its role to the fluctuating needs of capital, and vigorously safeguarding its connections to corporate power, higher education has become unknowingly imprinted with an astonishing variety of reactionary social practices as it unsuccessfully tries to hide that it is in cahoots with the repressive state apparatuses and the military-industrial complex, and works to create the hive known as the national security state. Impecunious students are taught to be dedicated to the hive (as indentured servants as a result of soaring tuition fees), which is conditioned by the pathogenic pressures of profit-making. Within the hive, the capitalist unconscious turns murderously upon what is left of the Enlightenment as the irresolutely corporate conditions under which knowledge is produced reduce the products of the intellect to inert commodities. Higher education offers mainly on-the-cheap analyses of how capitalism impacts the production of knowledge and fails, in the main, to survey ways of creating an alternative social universe unburdened by value formation, and, in the end, offers us little more than a vision of a discount-store democracy. In making capitalism aprioristic to civilized societies, corporate education has replaced stakeholders with shareholders and has become the unthinkable extremity towards which education is propelled under the auspices of the cash nexus – propelled by a hunger for profit as unfillable as a black hole that would extinguish use value if allowed to run its course.

Under earlier dispensations, education had many names – it was paidea, it was critical citizenship, it was counter-hegemonic, it was transformational, it was a lot of things. Over time, its descriptions changed as its objects changed, and now it is distinguished by a special nomenclature most often drawn from the world of management and business. While critical educators have striven to formulate their work clearly, and have defended their arguments with formidable weapons of dialectical reasoning, there is a new call by some Marxists and eco-pedagogues to expand the struggle as anti-capitalist agitation. This is to be welcomed, of course, but education as a revolutionary process will likely not seem time-honored enough for most readers to take seriously, with the exception perhaps of the work of Paulo Freire, whose storied corpus of texts exerts a continuous subterranean pressure on the critical tradition, and amply and brilliantly demonstrates its best features.

And what of Obama? Do his policies demonstrate the best features of liberal democracy and so many of us had hoped? Clearly and without question, Obama has hurt education reform immeasurably. Obama has really carried over the George Bush Jr. initiatives and rebranded them with some cosmetic touches. You are not a good educational leader when your Race to the Top initiatives tie federal funds for states and localities to their use of assessments of national 'college and career readiness' standards; when you set yourself on a mission to privatize or quasi-privatize public schools through an expansion of charter schools; when you evaluate teachers by linking an individual teacher's salary and employment status to student test scores; or when you pink slip teachers and principals in schools that have been designated as failing schools; and especially when your entire philosophy of education is driven by the logic of assessment and competition that includes merit pay for teachers, etc. To use federal leverage to get your initiatives in place, to sow distrust of public schools and to give preferential treatment to charter schools (that do not do as well as public schools overall even though they can cherry-pick their students and can refuse to admit students with learning disabilities), to create such a mess that teacher drop-out rates are at an all time high – the voluntary drop out rate for teachers is higher than the failure rate of students as nationally, 16% leave after the first year and approximately 45% leave within five years – is to give educational reform another kick in the teeth. Whether it is a Democrat or Republican in the White House does not seem to matter – the Democratic will wear hobnailed boots to kick out your teeth, the Republicans will use army surplus store boots from the invasion of Iraq to do the job.

What punishment is due to war criminals such as Obama? Dipping his Aesopian tongue in kerosene and igniting it with a smoldering lump of coal from the fire around which Afghan tribal leaders sit to mourn the death of family members, whose families have lost relatives in Obama's drone attacks? Will there ever be any justice in this regard for two US presidents who, after September 11, 2001 (9/11), launched two wars that have killed more than a million people and contributed to ongoing instability and violence that continue to this day? If we can put aside for a moment the sentimental inducements that accompany discussions of 9/11 in the public square, there is another 9/11 that we need to take into consideration: September 11, 1973, when Richard Nixon and Henry Kissinger helped to orchestrate a coup of Salvador Allende's government in Chile. Mark Weisbrot quotes Richard Nixon on why he wanted the Allende socialist government to be overthrown:

> President Richard Nixon was clear, at least in private conversations, about why he wanted the coup that destroyed one [of] the hemisphere's longest-running democracies, from his point of view: 'The main concern in Chile is that [President Salvador Allende] can consolidate himself, and the picture projected to the world will be his success. [...] If we let the potential leaders in South America think they can move like Chile and have it both ways, we will be in trouble'. (Weisbrot, 2013)

Nixon and Kissinger led the way in Chile for a rule of terror by coup leader Augusto Pinochet, to whom they gave the green light to assassinate Allende and strategic assistance from the US military:

> The U.S. government was one of the main organisers and perpetrators of the September 11, 1973 military coup in Chile, and these perpetrators also changed the world – of course much for the worse. The coup snuffed out an experiment in Latin American social democracy, established a military dictatorship that killed, tortured, and disappeared tens of thousands of people, and for a quarter-century mostly prevented Latin Americans from improving their living standards and leadership through the ballot box. (Weisbrot, 2013)

The rule of terror in Chile, courtesy of the US government, is nothing new. The Vietnam War is closer to home for most Americans. Listening to the transcripts of White House tape recordings between President Nixon and his advisors on April 25, 1972, and May, 1972 leads us to believe that the outcome could have been much worse for the North Vietnamese:

President Nixon: How many did we kill in Laos?
National Security Adviser Henry Kissinger: In the Laotian thing, we killed about ten, fifteen [thousand] ...
Nixon: See, the attack in the North [Vietnam] that we have in mind ... power plants, whatever's left – POL [petroleum], the docks.... And, I still think we ought to take the dikes out now. Will that drown people?
Kissinger: About two hundred thousand people.
Nixon: No, no, no. I'd rather use the nuclear bomb. Have you got that, Henry?
Kissinger: That, I think, would just be too much.
Nixon: The nuclear bomb, does that bother you? I just want you to think big, Henry, for Christsakes. (Blum, 2014)

May 2, 1972:

Nixon: America is not defeated. We must not lose in Vietnam. The surgical operation theory is all right, but I want that place bombed to *smithereens*. If we draw the sword, we're gonna bomb those bastards all over the place. Let it fly, *let it fly*. (Blum, 2014)

I have advocated for a critical patriotism (McLaren, 2013) in my work in critical pedagogy, a pedagogy that would identify and condemn crimes against humanity perpetrated by the United States, as a way of avoiding future tragedies. As a way of countering the attitude of government advisors such as Michael Ledeen, former Defense Department consultant and holder of the Freedom Chair at the American Enterprise Institute, who opines sardonically: 'Every ten years or so, the United States needs to pick up some small crappy little country and throw it against the wall, just to show the world we mean business' (Blum, 2014). In high school history classes, we do not hear much about the US atrocities during the Philippine-American War (1899–1902), the coup in Chile or about Pinochet's feared Caribellos; or the assassinations of Catholic priests organizing cooperatives in the Guatemalan towns of Quetzaltenango, Huehuetenango, San Marcos and Solola; or the failed coup against the Venezuelan government of Hugo Chávez in 2002; or the role of the Central Intelligence Agency (CIA) in destabilizing Latin American and Middle Eastern regimes throughout the centuries; or the history of the United States as the supreme master of focused and unidirectional aggression, whose intransigent martial will has made it the most feared country in history. Nor do we learn about the Zapatista uprising which occurred as a result of government oppression in the towns of the Selva, Altos, Norte and Costa regions of Chiapas, and took place in San Cristobal de las Casas, Las Margaritas, Altamirano, Oxchuc, Huixtan, Chanal and Ocosingo, and involved Tzotzils, Tzeltals, Tojolabals, Chols, Mams and Zoques.

What is of most concern in teacher education programs is not the impact that neoliberal capitalism has had on the way the United States deals with questions of public and foreign policy, and the implications of this for developing a critical approach to citizenship. What occupies the curricula in teacher education is the question of race and gender and sexual identity formations. And while, in itself, this is an important emphasis, identity formation is rarely problematized against the backdrop of social class and poverty, and the history of US imperialism. I do not want to downplay the importance of the struggles over race or gender or sexuality, and the history of the civil rights struggle. But

I believe that it is necessary to see such antagonisms both in relationship to a geopolitics of knowledge and in terms of the ways in which capitalism has reconstituted itself over the years.

We do more than embrace the Geist of solidarity; we work towards its world-historical attainment in the pursuit of truth. A commitment to truth is never unproductive because no transformative act can be accomplished without commitment. No true act of commitment is an exit from the truth, but tramps down a path along which truth is won (Fischman & McLaren, 2005). I do not want to use my political imagination to create something new out of the debris of the old, because that leads us to adapt our revolutionary work to that which already exists. My concern is to struggle to change the conditions of what already exists and to liberate agency for its own conditions of possibility in order to create what was thought to be impossible.

1 A New Epistemological Alternative

To look mainly to the European social tradition for guidance in the belief that the struggle for a socialist alternative to capitalism is the monopoly of the West would be to succumb to the most crude provinciality and a truncated ethnocentrism. Thomas Fatheuer (2011) has examined recent innovative aspects in the constitutions of Ecuador and Bolivia. In Ecuador, for instance, the right to a 'good life' – *buen vivir* – becomes a central objective, a bread-and-butter concern that cannot be relinquished. One of the subsections of the constitution deals with the rights to nutrition, health, education and water, for example. The concept of the good life here is more than economic, social and cultural rights. It is a basic principle that 'forms the foundation of a new development model (*regimen de desarrollo*)' (Fatheuer, 2011, p. 16). Article 275 states: '*Buen Vivir* requires that individuals, communities, peoples and nations are in actual possession of their rights and exercise their responsibilities in the context of interculturalism, respect for diversity and of harmonious coexistence with nature' (cited in Fatheuer, 2011, p. 16). Fatheuer distinguishes the concept of *buen vivir* from the Western idea of prosperity as follows:

> *Buen Vivir* is not geared toward 'having more' and does not see accumulation and growth, but rather a state of equilibrium as its goal. Its reference to the indigenous world view is also central: its starting point is not progress or growth as a linear model of thinking, but the attainment and reproduction of the equilibrium state of *Sumak Kausay*. (Fatheuer, 2011, p. 16)

Both Bolivia and Ecuador have utilized their constitutions to re-establish their states in a postcolonial context and are committed to the concept of plurinationalism and the preservation of nature. Here, the state promotes the ethical and moral principles of pluralistic society:

> *amaqhilla, ama llulla, ama suwa* (do not be lazy, do not lie, do not steal), *suma qamana* (*vive bien*), *nandereko* (*vida armoniosa* – harmonious life), *teko kavi* (*vida buena*), *ivi maraei* (*tierra sin mal* – Earth without evil, also translated as 'intact environment'), and *qhapaj nan* (*Camino o vida noble* – the path of wisdom). (Fatheuer, 2011, pp. 17–18)

The concept of *Pachamama* ('Mother Earth') and the rights of nature play a special role, designed to put human beings and nature on a foundation of originality, mutuality and dialogue, and the Defensoria de la Madre Tierra statute is designed to 'monitor the validity, promotion, dissemination and implementation of the rights of *Madre Tierra*', and forbid the marketing of Mother Earth (Fatheuer, 2011, p. 18). Here it is stipulated that the earth has a right to regenerate itself. It is important to point out that *buen vivir* is not a return to ancestral, traditional thinking, but is a type of *ch'ixi*, or a concept where something can exist and not exist at the same time – in other words, a third state where modernity is not conceived as homogeneous, but as *cuidadania*, or 'difference'; a biocentric world view that permits the simultaneous existence of contradictory states without the need for resolution towards a given pole, and that conceives of life in a way which is not informed by the opposition of nature and humans (Fatheuer, 2011). New indigenous discourses in Bolivia and those articulated by the Confederation of Indigenous Discourses of Educador advocate for an integral philosophy and a new plurinational, communitarian, collective, egalitarian, multilingual, intercultural and bio-socialist vision of sustainable development. They fight against a capitalism that militates against harmony inside and between society and nature (Altmann, 2013). Interculturality is seen as a relational and a structural transformation and an instrument of decolonization. It is something that must be created and it refers not only to groups but also structures based on respect, cultural heterogeneity, participative self-representation, communitarian forms of authority, mutual legitimacy, equity, symmetry and equality, and is applicable to monoethnic and multiethnic territories. Here, interculturality in combination with plurinationality is linked to a postcolonial refoundation of the modern state (Altmann, 2012).

John P. Clark (2013), in his magnificent work *The Impossible Community*, has offered an array of possible approaches to take from the perspective of communitarian anarchism. These include a revised version of the libertarian municipalism of the late Murray Bookchin, the Gandhian Sarvodaya movement in India, and the related movement in Sri Lanka called Sarvodaya Shramadana – the Gandhian approach to self-rule and voluntary redistribution of land as collective property to be managed by means of the *gram sabha* ('village assembly') and the *panchayat* ('village committee'). Sarvodaya Shramadana offers four basic virtues: *upekkha* ('mental balance'), *metta* ('goodwill towards all beings'), *karma* ('compassion for all beings who suffer') and *mundita* ('sympathetic joy for all those liberated from suffering'). Clark's (2013) work focuses on the tragedies and contradictions of development and his discussion of India is particularly insightful (see especially pp. 217–245 and the eloquently informative review of Clark's book by Sethness, 2013). More familiar to teachers are perhaps the examples of the Zapatistas and the Landless Peasants' Movement in Brazil. Clark mentions, as well, the indigenous Adivasi struggles and those by Dalits, fighting the paramilitaries of the transnational mining communities in India.

Instead of reducing citizens and non-citizens alike to their racialized and gendered labor productivity, as is the case with the neoliberal state apparatus, we wish to introduce the term *buen vivir* as an opposing logic to the way we approach our formation as citizen-subjects. We would advise the guardians of the neoliberal state – especially those who are now in the 'business' of education – to look towards *Las Americas* for new conceptions of democratic life that could serve as a means of breaking free from the disabling logic of neoliberalism that now engulfs the planet – a new epistemology of living that has so far not been a casualty of the epistemicide of the conquistadores past and present. We still adhere to the proposition that the human mind lives in a largely self-created world of illusion and error, a defective system of false reality from whence we can be rescued only by the development of a critical self-reflexive subjectivity and protagonistic agency. But we would add that such self-creation occurs under conditions not of our own making. Many of those conditions have been created by social relations of production and the way in which neoliberal capitalism has produced nature-human relations as a total world ecology linked to a racialized social division of labor and hyper-nationalism. Critical consciousness here becomes the inverse equivalent of the ignorance of our false consciousness under capitalist social relations of exploitation and alienation. Hence, we seek a social universe outside of the commodification of human labor, a universe deepened by direct and participatory democracy and a quest for *buen vivir*. Clearly, while we need a new epistemology of *buen vivir* and of Sarvodaya Shramadana to help stave off the epistemicide of indigenous knowledges by means of violent Eurocentric practices, we also need a class struggle of transnational reach.

If the new generation is to help throw off the chains forged by the centuries-old dogma of the capitalist class, then we cannot leave this challenge only to our youth. We need to offer them hope, but hope at the expense of truth can turn optimism into feelings of omnipotence and can lead to a fatal outbreak of hubris. We need to conjugate our hope with seeking new pathways to justice, despite the grim reality that the odds are not in our favor, and perhaps never will be.

Critical revolutionary pedagogy is non-sectarian and emphasizes ecumenical approaches, attempting to incorporate a Marxist humanist critique of alienation under capitalism into the doxa of critical pedagogy – a move that recognizes consciousness and external reality as consitutively entangled, and asserts that there must be an ethical dimension which gives priority to the oppressed, thereby rejecting many of the 'diamat' tendencies that held sway in the former Soviet Union and Eastern bloc countries. Such tendencies maintained that they could uncover a transparent reflection of reality and that a focus on human consciousness, self-management and agency within popularly based social movements was unscientific, and that the central focus should be on social relations of production. By contrast, human agency and human needs are not conceptualized by Marxist humanists as secondary or epiphenomenal to objective social forces. Consequently, reform and revolution are not mutually antagonistic relationships, but must be understood in a dialectical relationship to each other. Dialectics does not juxtapose reform and revolution, but mediates them as a 'both-and' relationship rather than an 'either-or' relationship. The same is true with ecology and the grounding antagonism between capital and labor, such that class struggle is at one and the same time an ecological struggle, taking to heart the Earth First slogan that there can be 'no jobs on a dead planet'.

Even the illustrious Marcuse in his Great Refusal (his analysis of the predatory capitalist system and neoconservatism or what he referred to as 'counterrevolution') displaces the dialectical quality of classical Hegelian and Marxist philosophy, betraying an incapacity to overcome contradiction in his lurching towards a metaphysical or antinomial (neo-Kantian) posture in which he vacillates between two poles of a contradiction, poles of which he regards as antiseptically independent rather than interpenetrating; at times he seemed tragically resigned to the perennial permanence of contradiction and paradox (Reitz, 2000). Here we can benefit from Marx's focus on Hegel's concept of self-movement through second negativity, which leads him to posit a vision of a new society that involves the transcendence of value production as determined by socially necessary labor time. Unlike the popular misconception about Marx's critique of Hegel – that Hegel's idealism was opposed to

Marx's materialism – Marx did not criticize Hegel for his failure to deal with material reality. When Marx noted that Hegel knows only abstractly spiritual labor, he was referring to the structure of Hegel's *Phenomenology* and philosophy as a whole, which was based on a dialectic of self-consciousness, in which thought returns to itself by knowing itself (Hudis, 2012). Marx's concept of transcendence, on the contrary, was grounded in human sensuousness, in the self-transcendence of the totality of human powers. Dialectics deals with the transformative contradictions that power the material historicity of capitalist life.

Hegel presented the entire movement of history in terms of the unfolding of the disembodied idea; in other words, he presented human actuality as a product of thought instead of presenting thought as the product of human actuality. Marx, therefore, inverts the relations of Hegel's subject and predicate. Marx criticized Hegel for failing to distinguish between labor as a trans-historical, creative expression of humanity's 'species being' and labor as the reduction of such activity to value production. We need to understand the dialectic, the description of the means by which reality unfolds, the nature of self-activity, self-development and self-transcendence, and the way that human activity subjectively and temporally mediates the objective world.

The presence of the idea – as negation – in human consciousness has the power to alter the natural world. Marx was not interested in the returning of thought to itself in Hegel's philosophy, but the return of humanity to itself by overcoming the alienation of the objective world brought about by capitalist social relations. In other words, the human being is the agent of the Idea; the Idea is not its own agent. The human being is the medium of the Idea's self-movement. Self-movement is made possible through the act of negation by negating the barriers to self-development. But negation, as Peter Hudis (2012, pp. 72–73) tells us, is always dependent on the object of its critique. Whatever you negate still bears the stamp of what has been negated – that is, it still bears the imprint of the object of negation. We have seen, for instance, in the past, that oppressive forms which one has attempted to negate still impact the ideas we have of liberation. That is why Hegel argued that we need a self-referential negation – a negation of the negation. By means of a negation of the negation, negation establishes a relation with itself, freeing itself from the external object it is attempting to negate. Because it exists without a relationship to another outside of itself, it is considered to be absolute – it is freed from dependency on the other. It negates its dependency through a self-referential act of negation. For example, the abolition of private property and its replacement with collective property does not ensure liberation; it is only an abstract negation which must be negated in order to reach liberation. It is still infected with its opposite, which focuses exclusively on property. It simply replaces private property with collective property and is still impacted by the idea of ownership or having (Hudis, 2012, pp. 71–73). Hudis writes:

> [Marx] appropriates the concept of the 'negation of the negation' to explain the path to a new society. Communism, the abolition of private property, is the negation of capitalism. But this negation, Marx tells us, is dependent on the object of its critique insofar as it replaces private property with collective property. Communism is not free from the alienated notion that ownership or having is the most important part of being human; it simply affirms it on a different level. Of course, Marx thinks that it is necessary to negate private property. But this negation, he insists, must itself be negated. Only then can the truly positive – a totally new society – emerge. As Dunayevskaya writes in P&R [*Philosophy and Revolution* (1973)], 'The overcoming of this "transcendence," called absolute negativity by Hegel, is what Marx considered the only way to create a truly human world, "positive Humanism, beginning from itself"'. (Hudis, 2005)

However, in order to abolish capital, the negation of private property must itself be negated, which would be the achievement of a positivity – a positive humanism – beginning with itself. While it is necessary to negate private property, that negation must itself be negated. If you stop before this second negation then you are presupposing that having is more important than being (Hudis, 2012). Saying 'no' to capital, for instance, constitutes a first negation. When the subject becomes self-conscious regarding this negation – that is, when the subject understanding the meaning of this negation recognizes the positive content of this negation – then she has arrived at the negation of the negation. In other words, when a subject comes to recognize that she is the source of the negative, this becomes a second negation, a reaching of class consciousness. When a subject recognizes the positivity of the act of negation itself as negativity, then she knows herself as a source of the movement of the real. This occurs when human beings, as agents of self-determination, hear themselves speak, and are able both to denounce oppression and the evils of the world and to announce, in Freire's terms, a liberating alternative. I fully agree with Reitz (2000, p. 263) that critical knowledge 'is knowledge that enables the social negation of the social negation of human life's core activities, the most central of which are neither being-toward-death [as Heidegger would maintain], nor subservience [as Kant would argue], but creative labor'. When subjects create critical knowledge, they then are able to appropriate freedom itself for the sake of the liberation of humanity (Pomeroy, 2004).

Life does not unfold as some old sheet strewn across a brass bed in the dusky attic of history; our destinies as children, parents, and teachers do not flow unilaterally toward a single vertigo-inducing epiphany, some pyrotechnic explosion of iridescent and refulgent splendor where we lay becalmed, rocking on a silent sea of pure bliss, or where we are held speechless in some wind-washed grove of cedars, happily in the thrall of an unbridled, unsullied and undiluted love of incandescent intensity. Our lives are not overseen by a handsome God who blithely sits atop a terra cotta pedestal and with guileless simplicity, quiet paternalism and unsmiling earnestness rules over his eager and fumbling brood, ever so often rumpling the curly heads of the rosy-cheeked cherubim and engaging the saints in blissful conversation about quantum theory. Were there such a God, wrapped in the mantle of an otherworldly Platonism and possessing neither moral obliquity nor guilt, who brings forth the world through supernatural volition alone, the world would be nothing but an echo of the divine mind. Hunger could be ended by merely thinking of a full belly and sickness eliminated by a picture of perfect health.

Most of us, however, sling ourselves nervously back and forth across the great Manichean divide of the drab of everyday existence, where, in our elemental contact with the world, our human desires, for better or for worse, tug at us like some glow-in-the-dark hustler in a carnival midway. We go hungry, we suffer, and we live in torment and witness most of the world's population crumpled up in pain. We do not have to witness a final miracle of eschatological significance to reclaim the world. What we do have to accomplish at this very moment is organizing our world to meet the basic needs of humanity.

2   Comrade Jesus: Christian Communism Reborn?

But the same message of meeting the needs of humanity was prevalent in the Bible, and occupied the message of Jesus. I do not suddenly mention this out of some otherworldly penchant, but for a concern for the here and the now. The majority of American citizens are Christians of some denomination or other and it is important to point out as an incontrovertible fact that the message of Jesus in the Gospels is focused on the liberation of the poor from captivity and oppression, thus in Luke 4:18–19: 'The Spirit of the Lord is upon me, because he has anointed me to preach good news to the poor. He has sent me to proclaim release to the captives and recovering of sight to the blind, to set at liberty those who are oppressed, to proclaim the acceptable year of the Lord.' Jesus was very much opposed to oppression and bondage and it was no secret that he excluded the wealthy from the kingdom of God, noted in this very clear passage from Matthew 19:16–24 (this authentic logion of Jesus is also described in Mark 10:17–25 and Luke 18:18–25):

> And, behold, one came and said unto him, Good Master, what good thing shall I do, that I may have eternal life? And he said unto him, Why do you ask me about what is good? there is none good but one, that is, God: but if thou wilt enter into life, keep the commandments. He saith unto him, Which? Jesus said, Thou shalt do no murder, Thou shalt not commit adultery, Thou shalt not steal, Thou shalt not bear false witness, Honor thy father and thy mother: and, Thou shalt love thy neighbour as thyself. The young man saith unto him, All these things have I kept from my youth up: what lack I yet? Jesus said unto him, If thou wilt be perfect, go and sell that thou hast, and give to the poor, and thou shalt have treasure in heaven: and come and follow me. But when the young man heard that saying, he went away sorrowful: for he had great possessions. Then said Jesus unto his disciples, Verily I say unto you, That a rich man shall hardly enter into the kingdom of heaven. And again I say unto you, It is easier for a camel to go through the eye of a needle, than for a rich man to enter into the kingdom of God.

Many of us – either openly or secretly – harbor a religious faith that often remains hidden between the lines of our manifestos and treatises. I have often maintained the position that the official church of Jesus has been implicated in the indefensible falsification of the gospel in order to protect the hierarchies of the church. But here I wish to amplify this idea by briefly summarizing the important work of José Porfirio Miranda. Miranda's work skillfully corroborates his own analysis of the Bible with those of ecclesiastically sanctioned studies by recognized and prominent Catholic exegetes. According to Miranda (1977, p. 203), Christian faith is supposed to 'transform humankind and the world'. Miranda (1980, 2004) claims the persecution of Christians for the first three centuries constrained Christians to present a version of Christianity that would no longer provoke repression. After the fourth century, the church acquired a dominant status in class society, and this was what then motivated the continuing falsification of the gospel.

The official teachings of the church falsify the gospel, since it is clear from reading the texts of the Bible that Jesus maintains an intransigent condemnation of the rich. Even liberation theology gets this wrong when it asserts that there should be a 'preferential option for the poor' – it is not an option, but, as Miranda notes, it is an obligation. We cannot shirk from this obligation without imputation of culpability and still remain Christians. There is no abstention from this struggle. The condition of the poor obliges a restitution since such a struggle is injustice writ large (Miranda, 1974). Jesus died for participating in political transgression aimed at liberating Judea from the Romans. According to Miranda, Jesus clearly was a communist, and this can convincingly be seen throughout the New Testament but particularly in passages such as John 12:6, 13:29 and Luke 8:1–3. Jesus went so far as to make the renunciation of property a condition for entering the kingdom of God. When Luke says, 'Happy the poor, for yours is the Kingdom of God' (Luke 6:20) and adds, 'Woe to you the rich, because you have received your comfort' (Luke 6:24), Luke is repeating Mark 10:25 when Jesus warns that the rich cannot enter the kingdom. The Bible makes clear through Jesus' own sayings that the kingdom is not the state of being after death; rather, the kingdom is now, here on earth. Essentially Jesus is saying that 'in the kingdom there cannot be social differences – that the kingdom, whether or not it pleases the conservatives, is a classless society' (Miranda, 2004, p. 20). Consider what Luke says in Acts:

> All the believers together had everything in common; they sold their possessions and their goods, and distributed among all in accordance with each one's need. [Acts 2:44–45]

> The hear of the multitude of believers was one and their soul was one, and not a single one said anything of what he had was his, but all things were in common.... There was no poor person among them, since whoever possessed fields or houses sold them, bore the proceeds of the sale and placed them at the feet of the apostles; and a distribution was made to each in accordance with his need. [Acts 4:32, 34–35]

Jesus did not say that the poor will always be with us, he said that the poor are with us all the time. Miranda (2004, pp. 58–60) cites numerous translation sources attesting that this statement should be translated as 'The poor you have with you at all moments [or continuously]. And you can do them good when you wish; on the other hand, you do not have me at all moments' [Mark 14:7]. According to Miranda (2004, p. 65), Jesus did not say 'my kingdom is not of this world' he said 'my kingdom does not come forth from this world' or 'my kingdom is not from this world' since we can retain the original meaning only if we consider the preposition 'ek' in the original Greek as meaning 'from', signifying place of origin or provenance. But did not Jesus advocate paying taxes? Rendering unto Cesar what is due Cesar? Jesus' remark about giving Cesar what is due Cesar is decidedly ironic, and not a capitulation to Roman authority (Miranda, 2004, pp. 61–65). Consider the following quotation cited by Miranda (2004, p. 53) concerning economic transactions found in the Bible:

> For the sake of profit, many have sinned; the one who tries to grow rich, turns away his gaze. Stuck tight between two stones, between sale and purchase, sin is wedged. [Ecclus 27:1–2]

Miranda (2004, p. 54) notes that Biblical scripture condemns the term 'interest' (the Hebrew word is 'neshet') numerous times: Exodus 22:24; Leviticus 25:36, 37; Deuteronomy 23:19 (three times); Ezekiel 18:8, 13, 17, 22:12; Psalm 15:5; Proverbs 28:8. And numerous times profit-making through commerce, loans at interest, and productive activity itself (the process of production) is condemned (production likely here referring to agriculture). Does not James condemn the acquisition of wealth by agricultural entrepreneurs (see James 5:1–6)? And does he not, in fact, attack all the rich (James 1:10–11)? In James 2:6 does he not say: 'Is it not the rich who oppress you and who hail you before the tribunals?' Does he not also say: 'See, what you have whittled away from the pay of the workers who reap your fields cries out, and the anguish of the harvesters has come to the ears of the Lord of Armies' (James 5:4)? Does it now surprise us that Jesus would call money, 'money of iniquity' (Luke 16:9, 11)? On this issue Miranda (2004, p. 55) writes:

> What this verse is doing is explaining the origin of wealth. Its intention is not to refer to *some* particularly perverse rich people who have committed knaveries which other rich people do not commit. The letter's attack is against *all* the rich.

This is the biblical reprobation of differentiating wealth as Luke vituperates those who have defrauded workers and impugns all the rich. According to Miranda (2004, p. 53), profit 'is considered to be the source of (differentiating) wealth'. Miranda continues:

> For James, differentiating wealth can be acquired only by means of expropriation of the produce of the workers' labor. Therefore, following Jesus Christ and the Old Testament, James condemns differentiating wealth without vacillation or compromise. Profit made in the very process of production is thus specifically imprecated. (Miranda, 2004, p. 55)

Miranda (2004, p. 73) explains further what this implies: 'Where there is no differentiating wealth, where economic activity is directly for the purpose of the satisfaction of needs and not for trade or the operations of buying and selling for profit, government becomes unnecessary'. The Bible attacks not only acquired wealth but the means by which such wealth is accumulated, which is the taking of profit or what could be considered a form of systemic or legalized exploitation. Even the prophets such as Micha and Amos understood that 'no differentiating wealth can be acquired without spoliation and fraud' (Miranda, 2004, p. 40). Miranda notes: 'If we want to know "Why communism?" the response is unequivocal: because any other system consists in the exploitation of some persons over others' (2004, p. 55). Miranda sees Jesus as the true God grounded in himself, meaning grounded in the establishment of justice and life now, at this very moment, since 'the hour is coming and it is now'. Miranda is uncompromising when he notes:

> A god who intervenes in history to elicit religious adoration of himself and not to undo the hell of cruelty and death that human history has become is an immoral god in the deepest sense of the word. A god who is reconciled or merely indifferent to the pain of human beings is a merciless god, a monster, not the ethnical God whom the Bible knows. We would be morally obliged to rebel against such a god, even if our defeat were inevitable. Equally immoral is the god for whom the end of injustice and innocent suffering is a secondary or subordinate imperative. (Miranda, 1977, p. 187)

The key point in Miranda's theological argument is that the eschaton has already arrived, the eschaton of justice and life for all, in the example of Jesus Christ. If Christians do not believe that the eschaton has already come, then they relegate Jesus to a nontemporal and eternal or Platonic realm – but the historical moment of salvation is not repeatable since Jesus is the definitive 'now' of history. If this were not the case, 'then the imperative of love of neighbor becomes an intro-self concept. It does not speak as a real otherness, because anodyne time, even if it is present, truly has no reason to command me more than any other time' (Miranda, 1977, p. 192). Christians cannot postpone the commandment to love their neighbor in the fathomless future, because this would make of God an unassimilable otherness, a perpetual language game in which postmodernists would love to participate without a commitment to any political imperative. And thus we could never be contemporaneous with God. Eternal life is not life after death but the defeat of death, that is, the defeat of suffering and injustice in the here and now. Of course, what should be condemned are the totalitarian police states that *claimed* to be communist (such as the Soviet Union) but which were, in the final instance, formations of state capitalism (see Dunayevskaya, 1992). William Herzog's various attempts at developing an historical-critical approach to investigate adequately the historical Jesus began with examining the eschatological-existential and theological-ethical meanings of the parables of Jesus. Herzog considered these approaches insufficient and it finally led him to reject such approaches in favor of a Freirean 'problem-posing' approach that involved a dialectical understanding of the parables of Jesus, i.e., reading them as microscenes within the macroscenerio in which they were told. Finally, Herzog (1994) attempted to understand these parables in relation to the social and economic world of agrarian societies and the political world of aristocratic empires. The major findings of Herzog's experiment revealed that the parables of Jesus were created to problematize systems of oppression and that the center of Jesus's spirituality was the call to social justice.

Jesus was likely no quietist who publicly repudiated his Messianic role, avoided political involvement and rejected the idea of leading a nationalist movement against the Romans. What is clear is that he was executed for sedition at the hands of the Romans and if he were not a Zealot, then is likely he was sympathetic to many of their principles (Brandon, 1967). For those Christians – especially the prosperity evangelicals who are so popular in the United States – who promote capitalism and equate faith with wealth, it would serve them well to reconsider their interpretation of the gospels and to consider the fact that communist predated Karl Marx through the teaching of the Bible (Miranda, 1974, 2004).

No matter how strained we may become in fathoming the calamity of capitalist globalization and its attending antagonisms, we cannot banish the harrowing realities of our times or thrust them out of mind by taking refuge in our books, our theories, our seminar rooms, or in the salons of our organizing committees. We have, after all, a new era to proclaim. Here educators committed to social transformation through incremental means can take heed from the words of Miranda:

> The true revolutionary abjures reformist palliatives, because these divert the efforts of the people most capable of fomenting rebellion against the bourgeois system into rejuvenating and refurbishing it; such palliatives thus constitute the system's best defense. By the same token, the revolutionary must find any change in the socioeconomic system to be a priori inadequate, if that change does not involve a radical revolution in people's attitudes towards each other. If exchange-value (that 'imaginary entity') and the desire for personal gain continue to exist, they will inevitably create other oppressive and exploitative economic systems. (Miranda, 1977, pp. 21–22)

The revolution is now, it is the dialectic regained and it is the people unchained.

Acknowledgments

This essay is a modified version of a recent article called 'Education Agonistes' that was published in *Policy Futures in Education* (McLaren, 2014a). It is also a reworking of a longer article, based on 'Education Agonistes' called 'Comrade Jesus: An epistolic manifesto' to be published in *Knowledge Cultures* (McLaren, 2014b). I have borrowed some sections of my own work from the following sources: 'Foreword' in *Inclusive Practices and Social Justice Leadership for Special Populations in Urban Settings: A Moral Imperative* (McLaren, 2015), and a promotional blurb for the book, *The Mis-measure of Education* by Jim Horn and Denise Wilburn (2013).

This chapter originally appeared as P. McLaren, On dialectics and human decency: Education in the dock, *Open Review of Educational Research,* 2(1) (2015), 1–25. Reprinted here, with minor edits, with permission from the publisher.

References

Ahmad, A. (2011). On post modernism. *The Marxist, 28* (January–March), 4–38.

Altmann, P. (2012). *The concept of interculturality in Ecuador – Development and importance for its agents* (Center for Area Studies Working Paper Series No. 1/2012). Center for Area Studies, Freie Universität Berlin.

Altmann, P. (2013). Good life as a social movement proposal for natural resource use: The indigenous movement in Ecuador. *Consilience: The Journal of Sustainable Development, 10*(1), 59–71.

Benjamin, W. (1936). The work of art in the age of mechanical reproduction. http://www.marxists.org/reference/subject/philosophy/works/ge/benjamin.htm

Blum, W. (2014). Edward Snowden (Anti-Empire Report, 129, June 6). http://williamblum.org/aer/read/129

Brandon, S. G. F. (1967). *Jesus and the zealots.* Charles Scribner's Sons.

Clark, J. P. (2013). *The impossible community: Realizing communitarian anarchism.* Bloomsbury.

Democracy Now. (2007, August 30). The privatization of education: How New Orleans went from a public school system to a charter school city. http://www.democracynow.org/2007/8/30/the_privatization_of_education_how_new#

Dunayevskaya, R. (1992). *The Marxist-humanist theory of state capitalism.* The News & Letters Committee.

Ebert, T. (2009). *The task of cultural critique.* University of Illinois Press.

Fatheuer, T. (2011). *Buen Vivir: A brief introduction to Latin America's new concepts for the good life and the rights of nature* (Heinrich Boll Foundation Publication Series on Ecology, vol. 17). Berlin: Heinrich Boll Foundation.

Fischman, G. E., & McLaren, P. (2005). Rethinking critical pedagogy and the Gramscian and Freirean legacies: From organic to committed intellectuals or critical pedagogy, commitment, and praxis. *Cultural Studies ↔ Critical Methodologies, 5*(4), 425–446. https://doi.org/10.1177/1532708605279701

Ford, G. (2014, March 5). Hillary and other assorted Barbarians at Russia's gate. *Black Agenda Report.* http://blackagendareport.com/content/hillary-and-other-assorted-barbarians-russia%E2%80%99s-gate

Grosfoguel, R. (2013). The structure of knowledge in Westernized universities: Epistemic racism/sexism and the four genocides/epistemicides of the long 16th century. *Human Architecture, 11*(1), 73–90.

Herzog, W. R. (1994). *Parables as subversive speech: Jesus as pedagogue of the oppressed.* Westminster/John Knox Press.

Horn, J., & Wilburn, D. (2013). *The mismeasure of education.* Information Age Publishers.

Hudis, P. (2005). Marx's critical appropriation and transcendence of Hegel's theory of alienation. Presentation to Brecht Forum, New York City, November.

Hudis, P. (2012). *Marx's concept of the alternative to capitalism.* Haymarket Books.

Leech, G. (2012). *Capitalism: A structural genocide.* Zed Books.

Lichtman, R. (1982). *The production of desire: The integration of psychoanalysis into Marxist theory.* Free Press.

McLaren, P. (1999). *Schooling as a ritual performance: Toward a political economy of educational symbols and gestures.* Rowman & Littlefield.

McLaren, P. (2006). *Rage and hope: Interviews with Peter McLaren on war, imperialism, and critical pedagogy.* Peter Lang.

McLaren, P. (2012). Objection sustained: Revolutionary pedagogical praxis as an occupying force. *Policy Futures in Education, 10*(4), 487–495. doi:10.2304/pfie.2012.10.4.487

McLaren, P. (2013). A critical patriotism for urban schooling: A call for a pedagogy against fear and denial and for democracy. *Texas Education Review, 1,* 234–253. http://txedrev.org/wp-content/uploads/2013/11/McLaren_A-Critical-Patriotism-for-Urban-Schooling_TxEdRev.pdf

McLaren, P. (2014a). Education Agonistes: An epistle to the transnational capitalist class. *Policy Futures in Education, 12*(4), 583–610.

McLaren, P. (2014b). The dialectic regained. *Knowledge Cultures, 2*(6).

McLaren, P. (2015). Foreword. In K. Esposito & A. Normore (Eds.), *Inclusive practices and social justice leadership for special populations in urban settings: A moral imperative.* Peter Lang.

Miranda, J. P. (1974). *Marx and the Bible: A critique of the philosophy of oppression.* Orbis Books.

Miranda, J. P. (1977). *Being and the Messiah: The message of St. John.* Orbis Books.

Miranda, J. P. (1980). *Marx against the Marxists: The Christian humanism of Karl Marx.* SCM Press.

Miranda, J. P. (2004). *Communism in the Bible* (R. R. Barr, Trans.). Wipf & Stock.

Monzo, L. D., & McLaren, P. (2014). Critical pedagogy and the decolonial option: Challenges to the inevitability of capitalism. *Policy Futures in Education, 12*(4), 513–525. doi:10.2304/pfie.2014.12.4.513

Palast, G. (2013, August 24). Confidential memo at the heart of the global financial crisis. *Vice Magazine.* http://readersupportednews.org/opinion2/279-82/19053-confidential-memo-at-the-heart-of-the-global-financial-crisis

Pomeroy, A. F. (2004). Why Marx, why now? A recollection of Dunayevskaya's *Power of negativity. Cultural Logic, 7.* http://clogic.eserver.org/2004/pomeroy.html

Reitz, C. (2000). *Art, alienation, and the humanities: A critical engagement with Herbert Marcuse.* State University of New York Press.

Robinson, W. I. (1996). *Promoting polyarchy: Globalization, US intervention, and hegemony.* Cambridge University Press.

Robinson, W. I. (2000). Social theory and globalization: The rise of a transnational state. *Theory and Society, 30*(2), 157–200. doi:10.1023/A:1011077330455

Robinson, W. I. (2004). *A theory of global capitalism: Production, class, and state in a transnational world.* Johns Hopkins University Press.

Robinson, W. I. (2008). *Latin America and global capitalism.* Johns Hopkins University Press.

Robinson, W. I. (2011a, May 8). Global capitalism and 21st century Fascism. *Aljazeera.* http://www.aljazeera.com/indepth/opinion/2011/04/201142612714539672.html

Robinson, W. I. (2011b, December 4). Global rebellion: The coming chaos? *Aljazeera.* http://www.aljazeera.com/indepth/opinion/2011/11/2011130121556567265.html

Sethness, J. (2013, June 16). The structural violence that is capitalism. *Truthout.* http://www.truth-out.org/opinion/item/16887-the-structural-genocide-that-is-capitalism

Weisbrot, M. (2013, September 14). Forty years on, much of Allende's dream has come true: The United States no longer has the same hegemonic stranglehold over countries within Latin America. *Aljazeera.* http://www.aljazeera.com/indepth/opinion/2013/09/2013913174222513256.html

CHAPTER 9

Rethinking Critical Pedagogy and the Gramscian and Freirean Legacies

From Organic to Committed Intellectuals or Critical Pedagogy, Commitment, and Praxis

Gustavo E. Fischman and Peter McLaren

1   Points of Departure

One of the now commonplace claims of critical pedagogy during its nearly 30-year history in the United States is that both the failures and successes of education are constructed in and through people's linguistic, cultural, social, and behavioral interactions, which are constrained and enabled by social relations of production and dominant cultural formations, ideological apparatuses, and institutional practices (Heras, 1999). These interactions are also shaped by the ways in which members of specific social groups understand, perceive, and act in, through, and on reality. For educators who work within the tradition of critical pedagogy, it is not enough to understand any given educational reality; there is a pedagogical mandate to transform it with the goal of radically democratizing educational sites and societies through a shared praxis. By emphasizing the importance of understanding and transforming pedagogical and social realities, it also points to the intrinsic relationship between education and the production and reproduction of labor-power.

A central and related aspect of critical pedagogy is the role of educators in the process of educational critique. Henry A. Giroux (1992) has described educators as "transformative intellectuals" because they take a critical stance toward their own practice and the practice of others to engage in debate and inquiry. In doing so, educators become active in shaping the curriculum, having a role in shaping school policy, defining educational philosophies, and working with their communities in diverse capacities. Transformative intellectuals are aware of their own theoretical convictions and are skilled in strategies for translating them into practice (Giroux, 1992, 2002). Giroux builds here on the Gramscian concept of praxis, or theoretically oriented action, and that of the intellectual, who has a prominent role to play in promoting an agenda for change.

Giroux's perspective presents several ideas and notions that are widely embraced by those associated with critical pedagogy. The social and political

© SAGE, 2005

dimensions of schooling, the need to understand and transform schools and society, and the key role that educators in these processes play are core themes shared by many critical educators. Although it is hard to quantify or even qualify the influence of critical pedagogues in North America, it would be hard to deny that as a collective movement it has produced one of the most dynamic and controversial educational schools of thought of the past 30 years.

The main goal of this article is to revisit the contributions of Antonio Gramsci and Paulo Freire to the foundational concept of ideology and related concepts of hegemony and the intellectual, with the aim of rethinking critical pedagogy and the notion of teachers as transformative intellectuals. It is our intention to rethink Gramsci's and Freire's contributions in a way that will be consistent with Borg and Mayo's (2002) warning against "scriptural readings" of texts.

We will argue that one of the advantages of using Gramsci's and Freire's framework in the complex task of rethinking critical pedagogy is that both authors made a vital departure from the concept of ideology as an inert compendium of static and agreed-on ideas to the concept of ideology as embodied, lived, and dynamic sets of social practices. In this conceptualization, ideologies connected to a broader system of intelligibility linked to the cultural logic of capitalism contribute to the development of hegemonic relations and regimes and are dialectically co-constructed by individuals and the social classes, groups, and institutions of which they are a part.

2   Points of Departure 1: Ideology and Hegemony

To grasp the complex relationship between ideology and hegemony, both constructs need to be seen as parallax relations, that is, from the perspective of the social agent at the present moment, with the understanding that this site of enunciation is in itself dialectically conditioned by this interplay. For Gramsci, a dominant class or class alliance necessarily requires two forms of control – coercion (sustained by politically regulated repression) and consent – in order to achieve hegemonic status. These forms of control function catalytically as allied practices that stipulate an ethical dimension tied to the forces of production. According to Gramsci,

> every state is ethical in as much as one of its most important functions is to raise the great mass of the population to a particular cultural and moral level, a level (or type) which corresponds to the needs of the productive forces of development, and hence to the interest of the ruling

> classes. The school as a positive educative function, and the courts as a repressive and negative educative function, are the most important State activities in this sense. (p. 258)

Hegemonic relationships not only play an ethical role but also a pedagogical one. Gramsci (1971) made it clear that "every relationship of hegemony is necessarily a pedagogical relationship" (p. 350) because

> a class is dominant in two ways, i.e., 'leading' and 'dominant'. It leads the classes which are allies, and dominates those which are its enemies. One should not count solely on the power and material force which such position gives in order to exercise political leadership or hegemony. (p. 57)

As a Marxist intellectual, Gramsci (1971) never failed to stress the importance of economic relations, insisting that the economy determines, in the last instance, the nature, type, and reach of the compromises and agreements that can be achieved among the dominant groups and the popular sectors. He further clarifies this point as follows:

> It is undoubtedly the fact that hegemony presupposes that account be taken of the interests and the tendencies of the groups over which hegemony is to be exercised, and that a certain compromise equilibrium should be formed – in other words that the leading group should make sacrifices of an economic corporate kind. But there is also no doubt that such sacrifices and such a compromise cannot touch the essential; for though hegemony is ethical-political, it must also be economic, must necessarily be based on the decisive function exercised by the leading group in the decisive nucleus of economic activity. (p. 161)

However, the notion of hegemonic rule was not well developed in Gramsci (Borg et al., 2002). Walter Adamson (1980) notes that the relationship between hegemony, state power, and forms of political legitimization was at times ambiguous and used in several different (and sometimes contradictory) senses:

> It is used, first of all, in a morally neutral and instrumental sense to characterize those bourgeois regimes that have proved capable of organizing mass consent effectively. But it is also used in an essentially ethical sense to characterize the functioning of a proletarian regulated society. Here is another instance in which the attempt to incorporate Machiavellian and

ethical state traditions raises perplexing and unresolved questions. Is the sort of consent being obtained the same in both cases? Or is consent in a bourgeois hegemony somehow passive and noncritical, while under proletarian auspices it would be active, participatory, and philosophical? If so, what more fully is the institutional basis of this latter sort of control? (p. 242)

We find that the Gramscian dichotomy of force and consent is not nearly sufficient or comprehensive enough to allow us to examine the complex character of hegemonic rule because these two terms do not permit a detailed analysis of the nuances and forms of political legitimization. Consequently, it makes more sense to view the terms *force* and *consent* in Adamson's (1980) terms: as "endpoints of a continuum that includes such intermediate positions as constraint (e.g., fear of unemployment), co-optation, and perhaps even Arendt's category of authority'" (p. 243).

In our view, Gramsci's (1971) work can help us in understanding the class contradictions that structure the subjectivities and self-activity (agency) of oppressed classes with the understanding that hegemony does not take place in an indeterminate terrain (Katz, 1997). In light of Gramsci's work, there is a need to understand the overdetermination of self-activity and subjective agency by larger structures of capitalist social relations within the global division of labor (especially in the context of a restructured labor demand). The concept of hegemony that is articulated by many post-Marxists is often recognized as a type of *trompe l'oeil* whereby forces of domination are willfully under-recognized as the structured equanimity of inevitability, chance, or irreversible fate. Historically, variable structural determinants of action are either detached from cultural formations and social practices or flatly ignored. Built into a number of theories of hegemony is the notion of the reversibility of cultural formations within specified conjunctures, as if such articulatory practices were asocial or ahistorical or otherwise severed from the chains of class determination. According to Katz (1997), this is clearly a misunderstanding of Gramsci and omits the entire problem of domination. Misappropriations of Gramsci's work (especially with the "radical democracy" school) have effectively caused domination to hemorrhage into a pool of relational negotiations in which certain ideological positions are won through consent. Here, we need to be reminded that intellectuals themselves are always the products of new forms of collective labor power brought about and consolidated by the forces of production.

Whereas Gramsci (1971) often stressed as a defining attribute the spirit or the will, Marx gave pride of place to production. Gramsci emphasized human consciousness as a defining attribute of humanity. Consciousness, akin to spirit, was linked to the notion of history as a form of becoming. Organized will becomes the basis of his philosophy. Although Gramsci acknowledges the link between humanity and production, he does not sufficiently emphasize the most important aspect of humanity's "complex of social relations": the satisfaction of human needs and the human necessity to produce (Hoffman, 1984). The satisfaction of human needs is the primary historical act and must be accomplished before men and women are in the position to make history. The human necessity to produce and reproduce thus underwrites all social relationships. For Gramsci, humanity is defined by concrete will, will plus historical circumstances, whereas for Marx, humanity is a response to and product of social and historical circumstances that are not primarily dependent on human will. Human relationships thus exist independently of the way in which people understand them. "Classical Marxism examined closely the repressive function of the class state, whereas Gramsci stressed the integrative function" (Brosio, 1994, p. 50).

The focus on the integrative function of the state is perhaps the key to understanding why, as Terry Eagleton (1991) maintains, Gramsci associates hegemony with the arena of civil society. This term is used by the Italian revolutionary to indicate a wide range of institutions that serve as intermediaries between the state and the economy: the church, schools, the press, the family, hospitals, political parties, and so on. We agree with John Holst (2002) that many leftist scholars have uncritically adopted a civil societarian view of Gramsci, underestimating Gramsci's attempt to connect civil society to the state. Here, we disagree fundamentally with the strict civil societarian view of Gramsci because Gramsci clearly saw civil society as part of the state. Both were "located in the superstructure that for Marxism has always been the domain of the state in the hands of the ruling class" (Holst, 2002, p. 106). Because Gramsci identified civil society as an arena used by the ruling class to exert its hegemony over the society, the struggle for Gramsci was not to transform civil society but rather, as Holst points out, "to build proletarian hegemony" (p. 106).

For our own purposes, it should be stressed that hegemony is as much related to antagonistic processes as it is to consensual individual and social practices of negotiation and/or exchanges that take place not only in the realm of the civil society but also in the everyday actions of families, the state, and the various political arenas. Ernesto Laclau and Chantal Mouffe (1986) argue that the concept of hegemony was originally tied to "an essentialist logic" in which only one authentic historical subject, "the working class," was able to develop truly counterhegemonic policies and practices. In their view, such a logic, rather than advancing the project of social change and social justice, covered over and obstructed multiple forms of struggle developed by several groups and social movements (e.g., those developed by indigenous peoples, ethnic groups, women, ecologists, human rights activists), which could not be reduced to or categorized according to the exclusive basis of the class position of their members. However, instead of throwing the baby out with the bathwater, Laclau and Mouffe propose to free the concept of hegemony of any kind of essentialism and reappropriate the potentially emancipatory characteristics of the concept. Best and Kellner (1991) maintain that for Laclau and Mouffe,

> hegemony entails a detotalizing logic of articulation and contingency that refuses the conception of the *a priori* unity or the progressive character of the working class or any other subject position. Rather, cultural and political identities are never given in advance, but must be constituted or articulated, from diverse elements. (p. 195)

Similar to the position articulated by Laclau and Mouffe (1986), Stuart Hall (1996; Hall & Donald, 1986) situates the Gramscian challenge as the struggle for a new social order. Hall's use of the term *articulation* is presented as a theoretically fecund means by which the double emphasis of Gramsci – that is, the emphasis on culture and structure, on ideology and material social relations – may be joined. What this double movement through the concept of articulation has achieved has been to conceptualize class and cultural struggles as interwoven and richly articulated (we will provide a critique of Hall's concept of articulation later in our discussion).

According to this formulation, groups and classes exist in a shifting and mediated relationship, in a structured field of complex relations and ideological forces stitched together out of social fragments and privileging hierarchies, in structured asymmetries of power, in contending vectors of influence, and in emergent, contingent alliances. When one examines ideology, one must not look for smooth lines of articulation or a set of seamless canonical ideas, but rather a regime of culture existing as a palimpsest of emergent and residual discourses. Hall's (1996) eloquent position on this issue is worth quoting at length:

> Gramsci always insisted that hegemony is not exclusively an ideological phenomenon. There can be no hegemony without "the decisive nucleus of the economic." On the other hand, do not fall into the trap of the old mechanical economism and believe that if you can only get hold of the economy, you can move the rest of life. The nature of power in the modern world is that it is also constructed in relation to political, moral, intellectual, cultural, ideological and sexual questions. The question of

> hegemony is always the question of a new cultural order. The question which faced Gramsci in relation to Italy faces us now in relation to Britain: what is the nature of this new civilization? Hegemony is not a state of grace which is installed forever. It's not a formation which incorporates everybody. The notion of a "historical bloc" is precisely different from that of a pacified, homogeneous, ruling class. It entails a quite different conception of how social forces and movements, in their diversity, can be articulated into strategic alliances. To construct a new cultural order, you need not to reflect an already-formed collective will, but to fashion a new one, to inaugurate a new historical project. (p. 170)

Along with Stuart Hall, Ernesto Laclau and Chantal Mouffe (1986) have developed a conception of hegemony as an ever-evolving set of political, economic, ideological, and cultural processes by which the dominant social sectors (or hegemonic bloc) elicit consent from the popular sectors. And yet hegemony is inseparable from conflicts and struggles over it. In this process, the struggle for control over the symbolic and economic domains of any given society and the role the state plays in such struggles cannot be diminished. The problem with the view of hegemony articulated by Laclau, Mouffe, and Hall is that in their emphasis, to distance themselves from what they consider to be a crude economism, they often seriously neglected the fundamental social contradiction between capital and labor and resecured the prohibitions on challenging the contradictions of capitalism while at the same time positing cultural struggles associated with changes in the mode of accumulation, exchange, and circulation of capital as superordinate over material relations of exploitation linked to production (i.e., to the extraction of surplus labor from workers who have nothing else to sell but their capacity to labor, their labor power).

Richard Brosio (1994) highlights Gramsci's realization "that hegemony must be ultimately anchored in economic strength – and ultimately physical power" (p. 48). Brosio also reminds us that although the state uses a combination of force and consent to maintain hegemony, it is important not to forget "that the exercise and maintenance of hegemony over subaltern groups is still a variation of class struggle" (p. 50). Brosio further cautions us not to forget the relationship of power to the educative aspects of hegemony:

> There is a tendency to stress Gramsci's important development of hegemony, the role of persuasion and consent, the seemingly willing participation by subaltern groups in their own domination; however, he was not naive about the relationship of power to this persuasive hegemony. (p. 49)

The characteristics of consent and coercion that underwrite Gramsci's model of hegemonic domination are fundamentally dynamic categories. Because they are dynamic rather than static relationships, they admit the possibility of rearticulation into counterhegemonic practices. We must not forget Gramsci's (1971) firm conviction "that ordinary men and women could be educated into understanding the coercive and persuasive power of capitalist hegemony over them" (pp. 49–50). And this means acknowledging the roots of capitalist exploitation as located within the extraction of surplus value from the surplus labor of workers by owners and the potential for resistance that resides with workers on whom the system of capital depends (even in the technology-driven world of the so-called information economy that supposedly thrives on "immaterial" labor).

3   Points of Departure II: Resistance, Agency, and the Organic Intellectual

The distinctive presence of the notions of collective will and consciousness in Gramsci's work are closely related to his concepts of resistance and agency. Gramsci described resistance as largely passive and unconscious and suggested that as any political movement develops, agency replaces resistance:

> If yesterday the subaltern element was a thing, today it is no longer a thing but a historical person, a protagonist; if yesterday it was not responsible because "resisting" a will external to itself, now it feels itself to be responsible because it is no longer resisting but an agent, necessarily active and taking the initiative. But was it ever mere "resistance", a mere "thing", mere "non-responsibility"? Certainly not. (p. 337)

Gramsci (1971) also argued that some intellectuals, particularly those who could be described as traditional, mistakenly understand the popular sectors as merely agents who resist hegemonic processes and who "don't even expect that the subaltern will become directive and responsible" (p. 337). Gramsci deeply understood the importance of the articulation of knowledge with passion and commitment, evidenced in the following remarks:

> the intellectual's error consists in believing that one can know without understanding and even more without feeling and being impassioned (not only for knowledge in itself but also for the object of knowledge): in other words that the intellectual can be an intellectual (and not a pure pedant) if distinct and separate from the people-nation, that is without

> feeling the elementary passions of the people, understanding them and therefore explaining and justifying them in the particular historical situation and connecting them dialectically to the laws of history and to a superior conception of the world, scientifically and coherently elaborated – i.e. knowledge. (p. 418)

For Gramsci, resistance was a sign of (subaltern) discontent rather than a conscious effort to promote social change. An immediate question uncoils: How is it possible to turn mere resistance into agency? The organic intellectual (specialized intellectuals each class develops) was Gramsci's answer.

Gramsci (1971) took up the challenge of articulating the extent to which the working class could generate its own intellectual force, building on his well-known conviction that "all men are intellectuals [...] but not all men have in society the function of intellectuals" (p. 9). His solution, the "organic intellectual," took a collective character within a working-class social formation in which the role of theory was organically linked with the ebb and flow of daily proletarian life. In this view, intellectuals should become an elaborate, historical expression of traditions, culture, values, and social relations. As Boggs (1984) notes, quasi-Jacobin ideological functions were still important intellectual tasks but now were required to be centered within the proletarian milieu (factories, community life, and culture). In this respect, intellectuals would be organic to that milieu only if they were fully immersed in its culture and language. Intellectuals therefore carried out universal functions that situated social activity within local and specific class struggles and in the defense of class interests. In effect, Gramsci was able to overcome conceptual positions based on a mechanical separation between the intellectual and popular realms, a position clearly demonstrated in the following commentary:

> the popular element "feels" but does not always know or understand; the intellectual element "knows" but does not always understand and in particular does not always feel. The two extremes are therefore pedantry and philistinism on the one hand and blind passion and sectarianism on the other. Not that the pedant cannot be impassioned; far from it. Impassioned pedantry is every bit as ridiculous and dangerous as wildest sectarianism and demagogy. [...] One cannot make politics-history without this passion, without the sentimental connection between intellectuals and people-nation. In the absence of such a nexus the relations between the intellectual and the people-nation are, or are reduced to, relationship of purely bureaucratic and formal order; the intellectuals become a caste, or a priesthood. (p. 418)

Gramsci, like Paulo Freire years later, urged intellectuals to develop a relational knowledge of and with the masses to help them become self-reflective. His unsurpassed understanding of the relationship between theory and practice stipulated an active participation in their social quotidian struggles and an investment in their future well-being. Hence, Gramsci (1971) urged intellectuals to live their intellectual lives in a state of ongoing praxis:

> The mode of being of the new intellectual can no longer consist in eloquence, which is an exterior and momentary mover of feelings and passions, but in active participation in practical life, as constructor, organizer "permanent persuader" and not just a simple orator. (p. 10)

Gramsci (1971) believed that intellectuals need to develop not only intellectual capital to engage with and on behalf of the masses but the social capital of trust and collective will necessary to bring about community-based liberatory praxis. Gramsci was constantly preoccupied by a concern that popular revolt would be absorbed into the prevailing hegemony or else mobilized into the direction of reactionary fascism.

Gramsci (1971) did not believe, like the anarchists and syndicalists of his day, that mass consciousness, or common sense, was innately rebellious. For Gramsci, mass consciousness was contradictory and rather formless by necessity, and the construction of a collective political will was always gradual and uneven and part of a counterhegemonic movement in which intellectuals play an increasingly important role. The challenge for Gramsci "was how to move beyond social immediacy without at the same time destroying spontaneous impulses" (pp. 40–41) so that common sense became good sense and spontaneity was transformed into critical consciousness.

4 Points of Departure III: From Organic to Committed Intellectuals

Working-class organic intellectuals were, for Gramsci, a fundamentally important expression of working-class life, critical agents that serve as vehicles for interrogating emergent patterns of thought and action, radicalizing subaltern groups, translating theory into strategy, and creating revolutionary subjectivity through the formation of continuous and multifaceted counterhegemonic activity and the development of a revolutionary historical bloc where divergent interests converge and coalesce around shared visions and objectives.

Although Gramsci (1971, p. 258) considered all individuals to be intellectuals, not all of them held positions or fulfilled the functions traditionally assigned to and developed by intellectuals. Most importantly for Gramsci, organic intellectuals of the working class not only resist hegemonic processes, but they also attempt to displace the old hegemonic order by leading their class or popular front into more elaborate forms of understanding capital's incessant drive for self-expansion, the antagonistic relation between labor and capital, and the political and ideological process of class rule. At the same time, organic intellectuals serve as role models who open the horizons of their class or popular front to secure a more equitable system of societal organization, which Gramsci believed must take the form of a socialist society that is committed to uprooting value production and breaking from capital's pernicious logic.

The role of the organic intellectual was to mediate between the good sense of subaltern groups and the formation of a counterhegemonic consciousness that can read the contextually specific and historically conjunctural contradictions inherent in society. According to Carroll and Ratner (1994), Gramsci

> held that all people are intellectuals in capacity, if not function. He believed that counter-hegemonic leadership emanates from intellectuals whose organic ties to subaltern groups enable them to achieve a unity of theory and practice and of thinking and feeling, thus mediating between the abstract and concrete in a manner foreign to traditional scholastic, ecclesiastic, and political elites. For Gramsci, the role of the intellectual is that of organizer and facilitator: instead of bringing correct consciousness to the masses "from without," the organic intellectual facilitates the practical movement from "good sense" (which resistant subordinates already possess) to a broader, counter-hegemonic consciousness that is sensitive to the specific conditions of a social formation at a given conjuncture. (p. 12)

In the search for the limits of what it means to be an intellectual, there exists among some scholars a lucid mistrustfulness of Gramsci's (1971) materialism. These scholars focus on Gramsci's concern with the intellectual function rather than on the function of the intellectual. As Ernesto Laclau (1990) has pointed out,

> the intellectual for Gramsci is not a segregated intellectual group but one that establishes the organic unity among a group of activities that, if left to themselves, would remain fragmented and dispersed. A union activist, in that sense, would be an intellectual. (p. 204)

Laclau (1990) emphasizes, however, that the process of building organic unity is not about the function of the intellectual but about the intellectual function. It is not focused on a class, nor can it be the exclusive preserve of an elite. Rather, it has the potential of emerging at all points of any social network: churches, hospitals, court houses, schools, and street corners; and once we accept the intellectual task as a function, does it matter who these intellectuals are and what their specific function in the larger social totality happens to be? Does it matter if they are priests, physicians, notaries, lawyers, teachers, nurses, dropouts, or gang members?

For Gramsci (1971), and also for Paulo Freire, political pedagogical actions are not an exclusive function of having the right knowledge but also of faithfulness to the event, in other words, of being in the right place at the right time. Is this a popular expression of the rejection of intellectual tasks? Not necessarily. This understanding deals with the ethical privilege of "being there" over "being something." By focusing on the relationships developed through hegemonic and counterhegemonic modalities, Gramsci highlighted the paradoxical practices in which the popular sectors engage, and he shows only one way out of this paradox. If society is to become democratic, the organic intellectuals of the popular classes must possess both knowledge of the problems facing them as well as practical solutions to those problems.

Gramsci (1971) saw democracy as essentially a dialectical movement between individual agency and structural location:

> But democracy, by definition, cannot mean merely that an unskilled worker can become skilled. It must mean that every "citizen" can "govern" and that society places him, even if only abstractly, in a general condition to achieve this. Political democracy tends towards a coincidence of the rulers and the ruled (in the sense of government with the consent of the governed) ensuring for each non-ruler a free training in the skill and general technical preparation necessary to that end. (pp. 40–41)

On one hand, Gramsci (1971) believed that the working class and the peasants (i.e., popular classes) are the only real determinant historical subjects that are able to effectively resist, challenge, and transform the hegemonic position of the bourgeoisie even though the popular classes have developed a contradictory consciousness that ultimately does not allow the elaboration of autonomous decisions or choices. On the other hand, organic intellectuals, on their own merits, are able to construct other models of consciousness in political and cultural arenas, and it is this process that, for Gramsci, constitutes the key to overcoming the shortcomings of these popular classes:

> Critical self-consciousness means, historically and politically, the construction of an *elite* of intellectuals. A human mass does not "distinguish"

> itself, does not become independent in its own right without, in the widest sense, organizing itself; and there is no organization without intellectuals, that is without organizers and leaders, in other words, without the theoretical aspect of the theory-practice nexus being distinguished concretely by the existence of a group of "specialized" in conceptual and philosophical elaboration of ideas. (p. 334)

One of the main challenges of Gramsci's (1971) framework, and one that is repeated by many in the field of education, is that of contesting the supposed categorical assumption that organic intellectuals must develop some sort of supranatural level of consciousness, avoiding or overcoming the contradictory personal and social struggles present in everyday life. At the same time, this valorization of the role of one small group of leaders and organizers replicates the heroic myths of romantic idealism of the past century, which in turn reflects its positivistic heritage, and a firm belief in the existence of a normal and teleological line of progress for all societies (i.e., from backward societies to capitalistic forms to socialist and finally communist societies).

5   Points of Departure IV: Critical Pedagogy, Commitment, and Praxis

Although we agree with Carl Boggs (1993) that today's critical intellectuals also embody some elements of Gramsci's (1971) organic model, we are concerned about the lack of interest in class politics and class struggle on the part of the emerging strata of postmodern intellectuals and their relationship to new social movements, including movements on a global scale. We further believe that Gramsci's appropriation by educational postmodernists has too often emphasized the priority of language and representation in the hegemonic processes of identity formation to the detriment of acknowledging how the social construction of race, class, and gender are implicated in the international division of labor. Postmodern educators have not sufficiently comprehended the importance of understanding and challenging the totalizing power of capitalism. Capitalism totalizes like nothing else; it is its totalizing character that renders capitalism unique (Carroll & Ratner, 1994). According to Marx (1983),

> it is not values in use and the enjoyment of them, but exchange value and its augmentation, that spur [the capitalist] into action. Fanatically bent on making value expand itself, he ruthlessly forces the human race to produce for production's sake. […] Moreover, the development of capitalist production makes it constantly necessary to keep increasing

the amount of the capital laid out in a given industrial undertaking, and competition makes the immanent laws of capitalist production to be felt by each individual capitalist, as external coercive laws. It compels him to keep constantly extending his capital, in order to preserve it, but extend it he cannot, except by means of progressive accumulations. [...] To accumulate, is to conquer the world of social wealth, to increase the mass of human beings exploited by him, and thus to extend both the direct and the indirect sway of the capitalist. (p. 17)

Of course, some of the blame for the retreat from class and class struggle on the part of many neo-Gramscians has to lie with the cultural studies exponents of Gramsci (1971), including Hall himself, and the way that Gramsci's notion of hegemony has been retranslated.

Fabiana Woodfin (2005) has undertaken an important analysis of Gramsci's work in terms of how it has been taken up and retranslated by cultural studies theorists and other "self-affirmed post-Marxists" in Europe and the United States. Woodfin's analysis focuses on the centrality of translation practices to ways of conceiving social change. According to Woodfin, the appropriation of Gramsci has often served the ironic purpose of arguing against Marx, a tendency that has produced a disturbing paradox within the field: on one hand, stalking the horizon of cultural studies are the neo-Marxist "culturalists" who, under Hall's lead, applaud Gramsci for his supposedly lack of emphasis on social determinism vis-à-vis class; on the other, there are the hardliner post-Marxists, such as Laclau and Mouffe, who criticize Gramsci for having been too preoccupied with issues of class. According to Woodfin,

> the former impose the concept of "articulation" between base and superstructure so that culture and politics may finally divorce economy, while the latter find political-economic considerations of the superstructure as "economistic" and no longer appropriate in post-industrial capitalist societies. Both ultimately encourage a cultural determinism that is just as insidious and politically paralyzing as its economic variant. Both dismiss Marxism as passé.

Woodfin (2005) initiates a critical translation practice of Gramsci's work that problematizes the "essentializing reduction of the diversity within Marxist theory" by Hall, Laclau, and others through a recontextualization of Gramsci's work that reveals "the continuing relevance of Marxism for informing a critical political practice that need not be – and indeed was not always – economistic or deterministic."

Woodfin (2005) traces the problem to the dispute within British cultural studies over how to best reengage with the Marxist tradition. In a belated response to the challenge of E. P. Thompson to reintroduce Marxism into an understanding of culture, Raymond Williams famously put forward the proposition that social being determines consciousness as a replacement for the mechanical base-determines-superstructure model, a move that, according to Woodfin, set the stage for the introduction of Gramsci into the project of British cultural studies.

Struggle was put at the center of cultural inquiry, whereas culture was redefined as a "whole way of struggle." But this "break into Marxism" that set the stage for Gramsci was short lived and, thanks to the work of Stuart Hall, Ernesto Laclau, Chantal Mouffe, and others, culminated in its opposite: a break out of Marxism (Woodfin, 2005).

Hall's (1996) attempt to intervene into the structuralism-culturalism dispute, a dispute that was famously framed by the Thompson/Williams debate but regrettably reduced by Hall into a conflict between crude economic reductionism and naive idealist humanism, included an outright rejection of the base-superstructure model (Woodfin, 2005). Woodfin describes how, through such a move, Hall positioned his project against Marxism rather than as an argument for the continuing relevance of a Marxism that exists beyond deterministic and economistic models. Rather than seeing the outcome of the Williams/Thompson debate in terms of a renewal of Marx's "being versus consciousness" dialectic, Hall rewrote the culturalist-structuralist dispute as the defining break away from Marxism. Woodfin draws our attention to the example of Hall's use of the term *articulation* (which Hall borrowed from Ernesto Laclau), which stresses the contingent and nonnecessary aspects of ideological elements and the relationship between ideological elements and social forces and also between different social groups within a particular social movement. Here, Woodfin (2005) describes Hall's use of the term *articulation* as representing "no less than a disjoining of the two dialectical antipodes of Marxism, whether one wishes to view it as base and superstructure, as being and consciousness, or as structure and experience."

Our use of Gramsci (1971) acknowledges the strategic centrality of class struggle in his work. We argue for a counterhegemonic coalition of social formations comprising committed intellectuals whose political bonds are interconnected and articulated through the unification of demands in heterogeneous, multifaceted, yet focalized anticapitalist struggles. This is not to limit counterhegemonic struggles to the productivist framework of unilinear labor struggles or Marxist "workerism," for instance, but rather to forge by means of a unified subaltern historical bloc new bonds between labor and new social movements without dismissing the potential of politically unorganized social sectors, such as the growing numbers of unemployed and homeless (Brosio, 1994).

One of the main goals of these diverse coalitions should be to suffocate the authoritarian power of the state and curb its ability to support other structures of oppression. To do so demands moving beyond localized radical struggles and the creation of networks of micropolitical struggles. This does not mean we reject community-based multiform politics, but rather stress the need to coordinate our single-issue and micropolitical efforts so that the power of the state's apparatus is not underestimated and can be effectively challenged. Of course, we also acknowledge that the state is not the all-encompassing and indomitable structure of domination that orthodox Marxists have often claimed, as there exist fault lines than enable challenges from below. But we also recognize that state formations, whereas more fluid in the context of global markets and the internationalization of capital, have not become obsolete. In fact, they are functionally necessary to promote the reproduction of capitalist social relations and their transnational expansion. Although we agree with Boggs (1993) that a reconstituted definition of the organic intellectual emphasizes transnational social movements that are not necessarily linked to social identity or class formation, we worry that such a dialectical movement between intellectuals and social forces or movements is insufficiently powerful, at present, to overturn the highly integrated power structures of global capitalism associated with the economic exploitation of the masses, ecological genocide, and bureaucratic domination.

And although we agree that economic and cultural relations can be – and often are – decoupled within capitalist society so that they appear to have an autonomous or semiautonomous existence outside of capitalist productive relations, we cannot maintain strongly enough that objective surplus labor grounds both cultural practices and social institutions. A focus on capitalist consumption and circulation does appear to segregate cultural formations and commodity relations from class antagonisms and to sever the practice of exploitation from that of consumption as a matter of personal choice or taste or preference or even lifestyle. We believe, however, the labor/capitalist dynamic at the point of production is what needs to be foregrounded. Here, we follow Hoffman (1984) in warning against a mechanical splicing apart of the Gramscian couplet of coercion and consent, as all political action must be premised on the idea of the coercive character of all relationships involving labor and capital. Failure to foreground the role of relations of production in explaining the dynamics of consent and coercion has led many post-Marxist or postmodernist scholars who champion the new social movements to overemphasize contingency and the reversibility of cultural practices at the level of the individual at the expense of challenging the structural determinations and productive forces of capital, its laws of motion, and its value form of labor. In effect, such a move replaces an undialectical theory of economic determination with a poststructuralist theory of cultural determination.

Post-Marxist or postmodernist critics do not see consent as a moment conceived within social coercion and brought about by productive practices (leading to the current crisis of overproduction in which higher levels of productivity has made capitalist accumulation more difficult to maintain). In contrast, the committed intellectual recognizes that so-called autonomous acts of consent are always already rooted in the coercive relationships of the realm of necessity (i.e., the labor-capital dialectic). Because coercion is the "ethical expression of the fact that people *have to* produce" (Hoffman, 1984, p. 212), it makes sense to view the dialectical relationship between coercion and consent as a dialectical unity. Hoffman (1984) asserts that "consent has to respond to coercion in order to 'negate' it. We have to avoid [...] a fatalistic social determinism [...] and a voluntaristic postulation of situations in which 'social pressures are non-existent'" (p. 210). Without acknowledging coercion as such, we are faced with a pedagogy grounded in antipolitics of free-floating critique. To borrow a description from Carroll and Ratner (1994), "politics becomes an anything-goes adventure – as exhilarating as it is strategically rudderless" (p. 14). Such politics renarrates class struggle against economic exploitation and between exploiters and the exploited as cultural struggles against dominant discourses of the 'haves' against those of the 'have nots.' This has the effect of camouflaging continuing efforts by the capitalist state to subsidize the wealthy few at the expense of the many and disguising in cultural garb the reality of class exploitation as the unmet needs of the majority. This is precisely the problem with those who advocate a "radical democracy" and who are preoccupied with formal equality of political rights but who refuse to challenge the value form of labor and property rights that form the foundation on which political rights are built.

Our position has some relevance for discussing the issue of race. For instance, by separating race and racism from the social relations of production and treating them mainly as issues of ethnicity and the politics of difference and diversity, the multiculturalist problematic operates effectively as a hegemonic scheme of peacefully managing the crisis of race, ethnicity, gender, and labor in countries such as the United States, a way of neutralizing the perennial conflicts in the system, of containing diversity in a common grid, of selling diversity to preserve the ethnocentric paradigm of commodity relations that structure the experience of life worlds within globalizing capitalism. According to E. San Juan (2003, 2004), an understanding of the hegemony of the United States as a racial polity must begin with a historical materialist approach grounded in the labor/capital dialectic, where class is seen as an antagonistic relation between labor and capital and where race is understood historically as a manifestation of the class-conflicted structure of capitalism and its political/ideological/judicial process of class rule (San Juan, 2003, 2004).

6   Points of Departure V: Committed Intellectuals and Critical Pedagogies

We wish to expand on the role of the organic intellectual by suggesting that the resisting, hegemonized, and fragmented subaltern needs to function not as a critically superconscious "organic intellectual" but as a committed one (Fischman, 1998). The committed intellectual is sometimes critically self-conscious and actively engaged but at other times is confused or even unaware of his or her limitations or capacities to be an active proponent of social change. Or as Paulo Freire (1989) has noted, "conscientization is not exactly the starting point of commitment. Conscientization is more of a product of commitment. I do not have to be already critically self-conscious in order to struggle. By struggling I become conscious/aware" (p. 46).

Critical consciousness always implies that the subject has some awareness of the immediate world that concerns him or her. As Freire (1989) came to recognize, a deep understanding of the complex processes of oppression and domination is not enough to guarantee personal or collective praxis. What must serve as the genesis of such an understanding is an unwavering commitment to the struggle against injustice. Only by developing an understanding that is born of a commitment to social justice can such an understanding lead to the type of conscientization necessary to challenge the hegemonic structures of domination and exploitation. The globalization of capital can be challenged and even defeated not simply by understanding its formation and dissembling operations but also by developing the will and the courage – the commitment – to struggle against it.

The committed intellectual is not someone who is interested only in resisting and defeating forms of cultural domination but rather someone for whom the end of all forms of exploitation is the focal point of his or her commitment to transform the world because, as Foucault (1980) has so famously indicated,

> the essential political problem for the intellectual is not to criticize the ideological contents supposedly linked to science or to ensure that his

own scientific practice is accompanied by a correct ideology, but that of ascertaining the possibility of constituting a new politics of truth. The problem is not changing people's consciousness – or what's in their heads – but the political, economic, institutional regime of the production of truth. (p. 133)

The problem with Foucault's formulation, in our view, is that his regime change for the production of truth puts too much stock in a diffuse theory of power, deemphasizing the role of the fundamental laws of motion of capital in shaping discursive regimes based on the relations of people to ownership of the means of production and the social division of labor and therefore neutralizing class as an economic category and rewriting it as a cultural or discursive identity.

The point is not to initiate a face-off between two equally dogmatic assertions – between advocates of structural determination (i.e., social determinations of race, class, gender, and sexuality) and proponents of universal contingency or between supporters of Marxist reflectionism and those who support a poststructuralist relativism (i.e. resistance to meaning as a result of an endless play of indeterminacy) or between vanguardists (who privilege the party over the self-activity of the proletariat) and antivanguardists (many who believe that alternatives to capital will arise automatically from the self-activity of the oppressed). These are, in our view, false alternatives. We believe that a better strategy is to develop a philosophy of praxis, that is, to work out a philosophically grounded vision of the future outside the precincts of capital's value form of labor (Hudis, 2004). One possible route would be to follow Gramsci's strategy of acquiring a critical understanding of hegemonic structures (civic, social, and state) that constrain human action within the debilitating labor-capital contradiction and value form of labor while at the same time emphasizing a commitment to revolutionary agency that will permit collective redefinitions of and strategies and tactics for social change (Carroll & Ratner, 1994).

Here, the committed intellectual distinguishes between philosophy and theory while attempting to integrate both into everyday praxis. Philosophy is appropriated without adopting the contemplative standpoint that defines much traditional theory. It does this by penetrating and grasping what Karel Kosik (1976, p. 1) calls the "thing itself." In other words, philosophy is positioned away from its traditional concern with inner life by bringing the ideas of mental and manual labor, and philosophy and reality together as a praxiological dimension of the committed intellectual as critical pedagogue. According to Peter Hudis (2004), philosophy "is distinct from theory in that it recognizes the profound relation between the subject and the world in seeking to grasp the 'thing itself.'" By "thing itself," Hudis refers, like Kosik, to "not only [...] external objects but also to the categories which underlay human cognition." He goes on to say that

> philosophy is different from theory as it is traditionally understood in that it does not take its premises for granted. Philosophy is not about "accepting" certain fixed truths which one then simply projects without further self-examination. Philosophy subjects everything to self-examination, even its own premises – not for the sake of just tearing things down (that would be sophistry) but as part of creating something new.

Hudis (2004) reminds us that although philosophy is a qualitatively superior form of cognition, it doesn't mean that we dispense with theory. This is because the practice of philosophy means taking part in rigorous theoretical debate and discussion. Because only through theoretic work can philosophical conclusions be adequately justified. But theory is, in itself, insufficient. In fact, what is necessary, according to Hudis, is a Marxist humanism that stipulates a qualitatively new approach that fuses theory and philosophy so that "thought ceases to take its premises for granted" (Hudis, 2004). Although we continue to justify our philosophical conclusions theoretically, we need to understand that cognition is not only about using theory to justify certain assumptions and claims – those must continue to be critically examined. A critical fusion of theory and philosophy prevents fixed conclusions from being projected by holding onto certain assumptions. Ideas themselves must, after all, be developed to their logical conclusion. Marxist humanist philosophers, however, are able to redefine the image of thought as the way that we think. Hudis asserts how Marxist humanist philosophy and its fusion of theory and philosophy is able to free thought "from a contemplative or formalist relation to reality by posing the reunification of mental and manual abilities in the individual." Here, philosophy and theory as they are joined together in a manner that enables their unity to permeate our very mode of being in all facets of our existence (in a manner that is faithful to Hegel's absolute method) are interpenetrated by voices from below enabling at the same time theory and practice to be concretized in each living individual. This gives each and every individual the capacity to become philosophers and to exercise such a capacity in the interest of understanding the meaning of contemporary life in order to change it. Here, theory and practice are not formally opposed but are unified and concretized in living and breathing individuals of history.

The committed intellectual recognizes that self-reflexivity or the capacity to engage in critical self-consciousness is not enough to resist both the repressive and integrative functions of hegemony. What is necessary is to find ways to actively intervene in the capitalist world order in ways that have the potential to transform that world. In other words, the committed intellectual works in diverse space and spheres in which new social movements intersect with more organically traditionalist socialist movements. What links the two groups of intellectuals is a common commitment to anticapitalist struggle and a provisional model of socialist democracy. As Brosio (1994) warns,

> the fact that working-class consciousness has not yet overcome this hegemony in the West causes one to think that becoming aware may not be enough, when one considers the advances which have been made by capital in its colonization of the quotidian, lived experiences of the masses since the time in which Gramsci wrote. Moreover, there are many persons in Gramsci's native country and elsewhere who understand the nature of their sophisticated oppression, but are unable to muster the power to stop it and finally overcome it. (p. 50)

The figure of the committed intellectual that we are developing never forgets that we live in a world of messy material relations that is part of the consolidation of a world market of expanding profits for the capitalist class. This material reality not only structures our consciousness and ferments our subjectivities into a colorless and odorless pulque but continually exploits human labor and strips people who are located in subaltern economic, social, and cultural positions of their fundamental humanity and self-worth (McLaren, in press). Exploitation not only alienates, it also destroys. It forces people to work and live in dangerous workplace environments; pollutes the earth with toxic, life-threatening chemicals; and teaches people that indignity and poverty are natural and unchangeable situations. It naturalizes wage labor and the private accumulation of profit and legitimizes the social division of labor within capitalist societies. It subjects workers to the selling of their only commodity, their labor power, to survive. At the same time, the committed intellectual supports the resistance and transformation of capitalist social relations by means of the collectivity of labor (both local and global but always united) struggling to abolish the private ownership of the instruments of labor and collectively producing them in the interests of all.

The committed intellectual does not view hegemonic or dominant discourses as seamless but rather views all discourses as fundamentally contradictory and conflictive; furthermore, discourses are never immune from the larger context of objective labor practices or regarded as disentangled from social relations arising from the history of productive labor. Recognizing that the international division of labor is refracted through race, class, and gender antagonisms, the committed intellectual confronts the capitalist world order with a race, class, and gender consciousness and a politics of respite and renewal. It does so without succumbing to essentialist positions or easy rhetorical discourses of good versus evil, populist nostalgia, possessive parochialism, or militant cultural particularism. At the same time, we continue to acknowledge the labor-capital antagonism as the most fundamental dialectical contradiction within capitalist society. On the issue of challenging exploitation from an ethics of persuasion, we agree with Ronald Glass's (2006) eloquent advice:

> While the task of countering these developments is daunting, there is also no doubt that organic intellectuals can clarify the moral landscape of politics and policy in order to articulate coherent programs that can forge alliances capable of resisting, challenging and overcoming hegemonic powers. However, as Paulo Freire reminded us, people's readiness to listen and to see the moral truths of reality is not dependent on the rightness or force of ethical argument alone; the persuasive power of moral argument cannot achieve its effect when it is divorced from organizing and action. The needed resistance to the dominant norms of the current reform movement won't be mobilized simply by making injustices or unfair practices evident through disclosures in popular electronic and print media, even though such channels are more helpful than publications in policy or scholarly outlets. After all, educational inequities and the harsh outcomes to be expected from present policies are already in plain sight, and not only for those suffering because of them. Since the wellsprings of action are obscure and bodily decisions both get shaped in habits and run ahead of conscious judgment, the most effective critiques of policy will likely emerge from concrete struggles for educational justice. (p. 2)

To conclude, three main ideas have guided our attempt to use Gramsci's and Freire's potent ideas in our formulation of the committed intellectual. First, their work facilitates an understanding of how the regime of capital functions in the political/pedagogical processes of schooling through historically specific, class, racial, ethnic, and gender differentiations. Second, Freire and Gramsci are good examples of the figure of the committed intellectual we are trying to elaborate here (Borg et al., 2002, pp. 147–179). Their work on the contradictory aspects of ideological formations offer us the much-needed critical means to understand the dialectical nature of subjection not only in terms of capitalist exploitation but also in relation to other forms of oppression (mainly sexism and racism, which are, of course, intimately linked to class exploitation) such as found in the mystification of the very capitalist, sexist, and racist ideologies and social practices that naturalize, sustain, and define hegemonic systems of oppression. Finally, Gramsci's concept of the organic intellectual and Freire's teachings on concientization (as well as Hudis's focus on the unity of mental and manual labor through the unification of theory and philosophy) offer fecund points of departure for understanding the possibilities inherent in critical agency by providing contemporary educators with a foundation on which to construct a critical pedagogy for a socialist future. This is the crucial difference when contrasted with the most prevalent forms of critical pedagogy. A critical pedagogy that incorporates the role of the committed intellectual is one that concomitantly posits socialism as a viable historical alternative outside the social universe of capital, a pedagogy that unhesitatingly and unapologetically names its vision as socialist and works unflaggingly toward its realization with the recognition that there are no ultimate guarantees of victory.

Acknowledgment

This chapter originally appeared as G. E. Fischman and P. McLaren, Rethinking critical pedagogy and the Gramscian and Freirean legacies: From organic to committed intellectuals or critical pedagogy, commitment, and praxis, *Cultural Studies ↔ Critical Methodologies*, 5(4) (2005), 425–447. Reprinted here, with minor edits, with permission from the publisher.

References

Adamson, W. L. (1980). *Hegemony and revolution: A study of Antonio Gramsci's political and cultural theory.* University of California Press.

Best, S., & Kellner, D. (1991). *Postmodern theory: Critical interrogations.* Guilford.

Boggs, C. (1984). *The two revolutions: Gramsci and the dilemmas of Western Marxism.* South End.

Boggs, C. (1993). *Intellectuals and the crisis of modernity.* State University of New York Press.

Borg, C., Buttigieg, J., & Mayo, P. (Eds.). (2002). *Gramsci and education.* Rowman & Littlefield.

Borg, C., & Mayo, P. (2002). Gramsci and the unitarian school. In C. Borg, J. Buttigieg & P. Mayo (Eds.), *Gramsci and education* (pp. 87–108). Rowman & Littlefield.

Brosio, R. A. (1994). *A radical democratic critique of capitalist education.* Peter Lang.

Carroll, W. K., & Ratner, R. S. (1994). Between Leninism and radical pluralism: Gramscian reflections on counter-hegemony and the new social movements. *Critical Sociology, 20,* 2.

Eagleton, T. (1991). *Ideology: An introduction.* Verso.

Fischman, G. (1998). Donkeys and superteachers: Structural adjustment and popular education in Latin America. *International Review of Education, 44,* 191–213.

Foucault, M. (1980). *Power/knowledge: Selected interviews and other writings 1972–1977* (G. Gordon, Ed.). Pantheon.

Freire, P. (1989). *Education for the critical consciousness.* Continuum.

Giroux, H. A. (1992). *Border crossings: Cultural workers and the politics of education.* Routledge.

Giroux, H. A. (2002). Rethinking cultural politics and radical pedagogy in the work of Antonio Gramsci. In C. Borg, J. Buttigieg & P. Mayo (Eds.), *Gramsci and education* (pp. 41–66). Rowman & Littlefield.

Glass, R. D. (2006). Moral and political clarity and education as a practice of freedom. In M. Boler (Ed.), *Democratic dialogue and education: Troubling speech, disturbing silence* (pp. 15–32). Peter Lang.

Gramsci, A. (1971). *Selections from the prison notebooks.* International Publishers.

Hall, S. (1996). Gramsci's relevance for the study of race and ethnicity. In D. Morley & K.-H. Chen (Eds.), *Stuart Hall: Critical dialogues in cultural studies* (pp. 411–441). Routledge.

Hall, S., & Donald, J. (Eds.). (1986). *Politics and ideology: A reader.* Open University Press.

Heras, A. I. (1999). Taking action with family and community members: Critical pedagogy as a framework for educational change. In Z. Cline & J. Necochea (Eds.), *Advances in confluent education* (2nd ed., pp. 73–107). JAI Press.

Hoffman, J. (1984). *The Gramscian challenge: Coercion and consent in Marxist political theory.* Basil Blackwell.

Holst, J. D. (2002). *Social movements, civil society, and radical adult education.* Bergin & Garvey.

Hudis, P. (2004). *Working out a philosophically grounded vision of the future* (Report to 2004 Convention of News and Letters Committees, Chicago). Unpublished manuscript.

Katz, A. (1997). Postmodern cultural studies: A critique. *Cultural Logic: An Electronic Journal of Marxist Theory and Practice, 1*(1).

Kosik, K. (1976). *Dialectics of the concrete: A study on problems of man and world.* R. Reidel Publishing Company.

Laclau, E. (1990). *New reflections on the revolution of our time.* Verso.

Laclau, E., & Mouffe, C. (1986). *Hegemony and socialist strategy.* Verso.

Marx, K. (1983). *Capital* (Vol. 1). Lawrence & Wishart.

San Juan, E., Jr. (2003). Marxism and the race/class problematic: A re-articulation. *Cultural Logic, 6.* http://eserver.org/clogic/2003/sanjuan.html

San Juan, E., Jr. (2004). Post-9/11 reflections on multiculturalism and racism. *Axis of Logic.* http://www.axisoflogic.com/cgi-bin/exec/view.pLarchive=79&num=13554

Woodfin, F. (2005). *Lost in translation: Recovering the critical in Gramsci's philosophy of praxis.* Unpublished master's thesis, Boise State University.

CHAPTER 10

From Liberation to Salvation

Revolutionary Critical Pedagogy Meets Liberation Theology

Peter McLaren and Petar Jandrić

1   Introduction

This conversation between Peter McLaren and Petar Jandrić brings about some of the most recent and deepest of McLaren's insights into the relationship between revolutionary critical pedagogy and liberation theology, and outlines the main directions of development of McLaren's thought during and after *Pedagogy of Insurrection*. In the conversation, McLaren reveals his personal and theoretical path to liberation theology. He argues for the relevance of liberation theology for contemporary social struggles, links it with social sciences, and addresses some recent critiques of *Pedagogy of Insurrection*. McLaren identifies the idolatry of money as the central point of convergence between liberation theology and Marxism. Developing this thought further, he asserts that Jesus was a communist. McLaren analyses the revolutionary praxis of liberation theology in Latin America, and concludes that the struggle needs to avoid violence and endure without losing tenderness. He analyzes the international politics of liberation theology and shows that liberation theology was demonized by the US administration because it works for the poor. McLaren then expands experiences from Latin America towards a global ethics of solidarity, criticizes Church positions on various matters, and insists on a critical approach to Church dogmas. He explores theoretical and practical dissonances between Marxism and Christianity, and expands them towards a more general dichotomy between the material and the spiritual. He explores the Christian eschaton – the arrival of the Kingdom of God – and links it to Marx's prophecy of the future socialist society. Finally, he explores ecumenical opportunities of liberation theology and firmly links it with the arrival of the socialist society.

Petar Jandrić (PJ): For anyone interested in critical pedagogy, Peter McLaren needs no introduction. As the "intellectual relative" of Paulo Freire (Freire, 1995, p. x), and one of the leading architects of contemporary critical pedagogy, Peter has left an invaluable mark in the past and present of the educational left. Yet, Peter has never looked backwards. Instead of lulling in the

© PETER MCLAREN AND PETAR JANDRIĆ, 2017

well-deserved secure position of a senior intellectual, in 2015 he published the ground-breaking book *Pedagogy of Insurrection* (McLaren, 2015) which develops a new emancipatory praxis at the crossroads between revolutionary critical pedagogy and liberation theology. Unsurprisingly, the book has immediately provoked a lot of attention. Some critics praised Peter's intellectual boldness and strength; other critics have attacked his thought in various ways and almost reached the level of hate language. The third group, and I readily admit to belong to that group, was confused, curious, yet careful. Brought up in excommunist East Europe, and myself deeply conflicted about religion, I could not help but ask: How is it possible that someone like Peter McLaren has made such a bold move towards religion and spirituality? What are the underlying reasons behind this move?

During the past few years, Peter and I have co-written several conversational pieces (i.e. McLaren & Jandrić, 2014, 2015). For the purpose of republishing one of these pieces in my forthcoming book (Jandrić, 2017), I wanted to update the text with Peter's insights in liberation theology. In the hope to get an additional page or two for the existing article, in Autumn 2016 I emailed Peter few questions. In only a couple of days, however, I received almost 10,000 words of Peter's writing at its best – sharp, bold, powerful, straight to the point testimony of many years of deep thinking about the relationship between revolutionary critical pedagogy and liberation theology. Peter's initial answers provoked more questions, then more answers, then even more questions [...] after several days of furious email exchange, this text had finally arrived into being.

Peter and I immediately understood that this conversation is much more than a mere extension of our ongoing work. Instead of rephrasing the content of his recent book, in this article Peter responds to a lot of critical feedback to *Pedagogy of Insurrection* (McLaren, 2015), looks into the historical roots of liberation, presents fresh ideas, and answers questions emerging from his recent work. Thus, this conversation brings about some of the most recent and deepest insights of Peter McLaren into the relationship between revolutionary critical pedagogy and liberation theology, and outlines the main directions of development of Peter's thought during and after *Pedagogy of Insurrection* (McLaren, 2015).

Peter McLaren (PM): I have greatly enjoyed working with you and since meeting you both online and in person have admired your keen intellect and your commitment to social justice in your work. My work over the past 30 years has been primarily in critical theory, critical pedagogy, Marxist humanist philosophy, and more recently, liberation theology. I look forward to our discussion.

2   The Path to Liberation Theology

PJ: Please describe your personal journey to liberation theology, Peter. Did you experience some kind of transcendental experience; did you arrive to liberation pedagogy by the way of intellectual development; or perhaps both?

PM: I am aware that many of your readers might be unfamiliar with the political history of South America, so please permit me to provide some context for my discussion of the theology of liberation. Before I begin, I need to tell you that I have not had any formal training in theology but as a Catholic convert and a Marxist educator, I have for a long time followed the work of a number of theologians associated with this tradition. In my teenage years I contemplated going into the priesthood but became swept away by the indulgences of every kind and stripe that were available in the 1960s and my life has been anything but priestly. I converted to Catholicism later in my life, in my 30s, having been raised an Anglican. But my mother, Frances Teresa Bernadette McLaren was, as you might guess from her name, Catholic and my father, Lawrence Omand McLaren, was brought up Presbyterian. They wanted to raise me in a religious tradition separate from theirs.

I became serious about revolutionary politics about the time of my conversion to Catholicism and at the same time I was drawn to numerous spiritual traditions. Around this time, too, I was receiving invitations to speak in Latin America and the Caribbean, eventually over the years working with educators and activist groups in Argentina, Mexico, Peru, Brazil, Colombia, Venezuela, Cuba, Puerto Rico, etc. Well, the late 1960s, 1970s, and 1980s were especially brutal years for campesinos, workers, activists, teachers, and revolutionaries throughout Latin America, especially in the Southern Cone. After the government assassination of six Jesuit scholars, their housekeeper and her daughter on 16 November 1989 on the campus of Universidad Centroamericana in San Salvador, El Salvador, the world finally started to take serious notice, especially since the Archbishop of San Salvador, Oscar Romero, had been assassinated in 1980 while offering mass in the chapel of the Hospital of Divine Providence after famously speaking out against poverty, social injustice, and torture.

PJ: During recent years, you often visited Venezuela and conversed with the late president Hugo Chávez. Were you involved with the Catholic Church during your visits to Venezuela?

PM: No, I did not make any connections with Catholic organizations during my visits. The limited but highly influential times that I spent in Venezuela were important in my formation as a revolutionary mostly by learning – despite my limited Spanish – from the local people. And while I remain a supporter of the Bolivarian revolution I acknowledge that there have been serious mistakes. For example, I was never supportive of Chávez's relationship with Iran, nor do I support the peace prize that Chávez's successor, President Maduro, presented to Vladimir Putin recently – especially given that at this very moment Putin is helping Assad to massacre thousands of innocent civilians in Aleppo. Russia's involvement in the Ukraine and its annexation of Crimea and the death squads in Russia exterminating political opponents are all disturbing realities. Yes, I understand the method in the madness and the concept of "the enemy of my enemy is my friend."

PJ: Can you place your personal path towards liberation theology in a broader historical perspective?

PM: Of course, much had been happening in Latin America and the Caribbean long before the abovementioned atrocities were reported in the international press – if we want to be historically expansive, we could say that the problems began with the European colonization of Las Americas, beginning in 1492 when the indigenous populations were enslaved or exterminated. But in more recent times we need only to look at Cuba. When Cuba moved to a people-centered economy in 1959, the USA organized the Bay of Pigs invasion, and in the ensuing years throughout Latin America the USA has been behind the establishment of military regimes that included Chile, Uruguay, Brazil, and Argentina.

As early as 1969, *The Rockefeller Report* (Rockefeller Foundation, 1969) identified liberation theology as a threat to the corporate interests and the security of the USA.

Then there was the clandestine Operation Condor (*Operación Cóndor* or *Plan Cóndor*; McSherry, 2005) that was a major plan of interservice and regional cooperation and a sharing of joint intelligence among the USA and the right-wing dictatorships of the Southern Cone of South America, including Argentina, Chile, Uruguay, Paraguay, Bolivia, and Brazil, in order to maintain an intelligence-sharing program of state terror and political repression. The program began in 1968 but was fully implemented by 1975 and was responsible for as many or more than 60,000 deaths up until 1989. In Argentina alone over 150 priests and nuns were killed, along with peasants, workers, intellectuals, and anyone associated with being part of or sympathetic towards leftist guerilla movements. The program – which can be traced to the infamous US School of the Americas (renamed the Western Hemisphere Institute for Security Cooperation because of its historical association with the training of Latin American death squads) – was created to advance joint counterinsurgency operations designed to eradicate communist subversives and ideas, and to suppress the influence of liberation theology and other oppositional political or ideological positions.

Through the Central Intelligence Agency (CIA), the US military, and the State Department, the US government helped to bring military dictatorships to power and secure their stability by imposing sanctions to destabilize the economies of socialist-leaning regimes and by supporting and training "black op" and execution squads. While the USA was not an official member of the Condor consortium, documents that were later uncovered revealed that during this time the USA provided major organizational, financial, and technical assistance to the repressive regimes involved. The secret papers of the 17th Conference of American Armies in Mar del Plata in 1987 revealed that the US military initiated numerous discussions about how to wage socio-psychological warfare against liberation theology, ecclesial, and base communities through LIC (Low Intensity Conflict) strategies using misinformation and ideological subversion (Duchrow, 1999). Of course, when the assassinations of the Jesuits broke into the news there was international pressure to shut down the death squads.

PJ: What caused so much resistance towards liberation theology? Why was it so threatening?

PM: Why was liberation theology so threatening? To answer that question we need to consider The Conference of Latin American Bishops that was held in 1968 in Medellín, Colombia. It was here that bishops from all over Latin America agreed that the church should take "preferential option for the poor." The bishops decided to form Christian base communities in which they would create literacy programs, and this captured the attention of Paulo Freire. The goal of the bishops was to support conditions so that the poor could liberate themselves from the "institutionalized violence" of poverty. The year that marked the beginning of Operation Condor was the same year – 1968 – that this conference in Medellín, Colombia, took place. What emerged from this conference was to become known as liberation theology.

However, John Paul II was very much opposed to communism and he considered liberation theology a dangerous development within the Church. In the late 1970s, shortly after he was elected Pope, he began to oppose liberation theology directly and the church hierarchy moved decidedly to the right. He put Joseph Cardinal Ratzinger (later Pope Benedict XVI) in charge of countering the theological interpretations and actions of liberation theologians. It was no accident that Pope John Paul II made numerous trips to Latin America. In 1983, the Pope visited Nicaragua to scold Father Ernesto Cardenal and to oppose liberation theology. I had the good fortune of meeting Ernesto Cardenal on a television show hosted by President Hugo Chávez in 2006. John Paul II defrocked Cardenal because of his participation in liberation theology. Fortunately, Pope Francis overturned this decision in 2014.

3   Pedagogy of Insurrection

PJ: Based on this brief historical introduction, let us jump into the moment here and now. Immediately after publishing, *Pedagogy of Insurrection* (McLaren, 2015) provoked a lot of attention. For instance, it came under heavy attack from a radical leftist anarchist educator, who claims that your work in the field of liberation theology is well below the standards for social science research. Can you please respond to this argument? What makes liberation theology real, alive, and relevant for social science and beyond?

PM: Well, one question would be: Are we talking about the Hegelian conception of science – dialectical reasoning – or the vulgar empiricist conception of science? Marx's concept of "value," for instance, has nothing to do with corporeal existence. Value is not a thing but a relationship. Dialectical reasoning brings "internal relations" to the forefront, which cannot be reduced to things – this issue needs to be interrogated from a different epistemological standpoint. And from an ethical standpoint – from the standpoint of the dispossessed, from the perspective of the oppressed, and also from the standpoint of the oppressor. It cannot remain neutral. Liberation theology displays a praxiological dimension of thought and action coming together to transform the world in the interests of justice. God becomes visible when people put their lives on the line for others, especially when they sacrifice themselves for those who are most vulnerable to exploitation and alienation and the ravages of capitalism. Vulgar empiricism and materialist dogmatism cannot help us grasp the idea behind the transaction between the capitalist and the laborer. What is sold in this exchange, Marx tells us, is not labor – but labor power. There is plenty of pseudo-Marxist theory out there, as well as anarchist theory that claims that theology is a flabby discipline. Of course, there is flabby theology, but it would be impertinent and glib to claim this for all theological traditions.

I think social science is very relevant for theology, and vice versa. Just as Marx's work revolutionized the science of history in his discovery of the workings of the mode of production by means of scientific dialectics, so Christian theology has revolutionized our understanding of faith. Theology challenges positivistic science and empiricism, but that does not render it unscientific. Liberation theologians may challenge the materialism of the anti-Hegelians, or they may take a different approach. Certainly, the principles of natural science are not the only principles by which to verify truth. But liberation theology needs social science as much as social science needs theology. We need to understand the world in order to change it – after all, this was a major imperative for Marx as it was for Jesus. Jesus taught us not through social science theories but through parables.

PJ: Theology and (social) science are written using radically different languages – therefore, we need to read them in radically different ways. Most of our readers will be familiar with reading one or another language of science. How should we go about reading the gospels?

PM: Both Jesus and Marx maintained a commitment to the poor and the powerless. In the case of Jesus, his story is the embodiment of the word of God. Theology helps us to gain a deeper understanding of the meaning of Jesus' life. Jesus comes to the encounter with the divine a new praxis, an incarnation that radiates love through a concretization of prophetic justice. Of course, when we attempt to fathom the paschal mystery, we are guided by our own history, our own formation, what the Germans refer to as *Bildung*. Here we adhere to historico-critical exegesis with an understanding that a purely scientific exegesis does not eliminate divergent interpretations, since it is impossible to rid ourselves of all of our theologio-dogmatic presuppositions. When we read the scriptures we have to acknowledge that our interpretations are guided by our own biographies and by suffering Christian communities throughout the ages who read the gospels through contextually specific eschatological, soteriological, and Christological themes – mainly with a kerygmatic intention. As Leonardo Boff (1987) would put it, reading the gospels is not the same as reading facts of history, because in such a reading you are dealing with history, the interpretation of history, and a profession of faith working together to understand the totality of Christianity from an apologetical viewpoint. Christ destroys all of our previous images of God, as Christ suffers for all the crucified of history. As Boff (1987) notes, this is a mystery inaccessible to discursive reason but capable of being understood through human praxis. We are resurrected through our refusal to cooperate with the social sin of this world.

Remember, Petar, that Paulo Freire wrote that the prophetic position of the Church "demands a critical analysis of the social structures in which [...] conflict takes place. This means it demands of its followers a knowledge of socio-political science, since this science cannot be neutral; this demands an ideological choice" (1973, p. 14). Here Freire admits to the notion that all science is a form of ideology and that there is an ideological choice in choosing particular types of science with which to clarify and deepen our understanding of the struggle for liberation. Part of the prophetic vision of the Church demands an engagement with social science that can help unpeel the veneer of mystification that keeps us from knowing reality. Freire writes that a prophetic perspective "does not represent an escape into a world of unattainable dreams. It demands a scientific knowledge of the world as it really is" (1973, p. 14). But note that for Freire, this scientific understanding of the world is found through praxis, through revolutionary praxis. Freire warns that "to denounce the present reality and announce its radical transformation into another reality capable of giving birth to new men and women, implies gaining through praxis a new knowledge of reality" (1973, p. 14). Freire criticizes the petit bourgeois dimension of the Church today and urges theologians to consider in their work the so-called Third World that exists within their own so-called First World – in the outskirts of their cities. And I would add – within our segregated inner cities.

PJ: Speaking of *Pedagogy of Insurrection* (2015), you have been attacked by a former admirer of your work as no better than historical tyrants who use God as a cover for their crimes. This is because you "came out" as a devout Catholic and very likely many of your leftist admirers assume you are an atheist. This kind of *argumentum ad hominem* is obviously wrong. Yet, I completely agree with Derek Ford's review, which says that publishing *Pedagogy of Insurrection* "is certainly a risky move for McLaren, for he risks both the condemnation of the Christian right as well as contemporary atheists. Interestingly, these two groups have quite a bit in common" (Ford, 2016).

What is the connection between left-wing and right-wing critiques of your work? Here, I am especially interested in critiques arriving from the left: the closer they are, the more they hurt. Some left-wing theorists, especially those arriving from anarchist circles, say that religion and capitalism are mutually foundational – in this view, religion simply does not work together with socialism. What do you make of this critique? How, and under which condition, can we divorce religion from capitalism and build a theist socialist future?

PM: I regard the particular attack to which you refer as an example of what Lenin would call an infantilism of the left. Which is not to say I regard all atheists in this way, far from it. But let us get to the bigger picture here. Of course I agree with Herbert Marcuse (2011) when he wrote in "The role of religion in a changing society" that no evaluation of that role can be made without meeting Marx's criticism of religion. I have never veered from this position. But Christianity, as Miranda notes (1974, 1980, 2004), is not something that should be absorbed into a religion. Marx attacks Christianity to the extent that it *has* been calcified into a religion. Marx was certainly anti-clerical but both Marx and Engels, I believe, saw their work as a continuation of the authentic message of Jesus. Marx applied the term "Christian" to himself in a letter to Ludwig Kugelmann in 1870, constantly made Biblical references throughout his works, and compared the persecutions against the international as the persecutions of primitive Christians by the Romans.

As a revolutionary Marxist humanist who works in the tradition of critical pedagogy, which I have developed over the years as "revolutionary critical pedagogy" – and as a Catholic – I have been greatly influenced by the work of the great Jesuit theologian and educator José Porfirio Miranda. So much of what I am offering as a response to your question is indebted to his work, especially his classic work, *Marx against the Marxists* (Miranda, 1980), that readers will need to seriously engage this work in order to get the details. In his world-shaking critique of capitalism, Marx regards people as endowed with the capacity to make history. Marx affirms "the cunning of reason" as the means by which human actors shape history. This type of reason is neither an abstraction, nor is it attached to the notion of history as some kind of abstract entity of its own that floats above the messy web of human strife and turmoil. Reason in this larger sense has, according to Marx, created the conditions of possibility for a truly humane society to emerge out of the ruins of capital. But the foundational issue here is: Why must a new society emerge from the extraction of surplus value from alienated labor?

The destruction of capital becomes, for Marx, the immanent form for a higher principle that makes possible capitalism's ability to cede its place to a communist society. Marx's entire corpus of works is orientated towards this historical eschatology in his denunciation of the worship of the god of money. The cunning or subtlety of reason creates the conditions of possibility for results that are contrary to those which the capitalists were pursuing. Miranda is very convincing here when he affirms that Marx appeals to this eschatological aspect of history – this affirming of the eschaton or Kingdom of God of which Jesus preached. This eschaton is occurring in history itself and not in some other world, some cosmic hinterland where people float around as disembodied spirits. Churches and Christians everywhere tragically refuse to hear this message. Marx has this eschatological awareness, his writings are full of it, and I do not have space here to recite all the instances in his writings where this is evident – they can be found in the works of Miranda.

PJ: Can you say a bit more about the eschatological aspect of history? How can it be confirmed; how does it link to liberation?

PM: We cannot affirm the existence of an eschaton unless we affirm the existence of a God guiding history. The eschaton for Christ meant that injustice and exploitation will disappear once and for all. Atheists reject the eschaton, clearly. I hold that both Jesus and Marx maintained the reality of the eschaton. Engels and Marx's work reveal this both implicitly and explicitly. The reason immanent in history is God. This I believe is reflected in the notion of hope that can be seen in the writings of both Marx and Engels. Clearly Marx understood Kant's categorical imperative as "bad infinity," that is, the eternal return of the same in which an imperative is reiterated but is never fully realized. Marx rejected Kant's anti-eschatological and anti-messianic attitudes of eternal deferment and postponement. And what about Hegel? Marx had a profound critique of Hegel's work but he did not dismiss Hegel's affirmation of the final end of history through an intervening Absolute that can bring the endless return of the same to a halt.

God is the intervening Absolute who relativizes the eternal return of the same and delinks us from it so that we can seize the torch of liberation. Jesus came to revolutionize the social structure of religion, not to occupy a throne reserved for him by "religious" functionaries of the state who have been made illustrious in the capitalist world by their unslakable thirst for power and class privilege. As Miranda argues, rebellion against religion is mandatory for anyone who wants to bring justice to the world. Charles Reitz, who has adumbrated a Marxist atheist position, is correct here in arguing for a communal politics of justice and commonwealth by means of a dialectical sublation of religion, surpassing its inadequacies yet preserving its worthwhile historical contributions. Here, Reitz (2015) starts with humanity's oldest philosophical and religious sources in Africa that reflects that "communally laboring humanity can be seen as the source of ethics." This ethics of caring, reciprocity, and the "golden rule" includes emancipatory religious practice, as in the civil rights movement. Here the struggle for justice includes the struggle against racism, sexism, patriarchy, and capitalism. Can we not hear the words of Jesus: "Woe to you rich, for your consolation is now" (Luke 6:24) or "Blessed are you poor; the reign of God is yours (Luke 6:20)?

4   The Idolatry of Money

PJ: In regards to religion, various leftist traditions significantly collide – Paulo Freire was a deep Christian believer, while Marx famously proclaimed religion as "the opium of the people" (Marx, 1843/1970). Your work is deeply situated in both traditions, and *Pedagogy of Insurrection* (McLaren, 2015) clearly leans towards the Latin American approach that sees Christianity as compatible with, and even beneficial to, revolutionary critical pedagogy. What are the reasons behind such direction of development of your thought?

PM: Freire has addressed the role of theologians and the Church – its formalism, supposed neutrality, and captivity in a complex web of bureaucratic rites that pretends to serve the oppressed but actually supports the power elite – from the perspective of the philosophy of praxis that he developed throughout his life. For Freire, critical consciousness (conscientization) cannot be divorced from Christian consciousness. Freire's attack on bourgeois subjective idealism as "naive consciousness" approaches the transformation of consciousness as a political act: to speak a true word, according to Freire, is to transform the world. The ruling class, from Freire's perspective, views consciousness as something that can be transformed by "lessons, lectures and eloquent sermons" (1973, p. 2). In this instance consciousness is essentially static, necrophilic (death-loving) as distinct from biophilic (life-loving), constitutes "an uncritical adherence to the ruling class" (1973, p. 2), and serves as a means of "emptying conscientization of its dialectical content" (1973, p. 3).

Freire calls for a type of class suicide in which the bourgeoisie take on a new apprenticeship of dying to their own class interests and experiencing their own Easter moment through a form of mutual understanding and transcendence. Freire argues that the theologians of Latin America must move forward and transform the dominant class interests in the interests of the suffering poor "if they are to experience 'death' as an oppressed class and be born again to liberation" (1973, p. 6). Or else, they will be implicated within a Church "which forbids itself the Easter which it preaches" (1973, pp. 5–6). Freire borrowed the concept of "class suicide" from Amilcar Cabral, the Guinea-Bissauan and Cape Verdean revolutionary and political leader who was assassinated in 1973. For Freire, insight into the conditions of social injustice of this world stipulates that the privileged must commit a type of "class suicide" where they self-consciously attempt to divest themselves of their power and privilege and willingly commit themselves to unlearning their attachment to their own self-interest. Essentially, this was a type of Easter experience in which a person willingly sacrifices his or her middle or ruling class interests in order to be reborn through a personal commitment to suffering alongside the poor.

Of course, this class suicide takes place in the context of a larger mission to end the social sin of poverty itself. It is a transformational process in which a person identifies with the poor and the oppressed and commits oneself to taking down all victims from the cross. Here we find an echo of the teachings of St Francis. Both Freire and St Francis understood that a transcendence of oppression – a striving upwards – in the struggle for liberation was not enough. As Leonardo Boff notes in his study of St Francis, a striving "upwards" away from the travails of the world through the attainment of a mystical consciousness is not enough. What is also needed, and even more so, is a "trans-descendence" – a kenotic act of self-emptying, an openness to the lives of those below – the poor, the stigmatized, the despised – and a willingness to integrate them into a community of love, kindness, and solidarity – a fraternal solidarity with those suffering from the scourge of life's deprivations. Christ encountered such trans-descendence in the wretched of the earth, in the crucified of history.

PJ: In theory, the concept of class suicide somehow seems much more viable than in practice.... How can we move on from theory to praxis?

PM: Let us examine some of Freire's positions here. Freire writes that the praxis by which consciousness is changed "is not only action but action *and* reflection" (1973, p. 3). He argues that theoretic praxis is only authentic when it maintains the dialectical movement between itself and the contextual specificity of the praxis one wishes to carry out, that is, when it is cognizant of the unity between practice and theory in which both are constructed, shaped, and reshaped. Authentic praxis, in other words, is a "dialectical movement which relates critical reflection on past action to the continuing struggle" (1973, p. 4). For Freire, a pedagogy of liberation involves "social praxis" that is all about "helping to free human beings from the oppression which strangles them in their objective reality" (1973, p. 4). Social praxis, as explained by Freire, is what drew me to the Latin American tradition of liberation theology, a theology that encourages the oppressed to create and recreate themselves in history in a concrete fashion rather than participate in what Freire calls "a reformed repetition of the present" (1973). Freire writes:

> I cannot permit myself to be a mere spectator. On the contrary, I must demand my place in the process of change. So the dramatic tension between the past and the future, death and life, being and non-being, is not longer a kind of dead-end for me; I can see it for what it really is: a permanent challenge to which I must respond. And my response can be none other than my historical praxis – in other words, revolutionary praxis. (1973, p. 7)

PJ: In *Pedagogy of Insurrection,* you write:

> Critical pedagogy is the lucubration of a whole philosophy of praxis that predates Marx and can be found in biblical texts. If we wish to break from alienated labor, then we must break completely with the logic of capitalist accumulation and profit, and this is something to which Marx and Jesus would agree. (McLaren, 2015, pp. 54–55)

If Marx and Jesus would agree with the break from alienated labor, why does contemporary revolutionary pedagogy need an additional layer of rituals and beliefs offered by Christianity? More generally, what are the unique emancipatory and educational potentials of Christianity, which cannot be found in traditional non-religious Marxism?

PM: My early work was on the topic of ritual – *Schooling as a Ritual Performance: Toward a Political Economy of Educational Symbols and Gestures* (McLaren, 1999). Here I followed the work of contemporary symbolic anthropologists – especially Victor Turner – in examining rituals as embodied metaphors and in relation to the construction of liminality. I applied these theories in a critical ethnography I undertook at a Catholic middle school in the Azorean community of Toronto. I was able to discern rituals of instruction, of accommodation, and how an anti-structure of resistance was possible under certain conditions. I also identified micro and macro rituals in school settings and how they can be both emancipatory and contribute to the reproduction of hierarchies of power and privilege. I articulated a theory of the teacher as a liminal servant and how the construction of liminality in the classroom can be the seedbed of true creativity, but at the same time a flashpoint for violence. Much of the important work in applied theater, in drama, and performance studies builds on conceptions of ritual. This can be seen in the writings of my late thesis advisor and mentor, Richard Courtney, and is paramount in the work of Augusto Boal – especially in his magisterial volume, *Theatre of the Oppressed* (2008), which was very much influenced by the work of his fellow Brazilian, Paulo Freire.

I was fortunate to participate in a public dialogue with Freire and Boal at the Rose Theater in Omaha, Nebraska, in the early 1990s. It was the first time Freire and Boal had appeared together in such a venue and I was honored to have been a part of this historic event. Symbols have a fecundity that become animated in rituals. They are brought to life, and live inside of us, through play, through rituals, and their elaboration can be seen in the evolution of drama and thought. Symbols are enacted and work synergistically with other symbols; I have termed this process "enfleshment." Here religious and secular symbols can, under specific historical and existential circumstances, hemorrhage into each other and can work in very liberating and also in very dangerous ways. Just think of Francoist Spain and the rituals that linked Catholic symbols to fascism.

According to Miranda (1980), Jesus was the first human being in history to denounce money as the object of idolatry, which centuries later Marx referred to variously as the Biblical idols of Baal, Mammon, and Moloch. In fact, when discussing the commodity form of production, he used these terms as much as he did the word "fetish." When Saint Paul talks about the "lust which is idolatry," he is referring to money. Book Three of *Capital* (Marx, 1981) makes clear that the capitalist mode of production is not the origin of class violence in capitalist society. As Miranda (1980) notes, the class division is created outside the sphere of production, when money becomes god, and it was this god that created the conditions of possibility for the capitalist mode of production. Money as exchange value stands outside production and circulation and yet dominates both. Money represents the autonomous existence of value as the concretization of human labor. It is when money no longer represents commodities, but when commodities represent money, that money becomes a god. Money is the god of all people living under the commodity mode of production and money had already become a god during the time of Jesus. In other words, the accumulation of capital is not enough to automatically create the mode of production we know today as capitalism, because it takes a certain type of historically produced civilization. The transformation of money into capital requires a certain kind of historical circumstance. Today, capitalism still functions as the institutionalization of the worship of Mammon.

Marx does a brilliant job of explaining how money was transformed into a god ruling human beings. Marx reveals how money is both the object and fountainhead of greed, of *auri sacra fames,* the product of a historically conditioned environment. According to Miranda (1980), Marx perceived the switching of the subject into an object and the transformation of the ends into the means as the centerpiece of the making of a false religion. Marx then applied this "conversion" to economics, to the production of value. Capital finds a way to exchange itself for a commodity that produces more value than the commodity itself – labor power. Capital moves into production through an exchange with labor power, via wage labor, which brings about the separation of the direct producers from the owners of the means of production. Interest-bearing capital is a fetish, a self-expanding value, and it expands its value independently of reproduction, which is a reversal of the relationship between persons and things – all pointing to Marx's anathematization of the worship of money as god. Miranda (2004) points out that at the very central point of his analysis of capital, at the very point where he uncovers the birth of money as a commodity, Marx cites two entire versus from the Apocalypse (Rev 17:13, 13:17). Marx offers a scientific elaboration of Christ's teaching about the god Mammon.

5   Jesus Was a Communist

PJ: The understanding of money as a god which rules human beings fascinates me. Can we say that it is one of the central points of connection between Christianity and Marxism?

PM: Jesus talked so much about economic sin that it is unfathomable why this is not a central part of the teachings of Christianity. The Lucan part of the Bible explicitly teaches communism (Acts 4:32; 4:34; 2:44; Luke 14:33). Miranda argues that the origin of the communist idea in the history of the West is not to be found in Plato or Marx but rather in the New Testament. The Bible clearly condemns acquired wealth and established wealth and also the means by which this wealth came to be – including various kinds of profit, such as interest on loans, and the expropriation of the produce of the workers' labor by agricultural entrepreneurs (James 5:1–6). Jesus is not against generalized wealth per se, such as the wealth of a people, but against relative or differentiating wealth. Someone cannot be rich while another remains poor. Mark 10:25 and Luke 6:20, 6:24, 16:19–31, 1:53 are interpreted by Miranda as arguing that there is no legitimately moral means of acquiring differentiating wealth and that Jesus maintains (Luke 16:29, 16:31) that the same condemnation of wealth can be found in the Old Testament.

Actually, three types of profit are attacked in the scriptures. The Bible itemizes its reproof of profit-taking as occurring through commerce (Ecclus 27:1–2), loans on interest (Exodus 22:24; Leviticus 25:36, 25:37; Deuteronomy 23:19; Ezekiel 18:8, 18:13, 18:17, 22:12; Psalm 15:5; Proverbs 28:8.), and productive activity or the process of production (James 5:1–6). There is something about the process itself of being able to grow rich that is wicked and unjust (Isaiah 53:9). The acquisition of wealth itself is possible only by exploiting the poor (Job 20:19; Psalm 37). Micah 2:1–2, as well as Isaiah 5:8, focus on how the rich keep acquiring property. Miranda (1974, 1980) makes a convincing case that the Bible condemns the exploitation suffered by the poor at the hands of the rich and creates an identity between the rich and the unjust (Isaiah 53:9). Jesus' teachings that enabled the first Christians to base their community on communism can be found in Mark 10:25, Luke 6:20, 24, Matthew 6:24, and Luke 16:19–31.

In fact, Miranda (1980) makes the claim that Jesus was a communist, which can be seen in John 12:6, 13:29, and Luke 8:1–3. Did not Jesus make the renunciation of property a condition for entering into the Kingdom of God? How can God make it possible for a rich person to enter the Kingdom of God? The answer is clearly provided by the Bible. According to Miranda this answer is: By ceasing to be rich (Mark 10:21, 25, 27) and giving away one's wealth to the poor. The scriptural exegesis undertaken by Miranda is, to me, thoroughly persuasive. As a revolutionary Marxist, I am certainly drawn to a number of Miranda's works, *Marx and the Bible* (1974) and *Marx against the Marxists* (1980).

PJ: Poverty is a central point of departure for Jesus, Marx, and Paulo Freire. Yet, the answers seem to collide. For Jesus, the poor will inherit the Kingdom of God; for Marx and Freire, the poor should take matters in own hands here and now....

PM: Jesus did not sacralize poverty or preach resignation to it because there will be some extraterrestrial compensation for it in the afterlife. That would be a glib and cynical assessment, and it erases the prophetic nature of such a pronouncement. To say the poor are blessed is not an involuntary justification of the relations and structures of exploitation. The poor are blessed because the coming of the Kingdom in the fullness of history will put an end – in the concrete sociological sense – to their poverty and suffering. Poverty is a form of structural sin that is incompatible with the Kingdom of God. I am not trying to reduce the Gospel to a manual for attaining political consciousness but maintaining that the Gospel has an inherent political dimension. As Gustavo Gutierrez notes,

> This conscienticizing of the preaching of the Gospel, which rejects any aseptic presentation of the message, should lead to a profound revision of the pastoral activity of the Church [...] the oppressed themselves should be the agents of their own pastoral activity. (1988, pp. 154–155)

Freire was a Christian and sympathetic to Marx, and while I never had a chance to discuss with Paulo the topic of liberation theology, I believe that it would have been a fascinating dialogue. For me, critical consciousness is something that is central to the movement of liberation theology. In the sense that Christians come to recognize not only their preferential option for the poor but, as I would put it, their preferential obligation and commitment to the poor. Critically conscious Christians do not only come to recognize their political formation as subjects – their standpoint epistemology – in relation to others, but also gain ontological and ethnical clarity on their role as Christians.

PJ: Christianity seems to have a fairly straightforward attitude to authority: "Let everyone be subject to the governing authorities, for there is no authority except that which God has established. The authorities that exist have been established by God" (Romans 13:1). How does liberation theology deal with this apparent contradiction between biblical messages and critical pedagogy? How can we simultaneously subject to the governing authorities, and engage in revolutionary struggle?

PM: Saint Paul, who was once a Pharisee, campaigned heavily against the legalism that perverted Christianity. Are we not justified by faith and not our adherence to the law? We need to seek to embody our own insight from our own age and not look to entrenched conceptions of the law established in very different historical epochs. We need to constantly renew our understanding of the gospels given the lessons of our own age. People wrestle with many statements made in the Bible that were historically and geopolitically specific to the times.

Liberation theologians focus on the socio-historical captivity of people in the grip of the pretentions of absolute authority and who are the gravest victims of the alienation brought about by capitalism. They seek a reciprocal salvation in their universal and ontological solidarity with the poor and with all of humanity, which is the possibility of our redemption and liberation. This is what critical pedagogy is about. Beginning with biographical experiences of the people, their lived, hermeneutical engagement with others, and interrogating those experiences in the context of those experiences being situated on a larger locus of the capitalist mode of production and what Jesus refers to as "the money of iniquity" (Luke 16:9, 11). A subversive praxis of faith challenges the systemization of governing authorities and their closed systems of authority and reprobates all measures of accumulating profit under the vice grip of their authority. Established authority that protects freedom and establishes the conditions of possibility of freedom from necessity and from senseless suffering can certainly be conserved, but in other instances when it works to despoil society it should be challenged by seeking a qualitative transformation of society in the interests of justice and solidarity.

6 To Endure without Losing Tenderness

PJ: In Latin America, liberation theology is far from a theory – instead, it is true emancipatory revolutionary praxis. In many cases, actually, practice has clearly pre-dated theory, so our conversation stands on the shoulders of a long radical tradition. What can we learn from the practical examples of liberation theology in Latin America?

PM: I am not sure, Petar, how many of your readers are old enough to remember two earth-trembling and maleficent incidents in El Salvador that occurred in the 1980s during the civil war that broke out during the military dictatorship from 1979 to 1992. I am referring to the five priests and two women who were murdered outside the Jesuit residence of the Universidad Centroamericana (UCA; founded in 1965), San Salvador, in November 1989. Those murdered were the university rector Ignacio Ellacuría, an internationally recognized liberation theologian; Segundo Montes, dean of the sociology department and director of the University Institute of Human Rights; Ignacio Martín Baró, head of the psychology department; theology professors Juan Ramón Moreno and Amando López; and Joaquin López y López, who headed the Fe y Alegria network of schools for the poor. Julia Elba Ramos, wife of the caretaker at the UCA and her daughter Celina were also killed (Ellacuría & Sobrino, 1993).

Prior to this horrendous event, in 1980, (the now beatified) Archbishop Óscar Arnulfo Romero was gunned down saying mass in a small hospital chapel. Before the military regime came to power in 1970s' El Salvador, a number of Jesuits there had begun rethinking and repivoting their work in a concerted attempt to embrace fully the preferential option for the poor that emerged from the conference in Medellín, Colombia, and to stand shoulder-to-shoulder and heart-to-heart with the poor and powerless campesinos. They understood this to mean actively supporting the rights of campesinos and civilian movements promoting social, economic, and political reform.

During the years of the military regime, it was Father Ignacio Ellacuría, rector at the UCA, who played an influential role during the tumultuous decade of military rule in reframing the university's mission that involved standing in solidarity with the country's impoverished majorities. Ensepulchred in a cemetery of silence and fear, the campesinos were in dire need of government reforms as well as protection from the church, which often stood silent in the face of large-scale torture and mass killings carried out by the heavily armed military regime. Echoing the language of Medellín, the university's 1979 mission was inextricably linked to the service of the people and, in fact, the mission of the university was in a large sense oriented by the oppressed campesinos themselves (Ellacuría & Sobrino, 1993).

Evidently, the Salvadoran government viewed Father Ignacio Ellacuría and the UCA as a serious threat to the USA's continued financial and political backing. The US-backed military dictatorship was well aware that if Salvadorean liberation theologians flagged the US Congress about human rights abuses by the government, it might withdraw its crucial financial support, weapons sales, and military training (including methods of torture) in the School of the Americas operated by the USA. The US-trained Atlocatl battalion (who trained the Salvadorean death squads) massacred thousands of unarmed peasants during the dirty war and hundreds were slain in El Mozote alone in 1981. They did not want the Catholic Church interfering in their practices of slaughtering innocent peasants whom they suspected of supporting guerrilla fighters. The government saw this reign of terror as a necessary step in ridding the country of a communist menace that, if not stamped out, would eviscerate the established Salvadorean ruling class.

PJ: Can we say that it was their Christian faith, and the backup of the institution of the Catholic Church, that made resistance so powerful?

PM: Certainly … but there was another factor at play among the Jesuits that made them so fearless. There was an influence on the Jesuits' work more immediate than Medellín's teaching of social justice: the example of the martyr Archbishop Óscar Romero. Shortly after the murders, Major Eric Warren Buckland, a senior US military advisor in El Salvador, testified that his Salvadoran counterpart, Colonel Carlos Armando Avíles Buitrago, chief of psychological operations for the Salvadoran Joint Command, informed him in advance of the planned killing. He later retracted his statement under pressure. Is it so incredible that at least one US official had knowledge of the plot to kill the Jesuits weeks before the event? And did nothing?

In my book, *Pedagogy of Insurrection* (McLaren, 2015), I wrote a last chapter that I named "Critical rage pedagogy." Here I unleashed a critical rage – using a combination of spoken word and other literary tropes – at the history of human atrocity.

To me, the Kingdom of God is not isolated to, say, a Beethoven symphony, Gregorian chants, the ecstasy of contemplating a mathematical formula, or to a painting by one of the great masters (although I certainly love art and music – not so much mathematics, I will confess). For me, the Kingdom of God is found more tangibly on the picket line, in solidarity with the suffering of those who are being brutalized everyday by capitalism by governments, by death squads and by religious edicts that marginalize them and exclude them from their full humanity. The Kingdom of God is found in the act of struggling and sacrificing for the other. Not speaking out for the other, since groups can very often speak for themselves, but speaking *alongside and with* others, as allies, as friends, as comrades, and as brothers and sisters in Christ.

PJ: Christians in Latin America went through some terrible experiences....

PM: It is difficult for some people outside of Latin America to comprehend the horrific suffering endured by Catholic priests and nuns in that part of the world during the dirty wars in the 1970s and 1980s, wars involving military dictatorships supported by the USA and death squads trained by the US military. In 1980 four US women, two Maryknoll nuns, an Ursuline nun, and a lay volunteer, were stopped by the military in El Salvador as they traveled from the airport on their way to work with impoverished campesino communities. With encouragement from their commander, a group of National Guardsmen took the women to a cow pasture where they were tortured, raped, and murdered. The rapes and assassinations of Maryknoll nuns, Sister Maura Clarke and Sister Ita Ford, Ursuline Sister Dorothy Kazel, and lay missionary Jean Donovan shocked the world. Sr Ita Ford was targeted specifically by US-backed Salvadoran death squads because she was an outspoken critic in defense of the poor. She wrote the following in a letter to her sister:

> You say you don't want anything to happen to me. [...] I'd prefer it that way myself – but I don't see that we have control over the forces of madness, and if you could choose to enter into other people's suffering, or to love others, you at least have to consent in some way to the possible consequences. Actually what I've learned here is that death is not the worst evil. We look death in the face every day. But the cause of the death is evil. That's what we have to wrestle and fight against. (Dear, 2006)

Many priests and nuns had committed themselves to those who had been victimized by military regimes; they had placed themselves squarely in solidarity with the crucified of history, those whose lives had been devastated by what Leonardo Boff calls the "international sin" of poverty (Boff, 1987, p. 118) and those who were brutally tortured and "disappeared" by the military regimes. Boff draws our attention to the case of Franciscan Father Ivan Bettencourt, a Colombian diocesan missionary who worked in the Olancho province of Honduras. In 1976, Bettencourt was tortured and killed along with US citizen Father Michael Cypher and 10 campesino organizers after speaking out and organizing against a local land grab in Honduras. This event became known as the "Horcones Massacre." Boff writes that Bettencourt was seized and interrogated, to force him to confess that he was a "Marxist subversive." They cut off his ears and interrogated him. They cut off his nose and interrogated him some more. They cut out his tongue and declared the interrogation at an end. They sliced his body to ribbons. He was still twitching so they machine-gunned him. Finally, they threw him into a well and hid the well under earth and rubble. Father Ivan died defending his brothers and sisters (Boff, 1987, p. 120).

PJ: These priests and nuns have exhibited remarkable stamina and courage. What can we learn from their stories and experiences?

PM: Some compare the courage and bravery of some of the renegade priests and nuns to that of Che Guevara. Che's motto was "Hay que endurecerse sin perder jamás la ternura" (One must endure [become hard, toughen oneself] without losing tenderness). Some see Che as a secular saint, who gave his life for the poor and the suffering in America Latina. Risking death for the cause of the crucified and impoverished of this world gives life meaning, and Che's legacy inspired millions throughout Latin America and the Caribbean. Priests informed by liberation theology saw their mission in light of the social gospel of Jesus Christ, that is, in terms of the political import of the message of Jesus, and bringing about the reign of the Kingdom of God, which included finding collective transcendence in the suffering servant through forgiveness, and through trust and faith in God. We cannot focus on the Christ of personal salvation alone, which is what many evangelicals would have us do. Our individual sins must be reflectively engaged and confronted in light of the gospel message, of course, but we cannot forget the social sins, such as capitalism, which we know is dependent for its survival on surplus value and the exploitation of human labor. Part of what we need to do is to evaluate the events in Jesus' life in light of the socio-historical context of his own life. This demands a social-scientific approach to the gospel message as well as historical-critical approaches. But the social justice aspect of the gospel of Jesus Christ cannot be denied.

I look at the US social order today in terms of the popularity at the moment of Donald Trump; there appears to be a blend of social Darwinism and the racial superiority of white Europeans, nationalism in the form of American exceptionalism and, of course, a religious triumphalism in terms of a God that has given the USA a providential role to play in history. Against this White Jesus of the diseased colonial imagination that secured the privilege of Whites is the Black Jesus, which grasps the perils of racism and imperialism and the prosperity gospel that has grown out of the prosperity gospel of US capitalism. Reggie Williams (2014) has written an interesting book, *Bonhoeffer's Black Jesus*, that illustrates the impact that the preaching of Adam Clayton Powell Sr, pastor of Harlem's Abyssinian Baptist Church, had on Dietrich Bonhoeffer when he was a Sloane Fellow at Union Theological Seminary in New York for the 1930–1931 academic year. His understanding of the Black experience of suffering, resistance, and transcendence helped him to understand what the Nazis were trying to do to the oppressed peoples of his homeland and also helped him understand the perils of developments within European Christianity.

PJ: What about armed revolutionary violence?

PM: Some scholars and activists cite Frantz Fanon to support acts of violence on the part of revolutionaries, in that Fanon believed violence helps colonized peoples overcome their inferiority complex and gives colonized subjects the necessary courage to continue their struggle. However, Peter Hudis offers a different perspective. In his magisterial book on Fanon, he cites recent studies by Marnia Lazreg and others, based on interviews with Front de Libération Nationale (FLN) militants, which maintain "that violence has, at best, an ephemeral 'cleansing' role. More often it dehumanizes and produces long-term distress in its participants" (Hudis, 2015, p. 121). Throughout the conflicts in Latin America throughout the 1970s and 1980s, priests certainly put their lives on the line to protect and serve the oppressed. Some joined revolutionary battalions to work as chaplains.

7   The First Religious War of the 21st Century

PJ: By standing on the side of the poor, liberation theology has entered the highest spheres of international politics.… How does this politics work in practice?

PM: I agree with Noam Chomsky who says that "the U.S. has often been bitterly opposed to Christianity" (cited in Chaudary, 2007) and describes the attacks on liberation theology by the US administration as "the first religious war of the 21st century" (cited in Rivage-Seul, 2016). Petar, to back up some of my claims, just read some of the following cables that were released by

Wikileaks. In 2013, Daniel Kovalik examined very revealing cables released by Wikileaks that were sent by the US Embassy to the Vatican. For example, in one cable headed "The 'Threat' of Liberation Theology" dated 6 May 2007, the Embassy reveals its unvarnished ideological stance against liberation theology in a message related to the visit of Pope Benedict XVI to Brazil:

> Another major contextual issue for the visit is the challenge to the traditional Church played by liberation theology. Pope John Paul (aided by the current pope when he was Cardinal Ratzinger) made major efforts to stamp out this Marxist analysis of class struggle. It had come to be promoted by a significant number of Catholic clergy and lay people, who in a political compromise sometimes sanctioned violence "on behalf of the people." The more orthodox form of liberation theology that sided with the poor and oppressed had undergone a reductionist reading that the Vatican sought to correct. To a large extent, Pope John Paul II beat down "liberation theology", but in the past few years, it has seen a resurgence in various parts of Latin America. (Kovalik, 2013)

Another cable from the US Embassy to the Vatican, on 14 January 2008, included a summary of Pope Benedict's current views on Liberation Theology:

> Also important – and disturbing – to the Holy See is the resilience of Latin American liberation theology. During his time as the powerful Prefect of the Congregation for the Doctrine of the Faith in the 1980s and 1990s, the then Cardinal Joseph Ratzinger opposed liberation theology for its overt sympathy for revolutionary movements. Some of the supporters of this theology – including former clerics – now occupy prominent political positions in countries like Bolivia and Paraguay, a phenomenon that one commentator has described as the secular reincarnation of liberation theology. For the Holy See, the Church Magisterium (the teachings of the Catholic Church) on social issues already advocates strongly for the rights of the underprivileged. This advocacy, often described as the Church's "preferential option for the poor", should not include clerics assuming high level governmental positions or running for office. In calling for a reduction of domestic tensions in Latin America, the Holy See hopes to prevent a climate fertile for activist, progressive clerics to coalesce with populist, authoritarian governments. (Kovalik, 2013)

What follows is an excerpt from a cable from 27 September 2005 released by the US Embassy in San Salvador, entitled, "El Salvador: The Declining Influence of The Roman Catholic Church." This cable states that

> In 1977, former Archbishop Oscar Arnulfo Romero adopted an outspoken stance in favor of "liberation theology" that alienated many of the church's most influential members. Archbishop Arturo Rivera y Damas followed Romero's example during his 1983–1994 tenure. Much changed in the years following the 1992 Peace Accords, which ended repression and violence on the part of government forces and guerrillas. With the selection of Fernando Saenz Lacalle as Archbishop of San Salvador in 1995, the Catholic Church entered a new era during which it withdrew its support for "liberation theology"; Saenz-Lacalle has placed a renewed emphasis on individual salvation and morality. However, an underlying division still exists within the Salvadoran Catholic Church vis-à-vis such political issues. (Kovalik, 2013)

The Embassy later explains that "[t]he Salvadoran Catholic Church has in effect been 're-Romanized'" (Kovalik, 2013). Kovalik comments on this cable as follows:

> what is left unspoken is that it was the murder of good people like Archbishop Romero that led to the Church "re-Romanizing" – a term with a double meaning, for it can properly mean that the Church is again in line with the Vatican in Rome (the intended meaning), but also that it has returned to the pro-Empire stance the Church has maintained (with limited interruption after the second Vatican Council in 1962) since 324 A.D. In other words, mission accomplished for both the Vatican and the U.S. (Kovalik, 2013)

Another cable from San Salvador, dated 24 June 2008, attempts its own historical overview of the FMLN (Frente Farabundo Martí para la Liberación Nacional or Farabundo Martí National Liberation). The Embassy offers a highly distorted picture when it writes:

> During the 12 year Salvadoran civil war (1980–92), the FMLN attempted to overthrow the government utilizing a strategy that included armed struggle, terrorism, socialist/communist political indoctrination. The liberation theology movement within the Catholic Church and labor unions largely supported these efforts. The group received monetary support and arms from the Soviet Bloc and Cuba. (Kovalik, 2013)

Here the liberation theology movement is unjustly painted as supporting terrorism with the clandestine support from the Soviet Union and Cuba. Absent from these overblown claims is the fact that the US-backed military and paramilitary death squads in El Salvador committed horrendous acts of terrorism against the civilian population that has been clearly documented. Furthermore, the leading proponents of the liberation theology movement, such as Archbishop Romero, condemned violence from both sides of the conflict. The release of these confidential cables from the US Embassy by Wikileaks, as reported by Daniel Kovalik, reveals the staggering extent of the current war against liberation theology by the US State Department. Given the history of coordinated US attacks on liberation theology, it is difficult to disagree with Noam Chomsky when he states that,

> the U.S. Army helped defeat liberation theology, which was a dominant force, and it was an enemy for the same reason that secular nationalism in the Arab world was an enemy – it was working for the poor. This is the same reason why Hamas and Hezbollah are enemies: they are working for the poor. It doesn't matter if they are Catholic or Muslim or anything else; that is intolerable. The Church of Latin America had undertaken "the preferential option for the poor." They committed the crime of going back to the Gospels. The contents of the Gospels are mostly suppressed (in the U.S.); they are a radical pacifist collection of documents. It was turned into the religion of the rich by the Emperor Constantine, who eviscerated its content. If anyone dares to go back to the Gospels, they become the enemy, which is what liberation theology was doing. (Cited in Chaudary, 2007)

PJ: Speaking with and speaking together with the poor is one of the central messages of both liberation theology and revolutionary critical pedagogy. In the capitalist world, however, the very act of speaking is privileged – so many people are excluded from full participation in economic, political, and other spheres....

PM: William Robinson (2004, 2014, 2016a, 2016b) has reported that approximately one third of humanity is locked out of productive participation in the capitalist economy. We can find a larger number of this group in Latin America. There has been a dramatic shift in the USA and other countries since the end of World War II from an admirable concern with social welfare to a preoccupation with social control and creating a national security state. There is a pronounced fear now among the ruling elite that outraged workers will rise up and protest living in what is fast becoming planet slum. Robinson notes that the role of the state in creating social cohesion through the accumulation of capital is fracturing as a result of the crisis of capitalist overaccumulation. Consequently, the state is fast losing its "legitimatizing" function, and we can see this now in the election cycle here in the USA when outsiders to the government – such as Trump – are rising up and urging people to demonize the surplus population through a logic overlain with hate and violence.

PJ: More often than not, the concept of surplus population (which is a terrible phrase in its own right) is linked to changes in the structure of employment caused by new technologies. What is the role of technology in this context?

PM: Not only is capitalism retooling itself, but also hiring practices for college graduates are likely to shift in an ominous direction. It likely will not be too long before Human Resource Professionals hired by your potential employer will determine your fitness for employment, extensions of credit, or admission to certain schools, based on computerized personality screening and data collection. For example, personality tests designed by computer programs that capture and evaluate your "Likes" on Facebook and other digital markers could follow you throughout your career or perhaps even "haunt" you. Wu Youyou, Michael Kosinski, Thore Graepel, and David Stillwell (Kosinski et al., 2013; Youyou et al., 2015) of Cambridge University's Department of Psychology and the Stanford University Department of Computer Science are developing a computer model of psychological assessment and personality profiling that assesses their subjects' personalities based on their "generic digital footprint" and employs what they call a "five-factor model" consisting of a standardized set of personality traits that measure Extraversion, Agreeableness, Conscientiousness, Neuroticism (sometimes named by its polar opposite, Emotional Stability), and Openness to Experience.

Computerized programs like this one – which the researchers argue are better equipped to assess personality traits than living and breathing human beings – are very likely to be utilized by future employers. This type of research goes much further than the "predictive analytics" used by Facebook and other social media sites. Certain algorithms or websites that you visit will determine that you are unsuited for jobs that you want. How has technology turned into such a companion of the security state? Freire maintained that "education for liberation does not merely free students from blackboards just to offer them projectors" (1973, p. 4). Computer science here has become completely domesticating. They are the result of the contradictions within their own power structures, serving capital by instrumentalizing our personalities and subjective agency.

Is this so surprising today, when public education is being turned into a series of investment opportunities? We see it in the retooling of colleges in order to serve better financial and military-industrial interests, in the overuse and exploitation of contingent faculty, in the growth of for-profit degree-granting institutions, in rising tuition and, not to mention, the assault on critical citizenship in favor of consumer citizenship. There are many struggles to take up in the making of the Kingdom of God.

PJ: Speaking of profiling technologies, computer science has become indeed domesticating. What is the role of social media in these developments?

PM: I worry, Petar, about social media. Yes, I can see the possibilities surrounding information sharing and communication across nations and impacting geopolitical arenas for the common good. But there is a dark side and it is everywhere. Google is a megacorporation, part of the social brain that masks itself as an innocent and innovative Silicon Valley offspring, spawned by computer and technology nerds sporting bow-ties and pocket protectors and looking for ways of bringing people together to share information. It pretends that it is autonomous from the imperatives and foreign policy decisions of the state and not in collusion with the military industrial complex, but in fact it is insinuated very seamlessly into the whole machinery of rule and hegemony of the ruling class, what Gramsci called the integral state. The patricians, proconsuls, and nomenclature of Google have become the custodians of secret dealings they have had with the US State Department. Google shares the same political DNA with the National Security Agency (NSA), the CIA, and the Pentagon. Google is a sentinel for US foreign policy, and charioteers for US imperialism. Their apparatchiks come from all the dark catacombs of the national security state.

8   Towards a Global Ethics of Solidarity

PJ: I am fascinated by your stories and examples from South America ... and I deeply sympathize with the message of liberation theology. Yet, Peter, I come from a radically different context – Eastern Europe – where various Christian denominations are traditionally on the side of the right. In Croatia, it is the Catholic Church that campaigns against gay marriages, and the right to abortion.... It is just last week that they had another rally. When you see those people protesting to penalize anything that deviates from their own vision of the social norm, it is hard to feel empowerment and emancipation. ... In this part of the world, unsurprisingly, lefties of all shapes and colors are very cautious towards religion. How do you go about such contradictions between liberation theology and our social reality?

PM: I am not surprised, Petar, about the Church in Croatia. We have a strong right-wing Catholic movement here in the USA that is decidedly against Pope Francis and liberation theology. Francis is not a proponent of liberation theology but of what developed in his native Argentina as *teologia del pueblo,* or theology of the people. It begins with the experiences of the oppression of people in the face of neoliberal capitalism and corporate globalization. The Catholic Church is not monolithic. There are fundamental ideological differences within the Church. I think that Pope Francis's experiences with the military dictatorship and his contact with fellow Jesuits who did support liberation theology made a powerful impact on him and helped him to adopt certain perspectives from liberation theology, such as a critique of global capitalism.

Liberation theologians openly contest certain positions taken by the established Church, just as Pope Francis does. Francis is more moderate in many of his views than many of the prominent exponents of liberation theology. Nevertheless, he has taken strong positions against global capitalism and environmental destruction that I welcome and applaud. Do we obscure the spiritual nature of the gospel by calling for more than just an identification with the poor but rather a robust confrontation with the rich and powerful? Do we administer to the poor without asking why they are poor? Here we need to recall the words of Brazil's Dom Hélder Câmara, whom Paulo Freire very much admired: "When I give food to the poor, they call me a saint; when I ask why the poor have no food, they call me a communist" (Câmara, 2009).

In 1965, as the famous Vatican II Council was coming to a close, Hélder Câmara led 40 bishops late at night into the Catacombs of Domitillia outside of Rome. After celebrating the Eucharist, they signed a document under the title of the Pact of the Catacombs, challenging themselves and others to live lives of evangelical poverty and to dedicate themselves to serving the two-thirds of humanity who live in poverty and deprivation. There are certainly ideological differences within the Church and in some countries – such as Croatia and Poland – the right-wing factions of the Church hold sway.

PJ: Your answer reflects political tensions between the left-wing and the right-wing political factions within the church. However, I am conflicted about much more "mundane" things, and the ones that the whole Catholic Church seems to agree about. Examples include the explicit position of the global Catholic Church against using condoms, against abortion, and against gay rights. In some areas of Africa, for instance, AIDS kills significant parts of the population, while the official church position – articulated, amongst others, by Pope Benedict XVI – claims that the HIV epidemic is "a tragedy that cannot be overcome by money alone, that cannot be overcome through the distribution of condoms, which even aggravates the problems" (cited in Butt, 2009). How do you go about such teachings and their consequences? More generally, how do you reconcile them with the message of liberation and emancipation?

PM: Yes, there are positions taken by the Church hierarchy that are firmly established and to which I remain in trenchant disagreement. And yes, they involve many of the same "mundane" issues to which you allude, but I do not think they are so much mundane as pervasive and impacting everyday life. I remember a Paulist father once telling me that I should never lose my critical approach to questions of dogma and faith. We want you to be a thinking Catholic, he told me. I do not believe the guardians of the faith would be very pleased with revolutionary priests accompanying guerilla armies as chaplains, such as Camilo Torres of Colombia or Gaspar Garcia Laviana of Spain. Yet I see their actions as heroic. We must act according to our conscience, in deep reflection and contemplation.

Going back to powerful analysis by Noam Chomsky, we should also consider the conditions in which these positions are being developed. Speaking about the US context, Chomsky says:

> There is a correlation, common in other parts of the world as well. When life is not offering expected benefits, people commonly turn to some means of support from religion. Furthermore, there is a lot of cynicism. It was recognized by party managers of both parties (Republicans and Democrats) that if they can throw some red meat to religious fundamentalist constituencies, like say we are against gay rights, they can pick up votes. In fact, maybe a third of the electorate – if you cater to elements of the religious right in ways that the business world, the real constituency, doesn't care that much about. (Cited in Chaudary, 2007)

These messages of the Church hierarchy are being heavily instrumentalized by politicians, who gain cheap votes over issues such as abortion or gay rights.

PJ: And what about spiritual aspects of these messages?

PM: I very much appreciate indigenous traditions and what they bring to discussions of spirituality. My approach is broadly ecumenical and includes Buddha, Mohammed, Krishna, and the Great Spirit of the native American traditions. Human welfare and wellbeing should be placed above the law. Condemnation of homosexuality in the Bible is very different from the way progressive individuals view homosexuality today, which is grounded in post-Enlightenment science (Rivage-Seul, 2008). It seems to some exegetes that what was forbidden was not homosexuality itself but heterosexuals engaged in homosexual acts (Rivage-Seul, 2008). Jesus himself was silent on the question of homosexuality. I agree with Boff when he writes that "The paradox of the cross is incomprehensible both to formal and to dialectical reason" (1987, p. 135), but this should not be used as a pretext for blind obedience to law. What is concealed in this mystery will be revealed through struggle – that is, through praxis – and not simply reflection or adherence to laws with which we disagree. Boff writes that "the incarnation is already present at the beginning of the universe" (1997, p. 178) and "the universe culminates in each individual in the form of consciousness" (1997, p. 121). He writes that "all energies and morphogenetic fields have acted synergistically so that each one might be born and be that singular and unique person that he or she is" and so it seems to me that we each have something very worthwhile to contribute to the debate through a cultivation of critical consciousness.

We have, all of us, been here since the beginning of the universe and are made out of star dust. And it is the guiding principles of the universe that brought us here, and that has resulted in the potential for our self-actualization, and that has taken 15 billion years of evolutionary processes. We had better start to listen to indigenous sages who have understood this far better than we Euro-Americans here in Babylon. We need to abandon our anthropocentric and mimetic desires and subject ourselves to a global ethics of solidarity, compassion, and fellowship so that our outer ecologies can be brought into cosmogenetic harmony with our ecology of the mind and spirit. And here we bring our maieutic processes of pedagogy into dialogue with a Freirean approach to conscientization. In other words, we bring together history, mind, and spirit. I reject a turgid monotheism that would cleave us from spiritual traditions that predate Christianity. In short, I would say that we must act in accordance with our own conscience.

9   Between the Material and the Spiritual

PJ: Are there any theoretical and/or practical dissonances between Marxism and Christianity in your theory? If there are, how do you go about them?

PM: While some might argue that traditional non-religious Marxism is not as equipped as theological traditions to engage fundamental questions pertaining to the hermeneutics of spirituality, there are numerous Marxist theorists who have written profoundly about issues of the spirit – here, I am thinking of Ernst Bloch, Walter Benjamin, and Erich Fromm, just to name a few. I think Marxism does address issues of the human spirit, but what interests me, in particular, is an engagement with a tradition that deals with a triune god. Of course, liberation theology comes in many forms: Chicano liberation theology; Latinx liberation theology; Native American liberation theology; African American liberation theology. Therefore, I do not want to limit liberation theology to the political theology that comes out of Europe, or to the Latin American liberation theology that is primarily Catholic and pastoral.

I work as a Marxist materialist but I believe there is a world beyond physicalism. That is a world of hope. Hope is conjugated in opposition to injustice and gestated in the struggle of humanity against inhumanity. Rubem Alves (cited in Boff, 1987, p. 124) writes of hope as follows:

> Hope is the presentiment that the imagination is more real, and reality less real, than we had thought. It is the sensation that the last word does not belong to the brutality of facts with their oppression and repression. It is the suspicion that reality is far more complex than realism would have us believe, that the frontiers of the possible are not determined by the limits of the present, and that, miraculously and surprisingly, life is readying the creative event that will open the way to freedom and resurrection.

Hope does not deliver us from suffering. But hope, I believe, can deliver us from the fear of suffering. It does this by giving us the courage to believe that we are not fated to live in misery, that light does shine through the cracks of the day-to-day sepulcher in which we find ourselves, in this cold and damp undercroft, in this darkness of inevitability.

PJ: What are the more general challenges that you encountered on the path of reconciliation between the spiritual and the scientific?

PM: Writing *Pedagogy of Insurrection* (McLaren, 2015) brought me face-to-face with questions that by no means have I worked out to my satisfaction. What I can say is that I certainly do not believe that knowledge is simply produced by the rational permutations of the brain. I do believe that it is possible to posit a divine consciousness that pervades our existence. I will note parenthetically or in passing only that there are some interesting speculative developments in theology centered around some ideas in quantum mechanics where field-based waves are seen as producing the hardware of the universe and the entities of the space-time domain, while the scalar or non-vectorial waves produce information without carrying energy and act like the software of the universe. The information that interconnects entities throughout space-time includes upward and downward causation, which helps to explain why the past is always present. Here, a definition of God might include the potentials of the universe for its self-creation, which might involve, for instance, tuning the universe to the evolution of complexity.

Here, Teilhard de Chardin's work (1959, 1964, 1965, 1966a, 1966b, 1968) becomes even more interesting and relevant. In this view, God can influence the course of revolution without interfering with the laws of nature. Some physicists argue that the original presence of this information can be ascribed to a transcendental creative act where the growth and development of this information is considered immanent. I am not well-versed enough in physics to evaluate this speculative argument. However, there are several practice-oriented codes of moral behavior that have been generated out of this work by Ervin Laszlo (2014), who has come up with a minimum moral code (live so that others can live) and a maximum moral code (act so as to further the evolution of a humanly favorable dynamic equilibrium in the biosphere). I would modify this, however, to include non-human animals. To me, holistic and local domains of consciousness are interdependent and material and mental domains are bidirectional so that when unconscious contents become conscious, this transition could possibly alter the unconscious memories left behind.

PJ: What are the ontological implications of this? Are you saying that something can exist beyond matter?

PM: Let us just say that I remain skeptical of the physicalist interpretation of reality that denies certain experiences that are connected to the transphysical. The idea of a nonemergent irreducible mind within a psychophysical world is worth considering in my estimation and this, of course, would take us to the Renaissance Neoplatonists and also to Bergson, Emerson, Schopenhauer, and Kant. Here I would need a broader theological framework that many Marxist traditions are not equipped to handle. An expanded view of mind is not, in my view, antithetical to Marxism. Consciousness is not a mere epiphenomenon of the material brain. We need new visionary taxonomies to help us understand anomalous experiences that cannot be explained by a physicalist interpretation. Does that mean that I believe the cosmos was created by an upwelling of the mind of God? Does that mean that Joseph of Copertino could actually fly? I do not spend a lot of time pondering these questions. I am more concerned with living with clarity and in preferential solidarity with those who are victims of the scandal of poverty and who belong to despised racial and ethnic groups and exploited social classes.

I am not here trying to push a neo-Platonist line of reasoning – yet, I remain open to various explanations of how the cosmos came into being. In my political work, I remain very much a historical materialist. I think this is the best approach for understanding the dialectical relationship between capitalism and labor (and materialism and idealism, for that matter) in the larger struggle for a socialist future. While I do not deny the material world, I am very interested in the nature of consciousness, and I would not in the least be surprised if consciousness exists independently of the brain, with the brain serving as a type of filtering device to gain access to the deep layers of the psyche. The brain here is conceived as a system that constrains the supraliminal conscious expression of normally inaccessible subliminal contents. And here I am echoing the work of F. W. H. Myers and William James and the work of contemporary researcher Edward F. Kelly (Kelly et al., 2007, 2015) and the notions of the subliminal self and the supraliminal self.

Now all of this interest I have in religious experiences, the nature of consciousness, etc., is mostly just engaging in thought games. One day perhaps I will be able to make more nuanced reflections about the nature of the cosmos, our role on this earth, and the place that faith plays in our lives. Yes, I do return over and over again to certain questions, figures, and memories. I return to questions "on the ground," questions that involve what Michelle Alexander calls "the new Jim Crow." The massive discrimination policies directed towards people of color in the areas of education, employment, public benefits; the mass incarceration of African-Americans and Latinos through the war on drugs and anti-crime policies; a criminal justice system responsible for creating and reproducing the racial hierarchy in the USA; or what could be called the American Caste System – the privatization of prisons ensuring large incarceration rates of prisoners of color.

PJ: I am interested in this dialectic between the material and the spiritual, the real and the mystical, the human and the divine ... and I guess that, in order to remain living in this world and with this world, one needs to find a certain balance between those radically different views to our earthly existence. How do you go about obvious and inherent differences and contradictions contained in these dichotomies? What keeps your materialist critique from plunging into pure mystics; what keeps your spiritual worldview attached to the material world?

PM: As a dissident educator whose resistance has been forged on picket lines, on marches, amidst military sweeps of unruly neighborhoods, in libraries, churches, seminar rooms, museums, revolutionary institutes, classrooms, clandestine meeting places, and public squares, I have always felt that I live in the interstices of internal contradictions, in the hinterlands of the unexcluded third, in the fructifying poetry of chaos and the absurdity of being, in the pluriverse of values in which we are pushed to make choices, where being and nonbeing interpenetrate amidst the explosion of metaphors and magical incantations, where everything transforms into something else, where whispers from primeval groves of evergreens turn into thunderclaps, where an infant's sigh turns into the oratory of a politician, where journeys begin at their destinations, where coherence mingles amicably with ambiguity.

As a teenager I was very interested in Theosophy, eastern religions, the Christian mystics, the desert fathers, and the lives of saints. I do not pay much attention in my recent work to Bruno Giordano, Marcion, Valentinus, Simon Magus, Appelles, or the Christological or ecclesial Gnosticism or Docetism that is associated with their teachings, which is not to say they do not offer some interesting points of debate. In this respect, however, I follow Jon Sobrino in defending the living, breathing, bleeding, and pulsating flesh of the man we call the Christ, the *ecce homo*. Of course I am inspired by the life of the saints and martyrs such as Saint Maximilian Kolbe, patron saint of drug addicts and political prisoners, whose prison cell I visited last year in Auschwitz. In my own work I have found it important to uphold the humanity of Christ without de-emphasizing Christ's divinity, and for me the humanity of Christ is best embodied historically in Jesus' birth, death, and resurrection, and all that occurred during his dispensation among us. Here I am emphasizing Christ walking among us, among the victims of the brutality of structural sin, among the sick, the homeless, the diseased, the despised, those who despair of life, those whose pilloried flesh stand as a testament to the injustice meted out by the powerful to the most vulnerable. In other words, I try to concern myself with the story or narrative of Christ, his narrative being that in no way denies Christ's divinity.

But we can very easily become lost in the unreality, the mystical body of Christ, or the Church, for that matter. Our humanness, our soft flesh, and breakable bones is what Sobrino (2001, p. 276) refers to as "the condition of possibility of salvation" through the "homo verus" (Sobrino, 2001, p. 278), that is, through Christ's constitutive relationship with God and history, and history and transcendence. We need, as Sobrino argues, a truly humanized Christ, not simply a demythified Christ produced in the libraries and sanctuaries of Rome by theologians of various ecclesiastical stripes. Let us not get too tangled up in what is real in Christ and what is divine, for what is truly human is that which can bring us victory over inhumanity, over the anti-Kingdom, through speaking truth to the demonic power ensepulchred in the vaults of alienation wrought by capitalism and its attendant antagonisms. So, for me, developing a philosophy of praxis means learning how to walk in history, as both the subject and the object of our human story, lacing up our thirsty boots and refreshing our parched spirit as we journey alongside the victims of social sin, moving from the historical to the transcendent through faith.

10   The Socialist Kingdom of God

PJ: An important aspect of Christian mystic – and the one you earlier identified as one of the main intersections between Christianity and Marxism – is the eschatological aspect of history. For Christians, this eschaton is the (arrival of) the Kingdom of God; for Marx and Engels, it is utopian socialism predicted as early as in the *Communist Manifesto* (Marx & Engels, 1848). Can you elaborate upon this eschaton a little deeper? What, for you, is the Kingdom of God?

PM: We have to honor the victims, speak to their lives of suffering in their theological reality. As Sobrino notes, the crucified peoples of this earth must not be remembered as some historical add-ons to our Sunday sermons but as those who were victims of the anti-Kingdom. After all, the anti-Kingdom is the Kingdom of Capital, of Wall Street and the world of value production (i.e. monetized wealth), of profit, of the exploitation and alienation of human labor, of private ownership of the means of production, of the market mechanism that forces capitalists (regardless of whether or not they are good people) to exploit workers, of the emergent transnational capital consolidated in a global capitalist historic bloc and the pillage zones of America Latina, and of the deregulated, informalized, and de-unionized capital-labor relation and the worldwide subordination of labor.

But here I need to emphasize something Sobrino (2001) has discussed at length in his many important writings. While we focus on the divine in Christ, we have forgotten the Kingdom of God of which Christ speaks. So when we identify as Catholics, why have we forgotten the primacy of creating the Kingdom of God and bringing it forth as Christ exhorted us to do? In my view, it is because our entire system operates as the anti-Kingdom. Christianity itself is undergirded by the imperatives of the anti-Kingdom in that it has attached itself to the imperatives of capitalism. To create the Kingdom of God means seeking the creation of a social universe outside of value production, or the production of profit for the rich. Creating the Kingdom of God means liberating the poor and this means ending the brutal war against the poor unleashed by the deregulation of the market. It means challenging the anti-Kingdom that stands against immigrants seeking a better life, against migrant workers, against refugees, and the intergenerationally reproduced barrios of planet slum. We focus instead on eternal life, on gnostic mysteries, and distance ourselves from the Kingdom of God with reality TV and the hundreds of TV channels we have at our disposal. We confuse the drive to increase material wealth with the drive to produce value, or create endless profits that can be expanded indefinitely.

In our forays into the hinterlands of mysticism, we cannot forget that the Kingdom of God is, in Sobrino's terms, a "type of historical-social-collective reality" (2001, p. 334) and not, as the old union song has it, a "pie in the sky when you die." The Kingdom of God is not some metaphor for an unearthly paradise, some ecclesiastical makeover of the earth in terms of the divine Christ or such that the holy and apostolic church becomes the prime sign or marker of the Kingdom. Clearly, for me, the Kingdom of God is not some place where well-heeled and aristocratic-looking souls lounge about in togas and golden wreaths. For me, the Kingdom of God is more likely found on the picket lines, in the temple cleared of the moneylenders, in a world where the rich no longer dominate, a world where death squads do not murder peasants with impunity, and where poor tenants do not confront racist landlords and developers do not build themselves towers in glorious homage to their wealth and power while others are forced to sleep under bridges.

PJ: Please explore some practical aspects of the eschaton. What are the main obstacles for its arrival? Where should we seek novel patterns of revolution for social justice?

PM: We have failed to reason dialectically, and to construct in our daily lives a philosophy of praxis grounded in a Christian Marxist humanism. Consequently, we are suffocating – here in the USA – in the furious winds of this Armageddon culture filled with doomsday pronouncements and with extreme right-wing conspiracy theories about a cabal of international bankers taking over the world and leaving the USA in the wake of the corporate globalist elite. This so-called cabal of corporate globalists has left poor whites barricaded in their crumbling towns and inner cities to be monitored by black helicopters from the United Nations and devoured by groups such as Black Lives Matter activists, immigrants of all stripes, Muslims, feminists, West Coast climate activists, and those who run the entertainment industry in the heart of Sodom. The Avenging Angel of the God of Money is a transnational capitalist billionaire and media personality who judges the entire world through the eyes of a circus ringmaster and a beauty pageant judge. Unbeknownst to the working classes, this is exactly the type of savior who will hurt their ranks the most. What has hurt them the most is not the elite political class who run the government, but the economic system that the government has been set up to defend.

The Kingdom of God is not suddenly going to appear after the apocalypse that is haunting us retroactively from the future has eliminated evil once and for all. The Kingdom of God is not designed to save capitalism but to replace it with a more just and humane system that is not driven by the profit motive. The eschaton is now, and it is the struggle for social justice that makes it immanent. We are not talking about the struggle shouldered by liberals singing their sundry progressive platitudes all the way to the offices of their investment bankers. The struggle for social justice stipulates that we come together and figure out how to create a social universe outside of capitalist value production, where the profit motive is eliminated. Education should play a significant role in this struggle, but it does not. This is why I have been trying to advance critical pedagogy as a transnational social movement to bring progressive educators together to face the problems of contemporary capitalism and to seek alternatives, because we are facing a capitalism that has continuously played a role in genocide, ecocide, and epistemicide, the latter referring to the abolition of ecologies of knowing of indigenous peoples.

The international law introduced by the 1948 United Nations Convention on Genocide makes it abundantly clear that the USA systematically sought the complete expiration of native Americans amounting to genocide against first nations peoples. Have we not recently destroyed the nation of Iraq? Have we not tortured and traumatized its population? Have we not soaked its gene pool in depleted uranium and ensured birth defects for generations to come? Has not the USA intervened militarily in approximately 50 countries since World War II? We have a long revolution ahead of us to stop such a global system of war and aggression and to replace capitalism with a socialist alternative.

The pattern of revolution for social justice – for socialism – will not be a straight line but will always be up and down, a path of walking through darkness and light, fighting inside the belly of the beast until, like Jonah, we are spit out onto the shore of hope. Is Jonah inside the belly of the whale not a story of entering the darkness, of being betrayed, of being the scapegoat, of being victimized by power, in order, finally, to land on the shore where we can be regain our breath, where we can be bathed in the light of truth? Is not the story of Jonah inside the whale, really an anti-sign, another way of rendering the doctrine of the cross? Is this not what is called "the paschal mystery"? As Rohr (2016) reminds us, mystery is not something that is impossible to understand, it is "something that you can endlessly understand," since at no point can you say, "I've got it!" Sometimes the descent is so great, so steep, that there seems no hope, just a vortex of horror and turmoil. It seems impossible at times to fathom how humanity can survive the horror of existence, especially during times of war, of economic catastrophe, of existential desperation and despair. How can God be found in this darkness? This truly is the paschal mystery.

PJ: Can you link this paschal mystery, the Christian eschaton described as the Kingdom of God, to Marx's prophecy of the future socialist society?

PM: I do see socialism as fitting in with the Kingdom of God announced by Jesus. Socialists in the past have sometimes made such a connection. Take the case of Helen Macfarlane. In 1850, Scottish governess, Helen Macfarlane, wrote polemical treatises supporting the Chartist movement. She was the first person to translate Hegel's philosophical writings into English and the first person to translate *The Communist Manifesto* into English. The Chartists were the first working-class movement to fight the British establishment in order to secure rights for the working class. For a time, Macfarlane supported Chartist leader Julian Harney in rebuilding the movement from a socialist and international perspective and refused to moderate the movement to win over the radical liberals. She allied herself with Marx and Engels and took on literary giants such a Thomas Carlyle and Charles Dickens. She interpreted Hegel as a humanist pantheist and she defined pantheism in humanistic terms. Her work reflects the Hegelian pantheism of David Strauss and her engagement with Marx and Engels helped her to radicalize Strauss's critical Hegelianism. For Hegel, the importance of the gospels was their symbolic content. For David Strauss, what was important about the gospels was their historicity – as myths that contained the Messianic desires of the early Christian communities (Black, 2014, p. XVII).

Feuerbach believed that theological knowledge was subjective and that the final criterion for the truth was to be found in the senses. Here the ego remains passive and determined by objective reality. For Marx, truth was found through historical praxis, through the negation of the negation. What is interesting about Macfarlane was her ability to merge the ideas of socialism, left Hegelianism, and Marxism with the teachings of Jesus and in doing so spiritualize the struggle for social justice. In 1850 she wrote:

> We Socialist-democrats are the soldiers of a holy cause; we are the exponents of a sublime idea; we are the apostles of the sacred religion of universal humanity. We have sworn by the God who *"made of one blood all nations of the Earth* that we will not pause till we have finished the great work – begun by the Nazarean – of man's redemption from the social miseries which destroy body and soul. (Macfarlane in Black, 2014, p. 22)

PJ: If the Kingdom of God is a "type of historical-social-collective reality" (Sobrino, 2001, p. 334), why should we not just stick to Marx and Engels' utopian socialism? Why, in this context, do we need a God?

PM: As a species on the verge of extinction, we have an ongoing obligation today to commit ourselves to build a network amongst the working class, the peasantry, and the urban cognitariat and precariat in order to break down the immutable hierarchies of power and privilege concomitant with the workings of capitalist society. In our struggle to achieve this, God will be revealed. As Miranda writes: "Only in a world of justice will God be" (1977, p. 45). The revolution therefore depends not on the man himself or the woman herself or on the collectivity (which would be merely expanded egoism), but on the Other. Providing for each according to his or her needs presupposes caring for people simply because they exist and are God's children. The social relations of capitalist exploitation can force us to yield but they cannot oblige us to obey. God is the moral imperative itself, the imperative to struggle against injustice and innocent suffering. God's presence in history, the true revelatory intervention of the God of the Bible in human history, occurs when we take up the struggle for social justice.

It is interesting to note that Marx and Engels entered an organization in 1872 that was founded by Wilhelm Weitling, the founder of German communism.

Weitling's organization was based on a communism grounded entirely in the gospel, as can be seen in his 1845 book, *The Gospel of a Poor Sinner* (Miranda, 1980). Marx was a great admirer of the Peasants' War organized and directed by Thomas Munzer in the 16th century. This was, in effect, the first anti-capitalist revolution. Munzer argued that the Kingdom of God is a condition of society without class differences, without private property, and without state powers opposed to the members of society.

11   The God of the Rich and the God of the Poor

PJ: Your work is a masterpiece of dialectics.... Where issues pertaining to ontology and epistemology pour into issues pertaining to politics and emancipation, there still is – even if only historically constructed – some sort of "division of work" between the different approaches and disciplines. What is the main strength of Marxism in the context of liberation theology?

PM: I return to the basic issues of the violence of capitalism, colonization, genocide, and the underlying epistemicide, which can be best understood as the destruction of epistemologies, ways of knowing, and ecologies of the mind of indigenous peoples throughout the world. Now for some proponents of liberation theology, communism as Marx envisioned is normative in the message of Jesus. And I have faith that the Kingdom of God will overcome the world of suffering precisely because I have faith in the people, the workers, the masses to defeat capital and bring about a more loving and human system for providing for the material needs of humanity. Terry Eagleton writes:

> I have argued already that reason alone can face down a barbarous irrationalism, but that to do so it must draw upon forces and sources of faith which run deeper than itself, and which can therefore bear an unsettling resemblance to the very irrationalism one is seeking to repel. (Eagleton, 2009, p. 161)

It is worth remembering, as Eagleton notes, "The Christian way of indicating that faith is not in the end a question of choice is the notion of grace. Like the world itself from a Christian viewpoint, faith is a gift" (2009, p. 138). Of course, this does not mean we cease examining our faith with evidence from the phenomenal world. Eagleton sees the great struggle today as one in which culture is pitted against civilization. He notes that "culture [...] is too much a matter of affirming what you are or have been, rather than what you might become" (2009, p. 165). And as for religion? Eagleton writes:

> What we know as Christendom saw itself as a unity of culture and civilization. If religion has proved far and away the most powerful, tenacious, universal symbolic form humanity has yet to come up with, it is partly on this account. What other symbolic form has managed to forge such direct links between the most absolute and universal of truths and the everyday practices of countless millions of men and women? What other way of life has brought the most rarefied of ideas and the most palpable of human realities into such intimate relationship? Religious faith has established a hotline from personal interiority to transcendent authority – an achievement upon which the advocates of culture can only gaze with envy. Yet religion is as powerless as culture to emancipate the dispossessed. For the most part, it has not the slightest interest in doing so. (2009, pp. 165–166)

But what of Marxism's potential in reconciling culture and civilization? Eagleton responds as follows:

> If Marxism holds out a promise of reconciling culture and civilization, it is among other things because its founder was both a Romantic humanist and an heir of Enlightenment rationalism. Marxism is about culture and civilization together – sensuous particularity *and* universality, worker and citizen of the world, local allegiances and international solidarity, the free self-realization of flesh-and-blood individuals and a global cooperative commonwealth of them. But Marxism has suffered in our time a staggering political rebuff; and one of the places to which those radical impulses have migrated is – of all things – theology. It is in some sectors of theology nowadays that one can find some of the most informed and animated discussions of Deleuze and Badiou, Foucault and feminism, Marx and Heidegger. (2009, p. 167)

What I find most important in Marxism is its explanation of how capitalism works to necessarily exploit workers and the environment, provoking workers to rise up and replace capitalism with socialism and eventually the state will wither under communism. Both Jesus and Marx have an eschatological view of history and, as Michael Rivage-Seul (2008) notes, Jesus challenges us to reject the worship of a divinized violence that feeds the "satanic military industrial complex" and practice a non-violent form of resistance against differentiating wealth.

PJ: In your work you talk about the development of critical consciousness among students. What does this mean?

PM: A commitment to the oppressed leads to action in and on the world on behalf of the aggrieved of this world. Critical reflection on that action leads to what I refer to as protagonistic agency, a praxis of liberation. Protagonistic agency pulls out of the darkness of probability and potentiality the reality of social change, bringing it into the realm of actuality. Through a concentration of will – a type of hyper-intentionality – critical educators can submerge their ideas in their unconscious where they can confront their fears and traumas surrounding the risks and reprisals that they may face in their struggle for social justice. Such a struggle in the Golgotha of their hearts can direct their ideas into the light of reflective awareness without over-identifying with their feelings because these ideas have now been conditioned to ratify a new reality rather than remaining trapped by the old. This is fundamentally a dialectical process, an embrace of absolute negativity that leads to new beginnings.

PJ: There are many different religions in the contemporary world. Can we generalize emancipatory and educational potentials of Christianity to all religious systems of belief, or should we be more careful about such generalizations?

PM: The realm of religion is the realm of myth, symbol, art, mystery, legend, theater, and poetry – realms where we can delve deeply into the meaning of life. I am an ecumenist and do not believe God is revealed only through Christianity. I have helped marry a couple during an Umbanda ceremony in Brazil, have received an award for defending African-Brazilian religion from attacks by Christian evangelists, have visited Buddhist temples in China, Taiwan, and Malaysia, prayed at the Vatican and at indigenous churches throughout Mexico, visited Shinto shrines in Japan and mosques in Turkey, and dialogued in Pakistan with both Sunni and Shia Muslims.

Do we believe that the Christian God is monolithic? In the Christian Bible there is a plethora of gods – the God of Empire that Christianity has supported since the fourth century, the God of Eve, the God of Abraham and Moses, the God of Cain, the God of Satan, and the God of Jesus. According to Rivage-Seul (2008), Jesus is the prophet whose revelation ultimately decided that the God of Moses and Abraham (the God of the poor and the suffering) was the true God of Israel. Should we believe that the rich and the poor worship the same God? Take Hitler, for example. Hitler claimed to be Christian, but he only used "religious" language as a propaganda tool and he stated in Goebel's diaries that "as soon as the war is over" the Nazis will go after "the real enemy" – the Catholics. Pius XII referred to Hitler as "an indispensable bulwark against the Russians" (Johnson, 1977, p. 490, as cited in Rivage-Seul, 2008, p. 109). According to Rivage-Seul, the God of the Bible is not neutral and could not have been the God of both Hitler and Yahweh. Was the God of Ronald Reagan the same God as the God of Reagan's "Godless communists" – the Sandinistas? Are the God of

Christian fundamentalism and the prosperity gospel not arrayed against Jesus who stands on the side of the poor and the oppressed?

Rivage-Seul (2008, p. 114) believes that liberation theology is closer theologically to the idea that God is experienced not just in nature but in history; is revealed primarily in Exodus; is concerned with justice as true worship; is class-biased in favor of the poor; endorses an ethic of love and self-sacrifice; protects freedom from exploitation; permits violence to defend the poor from exploiters; is anti-imperialist; considers the ultimate revelation of Jesus to be that God stands with the poor, and that an accumulation of riches presumes an engagement with forms of exploitation. We should always be careful about what we generalize to other religious systems of belief. If I were to generalize, however, it would be from the perspective of a theology of liberation. I would never want to generalize precepts and principles from any organization that serves mainly to strengthen and reproduce systems of power and privilege that serve the rich at the expense of the poor. To support the reproduction of the power and privilege of the rich would be counter to the teachings of Jesus, who was against any system that produced differentiating wealth or what some call today "economic inequality." Such a term is too weak for me. I would call it, plain and simple, capitalist exploitation.

Acknowledgment

This chapter originally appeared as P. McLaren and P. Jandrić, From liberation to salvation: Revolutionary critical pedagogy meets liberation theology, *Policy Futures in Education*, 15(5) (2017), 620–652. Reprinted here, with minor edits, with permission from the publisher.

References

Black, D. (Ed.). (2014). *Helen Macfarlane: Red republican: Essays, articles and her translation of the* Communist Manifesto. Uncant Publishers.

Boal, A. (2008). *Theatre of the oppressed (get political)*. Pluto Press.

Boff, L. (1987). *Passion of Christ, passion of the world: The facts, their interpretation and their meaning yesterday and today* (R. R. Barr, Trans.). Orbis Books.

Boff, L. (1997). *Cry of the earth, cry of the poor* (P. Berryman, Trans.). Orbis Books.

Butt, R. (2009, March 17). Pope claims condoms could make African Aids crisis worse. *The Guardian*. https://www.theguardian.com/world/2009/mar/17/pope-africa-condoms-aids

Câmara, D. H. (2009). *Dom Hélder Câmara: Essential writings*. Orbis Books.

Chaudary, A. (2007, April-May). On religion and politics: Noam Chomsky interviewed by Amina Chaudary. *Islamica Magazine*, 19. https://chomsky.info/200704/

Dear, J. (2006, December 6). Ita, Maura, Dorothy and Jean. *National Catholic Reporter*. https://www.ncronline.org/blogs/road-peace/ita-maura-dorothy-and-jean

Duchrow, U. (1999). Europe and global economic justice. In A. R. Morton & J. Francis (Eds.), *A Europe of neighbours? Religious social thought and the reshaping of a pluralist Europe* (pp. 125–140). The University of Edinburgh.

Eagleton, T. (2009). *Reason, faith and revolution: Reflections on the God debate*. Yale University Press.

Ellacuría, I., & Sobrino, J. (Eds.). (1993). *Mysterium liberationis: Fundamental concepts of liberation theology*. Orbis Books.

Ford, D. R. (2016). Review of Peter McLaren (2015), *Pedagogy of insurrection: From resurrection to revolution. Texas Education Review*. http://txedrev.org/wp-content/uploads/2016/04/ Ford_Final_pedagogy-of-insurrection-review_4-14.pdf

Freire, P. (1973). Education, liberation and the Church. *Study Encounter*, 9(1), 1–16.

Freire, P. (1995). Preface. In P. McLaren (Ed.), *Critical pedagogy and predatory culture* (pp. ix–xi). Routledge.

Gutierrez, G. (1988). *A theology of liberation: History, politics, and salvation* (C. Inda & J. Eagleson, Trans.). Orbis Books.

Hudis, P. (2015). *Frantz Fanon: Philosopher of the barricades*. Pluto Press.

Jandrić, P. (2017). *Learning in the age of the digital media*. Sense.

Johnson, P. (1977). *A history of Christianity*. Atheneum.

Kelly, E. F., Crabtree, A., & Marshall, P. (Eds.). (2015). *Beyond physicalism: Toward reconciliation of science and spirituality*. Rowman & Littlefield.

Kelly, E. F., et al. (2007). *Irreducible mind: Toward a psychology for the 21st century*. Rowman & Littlefield.

Kosinski, M., Stillwell, D., & Graepel, T. (2013). Private traits and attributes are predictable from digital records of human behavior. In: *Proceedings of the National Academy of Sciences (PNAS)*, 110(15), 5802–5805. https://doi.org/10.1073/pnas.1218772110

Kovalik, D. (2013, March 5). US still fighting "threat" of liberation theology. *Counterpunch*. http://www.counterpunch.org/2013/03/05/us-still-fighting-threat-of-liberation-theology/

Laszlo, E. (2014). *The self-actualizing cosmos: The Akasha revolution in science and human consciousness*. Inner Traditions.

Marcuse, H. (2011). The role of religion in a changing society. In D. Kellner & C. Pierce (Eds.), *Psychology, psychoanalysis and emancipation: Collected papers of Herbert Marcuse, Volume 5* (pp. 182–188). Routledge.

Marx, K. (1843/1970). *Critique of Hegel's 'Philosophy of right'* (A. Jolin & J. O'Malley, Trans.). Cambridge University Press.

Marx, K. (1981). *Capital, Vol. III*. Vintage.
Marx, K., & Engels, F. (1848). *The communist manifesto*. https://www.marxists.org/archive/marx/works/1848/communist-manifesto/index.htm
McLaren, P. (1999). *Schooling as a ritual performance: Toward a political economy of educational symbols and gestures*. Rowman & Littlefield.
McLaren, P. (2015). *Pedagogy of insurrection: From resurrection to revolution*. Peter Lang.
McLaren, P., & Jandrić, P. (2014). Critical revolutionary pedagogy is made by walking – In a world where many worlds coexist. *Policy Futures in Education, 12*(6), 805–831.
McLaren, P., & Jandrić, P. (2015). The critical challenge of networked learning: Using information technologies in the service of humanity. In P. Jandrić & D. Boras (Eds.), *Critical Learning in Digital Networks*. Springer.
McSherry, J. P. (2005). *Predatory states: Operation Condor and covert war in Latin America*. Rowman & Littlefield.
Miranda, J. P. (1974). *Marx and the Bible: A critique of the philosophy of oppression*. Orbis Books
Miranda, J. P. (1977). *Being and the Messiah: The message of St. John*. Orbis Books.
Miranda, J. P. (1980). *Marx against the Marxists: The Christian humanism of Karl Marx* (J. Drury, Trans.). Orbis Books.
Miranda, J. P. (2004). *Communism in the Bible* (R. R. Barr, Trans.). Wipf & Stock.
Reitz, C. (2015). *Philosophy & critical pedagogy: Insurrection & commonwealth*. Peter Lang.
Rivage-Seul, M. (2008). *The emperor's God: Imperial misunderstandings of Christianity*. Institute for Economic Democracy Press.
Rivage-Seul, M. (2016). Chomsky on U.S. war vs. liberation theology. https://mikerivageseul.wordpress.com/2012/04/28/chomsky-on-u-s-war-vs-liberation-theology/
Robinson, W. I. (2004). *A theory of global capitalism: Production, class, and state in a transnational world*. Johns Hopkins University Press.
Robinson, W. I. (2014). *Global capitalism and the crisis of humanity*. Cambridge University Press.
Robinson, W. I. (2016a, April 12). Sadistic capitalism: Six urgent matters for humanity in global crisis. *Truthout*. http://www.truth-out.org/opinion/item/35596-sadistic-capitalism-six-urgent-matters-for-humanity-in-global-crisis
Robinson, W. I. (2016b, January 1). Reform is not enough to stem the rising tide of inequality worldwide. *Truthout*. http://www.truth-out.org/news/item/34224-reformis-not-enough-to-stem-the-rising-tide-of-inequality-worldwide
Rockefeller Foundation. (1969). *The Rockefeller report*. https://www.rockefellerfoundation.org/app/uploads/Annual-Report-1969.pdf
Rohr, R. (2016, October 16). The path of descent. Center for Action and Contemplation. http://centerforactionandcontemplation.cmail19.com/t/ViewEmail/d/A2C391CB09818C45/12E9998DA07E136EC67FD2F38AC4859C

Sobrino, J. (2001). *Christ the liberator*. Orbis Books.
Teilhard de Chardin, P. (1959). *The phenomenon of man*. Harper and Row.
Teilhard de Chardin, P. (1964). *The future of man*. Harper and Row.
Teilhard de Chardin, P. (1965). *The appearance of man*. Harper and Row.
Teilhard de Chardin, P. (1966a). *The vision of the past*. Harper and Row.
Teilhard de Chardin, P. (1966b). *Man's place in nature*. Harper and Row.
Teilhard de Chardin, P. (1968). *Science and Christ*. Harper and Row.
Williams, R. (2014). *Bonhoeffer's Black Jesus: Harlem Renaissance theology and an ethic of resistance*. Baylor University Press.
Youyou, W., Kosinski, M., & Stillwell, D. (2015). Computer-based personality judgments are more accurate than those made by humans. *Proceedings of the National Academy of Sciences (PNAS)*, *112*(4), 1036–1040. https://doi.org/10.1073/pnas.1418680112

CHAPTER 11

The Abode of Educational Production
An Interview with Peter McLaren

Jordy Cummings

Jordy Cummings (JC): You're from Toronto, and politicized in the era of the New Left, after attending grad school at Massey College and even taking a course with Foucault.... Is there anything particular to Toronto's culture that has inspired you, as an educator, an activist and a socialist?

Peter McLaren (PM): I left Toronto kicking and screaming since I couldn't find a tenure-track university position in Canada, but the renowned American educator Henry A. Giroux (what irony, he is now a Canadian citizen!) had helped me find a position in Miami University of Ohio, and who could resist that offer? Working with Henry was an education on its own that could never be purchased. Henry has a generosity of spirit that still staggers me. Toronto, ah yes. Well, as far as my perceptions of schooling and society goes, there was *This Magazine Is about Schools* that I read in the late sixties and into the seventies, edited by George Martell and Satu Repo. It was housed, as I recall, in Rochdale College, where I frequently hung out with friends. It became *This Magazine* sometime in the seventies, I think. I learned a lot from reading that magazine but I was never a subscriber, but rather an intermittent reader. Which probably accounts for why I didn't have much of a coherent theoretical trajectory when I started to write professionally in 1979. I was never recruited by left organizations, nor did I really attempt to join political groups, even school activists.

When I published *Cries from the Corridor*, my diary chronicling my experience as an elementary school teacher in the Jane-Finch Corridor, I was basically your missionary liberal educator with a rucksack stuffed with some radical ideas, and the Canadian left as I recall was pretty snobbish, maybe that residue of British colonialism, and I was told that my professors at OISE (where I did my doctorate) resented all the publicity I received from that book. I think, too, that when I left for the US, there was this feeling that I was abandoning Canada. And while I am a dual-citizen and might not be as thoroughly Canadian as Pierre Berton, I consider myself died-in-the wool Canadian. I was always hoping to receive offers to return and teach in Canada but they never came. I would have returned in a heartbeat.

Maybe the biggest political lesson I learned was walking down Yonge Street in Willowdale in 1968 on whatever the hallucinogen of the day was, and flipping off a Metro cop. I was thrown into a black and white and taken to jail, where I was systematically beaten with a flashlight during the night. I still have a raised section of my skull that you can feel – my wife Wang Yan calls it my "dragon forehead." My subsequent trip to California that year was fraught with similar incidents, and I won't list those now. But, thanks to the bohemian culture of downtown Yorkville, where I spent years in the coffee houses and hippie lofts, and romantic moments with pre-Raphaelite looking lovers in velvet gowns in the shadows of Philosopher's Walk on the University of Toronto campus, you could confidently say that prior to leaving Canada, I felt I had imbibed the spirit of the Beat Poets, and consumed as much of underground culture that I could hold in one brainpan without flipping out – poetry, philosophy, Eastern religion, psychedelic drugs, all kinds of new ideas – gestalt theory, rational emotive therapy, Irving Layton, Leonard Cohen, Joni Mitchell, Buffy Saint-Marie, Gregory Bateson, R.D. Laing, general semantics, psychoanalysis, anarchism, acid rock, John C. Lilly, the occult, pyramid energy, theosophy, Darwin, Zen Buddhism, the Bloomsbury group, the Inklings, Dadaism, McLuhan, Gordon Lightfoot, Luke and the Apostles (my guitar teacher was Toronto's own David Wilcox), Catholic saints, well where should I stop? Stompin' Tom Connors?

Even throughout the torment and joy of those troubling and troubled years, I watched Hockey Night in Canada with my dad, and reminisced about how we would go curling together in matching sweaters during the four years my family spent in Winnipeg. I really miss those days. That eclecticism no doubt influenced my (thankfully short lived) attraction to postmodernism in the mid-1980s. I think Toronto is one of the great cities of the world, and I have visited many of them. But perhaps my perceptions of the city are dipped in an all-too saccharine romanticism that from time-to-time plagues me and my thinking.

One thing that I learned from my countercultural days in Toronto was that you make your path by walking and before you can travel the path, you have to become the path. This is the essence of praxis. I had become the path away from Willowdale, away from my home in the Beaches, away from everything I knew in order to step into the void of the United States. But I had yet to find a path towards something, towards an understanding of capitalist society and what would constitute a socialist alternative. My first impression of the United States was of the vastness of the armies of the homeless, haunted by the slow death that stalked the dispossessed in the so-called most progressive democracy in the world, or so the US was described in those days. It would take me years to understand that when the spectre of progress twists his hourglass watch upside down to mark the death-rattle countdown of those millions who are dying on city streets of preventable diseases and who lay unattended in hospital beds crammed into the corridors of decaying urban medical centers, he is present around the world wherever the logic of capital prevails. The pitted and pock-marked lungs of his victims are now unfillable, their life force fading behind curtains of dust and dead memories. These casualties of 'progress' are not restricted to one country. And they are not necessarily living in the streets. They are in office buildings, schools, monasteries, sanctuaries, offices, and shopping malls. They are often our own children, our relatives, our friends, ourselves.

JC: The theme of this issue is "Capitalism in the Classroom". What does it mean, to you to be an anti-capitalist and a Marxist in a pedagogical setting, both in practical and theoretical terms? Relatedly, what kind of shifts have you been seeing, and how can Marxist theory account for these shifts? It seems to me, as an educator, that this is an uneven, dialectical process. On one hand, we see an increase in online courses and a casualization of the academic profession. On the other hand, the range of information available to scholars has increased. As a Marxist, what do you make of all of this, and how does it affect your praxis?

PM: Clearly from where I sit, a spontaneous wave of indignation has swept throughout the United States, an uprush of animosity against intolerable indignities suffered by the working-class, and people of color. The social character of our life-activity, forged by the hammer blows of value-producing labor and stamped by the impact press of capitalist social relations, rests on the pervasive dependence and dehumanization of workers, the ever-increasing interdependence of capital and labor. The ontological conception of alienation was unpacked magnificently by Marx and that was what first drew me to his work. There is nothing more alienating than schools, which serve as conceptual, emotional, and epistemological prisons for too many students.

The miasmic system of capitalism in which we are inextricably enmeshed is one whose flexibility, omnipresence and omnivalence of oppression has been as expansive as the air that we breathe. But our labor power is both key to our enslavement and our liberation. Everywhere people are clamoring for justice. We have been stricken to the quick by an outlawry and scoundrelism exercised with prideful efficiency by the ruling class but the problem is not with personal behavior of capitalists, as egregious as that might be, but with the structure of capitalism itself. Youth here in the United States are fed up with war, yet I teach classes where the entire population of students who enrolled in my courses have never not known a time where their country was at war. At this time of endless wars against terror, there are no wistful interludes between wars. Wars today are forever ongoing and we merely suffer between the exasperating diminuendos and crescendos of events.

Now, for instance, the latest crescendo is the push forward by the Islamic State. We are a society that fights symptoms and refuses to treat the root causes of our ongoing crises – of the environment, of terrorism, of resources, of personal security, of education and so on. One of the most entangling of these disconcerting relationships is how capitalism structures, organizes and mediates all of these antagonisms in contextually specific ways. In the current interregnum we are, for all intents and purposes, existing as human capital. We have sold our life-activity to other people and some sections of the population (such as the African American populations who are being replaced as cheap labor by the Latino/as), are relegated to surplus populations that are unable to sell their labor-power. To acknowledge that we live in a capitalist society is to tremble and shudder. Witness today the prodigious and virulent expansion of surveillance technology beyond the exigencies of any agreed-upon notion of decency, technologies that efface the divisions between the real, the hyperreal and the suprareal and lock us into a scenario much worse that even Orwell envisioned, a scenario where will become willing agents of capital.

We have sold our labor-power for a wage and we can only use those silver dollars squeezed out of the profit ledger of the capitalist to cover the eyes of our corpse and hope that the ferryman of Hades will convey our soul across the waters of the Styx or Acheron as quickly as possible. We are prone in this society to be critical of primary assumptions and of course to protect them from attack. They are solemnly made sacerdotal, and hide behind religious prerogatives. As I have argued for decades, the capitalist marketplace is the new God. I live in Old Town, Orange, in California and the most convenient coffee shop for me is in a Wells Fargo bank. Truly, the building from the inside looks like a cathedral. My friend at UC Santa Barbara, Bill Robinson, notes that the negative of an anti-capitalist movement does not necessarily involve the positive (and here we can clearly see he is echoing Hegel's negation of the negation) of an alternative post-capitalist or socialist project. Which is precisely why, along with my Marxist humanist comrades, I have called long and hard for a philosophy of praxis grounded in absolute negativity. Here, I have been influenced greatly by the work of Hegel and Marx, and Dunayevskaya's theory of state capitalism. I've learned that you can't separate Hegel's dialectical method from this Absolute Idea (the transcendence of the opposition between theory and practice). Just as Hegel advised us to always, ceaselessly, call into question the grounding ideas from which a phenomenon is grasped, we need to break down external as well as internal barriers to liberation through a philosophy of praxis grounded in absolute negativity.

Regrettably, Marx's ideas have been ripped out of their revolutionary soil by decades of toxic bombardment by the corporate media and repotted in greenhouse megastores where, under hydrofarm compact fluorescent fixtures, they can be deracinated, debarked and made safe for university seminars and condominium living alike for highly committed twentysomethings who like to whistle to ballpark tunes in their faux Victorian bathtubs. For me, Marx provides a dizzying macro-level montage of society filled with autonomous narratives that evoke ineluctable paradoxes that take on new meaning when put all together. In other words, what I find most useful in Marx is his dialectics of internal relations, how all of social life is internally related. To stick with a film metaphor, Marx gives you that tracking shot with voiceover spiked with the ambient noise of workers marching forward ... a relentless tracking shot that won't let you escape ... and you have to follow it. Once the setting of the drama has been established, you become the protagonist and you are obligated to play the drama out. As we struggle for the supersession of property and labor determined by need and external utility, we look to Marx for direction in building a new society based on co-operation and production absent the pressures of external determination, where all manner of people interact and collaborate in freely associated, spontaneous and unpredictable ways.

As a teacher, I am interested in how global capitalism is dialectically interwoven with underdevelopment, and how this process is related to the production of knowledge, specifically in school systems and how such school systems teach us how to think, to research, and to develop our methodological skills that often leave us degage and docile. Prior to the ascendency of neoliberal capitalism, the primary mission of mass schooling was to create the "deep character" of the nation state by legitimizing the superiority of elite culture, trans-coding the culture of the ruling class with the culture of the nation state so that both were essentially seen as 'natural' symmetrical reflections of each other. Schools were important mechanisms in the invention of the identity of the modern nation state in the era of industrialization and played an important role in developing the concept of the citizen (a concept always contested by many groups, including conservatives, liberals and radicals).

However, schools today (since the mid-1980s), are discernibly shifting their role from building the nation state and creating democracy-minded citizens to serving the transnational corporations in their endless quest for profits. The nation state, it appears, is losing its ability to control capital by means of controlling the transnational corporations. Corporations have become in many instances more powerful than nation states (although I am not diminishing the role of nation states here). Schools that were once an important political entity that had a public code-setting agenda in creating conventional rules and regulations to be followed by each citizen are fast becoming part of the private sector bent on creating consumers within the capitalist marketplace. As society abandons its outmoded historical garb and takes on new forms, the perpetuity of the existing social order is increasingly called into question. So-called non-political forces – those associated with financial and commodity markets – are now the dominant forces of indoctrination and code setting within our market society and this has greatly impacted education.

Our collaborative existence as consumers has produced a closure on meaning through the very activity of opening up our desire to consume market commodities by means of a default set of blinders created by a capitalist imaginary that provides the formula or criteria of choice. Industrial capitalist schooling was occupied with conventional problem solving designed to provide students with the rules and conventions to solve particular problems via rule-based reasoning. Knowing the rules of the democratic state was the most important goal and this was often taught by means of a text book-assignment-recitation pattern. With the advent of consumer society and the replacement of Western high culture with transnational corporate culture (which relies on well-trained technical workers), the focus has moved away from conventional thinking to technical thinking. What this ultimately excludes, of course, is critical reflection, or producing knowledge from real-life problems or what Richard Quantz calls "meaningful action."

Meaningful action does not always take place in situations where relevant knowledge is available or where people are aware what the right choices and actions might be. Meaningful knowledge does require some knowledge of technical reasoning but it requires as well the ability to interpret and critique – to make moral choices and to commit to some action even when relevant knowledge is not available. It requires larger patterns of understanding and reasoning – and it requires us to create and recreate its own foundations and goals as it goes along. Given the abandoning of political institutions such as schools by the state, the focus has been on technical problem solving as a means-ends reasoning that involves selecting from available rules those that will help individuals achieve a particular given end. In short, critical reflection is not a priority. It is in fact, the enemy of today's education, even as schools tout the value of critical literacy and social justice agendas. Being a Marxist educator means that I see education as a path to socialism. Simply put, my struggle as a teacher is to create protagonist agency to fight three very powerful forces, what I call the 'triplecides' – genocide, ecocide and epistemicide. I see capitalism as a form of genocide (see the work of Gary Leech) and a number of my students have been developing the field of ecopedagogy (turning traditional forms of environmental education on their heads) – addressing the issues of ecocide, sustainability, ecosocialism and alternative epistemologies found often in first nations cultures.

The moral imperative behind today's neoliberalism reflects a distinct form of neo-mercantilism. The move in the US economy in the 1970s towards financialization and export production helped to concentrate wealth in the hands of CEOs and hedge-fund managers – and, as Chomsky and others have noted, this led to a concentration of political power, which in turn leads state policies to increase economic concentration, fiscal policies, deregulation of the economic, and rules of corporate governance. Neoliberalism as it factors the field of education reflects the logic of possessive individualism, urging all citizens or potential citizens to maximize their advantage on the labor market; and for those who are unable to accomplish this requirement – a requirement, by the way, that functions as a moral imperative – such as undocumented workers, they must as a non-market underclass live in a bottom-tiered netherworld of sweatshop labor that serves those of more fundamental worth to the social order – the more successful capitalist class.

All that is to have worth in neoliberal democracies must be directly linked to the functional needs of capitalism, so that capitalism and the capitalist class can reproduce itself along with capitalist society, and the capitalist worldview that legitimates the entire process. So here we can see neoliberalism linked to legal systems and mechanisms of legitimation that will help secure the market as the only authentically potent form of political and social organization. The state, in other words, becomes synonymous with the market. Certainly global financial institutions such as the International Monetary Fund and the World Bank comprise the ramparts behind which neoliberal ideology is to be protected at all costs, and it is important to view these institutions as basically controlled by the wealthy western powers, the United States in particular. And it is in this sense that neo-liberal ideology is an imperialist ideology. Anything left outside market forces would be under suspicion of being subversive of civilization – after all, there is no alternative to neoliberal capitalism. We could even say that we are living in a neoliberal modernity, in which the capitalist class is gaining power by dispossessing the working-class and selling or renting to the public what was commonly owned.

Neoliberalism is a revolution from above on the part of the transnational capitalist class to give ever more structural advantage to the global capitalist production system. Between this global ruling-class and the working class still exists the shrinking middle class, a fragile buffer between the rich and the poor. According to sociologist Bill Robinson, we inhabit a loosely constituted historic bloc, a social base in which the transnational capitalist class produces the consent of those drawn into this bloc and exercises moral, political and economic leadership – hegemonic leadership in the classical Gramscian sense. My focus as a Marxist is on this emerging transnational hegemony – this new historic bloc based on the hegemony of transnational capital – where, of course, the US is definitely playing a leading role.

While national capital, global capital and regional capitals are still prevalent, the hegemonic fraction of capital on a world scale is now transnational capital. The purpose of the transnational ruling class is the valorization and accumulation of capital and the defense and advance of the emergent hegemony of a global bourgeoisie and a new global capitalist-historical bloc. This historical bloc is composed of the transnational corporations and financial institutions, the elites that manage the supranational economic planning agencies, major forces in the dominant political parties, media conglomerates, and technocratic elites. Capitalism, which Marx portentously argued was written in letters of blood and fire, continues to be reproduced as robbery, as outlawry. As a Marxist educator, I raise these issues with my colleagues, with my students, but mostly I raise them in the context of arguing that critical pedagogy must not remain solely in the classroom but become part of a transnational social movement.

JC: The sixth edition of your classic *Life in Schools,* one of the few Marxist texts on teacher-education, has just been issued, updated for the Obama era. What were you trying to do with this book, and what kind of impact has it had? In turn, what kind of Obama-era shifts have provoked shifts or tweaks within the book? Finally, have you received any "pushback" or red-baiting around the impact of this book?

PM: The book has had a number of publishers, and the fifth edition was Pearson. Yes, the textbook and assessment company that produces standardized texts, that is singled out by progressive educators as one of the companies that is destroying public education. It owns Penguin Books and the Financial Times and operates in over seventy countries. I mention in the latest edition that after scheduling a meeting with a Pearson editor to discuss the new sixth edition, and after making copious notes and presenting them to her in the lobby of the Mark Twain hotel in San Francisco, she told me that my ideas were "too complex", that Pearson was too "corporate" and that American students could not really absorb the difficult concepts I present in *Life in Schools.* There was not going to be a sixth edition, I was told. In fact, she told me that Pearson was dropping the book.

I asked her if it was because I critiqued the company in the fifth edition of the book, and she said no, that was not the reason. She tried to soften the blow by offering me twenty free copies of the book. And of course the rights resorted back to me, and within ten minutes I had found another publisher. How was it possible to find another publisher in that short time span? Well, my meeting with Pearson took place during the annual convention of the American Educational Research Association and after the book was dropped by Pearson, my wife, Wang Yan, and I walked across the street to the lobby of the Hilton. Once inside, I noticed a grey-haired fellow frantically waving to me. It was my old friend Dean Birkenkamp, the head of Paradigm Publishers. He shouted across the room, "Is there any way I can get the rights to your *Life in Schools?*" I was a taken aback at my good fortune and of course the deal was sealed within minutes. Yes, the book is updated but the problem is when you do a new edition of the book you have to remove the same amount of the old material as you add in the new material. And I have trouble losing what I feel is very good work. But I made room for Obama.

Obama has hurt education reform immeasurably. Obama has really carried over the George Bush Jr. initiatives and rebranded them with some cosmetic touches. You aren't a good educational leader when your Race to the Top initiatives tie federal funds for states and localities to their use of assessments of national "college and career readiness" standards; when you set yourself on a mission to privatize or quasi-privatize public schools through an expansion of charter schools; when you evaluate teachers by linking an individual teacher's salary and employment status to student test scores; or when you pink slip teachers and principals in schools that have been designated as failing schools; and especially when your entire philosophy of education is driven by the logic of assessment and competition that includes merit pay for teachers, etc. To use federal leverage to get your initiatives in place, to sow distrust of public schools and to give preferential treatment to charter schools (that don't do as well as public schools overall even though they can cherry-pick their students and can refuse to admit students with learning disabilities), to create such a mess that teacher drop-out rates are at an all time high – the voluntary drop out rate for teachers is higher than the failure rate of students as nationally, 16 percent leave after the first year and approximately 45 percent leave within five years – is to give educational reform another kick in the teeth. Whether it's a Democrat or Republican in the White House doesn't seem to matter – the Democrats will wear hobnailed boots to kick out your teeth, the Republicans will use army surplus store boots from the invasion of Iraq to do the job.

I'm surprised that the book is doing so well in classrooms across the US, because of the political climate here. The works of Paulo Freire and Rudy Acuna were banned in Tucson, Arizona's public school system, there is a wave a evangelical fervour percolating throughout the US, particularly with the Tea Party folks, and "socialism" is a hot word. University undergraduates and sometimes graduate students – and their parents – can get riled up if they think they are being encouraged to criticize the United States. Again, at UCLA, I was labelled "the most dangerous professor at UCLA" during the Bush Jr. administration. Death threats, of course. Hate mail, yes. Not so much now as during the Bush Jr. administration but yes, it is there. There is at least one evangelical book that recently cited me as a grave danger to the young minds of America. And yes I get the usual Commie in the Classroom criticism, and the Cuban American community frequently gets on my case because of my book about Paulo Freire and Che Guevara. But the support I receive is so much stronger, and that is what keeps me going. And good friends. When you come under criticism you quickly learn who are your fair-weather friends, and who are your true friends.

And now I am teaching at Chapman University, a private university located in one of the most conservative and most 'charming' cities in the United States, the city of Orange. Well, after 20 years at UCLA I was made an offer by Chapman that I accepted. There is a small community of Freireans whom I very much enjoy working with and who walk their talk. You really do need other like-minded people to work with if you want to survive university life. That's why I decided to join the faculty here. The College of Education Studies has a progressive Dean, Don Cardinal, who is just about the best leader you could imagine. If you enter Chapman from one side of the campus, you see a statue of Margaret Thatcher, then Ayn Rand, then Milton Friedman, and then Ronald Reagan, so your blood might curdle if you are a leftist. But if you approach Chapman from another route, you will encounter statues of Marin Luther King, Benito Juarez and, yes, Paulo Freire. I have found Chapman to honour diverse viewpoints and to encourage critical thinking. And the faculty here is highly committed to social justice. We also have Dodge College, one of the top film schools in the country. While I teach regularly, I often spend half the week working in America Latina with different organizations, teachers unions, indigenous populations, and more recently the Europeans have been inviting me to participate in discussions about education.

JC: You are very influenced by the work of Paulo Freire and emancipatory education. Can you tell *Alternate Routes* a little bit about how you came to be inspired by Freire and how academics can make use of his work?

PM: I met Paulo Freire through the esteemed educational scholar and public intellectual Henry Giroux and one of his close friends, Donaldo Macedo who is a professor of linguistics. Henry A. Giroux had helped bring me to Miami University of Ohio, after the controversy over my book, *Cries from the Corridor,* made it impossible for me to land a full-time professorship in Canada during that time (although I did manage a one-year appointment at Brock University with help from John Novak, a prominent Deweyan educationalist). Henry introduced me to Paulo during a conference in Chicago in 1985 and later,

Donaldo Macedo helped to facilitate and solidify our relationship. My formation as a teacher has been forged and tempered in the crucible of Freire's copious and courageous works and my life profoundly shaped and keenly affected by the leadership and teachings of Paulo Freire. Paulo in his formidable generosity of spirit wrote several prefaces to books of mine, invited me to Cuba and Brazil, and while in Brazil hosted me in his university and his home. A mentor and friend over the ensuing years, he modeled the kind of educator I wanted to become. I have been fortunate to have met several world-historical figures who exemplify the best of our revolutionary spirit, and I would consider Hugo Chávez another such individual. Freire, Chávez, Marx – these are figures of inescapable relevance for revolutionary critical pedagogy, all in different ways.

While the legacy of Paulo Freire stands immeasurably beyond us as individuals, his world-historical vision of a just and equitable democratic society nevertheless serves as a quilting-point and guide to the future of education for millions of progressive educators worldwide. Revisiting the legacy and vision of Paulo Freire today chillingly reminds us that the dreams that have been programmed into today's sterile educational instruments of test-taking, accountability, technocratic thinking, and managerial control have led to an abandonment of the search for what it means to live critically, creatively and democratically in the service of those who have been marginalized and excluded in today's immiserated capitalist society. We would do well as educators to read today's 'businessification' and corporatization of education against the liberatory vision of Paulo Freire with the hope that we can and will regain the vision of a critical democracy to which Freire's storied corpus of works points and build the kind of democracy that lives up to its principles and pronouncements. Whether this can be done within a capitalist society is doubtful; in fact, I do not believe it can be done. It has become clear to me in traveling to approximately thirty countries in the course of my educational work, that Paulo Freire is still very much alive in the hearts and minds of all those teachers, administrators, cultural workers, and students who still choose to dream. We need to read the world as well as the world, that is, we need to be able to transcend through absolute negativity those barriers that keep us from realizing our full humanity.

Teachers need to be spokespersons for agency, the embodiment of a critical praxis – I call this protagonistic agency. With wide-eyed awareness, Freire serves notice that not only must we raise questions that the world refuses to raise but is incapable of raising at this historical moment. There is always a quixotic aspect of risk-taking in our attempts to transform the world through critical pedagogy. And we need to remember that critical pedagogy is a necessary but not sufficient for bringing about the socialist revolution. Freire would advise us, his comrades, not to reproduce his work, to import his work as we would some foreign commodity into our classrooms but to re-invent his ideas in the contextual specificity of where we found ourselves in our struggles, and by this he meant, socially, economically, culturally, geopolitically and the like. Critical educators who have been influenced by Freire recognize that history is always open and refuse to postulate history as a determinate truth, relinquishing the subjective in the making of history. There are no iron laws of history, since history works backwards, retrospectively, like Benjamin's Angel of history, caught in the swirling storm from paradise. For critical educators, ends and means must be interdependent. We can't read off from science our moral goals. Even if scientific laws of history obtained they cannot a priori stipulate moral ends because that would make moral ends meaningless.

Freire clearly worked within a dialectical materialist epistemology that attempted to posit a dialectical relationship between the objective world and our subjective understanding and knowledge of that world. Freire was concerned with the 'dialecticity' between consciousness and the world where he views critical consciousness as a type of metaconsciousness or "consciousness as consciousness of consciousness," as what I have come to term, "protagonist agency" or a type of intentionality towards the world that is intent on transforming the world as much as understanding the world. This means seeking ontological and ethical clarity in our relations with the world and with other human beings.

JC: You have an international reputation, having worked with the Bolivarians in Venezuela, the MST in Brazil among many progressive elements in Latin America. What kind of innovation is happening, in particular, within the context of the Bolivarian process? Can any of these innovations be translated into a Canadian or American context?

PM: I'm not an expert on the Bolivarian process. For that kind of expertise, you would need to read the important work of Michael Lebowitz and Marta Harnecker. Recently, Instituto McLaren de Pedagogía Crítica y Educación Popular helped to sponsor a lecture in Mexico City where Marta Harnecker appeared as the keynote – the conference is called Volver a Marx. We at Instituto McLaren are helping to organize that conference every year and we have been holding it in various cities throughout Mexico. We are trying to interest the general public – workers, students, artists, teachers, managers, farmers, indigenous groups, in the ideas of Marx as a way to initiate transformation and change. I certainly admire the potential of the communal councils of the Bolivarian Revolution, which serve as public pedagogical sites for socialism and endogenous development, and to what Michael Lebowitz calls 'a vehicle for changing both circumstances and the protagonists themselves', and deepening the struggle for socialism for the twenty-first century. Such a struggle is founded on revolutionary practice, famously described by Lebowitz, after Marx, as 'the simultaneous changing of circumstances and self-change'. The new socialist society stresses that the control of production is vested in the producing individuals themselves. Productive relations are social as a result of conscious choice and not after the fact. They are social because, as Lebowitz (2013) perceptively notes, as a people we deliberately choose to produce for people who need what we can produce.

Since more than seventy percent of university students came from the wealthiest quintile of the population, Chávez instituted the Bolivarian University System, in which the students themselves were able to participate in the management of their institution. Education was designed to promote citizen participation and joint responsibility, and to include all citizens in the creation of a new model of production that stressed endogenous development, that is, an economic system that was self-sufficient and diversified. Misiones were created to create a social economy and a diversity of production, and designed to meet the needs of Venezuela's poor and to counteract Venezuela's oil dependency. Higher education was de-concentrated from the urban centers in order to assist rural communities. I remember how much I enjoyed teaching at the Bolivarian University of Venezuela, located near the Central University of Venezuela – part of Mission Sucre, which provides free higher education to the poor, regardless of academic qualification, prior education or nationality – housed in the ultra-deluxe offices of former PDVSA oil executives that Chávez had fired for their attempt to bring down the government. College enrolment doubled under Chávez. Student projects were insolubly linked to local community improvement. At a graduation ceremony in the early years of the university, Chávez famously said: "Capitalism is machista and to a large extent excludes women, that's why, with the new socialism, girls, you can fly free."

Chávez set up a structure to offer employment for the graduates of UBV through a presidential commission that enabled new graduates to be placed around the country in development projects. The graduates would receive a scholarship that was slightly above the minimum wage. Some of these projects involved Misión Árbol (Tree Mission), recovering environments damaged by capitalism such as the Guaire River. When I was first invited to Venezuela by the government to help support the Bolivarian revolution, I remember speaking at the Central University of Venezuela. The students who attend this university are mainly the children of the ruling elite. Not many were Chavistas, well, at least not when I spoke there. After I announced to the students present that I was a Chavista (Soy Chavista!), I was told later that some students in retaliation had ripped my portrait off of a mural students had created of critical theorists. Yet I was able to have very good conversations with some of the students there in the years that followed.

Education under Chávez was education for the creation of a "multipolar" world. For Chávez, education either meant giving life support to capitalism's profit-orientation in such a way as to bolster the remains of the welfare state, or education meant recreating a socialism for the twenty-first century. Chávez was not concerned with incorporating the oppressed within the liberal-democratic framework, but rather in changing the framework through the reorganization of political space through education, that is, through making the state function in a nonstate mode by reorganizing the state from the bottom up through the education and initiatives of the popular majorities. Socialism, Chávez understood, could be sustained only by the subjective investment of those involved in the process.

Under Chávez, Venezuelan education was not only geared to help provide universal access to education (as Venezuela's poor had been shut out for generations), in particular, to those traditionally disadvantaged and/or excluded groups such as the urban and rural poor, those of African descent, and indigenous communities, but to help prepare the next generation of Venezuelans to enhance the conditions of possibility of a socialist alternative to capitalism. Venezuelan education aspired to be a combination of Freirean-influenced critical and popular education, where horizontal and dialogic (subject-subject) relationships were pursued using holistic, integral and transdisciplinary pedagogies and methodologies based on andragogical principles for a liberating and emancipatory education. Under Chávez, little attempt was made to distance educational reform from a politicized approach. Education reform clearly directed itself towards an organic form of endogenous socialist development of the social-community context as part of a larger struggle for a participatory-protagonistic democracy. Against the privatization of education and approaches hegemonized by the neoliberal education industry, and its consumerist role grounded in egoism, competition, elitism and alienation, Venezuelan education aspired to be humanistic, democratic, participatory, multi-ethnic, pluri-cultural, pluri-lingual and intercultural.

The development of a critical consciousness among the population was crucial, as was an integration of school, family and community in the decision-making process. Venezuelan education favored a multidisciplinary approach linking practice and theory, curriculum and pedagogy, with the purpose of creating social, economic and political inclusion within a broader vision of endogenous and sustainable development, and with the larger goal of transforming a culture of economic dependency to a culture of community participation. This approach, for example, underwrote the courses at UBV where mentorship was provided to students who undertook projects in their local communities. Over ninety-three percent of Venezuelans aged fifteen and over can read and write. The Venezuelan government has more than ninety institutions of higher education and remains committed to the idea that every citizen should be able to have a free education. Education was conceived within an integrationist geo-political conception of Latin American countries in a way that enabled Latin Americans to challenge economic dependency fostered on them by the imperialist powers, to resist colonialist globalization projects, and to create spaces where students could critically analyze local problems from a global perspective. Chávez's approach of *municipalización* refused to isolate universities from the rest of society and geographically de-concentrated the traditional university infrastructure and took the university to where the people are, to municipalities that had traditionally been underserved as well as factories and prisons. Canadians and Americas can learn a lot from these important initiatives.

JC: As of late, you have become a poet. As someone who does cultural analysis, I'm wondering if you can help me develop a Marxian take on the idea of "Poetic Knowledge"? How can we conceive "poetic knowledge" from a materialist standpoint?

PM: I like your question but I haven't produced any systematic analysis of poetic knowledge, although I am certainly drawn to the concept.

As an undergraduate at the University of Toronto, I was influenced by the power of myths, rituals, symbols and this was motivated in part in my study of Old English and Middle English and eventually Elizabethan drama. Later, I incorporated my interest in rituals and symbols into my own ethnographic work, influenced mostly through the comparative symbology of the anthropologist Victor Turner. When I was 19 I met the poet Allen Ginsberg, and spent time with Timothy Leary, and I was very much involved in the Yorkville scene in Toronto. Between San Francisco, Los Angeles, and Toronto, there was a lot going on. I was quite the fan of Andre Breton – and you know, the morning star anarchist rebellion work of Guy Debord and others. The Situationists International influenced me. So did Claire Cahun. My interest continued up through to my reading of Benjamin. Recently I visited the Trotsky museum (for the third time) in Mexico City and was quite captivated of the photos of Trotsky, Diego Rivera and Breton.

Writing for academic journals is painful, and to make it less so, I often use images from my dreams and approach topics in a very unorthodox fashion. Some readers like it, some don't, some think it is pompous for an academic to view his or her work as art, others appreciate it. Scattered throughout my dreams lately have been disturbing dystopian images; I recall one such dream recently where I discover myself squatting atop a Gothic cathedral, whose gargoyles perched below my feet are spouting the blood of history's time-enduring saints to quell the maelstrom of angry crowds below – crowds made up of the powerless, the forgotten, the excluded, victims caught in the crossfire of capitalism (the result of watching too many Zombie or vampire films, no doubt). I peer down at the collarless, blood-covered, and spindle-shanked figures below, shafts of brilliant light slicing through the clouds that hover hesitatingly over the entangled gloom, and then the noxious exhalation and clouds of putrid effluvia wafting upwards from the dank and pungent sewer mist rises to meet the light, and suddenly everyone is playing and celebrating in the city streets, like neighborhood kids who have yanked open a fire hydrant during a heat wave. It is then, in my dream, that a heaven-sweeping yearning to return the planet back to its pristine state wells up in me and I leap into the shadows below. That's about the time I usually wake up. Right after I have been swallowed by the darkness. For me, the challenge becomes thrusting our heads higher than cathedrals, through the confines that limit the imagination, through the boundaries of terminate optimism to a boundless hope so that we can create a world beyond our corrupted self-interest. Without starting to sound or think like Obama. We all have our dreams and nightmares and while I tend to pain our unmooredness or rudderlessness as dystopian it could easily be described under a different name.

Life does not unfold as some old sheet strewn across a brass bed in the dusky attic of history; our destinies as children, parents, and teachers do not flow unilaterally toward a single vertigo-inducing epiphany, some pyrotechnic explosion of iridescent and refulgent splendor where we lay becalmed, rocking on a silent sea of pure bliss, or where we are held speechless in some wind-washed grove of cedars, in the thrall of an unbridled, unsullied and undiluted love of incandescent intensity. Our lives are not overseen by a handsome God who blithely sits atop a terra cotta pedestal and with guileless simplicity, quiet paternalism and unsmiling earnestness rules over his eager and fumbling brood, ever so often rumpling the curly heads of the rosy-cheeked cherubim and engaging the saints in blissful conversation. Were there such a God, wrapped in the mantle of an otherworldly Platonism and possessing neither moral obliquity nor guilt, who brings forth the world through supernatural volition alone, the world would be nothing but an echo of the divine mind. Hunger could be ended by merely thinking of a full belly and sickness eliminated by a picture of perfect health.

Most of us, Jordy, sling ourselves nervously back and forth across the great Manichean divide of the drab of everyday existence, where, in our elemental contact with the world, our human desires, for better or for worse, tug at us like some glow-in-the-dark hustler in a carnival midway. We go hungry, we suffer, and we live in torment and witness most of the world's population crumpled up in pain. We don't have to witness a final miracle of eschatological significance to reclaim the world. What we do have to accomplish at this very moment is organizing our world to meet the basic needs of humanity. I don't now if there is something poetic in this. If I have developed a poetics of revolution, then it attempts to endow critical pedagogy with a mission of reconciling love and justice. Is love without justice meaningless? Or could love without justice be complicit in the reproduction of deep-seated structural injustices? I approach the Bible as a work of great poetry. I find that I am able to reach students – don't forget that I live in Orange County, behind the Orange Curtain and there is an evangelical church on nearly every street corner – with the message of socialism through biblical references.

Recently I've re-engaged the work of the Jesuit thinker, José Porfirio Miranda, who argues with verve and passion that the official teachings of the church falsify the gospel, since it is clear from reading the texts of the Bible that Jesus maintains an intransigent condemnation of the rich. Even liberation theology gets this wrong when it asserts that there should be a "preferential option for the poor" – it is not an option, but, as Miranda notes, it is an obligation. We cannot shirk from this obligation without imputation of culpability and still remain Christians. There is no abstention from this struggle. The condition of the poor obliges a restitution since such a struggle is injustice writ large. Jesus died for participating in political transgression aimed at liberating Judea from the Romans. According to Miranda, Jesus clearly was a communist, and this can convincingly be seen throughout the New Testament but particularly in passages such as John 12:6, 13:29 and Luke 8:1–3. Jesus went so far as to make the renunciation of property a condition for entering the kingdom of God. When Luke says, "Happy the poor, for yours is the Kingdom of God" (Luke 6:20) and adds, "Woe to you the rich, because you have received your comfort" (Luke 6:24), Luke is repeating Mark 10:25 when Jesus warns that the rich cannot enter the kingdom. The Bible makes clear through Jesus' own sayings that the kingdom is not the state of being after death; rather, the kingdom is now, here on earth. Essentially Jesus is saying, according to Miranda, that the kingdom is a classless society. There is something revolutionary in this, and something immediately poetic.

While history may be indifferent to the pontifications and bloviations of both church pulpit and lecture hall, there are few places now to turn for poetic inspiration given the commodification of the life world, not even to the receding forests where death mocks us, dancing on the leaves of jimsonweed (you can see it if you focus your imagination).

JC: Any final thoughts on "capitalism in the classroom" in the post-2008 era of lean production and assembly line education? Are there any cracks in the facade that give you hope that a different education is possible in a North American context?

PM: I wrote *Cries from the Corridor* in the mid-1970s and it was published in 1980. It was a descriptive account of Jane-Finch that operated from an unconscious missionary, blaming-the-victim ideology. As I grew in my understanding, I remedied this situation by publishing *Cries from the Corridor* as *Life in Schools* nine years later, three years after *Schooling as a Ritual Performance* was published, which was a analysis of a Canadian Catholic school. *Schooling as a Ritual Performance* received the usual criticism but also many accolades as an example of critical ethnography, such as a glowing review in the *London Times*. But I always knew that *Life in Schools* would have a larger and more lasting readership, so moving ahead and correcting many mistakes with *Cries from the Corridor* was important to me, and having the opportunity to create a text that is not just about pedagogy but also pedagogical in its format was welcomed. I hope there is another edition down the road, and what that road will bring is forbiddingly unclear. I often urge teachers under the press of modern social competition linked to capitalism not to be deceived by the timeless tenor of capitalist life. But, of course, an overtone of guileful distinction creeps into the comparison of capitalism and socialism, especially here in the USA, where Fox News equates socialism with the National Socialist German Workers' Party commonly known as the Nazis. Try talking about socialism in the corporate media and you won't get far, unless you are on one of the very few progressive programming slots.

Recently I published an article, "Education Agonistes: An Epistle to the Transnational Capitalist Class," where I drew attention to the development, integration and consolidation of the transnational capitalist class, transnational state capitalism and the emergence of the superclass. These ideas, of course, have been developed by Bill Robinson, Jerry Harris and others. Some theorists think that the BRICS (Brazil, Russia, India, China, and South Africa) offer a counterweight to the G-7 countries. The BRICS are really helping to integrate global capitalism worldwide, although their political strategies vary and are indeed complex and their politics might appear counter-hegemonic at times. So my position is that any counternarratives we want to put forward, any revolutionary practices we wish to engage, must grasp the nature of transnational state capitalism in the current world-historical context. Take a look at the crisis of 2008. It was not created by the policies and whims of some cabal of banksters; rather the crisis was and is structurally rooted in the nature of capital. The crisis is structural. Some right-wing critics agree that the crisis is indeed structural but they think it has to do with public debt. On the contrary, the root of the crisis can be found not only or mainly in the reality of public debt and political corruption – clearly there has been a contagion of frantic recklessness on the part of banksters and hedge fund slime-masters – but in issues of profitability and renewed capital accumulation. As capital consumes a greater share of the social wealth, the only source of profit and value becomes living labor and as long as the share of living labor relative to capital declines due to increases in productivity and technological innovation, there remains a tendency of the rate of profit to decline. And as Peter Hudis and others have noted, we have seen since the 1970s an acute situation whereby living labor at the point of production has been replaced by new and advanced labor saving devices (and sometimes this pushes us towards exosomatic evolution where we are compelled to give subjective selves away by transforming ourselves into a machine).

What we are seeing as a response to the falling rate of profit is a desperate and slovenly unimaginative attempt by governments to redistribute value from labor to capital by imposing economic austerity that is part and parcel of today's immiseration capitalism. We can't tame capitalism through planned production, or by trying to provoke the ruling class to recognize the clear intimation that their transitory powers are destroying the planet or by trying to resurrect Keynes from his ashes scattered on the Downs at Tilton, in Sussex; rather, we need to theorize how to abolish capitalism through a new kind of labor and human relations that has no use for value production. But we can't abolish capitalism and leave in tact the ideological causes that engendered it, or we will build even more exploitative systems of survival. But the road must lead to socialism or we will have to contend with the consequences of social dissolution on a scale never before imagined, of social convulsion that will shred the planet of all life.

Look what happened in Greece. Bill Robinson reveals how, in the wake of 2008, the transnational state failed to intervene to impose regulations on global finance capital. But it did intervene to impose costs of devalorization on labor. Goldman Sachs advised Greek financial authorities to pour state funds into derivatives to make their national accounts look good. This way they could attract loans and bond purchases. But then, as Robinson points out, Goldman Sachs began participating in "credit default swaps" (speculation on sovereign debt) which is a type of parallel derivative trading where they bet on the possibility that Greece would default. The cost of borrowing for Greece became prohibitive as a result, increasing interest rates dramatically. The whole situation raised the prospect of sovereign debt default while Goldman Sachs made enormous profits. And of course, all of this made it possible for the EU and IMF to offer Greece bridge loans on the basis of accepting massive austerity measures.

The bailouts of transnational capital represent, as Robinson notes, a transfer of the devaluation of capital onto labor, onto the working and popular classes. So here we are, teachers, educators, living in the belly of the beast, watch all of this going on. We watch the actions of ALEC, or the American Legislative Exchange Council advancing precisely, this transnational corporate agenda. We see connections between the state, corporations,, surveillance, militarization of the police. It is all frightening. When we look at the militarization of the police, we see the execution of young black males. As Robinson has noted, African-Americans went from being the super-exploited sector of the working class to being marginalized as employers switched from drawing on black labor to Latino/a immigrant labor as a super-exploited workforce. African-Americans are now structurally marginalized than they have ever been in recent history and they are slated for the school-to-prison pipeline of mass incarceration and police and state terror. Capital has fused with reactionary state power, and the white working class awaits its salvation from the Tea Party and their ilk.

The road to socialism is made by the path of critical pedagogy. It is achieved by bringing teacher activists together with labor struggles at the point of production, political struggles at the point of reproduction, and political struggles in political society. Kees van der Pijl and Bill Robinson and others, have written more extensively about this. Richard Kahn, Sam Fassbinder, Tina Evans, David Greewood, Steve Best and others have studied these implications in the context of ecopedagogy and animal rights. We have an enormous challenge before us. The best advice I can give to North Americans who want to improve education is to fight poverty. Study after study has shown that students fare better in societies that are more equal, where the gap between the rich and the poor has been appreciably closed. But even this is not enough. We must create a social universe where the idea of economic inequality is unthinkable. We will not be pulled into the future by a carriage with chestnut-coloured warmbloods with ribbon-braided tails. Likely we will be pushed into the unknown by our own ignorance and by meekly following the coattails of those who purchase our labor-power. Freire urges us to be a subject of history and not a casualty. The stakes are high. They always are.

Acknowledgment

This chapter originally appeared as J. Cummings, The abode of educational production: An interview with Peter McLaren, *Alternate Routes* (Special issue: *Neoliberalism and the degradation of education*), 26 (2015), 354–375. Reprinted here, with minor edits, with permission from the publisher.

CHAPTER 12

Karl Marx, Digital Technology, and Liberation Theology

Peter McLaren and Petar Jandrić

1 Karl Marx and Digital Technology

Petar Jandrić: Your early work has been strongly influenced by postmodernism. For more than a decade, however, it has slowly but surely entered "the Marxist-humanist trajectory" spanning from authors with various Marxist tendencies and the neo-Marxism of the Frankfurt School to the original works of Marx (McLaren et al., 2008). The shift from postmodern Peter to Marxist Peter has been elaborated fairly extensively – for instance, in conversations with Marcia Moraes and Glenn Rikowski published in *Rage and Hope* (2006). Please summarize it in few sentences.

Peter McLaren: One of the foundational social relations that interdicts a student's access to resources necessary to see the world critically is, I believe, class exploitation. An exploitation that despoils communities and dispossesses workers of their humanity. Education opposes schooling. Education is that which intrudes upon our instincts and instruments of mind and augments them; it pushes us our thoughts along the arcs of the stars where our thoughts can give rise to new vistas of being and becoming and to new solidarities with our fellow humans. Our responsibilities for creating critical citizens should be proportional to our privilege. Today a good education is no longer seen as a social responsibility but as picking carefully from an array of consumer choices provided by a number of new companies and corporations. We now offer endless arrays of remedies for new kinds of learning disabilities. Just take your pick. As early as the 1980s, I was asking myself: How do we react to the cries of help from the youth of today, whose full-throated screams meet the immemorial silence of the pedagogical tradition? An answer to this question mandated a move away from the ironic distantiation and self-indulgent detachment of the vulgar divas of the academy who clearly chose identity politics over class politics (and in so doing became complicitous in the very relations of inequality they officially rejected) by a close reading of Marx and Marxist theorists, culminating with engaging the work of Marxist educators.

PJ: Departing from the Frankfurt School of Social Science, contemporary critical theories of technologies have developed into various directions (including, but not limited to, the elusive fields of postmodernism). Some of these theories ended up quite far from their Marxist roots; nowadays, they seem stuck at the place which you left more than a decade ago. Can you elaborate your return to Marxism as a theoretical base for reinvention of critical education in the context of information and communication technologies?

PM: Well, I began with an autonomous Marxist focus – the self-activity of the working class – and I was initially drawn to the work of important thinkers such as Antonio Negri, Michael Hardt, Raniero Panzieri, Mario Tronti, Sergio Bologna, Mariorosa Dalla Costa, Francois Berardi, and others, although I didn't explicitly deal with their work in my writings on education. I moved towards an appreciation of more classical Marxist critique, the work of Mas'ud Zavarzadeh, Teresa Ebert, for instance, then I became interested in the Marxist humanism of Peter Hudis, Kevin Anderson and Raya Dunayevskaya, and of course the work of British educators Paula Allman, Mike Cole, Dave Hill and Glenn Rikowski. So I began with an interest in what has been described as a new era of capitalist development that was variously described under the epithets 'post-industrialism', 'post-Fordism' or 'postmodern capitalism'.

Here the emphasis was on information age capitalism via information technologies – computers and telecommunications – used by capital to create capital mobility across national boundaries and eventually the national security state of widespread societal surveillance. Even though my many visits to Latin America convinced me that we have not in any way left the smokestack era of factory production, I became interested in the various ways that capital has penetrated the entire society by means of technological and political instruments in order to generate a higher level of productivity and in order to monitor and reconstitute its response to the self-organization of the working class through these new technologies. Of course, innovations in the context of knowledge production and communication in the new information society do not merely serve as instruments of capitalist domination, but can be employed in creating alternative and oppositional movements in the larger project of transforming capitalist society into a socialist alternative.

PJ: There has been a lot of water under the bridge since Marx developed his theories. Please address some contemporary challenges to his dialectical thought.

PM: I am critical of autonomous Marxists such as Hardt and Negri who, in books such as *Empire* (2001), argue that the multitude, who have amassed the necessary 'general intellect', are now in place as a web of resistance to capitalism – and they have done so simply by refusing to reproduce capitalism, without any unifying philosophy of praxis. Marxist-humanist theorist Kevin

Anderson correctly sees this as a rejection of transcendence in favor of immanence (i.e. a rejection of Hegel). He writes:

> This gaping flaw in Empire is rooted in the type of philosophical outlook they have embraced, one that radically rejects all forms of what they term transcendence in favor of staying on the plane of immanence, i.e., taking elements within the given social reality as one's point of departure.

But we do not have to choose between such one-sided alternatives. Consider Hegel's standpoint, as summed up by Theodor Adorno of the Frankfurt School: 'To insist on the choice between immanence and transcendence is to revert to the traditional logic criticized in Hegel's polemic against Kant' (Adorno, Prisms, p. 31). In fact, Hardt and Negri regularly attack Hegel and the Enlightenment philosophers as conservative and authoritarian, while extolling pre-Enlightenment republican traditions rooted in Machiavelli and Spinoza. What they thereby cut themselves off from is the dialectical notion that a liberated future can emerge from within the present, if the various forces and tendencies that oppose the system can link up in turn with a theory of liberation that sketches out philosophically that emancipatory future for which they yearn.

Marx certainly overcame the pre-Hegelian split between immanence and transcendence. The working class did not exist before capitalism and was a product of the new capitalist order, and was therefore immanent or internal to capitalism. At the same time, however, the alienated and exploited working class fought against capital, not only for a bigger piece of the pie, but also engaged in a struggle to overcome capitalism itself, and was in this sense a force for transcendence (the future in the present) (Anderson, 2010, pp. 11–12).

Here we see, as with Habermas, a rejection of all forms of radical transcendence and a refusal to conceptualize dialectically an alternative to capitalism. As Anderson notes, doing so inspires a fear of utopianism, or worse, authoritarianism and colonial hubris. For Habermas, Hardt, Negri and Holloway, there appears to be a fear of the Promethean side of Marx's humanism that, Anderson notes, points towards transcendence of the given. Thus, in the case of Habermas, we return to a reformist liberalism, and Hardt and Negri are moving towards a poststructuralist radicalism.

The solution, as Anderson proposes, is to 'stare negativity in the face' (to cite Hegel), and work within a variegated dialectics that takes into consideration race and ethnicity, gender, sexuality and youth. We cannot just refuse to take state power, as John Holloway and others recommend, since the state with its pernicious logic of domination will continue to exist until we have created a new social order, one that consists of freely associated labor on a world scale.

PJ: Marx's attitudes towards technology are often generally outlined by the famous quote from *The Poverty of Philosophy: Answer to* The Philosophy of Poverty *by M. Proudhon*: "The windmill gives you society with the feudal lord; the steam mill, society with the industrial capitalist" (Marx, 1955). In order to reinvent his critique in the network society, therefore, it is reasonable to ask: What do information and communication technologies give us regarding the contemporary relationship between capital and labor?

PM: Capital's political command over labor-power is the central antagonism facing capitalist societies worldwide. I agree with some of the autonomist Marxists that capitalism does use technological renovation as a weapon to defeat the working class and that this certainly helps to explain capital's tendency to expand the proportion of dead or "constant" capital as against living or "variable" capital involved in the production process. The proliferation of information and communication technologies has to be understood in the context of the struggle between capital and labor. But capital still remains dependent on collective labor as the source of surplus value. So capitalism has to constantly reorganize itself through a re-composition of the state – today we find this as an inexorable push towards social fascism – and to recompose the workforce – whether under the umbrella of lifelong learning strategies, telecommunications, flexible labor policies, a growth of the service economy, and the criminalization of those who cannot compete in the workforce and then privatizing the prisons and turning them into sites of surplus value production.

Clearly, the world could be headed towards the type of informatics dystopia dominated by the guardians of the security state, as Assange notes. But that of course does not rule out entirely the use of information and communication technology to create sites of resistance and transformation. As technological innovation becomes a permanent feature of capitalist relations of production within the new network society, production becomes intensified around cultivating new consumers by producing "transhumans" with new needs, as countries in the global periphery are turned into a giant factory and others are turned into giant fortresses of consumption. Network society is trapped within structured inequalities and there is strong evidence that information and communication technology is further entrenching such structured inequality rather than abating it.

As long as capital governs technology (and not the other way around) in its attempts to commodify every niche of the lifeworld, technology will perilously serve as an instrument of converting all aspects of nature into commodity-form, and rupturing and turning into raw materials whatever planetary metabolism remains life-sustaining. The technoscientific agenda of capital is ominous and has resulted in epistemicide and the destruction of many indigenous approaches to the relationship between humans and planetary ecosystems. While there are efforts to create counter-knowledges that take into account self-reflexivity and recursive interactions between nature and technology, how can they be de-linked from capitalist appropriation of social knowledge in all of its forms? Marx talked about the possibility of machines becoming organs of participation in nature. But capital will always hijack this process which is why we need to create a social universe that is not ruled by the sovereignty of labor's value form.

The violently wielded dominative power of machine technology cannot be contested through the creation of a non-capitalist commonwealth based on democratic principles. We can't turn our intellectual activity into intellectual capital so that it becomes an appropriated commodity form by universities or other corporatized entities. The same with online teaching in virtual learning factories where what cannot be digitalized loses value and significance.

2 Karl Marx and Liberation Theology

PJ: What are the main points of convergence between liberation theology and the works of Karl Marx?

PM: In his 1980 masterwork, *Marx against the Marxists: The Christian Humanism of Karl Marx*, José Porfirio Miranda, who was educated at the Pontifical Biblical Institute in Rome and who had previously studied sociology in the Frankfurt School, argues that Marx was a Christian humanist who understood the extortionate and unscrupulous characteristics of Christianity and how it was turned into a fraudulent and profiteering caricature of the Gospels when Christianity became the God of empire. Post-Vatican era liberation theologians such as Miranda have recognised and attempted to transcend the role of the Church as reproductive of structural sin (the social relations of capitalist exploitation) to the form of liberating praxis, creating the conditions of possibility to find justice in history. According to Boff (1982, p. 96), in the first post-Vatican II era (1965–1970) there arose an extraordinary effort on the part of the clergy to divest itself of the signs of power, to enter more deeply among the people, living their ministry not as someone above and beyond the faithful (priest), but as a principle of encouragement, unity, and service (ordained minister).

In the second post-Vatican age (1970–1980), campesinos and lay people began to organize themselves into base communities, "where there is an experience of a true ecclesiogenesis" (Boff, 1982, p. 96).

Boff (1982, p. 98) contends that the poor serve as the sacrament of Christ, who, "as eschatological judge [...] judges each one according to the love that either liberates from poverty or rejects its plea". The idea of God as eschatological judge permeates Miranda's magisterial works of liberation theology. Rather than antiseptically cleaving liberation theology from Marx's historical-dialectics, as one often discovers in the congeries of opinions of liberation theologians, Miranda sees their intimate connection as a leavening of social justice. Neil Hinnem (2013) is correct is locating the convergence between Miranda's understanding of the biblical perspective on history and Marx's historical-dialectics in Miranda's articulation of orthopraxis and his concept of historical events, the most important event for Miranda being the intervention of Yahweh into human history. As Hinnem (2013) writes:

> History is not an evolutionary process: rather, it is punctuated by revolutionary events. For Miranda, these events are the interventions of God in history for the sake of human justice, culminating in the Christ event, ushering all believers in the Kingdom of God. This event leads, consequently, to the Kingdom's underlying hope, its absolute command, that justice be achieved. "In the historical event of Jesus Christ", writes Miranda, "the messianic kingdom has arrived."

For Miranda, the Bible is a subversive document that preached communism long before the time of Karl Marx. Miranda sees much in common between history as liberation from alienation as described by Marx, and the eschaton, or the divine plan for the realization of the Kingdom of God.

PJ: An important aspect of Christian mystic – and the one you earlier identified as one of the main intersections between Christianity and Marxism – is the eschatological aspect of history. For Christians, this eschaton is the (arrival of) the Kingdom of God; for Marx and Engels, it is utopian socialism predicted as early as in the *Communist Manifesto* (Marx & Engels, 1976). Can you elaborate upon this eschaton a little deeper? What, for you, is the Kingdom of God?

PM: We have to honor the victims, speak to their lives of suffering in their theological reality. As Sobrino notes, the crucified peoples of this earth must not be remembered as some historical add-ons to our Sunday sermons but as those who were victims of the anti-Kingdom. After all, the anti-Kingdom is the Kingdom of Capital, of Wall Street and the world of value production (i.e. monetized wealth), of profit, of the exploitation and alienation of human labor, of private ownership of the means of production, of the market mechanism that forces capitalists (regardless of whether or not they are good people) to exploit workers, of the emergent transnational capital consolidated in a global capitalist historic bloc and the pillage zones of America Latina, and of the deregulated, informalized, and de-unionized capital-labor relation and the worldwide subordination of labor.

But here I need to emphasize something Sobrino (2001) has discussed at length in his many important writings. While we focus on the divine in Christ, we have forgotten the Kingdom of God of which Christ speaks. So when we identify as Catholics, why have we forgotten the primacy of creating the Kingdom of God and bringing it forth as Christ exhorted us to do? In my view, it is because our entire system operates as the anti-Kingdom. Christianity itself is undergirded by the imperatives of the anti-Kingdom in that it has attached itself to the imperatives of capitalism. To create the Kingdom of God means seeking the creation of a social universe outside of value production, or the production of profit for the rich. Creating the Kingdom of God means liberating the poor and this means ending the brutal war against the poor unleashed by the deregulation of the market. It means challenging the anti-Kingdom that stands against immigrants seeking a better life, against migrant workers, against refugees, and the intergenerationally reproduced barrios of planet slum. We focus instead on eternal life, on gnostic mysteries, and distance ourselves from the Kingdom of God with reality TV and the hundreds of TV channels we have at our disposal. We confuse the drive to increase material wealth with the drive to produce value, or create endless profits that can be expanded indefinitely.

In our forays into the hinterlands of mysticism, we cannot forget that the Kingdom of God is, in Sobrino's terms, a "type of historical-social-collective reality" (2001, p. 334) and not, as the old union song has it, a "pie in the sky when you die." The Kingdom of God is not some metaphor for an unearthly paradise, some ecclesiastical makeover of the earth in terms of the divine Christ or such that the holy and apostolic church becomes the prime sign or marker of the Kingdom. Clearly, for me, the Kingdom of God is not some place where well-heeled and aristocratic-looking souls lounge about in togas and golden wreaths. For me, the Kingdom of God is more likely found on the picket lines, in the temple cleared of the moneylenders, in a world where the rich no longer dominate, a world where death squads do not murder peasants with impunity, and where poor tenants do not confront racist landlords and developers do not build themselves towers in glorious homage to their wealth and power while others are forced to sleep under bridges.

PJ: Can you link the Christian eschaton described as the Kingdom of God, to Marx's prophecy of the future socialist society?

PM: I do see socialism as fitting in with the Kingdom of God announced by Jesus. Socialists in the past have sometimes made such a connection. Take the case of Helen Macfarlane. In 1850, Scottish governess, Helen Macfarlane, wrote polemical treatises supporting the Chartist movement. She was the first person to translate Hegel's philosophical writings into English and the first person to translate The *Communist Manifesto* into English. The Chartists were the first working-class movement to fight the British establishment in order to secure rights for the working class. For a time, Macfarlane supported Chartist leader Julian Harney in rebuilding the movement from a socialist and international perspective and refused to moderate the movement to win over the radical liberals. She allied herself with Marx and Engels and took on literary giants such a Thomas Carlyle and Charles Dickens. She interpreted Hegel as a humanist pantheist and she defined pantheism in humanistic terms. Her work reflects the Hegelian pantheism of David Strauss and her engagement with Marx and Engels helped her to radicalize Strauss's critical Hegelianism. For Hegel, the importance of the gospels was their symbolic content. For David Strauss, what was important about the gospels was their historicity – as myths that contained the Messianic desires of the early Christian communities (Black, 2014, p. XVII).

Feuerbach believed that theological knowledge was subjective and that the final criterion for the truth was to be found in the senses. Here the ego remains passive and determined by objective reality. For Marx, truth was found through historical praxis, through the negation of the negation. What is interesting about Macfarlane was her ability to merge the ideas of socialism, left Hegelianism, and Marxism with the teachings of Jesus and in doing so spiritualize the struggle for social justice. In 1850 she wrote:

> We Socialist-democrats are the soldiers of a holy cause; we are the exponents of a sublime idea; we are the apostles of the sacred religion of universal humanity. We have sworn by the God who "made of one blood all nations of the Earth", that we will not pause till we have finished the great work – begun by the Nazarean – of man's redemption from the social miseries which destroy body and soul. (Macfarlane in Black, 2014, p. 22)

PJ: If the Kingdom of God is a "type of historical-social-collective reality" (Sobrino, 2001, p. 334), why should we not just stick to Marx and Engels' utopian socialism? Why, in this context, do we need a God?

PM: As a species on the verge of extinction, we have an ongoing obligation today to commit ourselves to build a network amongst the working class, the peasantry, and the urban cognitariat and precariat in order to break down the immutable hierarchies of power and privilege concomitant with the workings of capitalist society. In our struggle to achieve this, God will be revealed. As Miranda writes: "Only in a world of justice will God be" (1977, p. 45). The revolution therefore depends not on the man himself or the woman herself or on the collectivity (which would be merely expanded egoism), but on the Other. Providing for each according to his or her needs presupposes caring for people simply because they exist and are God's children. The social relations of capitalist exploitation can force us to yield but they cannot oblige us to obey. God is the moral imperative itself, the imperative to struggle against injustice and innocent suffering. God's presence in history, the true revelatory intervention of the God of the Bible in human history, occurs when we take up the struggle for social justice.

It is interesting to note that Marx and Engels entered an organization in 1872 that was founded by Wilhelm Weitling, the founder of German communism. Weitling's organization was based on a communism grounded entirely in the gospel, as can be seen in his 1845 book, The Gospel of a Poor Sinner (Miranda, 1980). Marx was a great admirer of the Peasants' War organized and directed by Thomas Munzer in the 16th century. This was, in effect, the first anti-capitalist revolution. Munzer argued that the Kingdom of God is a condition of society without class differences, without private property, and without state powers opposed to the members of society.

PJ: Your work is a masterpiece of dialectics.... Where issues pertaining to ontology and epistemology pour into issues pertaining to politics and emancipation, there still is – even if only historically constructed – some sort of "division of work" between the different approaches and disciplines. What is the main strength of Marxism in the context of liberation theology?

PM: I return to the basic issues of the violence of capitalism, colonization, genocide, and the underlying epistemicide, which can be best understood as the destruction of epistemologies, ways of knowing, and ecologies of the mind of indigenous peoples throughout the world. Now for some proponents of liberation theology, communism as Marx envisioned is normative in the message of Jesus. And I have faith that the Kingdom of God will overcome the world of suffering precisely because I have faith in the people, the workers, the masses to defeat capital and bring about a more loving and human system for providing for the material needs of humanity. Terry Eagleton writes:

> I have argued already that reason alone can face down a barbarous irrationalism, but that to do so it must draw upon forces and sources of faith which run deeper than itself, and which can therefore bear an unsettling resemblance to the very irrationalism one is seeking to repel. (Eagleton, 2009, p. 161)

It is worth remembering, as Eagleton notes, "The Christian way of indicating that faith is not in the end a question of choice is the notion of grace. Like the world itself from a Christian viewpoint, faith is a gift" (2009, p. 138). Of course, this does not mean we cease examining our faith with evidence from the phenomenal world. Eagleton sees the great struggle today as one in which culture is pitted against civilization. He notes that "culture [...] is too much a matter of affirming what you are or have been, rather than what you might become" (2009, p. 165). And as for religion? Eagleton writes:

> What we know as Christendom saw itself as a unity of culture and civilization. If religion has proved far and away the most powerful, tenacious, universal symbolic form humanity has yet to come up with, it is partly on this account. What other symbolic form has managed to forge such direct links between the most absolute and universal of truths and the everyday practices of countless millions of men and women? What other way of life has brought the most rarefied of ideas and the most palpable of human realities into such intimate relationship? Religious faith has established a hotline from personal interiority to transcendent authority – an achievement upon which the advocates of culture can only gaze with envy. Yet religion is as powerless as culture to emancipate the dispossessed. For the most part, it has not the slightest interest in doing so. (2009, pp. 165–166)

But what of Marxism's potential in reconciling culture and civilization? Eagleton responds as follows:

> If Marxism holds out a promise of reconciling culture and civilization, it is among other things because its founder was both a Romantic humanist and an heir of Enlightenment rationalism. Marxism is about culture and civilization together – sensuous particularity and universality, worker and citizen of the world, local allegiances and international solidarity, the free self-realization of flesh-and-blood individuals and a global cooperative commonwealth of them. But Marxism has suffered in our time a staggering political rebuff; and one of the places to which those radical impulses have migrated is – of all things – theology. It is in some sectors of theology nowadays that one can find some of the most informed and animated discussions of Deleuze and Badiou, Foucault and feminism, Marx and Heidegger. (2009, p. 167)

What I find most important in Marxism is its explanation of how capitalism works to necessarily exploit workers and the environment, provoking workers to rise up and replace capitalism with socialism and eventually the state will wither under communism. Both Jesus and Marx have an eschatological view of history and, as Michael Rivage-Seul (2008) notes, Jesus challenges us to reject the worship of a divinized violence that feeds the "satanic military industrial complex" and practice a non-violent form of resistance against differentiating wealth.

3   Karl Marx and Christian Spirituality

PJ: In *Pedagogy of Insurrection*, you write:

> Critical pedagogy is the lucubration of a whole philosophy of praxis that predates Marx and can be found in biblical texts. If we wish to break from alienated labor, then we must break completely with the logic of capitalist accumulation and profit, and this is something to which Marx and Jesus would agree. (McLaren, 2015, pp. 54–55)

If Marx and Jesus would agree with the break from alienated labor, why does contemporary revolutionary pedagogy need an additional layer of rituals and beliefs offered by Christianity? More generally, what are the unique emancipatory and educational potentials of Christianity, which cannot be found in traditional nonreligious Marxism?

PM: My early work was on the topic of ritual – *Schooling as a Ritual Performance: Toward a Political Economy of Educational Symbols and Gestures* (McLaren, 1999). Here I followed the work of contemporary symbolic anthropologists – especially Victor Turner – in examining rituals as embodied metaphors and in relation to the construction of liminality. I applied these theories in a critical ethnography I undertook at a Catholic middle school in the Azorean community of Toronto. I was able to discern rituals of instruction, of accommodation, and how an anti-structure of resistance was possible under certain conditions. I also identified micro and macro rituals in school settings and how they can be both emancipatory and contribute to the reproduction of hierarchies of power and privilege. I articulated a theory of the teacher as a liminal servant and how the construction of liminality in the classroom can be the seedbed of true creativity, but at the same time a flashpoint for violence. Much of the important work in applied theater, in drama, and performance studies builds on conceptions of ritual. This can be seen in the writings of my late thesis advisor and mentor, Richard Courtney, and is paramount in the work of Augusto Boal – especially in his magisterial volume, *Theatre of the Oppressed* (2008), which was very much influenced by the work of his fellow Brazilian, Paulo Freire.

I was fortunate to participate in a public dialogue with Freire and Boal at the Rose Theater in Omaha, Nebraska, in the early 1990s. It was the first time Freire and Boal had appeared together in such a venue and I was honored to have been a part of this historic event. Symbols have a fecundity that become animated in rituals. They are brought to life, and live inside of us, through play, through rituals, and their elaboration can be seen in the evolution of drama and thought. Symbols are enacted and work synergistically with other symbols; I have termed this process "enfleshment." Here religious and secular symbols can, under specific historical and existential circumstances, hemorrhage into each other and can work in very liberating and also in very dangerous ways. Just think of Francoist Spain and the rituals that linked Catholic symbols to fascism.

According to Miranda (1980), Jesus was the first human being in history to denounce money as the object of idolatry, which centuries later Marx referred to variously as the Biblical idols of Baal, Mammon, and Moloch. In fact, when discussing the commodity form of production, he used these terms as much as he did the word "fetish." When Saint Paul talks about the "lust which is idolatry," he is referring to money. Book Three of *Capital* (Marx, 1981) makes clear that the capitalist mode of production is not the origin of class violence in capitalist society. As Miranda (1980) notes, the class division is created outside the sphere of production, when money becomes god, and it was this god that created the conditions of possibility for the capitalist mode of production. Money as exchange value stands outside production and circulation and yet dominates both. Money represents the autonomous existence of value as the concretization of human labor. It is when money no longer represents commodities, but when commodities represent money, that money becomes a god. Money is the god of all people living under the commodity mode of production and money had already become a god during the time of Jesus. In other words, the accumulation of capital is not enough to automatically create the mode of production we know today as capitalism, because it takes a certain type of historically produced civilization. The transformation of money into capital requires a certain kind of historical circumstance. Today, capitalism still functions as the institutionalization of the worship of Mammon.

Marx does a brilliant job of explaining how money was transformed into a god ruling human beings. Marx reveals how money is both the object and fountainhead of greed, of *auri sacra fames*, the product of a historically conditioned environment. According to Miranda (1980), Marx perceived the switching of the subject into an object and the transformation of the ends into the means as the centerpiece of the making of a false religion. Marx then applied this "conversion" to economics, to the production of value. Capital finds a way to exchange itself for a commodity that produces more value than the commodity itself – labor power. Capital moves into production through an exchange with labor power, via wage labor, which brings about the separation of the direct producers from the owners of the means of production. Interest-bearing capital is a fetish, a self-expanding value, and it expands its value independently of reproduction, which is a reversal of the relationship between persons and things – all pointing to Marx's anathematization of the worship of money as god. Miranda (2004) points out that at the very central point of his analysis of capital, at the very point where he uncovers the birth of money as a commodity, Marx cites two entire versus from the Apocalypse (Rev 17:13, 13:17). Marx offers a scientific elaboration of Christ's teaching about the god Mammon.

PJ: The understanding of money as a god which rules human beings fascinates me. Can we say that it is one of the central points of connection between Christianity and Marxism?

PM: Jesus talked so much about economic sin that it is unfathomable why this is not a central part of the teachings of Christianity. The Lucan part of the Bible explicitly teaches communism (Acts 4:32; 4:34; 2:44; Luke 14:33). Miranda argues that the origin of the communist idea in the history of the West is not to be found in Plato or Marx but rather in the New Testament. The Bible clearly condemns acquired wealth and established wealth and also the means by which this wealth came to be – including various kinds of profit, such as interest on loans, and the expropriation of the produce of the workers' labor by agricultural entrepreneurs (James 5:1–6). Jesus is not against generalized wealth per se, such as the wealth of a people, but against relative or differentiating wealth. Someone cannot be rich while another remains poor. Mark 10:25 and Luke 6:20, 6:24, 16:19–31, 1:53 are interpreted by Miranda as arguing that there is no legitimately moral means of acquiring differentiating wealth and that Jesus maintains (Luke 16:29, 16:31) that the same condemnation of wealth can be found in the Old Testament.

Actually, three types of profit are attacked in the scriptures. The Bible itemizes its reproof of profit-taking as occurring through commerce (Ecclus 27:1–2), loans on interest (Exodus 22:24; Leviticus 25:36, 25:37; Deuteronomy 23:19; Ezekiel 18:8, 18:13, 18:17, 22:12; Psalm 15:5; Proverbs 28:8.), and productive activity or the process of production (James 5:1–6). There is something about the process itself of being able to grow rich that is wicked and unjust (Isaiah 53:9). The acquisition of wealth itself is possible only by exploiting the poor (Job 20:19; Psalm 37). Micha 2:1–2, as well as Isaiah 5:8, focus on how the rich keep acquiring property. Miranda (1974, 1980) makes a convincing case that the Bible condemns the exploitation suffered by the poor at the hands of the rich and creates an identity between the rich and the unjust (Isaiah 53:9). Jesus' teachings that enabled the first Christians to base their community on communism can be found in Mark 10:25, Luke 6:20, 24, Matthew 6:24, and Luke 16:19–31.

In fact, Miranda (1980) makes the claim that Jesus was a communist, which can be seen in John 12:6, 13:29, and Luke 8:1–3. Did not Jesus make the renunciation of property a condition for entering into the Kingdom of God? How can God make it possible for a rich person to enter the Kingdom of God? The answer is clearly provided by the Bible. According to Miranda this answer is: By ceasing to be rich (Mark 10:21, 25, 27) and giving away one's wealth to the poor. The scriptural exegesis undertaken by Miranda is, to me, thoroughly persuasive. As a revolutionary Marxist, I am certainly drawn to a number of Miranda's works, *Marx and the Bible* (1974) and *Marx against the Marxists* (1980).

PJ: Poverty is a central point of departure for Jesus, Marx, and Paulo Freire. Yet, the answers seem to collide. For Jesus, the poor will inherit the Kingdom of God; for Marx and Freire, the poor should take matters in own hands here and now....

PM: Jesus did not sacralize poverty or preach resignation to it because there will be some extra-terrestrial compensation for it in the afterlife. That would be a glib and cynical assessment, and it erases the prophetic nature of such a pronouncement. To say the poor are blessed is not an involuntary justification of the relations and structures of exploitation. The poor are blessed because the coming of the Kingdom in the fullness of history will put an end – in the concrete sociological sense – to their poverty and suffering. Poverty is a form of structural sin that is incompatible with the Kingdom of God. I am not trying to reduce the Gospel to a manual for attaining political consciousness but maintaining that the Gospel has an inherent political dimension. As Gustavo Gutierrez notes,

> This conscienticizing of the preaching of the Gospel, which rejects any aseptic presentation of the message, should lead to a profound revision of the pastoral activity of the Church [...] the oppressed themselves should be the agents of their own pastoral activity. (1988, pp. 154–155)

PJ: Socialist society may indeed be very close to the Kingdom of God, yet Marxist and Christian methods for achieving the eschaton seem quite different. In the Communist Manifesto, Marx and Engels write "Workers of the world, unite. You have nothing to lose but your chains!"[1]; *Matthew 5:5 says "Blessed are the meek: for they shall inherit the earth." What about these differences in views to human agency, Peter? What is their relationship to labour?*

PM: For Marx, human beings clearly are subjects, subjects of history. The subject of history is related to Marx's concept of living labour, of labour-power, the potential for labouring, the capacity for labour, its possibility and potency. It is living labour that is present in time and throughout human history as possibility, whereas objectified labour serves the means and instruments of production and has no role in liberation from oppression. Marx describes how the capitalist production process makes relationships between persons seem as relationships between things. For Marx, capital grounds all social mediation as a form of value, and that the substance of labour itself must be interrogated because doing so brings us closer to understanding the nature of capital's social universe out of which our subjectivities are created. Because the logic of capitalist work has invaded all forms of human sociability, society can be considered to be a totality of different types of labour. What is important here is to examine the particular forms that labour takes within capitalism. In other words, we need to examine value as a social relation, not as some kind of accounting device to measure rates of exploitation or domination. Consequently, labour should not be taken simply as a 'given' category, but interrogated as an object of critique, and examined as an abstract social structure.

For Marx, the commodity is highly unstable and non-identical. Its concrete particularity (use-value) is subsumed by its existence as value-in-motion or by what we have come to know as "capital". Value is always in motion because of the increase in capital's productivity that is required to maintain expansion. The dual aspect of labour within the commodity (use-value and exchange value) enables one single commodity – money – to act as the value measure of the commodity. Thus, the commodity must not be considered a thing, but a social relationship. You could describe the "soul" of capitalist production as the extraction from living labour of all the unpaid hours of labour that amounts to surplus-value or profit. Marx's analysis of the fetishism of the commodity form bears a strong kinship to the New Testament's references to "false gods". But, as Lebacqz (1986, p. 107) argues,

> in spite of its affinity with Marx's analytic methods and social goals, the view of justice provided in liberation theology is not simply a new version of "to each according to need". Justice is not a simple formula for distribution. Justice would not be accomplished merely by offering programs that meet basic needs of the poor. Justice requires the kind of liberating activity that characterizes God's behaviour toward the poor and oppressed [...] there is no separation of "love" and "justice". God's justice is God's love or compassion on those who suffer. God's love is God's justice or liberation of the oppressed.

Marx was a humanist, and this is clear in both his private letters but also his published works, but whether he was a Christian humanist as Miranda maintains remains very much an open question.

PJ: Marxism aims at social change through collective action, while Christianity is much more focused to individual development. Obviously, this is not an either-or relationship – as Paulo Freire (1972) would say, collective acts of emancipation are necessarily preconfigured by individual consciousness. What is your take on this tension between (Christian) individualism and (Marxist) collectivism?

PM: The emphasis in Christianity on otherworldliness (don't worry if the bad people are not caught and punished, they will be punished in the afterlife) has often been used as a moral justification for the consecration of deception, either by encouraging passive resistance to exploitation or labelling the unmasking of deeper truths about empire as too subversive, too "anti-American" – a posture that tends to make people unworldly or uncaring about others. Yet, as De La Torre (2015, p. 162) warns: "History demonstrates the futility of simply denouncing unjust social structures for those whom the structures privilege will never willingly abdicate what they consider to be their birthright". The mere moral exercise of political power through passive protest is not a convincing answer since the idea of the moral exercise of political power ignores what political power is: the state is (not as an abuse but by definition) "the monopoly of legitimate violence". While parts of the state machine may be "very peaceful", the threat of violence, backed up by armed forces, is always presupposed. And the practice of politics, whether in office or in opposition, is always war (mainly class war) carried on by other means. Non-violent politics is a contradiction in terms (Collier, 2001, p. 104).

So instead of fighting to change the structures of oppression, people either focus on remaking themselves as individuals into better persons (there are plenty of self-help books out there) or they become indelibly indifferent to politics or political change.

Marxism rejects this Cartesian sense of "liberty of indifference" (changing oneself rather than changing the world) and "the preference for autoplastic solutions which underlies it" (Collier, 2001, p. 100). While one is necessarily changed by changing the world (what we call praxis), that does not mean that all attempts to change ourselves are unnecessary or futile – since resistance to oppression requires us to adapt to changing circumstances, and adaptation requires all kinds of strategies of self-change. After all, in his "Theses on Feuerbach", Marx (1976) writes that: "The coincidence of the changing of circumstances and of human activity or self-changing can be conceived and rationally understood only as revolutionary practice". If we act as if the eschaton has already arrived, and we are preparing for the reign of God, then is this not a necessarily a quixotic predicament, but a form of pre-figurative politics.

Letting the reign of God be prefigured in our present lives, whether we image that reign to be a communist society or the Kingdom of God, there is no guarantee that our good actions will bring about its completion – but if we postdate our best ethics to the future communist society or Kingdom of God, then our good actions will, at least, have intrinsic values in themselves. Our organisation and actions should prefigure the socialist revolution or the coming of the Kingdom of God. While it may be true that means do not always resemble ends, Collier argues that "[s]o long as human authority exists, it should as far as possible be organized so that the greatest power serves the least powerful with all its might" which in its contemporary form is called "the dictatorship of the proletariat" (Collier, 2001, p. 122).

PJ: Both the Bible and the works of Marx can be read in many different ways – I surely don't need to remind you of historical atrocities which resulted from certain readings of both doctrines. ... While it is tempting to seek concordances between seminal Christian and Marxist texts, I would like to ask a more fundamental philosophical question: How commensurable are the philosophies of Marxism and Christianity?

PM: Denys Turner (1983) has contributed some important insights with respect to the compatibility of Marxism and Christianity that are worth repeating here. Both Marxism and Christianity are compatible with a materialist theory of history yet hold to a denial of ontological materialism. We are talking here not about a formal or Cartesian logical consistency between Marxism and Christianity but a dialectical consistency.

It is true that there exists no coherent synthesis between Christian doctrines and Marxist theory, but that all the more makes it imperative that we abandon the rhetorical homologies often found in liberation theology – "the anawim [the poor and the oppressed referred to in the Old Testament] become the proletariat, liberation becomes redemption politicised, alienation is original sin [...] the priesthood metamorphosized into Lenin's revolutionary leadership" (Turner, 1983, pp. 211–212). These homologies are useful, politically, to inspire the struggle of impoverished communities against well-armed death squads, but they must not be viewed as strict equivalences, since this could lead to uncritical forms of triumphalism.

PJ: I'm glad we're on the same page!

PM: While Marxism and Christianity seem to be incommensurable languages, both are constitutively necessary to explain reality and to understand what forces and relations shape the human condition. Both are part of the praxis of history and can be viewed as historically conditioned action systems, defined by their relationship to historical contingencies. As Turner (1983) reminds us, Marxism requires abolishing the conditions which require it – capitalist exploitation. Similarly, according to Turner, Christianity will realize itself only at the cost of its abolition as Christianity since its realization will become a fully human reality rather than a sacred reality – a fully socialized humanity and a fully humanized society consisting of love.

However, as Turner (1983) cogently argues, because God is non-identical with the contingencies of any particular form of history, our full humanity can only be known through aspirations for liberation which cannot be realized in practice. We need to secure the conditions of that absence of a presence which we can only symbolize and understand heuristically. We cannot love, we cannot be free, we cannot know God, we cannot know how we can live without oppression, because the Kingdom of God has not been realized; we can only work as Christians and Marxists to secure the conditions of the possibility of loving and living freely. Under capitalism, under the prevailing institutional structures of exploitation, love and freedom can only ever be ideological. We can only anticipate love in its absence, we can never truly see love fulfilled under the conditions of capitalism. In the conditions of bourgeois society, any further claims about love are only ideological. In a world of dehumanised, alienated social relationships, we can only symbolize love through its absence, and so we can say that love, and generosity, and goodness, and Christ are present in this world but present only in the form of their absence.

4 The Christian Morality of Dialectical Materialism

PJ: Speaking of the conditions of freedom, and of anticipation, we enter directly into the area of morality. Christian morality is quite theoretically robust, yet, as Rosen (2000, p. 21) says, "the question whether Marx's theory has a moral or ethical dimension is one of the most controversial of all issues of Marx interpretation". What is your take on that question?

PM: Marxism is, in this sense, morality itself, because, as Turner (1983, p. 215) argues: "it consists in the knowledge of what to do given the 'facts'". Marxism is the fundamental science of capitalism and reveals morality in capitalist society to be ideologically bourgeois. Marxism is thus all that morality can be – it represents the outer limits of morality – given today's existing conditions of capitalist exploitation and oppression. Marxism is "the theory and the practice of realizing the conditions of the possibility of morality" (Turner, 1983, p. 215), while at the same time, it is not possible for Christianity to be regarded as coterminous with Marxism even when Marxism "is demonstrably the scientifically warranted response to 'the conditions of any particular historical epoch'" (Turner, 1983, p. 213). And this is true "even if it follows from the fact that Christianity can know itself and the nature of its praxis only through the Marxist criticism of it" (Turner, 1983, p. 213). So while Marxism argues about "the impossibility of moral knowledge in capitalist conditions", it exists as a revolutionary form of praxis in that it points out how it is impossible for capitalism to conform to its own truth in practice "since conformity is structurally impossible for capitalism" (Turner, 1983, p. 213).

Christianity attempts to "symbolize the depths of what is to be human in the form of a sacredness, in the form of the refusal to admit what is most fully human could be compatible with the conditions of alienation and exploitation which historically obtain" (Turner, 1983, p. 213). Thus, Christianity recognizes love as the point of its praxis but it is a love which, under capitalism, can only be anticipated. Turner makes a prescient point when he argues that the absence of morality in Marxism is not in any sense a "mere a moralism" because it reveals that it is capitalism, not Marxism, which is a moralistic. In other words, Marxism reveals the "platitudinous imperatives, so forthcoming from Christians, to 'love' within conditions of gross and systematic exploitation" (Turner, 1983, p. 216) and Christianity's "transhistorical pretentiousness" in believing that Christ's presence in history is not historically contingent, that is, not dependent on any particular historical or economic conditions.

Adopting a transcendent morality among Christians is what Turner rejects as Christian "fidelism" which focuses on the Kingdom of God being "within you". This is not to deny the presence of God, but that such presence is not in the form of some supernatural text which has already been written; rather, "the unwritten text is present in the struggle to write it" (Turner, 1983, p. 219). This is very much like the popular proverb by Antonio Machado that one makes the road by walking (*Caminante, no hay camino. Se hace camino al andar*). Both Marxism and Christianity have the resources within their own traditions for rejecting immorality – for instance, for rejecting meta-moral principles where, for example, communist society is made into a moral absolute or Christianity is presented as an already written moral text to which only Christians or particularly enlightened Christians have access.

According to Turner, Marx rejected theism as false, because it "supposes an opposition between God and man" (Turner, 1983, p. 165) and he criticises atheism "because it accepts the terms which theism lays down and can speak of man only indirectly, that is, via the negation of theism" (Turner, 1983, p. 165). Marx rejected the theologically and politically conservative Christianity of his day, as well as the radical Christianity that made its appearances throughout his lifetime. Marx claims that questions pertaining to the existence of God arise only among those who fail to understand their own natural human origins. Turner recognised that Marx rejected contemporary immanentist theologies because he viewed them as a partial regression to negative atheism itself. While Marx rejected negative atheism, Turner does not take that to mean Marx was not an atheist.

PJ: I could somehow swallow that Marx was not a (complete) atheist, but it cannot be disputed that he was very anti-clerical. How does liberation theology, with its close relationships to the Church, absorb Marx's negativity towards its own being?

PM: Marx was anti-clerical, and so would any rational person be during the time of Marx who recognised that Jesus was the antithesis of clericalism, a clericalism whose world-denying conciliar prohibitions infected by monarchism and paternalism, disallowed justice for all. It was a temporal power that germinated autocracy and was leavened by obedience to a hierarchy that almost always sided with the imperial and structural intentionality of the state. It was clear to Marx and like-minded others that the ecclesiology that developed from the law, especially canon law, gave the papacy unrestricted power over the laity, resulting in a religious hubris of unrelenting fidelity to empire. It had ripped away from early Christianity sanctioned disobedience to imperial law. Now it demanded compliance to the dictatorship of the ruling class and its despotic commands often leading to brutishness, cruelty and unvarnished terror, to prioritizing sacred laws over human welfare and making the Law of Christ coextensive with the Law of Empire and its imperial covenant directed at capital accumulation by dispossession.

In liberation theology, however, there must be a principled intransigence towards authoritarian power rather than a creative adaptation to it, an ecclesiogenesis[2] that lives in dialectical tension between the pneumatological[3] and doctrinal aspect of the church and the base of the Church of the Poor. The Church proclaims a Kingdom of God that it can never put into practice, similar to capitalism that installs the very conditions (wage labour, value augmentation, social relations of production) under which wealth and prosperity are available onto to a few. Yet both cannot abandon the teachings they cannot follow.

PJ: Are there any theoretical and/or practical dissonances between Marxism and Christianity in your theory? If there are, how do you go about them?

PM: While some might argue that traditional non-religious Marxism is not as equipped as theological traditions to engage fundamental questions pertaining to the hermeneutics of spirituality, there are numerous Marxist theorists who have written profoundly about issues of the spirit – here, I am thinking of Ernst Bloch, Walter Benjamin, and Erich Fromm, just to name a few. I think Marxism does address issues of the human spirit, but what interests me, in particular, is an engagement with a tradition that deals with a triune god. Of course, liberation theology comes in many forms: Chicano liberation theology; Latinx liberation theology; Native American liberation theology; African American liberation theology. Therefore, I do not want to limit liberation theology to the political theology that comes out of Europe, or to the Latin American liberation theology that is primarily Catholic and pastoral.

I work as a Marxist materialist but I believe there is a world beyond physicalism. That is a world of hope. Hope is conjugated in opposition to injustice and gestated in the struggle of humanity against inhumanity. Rubem Alves (cited in Boff, 1986, p. 124) writes of hope as follows:

> Hope is the presentiment that the imagination is more real, and reality less real, than we had thought. It is the sensation that the last word does not belong to the brutality of facts with their oppression and repression. It is the suspicion that reality is far more complex than realism would have us believe, that the frontiers of the possible are not determined by the limits of the present, and that, miraculously and surprisingly, life is readying the creative event that will open the way to freedom and resurrection.

Hope does not deliver us from suffering. But hope, I believe, can deliver us from the fear of suffering. It does this by giving us the courage to believe that we are not fated to live in misery, that light does shine through the cracks of the day-to-day sepulcher in which we find ourselves, in this cold and damp undercroft, in this darkness of inevitability.

PJ: Marx was a scientist, and his worldview is based on dialectical materialism. Liberation theology is religious, and its worldview is based on faith. How do you reconcile these radically different approaches to reality?

PM: Today in our efforts to create a society constructed upon principles of social justice we have approached our projects as scientifically distilled data – big data serves both as our compass and our destination. But allegiance to data removes the consensus-generating process that is part of collective reflection and systematic rationality, as Miranda explains so well. Interpersonal dialogue has to be part of the object of study and rational reflection – since relations between people are the basis of the relations between things. We can't forget this. As Miranda (1980, p. 306) notes, the "communitarian process leading to consensus can evade the arbitrariness or naivete of extrascientific motives only if we, in all frankness, realize that dialogic discussion does exist, that it is moral in character, and that it is thus a matter of conscience". Without this consideration articulated by Miranda, and reflected in Paulo Freire's *Pedagogy of the Oppressed* (1970), we will etherise the role that our conscience must play and fall prey to corruption and self-interest.

We can't separate norms and facts, facts and value, for this expunges meaning from history, and both Marx and the teachings of the gospels recognise this. As Miranda (1980, p. 307) notes, "The eschaton of Marx, which is the same as that of the gospel, is what gives meaning to history". The project of immanentizing the eschaton is one that has historically struck fear in the hearts of conservatives who use the term pejoratively because it refers to attempts to bring about the Kingdom of God in the immanent world. The conservatives equate this with socialism, communism, anti-racism and even Nazism. But reading the Gospel from below mandates that such a project is already in the making, with the intervention of Christ into human history. It is rejected by conservatives for fear of the rise of totalitarianism. But at the root of such fear is that panic in the hearts of those who stand to lose their wealth and status should a state of egalitarianism and equality be achieved.

PJ: What is the main message of Marx's work for liberation theology positioned in, against, and beyond contemporary capitalism (cf. Holloway, 2016)?

PM: All of us can become blinded by virtue of our own interests, whether we are atheists, agnostics, Christians, Christian communists, or members of other religious faiths. For example, the capitalist does not realize that what is sold in the transaction between the capitalist is labour-power, not labour – sold at its exchange value, and so the capitalist is wilfully blinded to the fact that labour-power produces much more than it is worth simply as exchange value (the labourer works much more than it takes to reproduce his or her own necessities for survival) and operates out of a motivated amnesia that the capitalist has been stealing surplus value from his workers. The Christian and the capitalist rarely think deeply about Marx's notion of value, and both adhere to the empiricist expression "price of labour", which hides the fact that the wage system is, in reality, a form of slavery. This, according to Marx, is an epistemological issue as much as a moral issue. As Miranda points out, Marx did not adhere to a materialist dogmatism that limited epistemology to social class. He recognized that the very mechanism of cognition itself is ideological, and that there are moral values embedded in the process of cognition – that within the apologetics and empiricist ideologies of economists there exists hidden interests which he viewed as ideological.

It is worth remembering Miranda's (1980, p. 303) insight: "Empiricism sticks to things. Marx dissolves things into relations between persons because conscience is not troubled by any moral obligation whatsoever when it confronts things". Hence, it is important for both Christians and Marxists to remember that exploitation and oppression can only be overcome by a sincere willingness to know the truth. Yes, truth is always partial, contingent and contextual, but it can be known. Which is why I believe the work of Marx is so essential to Christianity and why liberation theology needs to be continually reinvented for the current times, especially after such brutal efforts by the Reagan administration and Pope John Paul II to silence it, and efforts by right-wing dictatorships throughout Latin America to crush it by murdering priests and exponents of the Church of the Poor in the 1970s and 1980s. Today, especially today, the world needs liberation theology, which, by the way, is not restricted to Christianity or Christians but to all those who seek justice in these exceedingly brutal times.

Acknowledgments

This article presents a selection of material published in following articles: P. McLaren and P. Jandrić, Critical revolutionary pedagogy is made by walking – in a world where many worlds coexist, *Policy Futures in Education*, 12(6) (2014), 805–831; P. McLaren and P. Jandrić, From liberation to salvation: Revolutionary critical pedagogy meets liberation theology, *Policy Futures in Education*, 15(5) (2017), 620–652; P. McLaren and P. Jandrić, Karl Marx and liberation theology: Dialectical materialism and Christian spirituality in, against, and beyond contemporary capitalism, *Triple C: Communication, Capitalism & Critique*, 16(2) (2018), 598–607; and P. McLaren and P. Jandrić, The critical challenge of networked learning: Using information technologies in the service of humanity, in P. Jandrić and D. Boras (Eds.), *Critical Learning in Digital Networks* (Springer, 2015). Some parts of the text have been previously republished in English language in P. McLaren and P. Jandrić, Peter McLaren's liberation theology: Karl Marx meets Jesus Christ, in J. S. Brooks and A. Normore (Eds.), *Leading against the grain: Lessons for creating just and equitable schools* (pp. 39–48) (Teachers College Press, 2017); P. McLaren, *Pedagogy of insurrection: From resurrection to revolution* (Peter Lang, 2015); P. Jandrić, *Learning in the age of digital reason* (Sense, 2017). Some parts of the text have been previously republished in other languages in P. McLaren and P. Jandrić, Critical revolutionary pedagogy in and for the age of the network, *Philosophy of Education*, 14(1) (2015), 106–126; and P. McLaren and P. Jandrić, Kultura borbe protiv neoliberalnog kapitalizma, *Zarez*, 398–399(16) (2014), 8–9. Reprinted parts of the text have been reformatted, abridged, and otherwise reshaped for the purpose of this article.

This chapter originally appeared as P. McLaren and P. Jandrić, Karl Marx, digital technology, and liberation theology, *Beijing International Review of Education*, 1(2–3) (2019), 544–569. Reprinted here, with minor edits, with permission from the publisher.

Notes

1 We are well aware that this phrase is a popularisation, which does not exist in the *Communist Manifesto* – yet, it does adequately describe the dichotomy between Marxist and Christian views to human agency.

2   The term 'ecclesiogenesis' is used by liberation theologian Leonardo Boff to describe the new ecclesiological experience within the Basic Christian Communities created in Latin America in which attempts are made by popular constituencies to create authentic Christian communities. Participants see this as creating a new form of church outside of the institutional structures of the traditional Catholic hierarchy (see Boff, 1986).
3   In Christianity, the term 'pneumatology' refers to the study of the Holy Spirit.

References

Anderson, K. (2010, August 18). Overcoming some current challenges to dialectical thought. *International Marxist-Humanist*. http://www.internationalmarxisthumanist.org/wp-content/uploads/pdf/anderson-overcoming-some-current-challenges-to-dialectical-thought-20100818.pdf

Black, D. (Ed.). (2014). *Helen Macfarlane: Red republican: Essays, articles and her translation of the* Communist Manifesto. Uncant Publishers.

Boal, A. (2008). *Theatre of the oppressed (get political)*. Pluto Press.

Boff, L. (1982). *Francis of Assisi: A model of human liberation* (J. W. Diercksmeier, Trans.). Orbis Books.

Boff, L. (1986). *Ecclesiogenesis: The base communities reinvent the church*. Orbis Books.

Collier, A. (2001). *Christianity and Marxism: A philosophical contribution to their reconciliation*. Routledge.

De La Torre, M. (2015). *The politics of Jesus: A Hispanic political theology*. Rowman and Littlefield.

Eagleton, T. (2009). *Reason, faith and revolution: Reflections on the God debate*. Yale University Press.

Freire, P. (1970). *Pedagogy of the oppressed*. Herder and Herder.

Gutierrez, G. (1988). *A theology of liberation: History, politics, and salvation* (C. Inda and J. Eagleson). Orbis Books.

Hardt, M., & Negri, A. (2001). *Empire*. Harvard University Press.

Hinnem, N. (2013). Marx and the Bible. *The Oxford Left Review, 11*, 31–37.

Holloway, J. (2016). *In, against, and beyond capitalism: The San Francisco lectures*. PM Press/Kairos.

Lebacqz, K. (1986). *Six theories of justice: Perspectives from philosophical and theological ethics*. Augsburg.

Marx, K. (1955). *The poverty of philosophy: Answer to* The philosophy of poverty *by M. Proudhon*. Progress.

Marx, K. (1981). *Capital, Vol. III*. Vintage.

Marx, K., & Engels, F. (1976). The Communist manifesto. In *Marx-Engels-Collected-Works (mecw)*, Volume 6. https://www.marxists.org/archive/marx/works/1848/communist-manifesto/index.htm

Marx, K. (1976). Theses on Feuerbach. In *Marx-Engels Collected Works, Volume 5*. http://marxists.anu.edu.au/archive/marx/works/1845/theses/original.htm

McLaren, P. (1999). *Schooling as a ritual performance: Toward a political economy of educational symbols and gestures*. Rowman & Littlefield.

McLaren, P. (2015). *Pedagogy of insurrection: From resurrection to revolution*. Peter Lang.

McLaren, P. (Ed.). (2006). *Rage and hope: Interviews with Peter McLaren on war, imperialism, and critical pedagogy*. Peter Lang.

McLaren, P., McMurry, A., & McGuirk, K. (2008). *An interview with Peter McLaren*. University of Waterloo. http://english.uwaterloo.ca/PeterMcLareninter-view.pdf

Miranda, J. P. (1974). *Marx and the Bible: A critique of the philosophy of oppression*. Orbis Books.

Miranda, J. P. (1977). *Being and the Messiah: The message of St. John*. Orbis Books.

Miranda, J. P. (1980). *Marx against the Marxists: The Christian humanism of Karl Marx* (J. Drury, Trans.). Orbis Books.

Miranda, J. P. (2004). *Communism in the Bible* (R. R. Barr, Trans.). Wipf & Stock.

Rivage-Seul, M. (2008). *The emperor's God: Imperial misunderstandings of Christianity*. Institute for Economic Democracy Press.

Rosen, M. (2000). The Marxist critique of morality and the theory of ideology. In E. Harcourt (Ed.), *Morality, reflection and ideology* (pp. 21–43). Oxford University Press.

Sobrino, J. (2001). *Christ the liberator*. Orbis Books.

Turner, D. (1983). *Marxism and Christianity*. Blackwell.

CHAPTER 13

Conclusion: The Future of Critical Pedagogy

I have been invited to comment on the future of critical pedagogy. What is the future of critical pedagogy? Has its tacit and enduring framework of liberation of the oppressed from forces and relations of exploitation been slowly and painstakingly whittled away by the unalloyed inertia of a long and protracted struggle that has lasted numerous decades? Or by the seemingly inexhaustible forces of the right? Has critical pedagogy been reduced to a shadow of its former self which once proclaimed an earth-shaking message so inhospitable to the laws of motion of capital that it was just as easy to imagine it was carried on a beam of light from the Pleiades star cluster than from a tiny schoolhouse in Pernambuco, Brazil, filled with sugarcane harvesters intent on reading both the word and the world. Is critical pedagogy at this present moment but a fleeting residue of its former association with Paulo Freire, whose pathfinding intervention into the dross and drudgery of the banking model of teaching brought hope and promise to those thirsting for liberation and helped teachers find their backbones in confronting the breathtakingly superficial pageantry of commodity culture and the swindle of neoliberalism that had formed its sacred center in capitalist relations of production, in the commodification of our subjectivity, in the transformation of relations between people into relations between things? Have critical educators been reduced to circuit preachers bullwhipped by their congregations who have stubbornly refused any message that stipulates that they sacrifice the comforts of this world? Has the critical educator, personified by Freire, become the impotent interlocuter of times past, who has now gone to seed in distant pastures. Has Freire become the educational talisman for students to cite, so that they can earn their credentials as criticalists? Is the potent brew of critical consciousness afforded by a pedagogy of the oppressed now just a cup of thin gruel passed from student to student in what remain of critical pedagogy seminars in the age of Trump?

Those are far too cynical questions, in my opinion, yet they deserve a response.

∙ ∙ ∙

If Freire's work has been decaffeinated over the years such that it no longer proves a threat to the ruling class any more than the work of Freire's educational precursors, then why, moments before his inauguration in early 2019, did Brazilian President Jair Bolsonaro tweet, "One of the goals to get Brazil out

© KONINKLIJKE BRILL NV, LEIDEN, 2019

of the worst positions in international education rankings is to combat the Marxist rubbish that has spread in educational institutions." And why, on the campaign trail, did Bolsonaro say that he wanted to "enter the Education Ministry with a flamethrower to remove Paulo Freire" (Bolsonaro to Erase Freire and Feminism from Textbooks, 2019)? Clearly Freire is a figure whose work needs to be reckoned with. If anything, his work is more relevant today than at any other time in its history.

If we look at the Chicago teachers who have recently inspired a national teacher uprising, then surely the critical tradition is holding sway. Whether they identify as Freirean educators or not, these rank-and-file teachers clearly have embraced Freire's spirit in challenging the corporate-driven takeover of public education. Disgruntled and fed up Chicago teachers have made striking respectable again. And they have made teachers excellent role models to follow once again. And what about the cadres who turn out books about or inspired by critical pedagogy? Are they just keeping up with educational fashion? The issues facing humanity are too serious for critical pedagogy to continue as a fashion statement. Clearly, it is the case that critical pedagogy has found a home in America Latina. In fact, writings produced by critical educators are often translated and used as a bulwark against fascism throughout countries spread across the world. While it may seem to some that critical pedagogy does not have a direct link to policy decisions traceable to local, regional or national arenas of education, it has impacted the field of education organically, by serving systematically and habitually as a moral compass for the way we treat each other in the classroom and by contributing to the epistemological, ontological and axiological stances we take in the production of knowledge and how we situate our actions in the larger environmental ecosystems that nourish us. And very often the impact is not necessarily felt in our own geopolitical backyards but in policies and practices developed by educators in other countries.

Critical pedagogy uncovers or otherwise identifies the enduring historical forces in educational discourses, practices, and values. These discourses, practices and values have been transformed over time and their common sense outcome in many instances has been historically relativized to encourage us to see what isn't there. Critical educators polemically reposition their critiques of education in capitalist society according to the contextually specific challenges that are unfolding at significant historical junctures and in doing so engage in dialectical reversals of received common sense such that the strange becomes familiar and the familiar strange. The challenge is to fathom not only why individuals remain ensepulchered within their received ideological formations – sometimes called the prison house of language – despite being presented with unwelcomed truths but also why they participate in the very activities which generate those dangerous truths while maintaining the appearance of being unbiased and open minded. Those of us who use the language of critical pedagogy in our work have been accused by the punishingly self righteous doyens on the right of being manipulated by proponents of "cultural Marxism." Here, the alt right maintains that the books of the Frankfurt School and some postmodernist theorists have allegedly served as ideological "anchor babies" smuggled into university libraries and planted on the shelves by communist sympathizers in order to carry out the unfinished work of the Soviet Union's assault on American freedoms. In other words, critical educators are accused of being knowing participants in the destruction of the United States after the Soviet Union disappeared into the quicksand of history. According to this logic, critical educators are functioning as witting puppets carrying out the orders of their Hidden Master (George Soros? The ghost of Hugo Chávez?) who is unleashing forces of destruction on the free world from some secret hideaway, perhaps located in the Vatican or in the catacombs of Paris.

Someone might intemperately ask at this point: Should an educational philosophy turned pedagogical movement be employed by teachers to challenge unassailably the growth of fascism here in the US and around the world, and shouldn't the bully boy populism of Donald Trump be dealt with at the ballot box rather than by cadres of teachers working from an ethics of social justice? I would simply answer this question with the following provision: If you feel compelled to ask this question, then perhaps teaching is not the right calling for you.

Freire's conceptual categories created by naming the world in order to transform it are always heuristic, and while they cannot capture the totality of the world they are useful in identifying certain important aspects of the world that can be transformed. Freire's work, grounded in a thoroughly Marxist, or dialectical materialist, theory of knowledge is also influenced by his Christian faith. Over time the exhausted epistemics of critical pedagogy have been supplemented by a conceptual polyamory that has tried at times to pull Freire's work more towards the left (revolutionary critical pedagogy) or towards the center (progressive liberal pedagogy). The work being produced in the field of liberation theology (McLaren & Jandrić, in press) puts a singular demand on those who have religious faith, the centerpiece of which is a demand for freedom and social justice. The knowledge co-created among students and among teachers and students working together in critical encounters with freedom is designated for use in developing social justice programs designed to bring structural change in an oppressive society. But what does political praxis in the service of permanent human liberation entail?

It means recognizing that the structure of reality is never permanent and although it is often reified in order to appear to be permanent, that can never really be the case because the structure of reality is never finished. Changing the structure of reality means acknowledging the alterity which permeates the world and understanding that knowledge never reflects the world but always refracts it and we need to take responsibility for this refraction, this reduction of the strangeness of the world to the familiar. In challenging the social relations that structure reality, we necessarily change the very formation of our own selves in the process, and this dialectical exchange flies directly in the face of what many feel about popular religiousness – that it foments helplessness in the face of the "perversity" and "antisolidarity nature" of capitalism and its "absolute insensitivity to the ethical dimension of existence" (Freire, 1997, p. 88). Freire writes:

> The issue around liberation and its practice is not fighting against the religiousness of the popular classes, which is a right of theirs and an expression of their culture, but rather overcoming, *with* it, the vision of a God at the service of the strong for a God on the side of those with whom justice, truth, and love should be. What marked popular religiousness – resignation and annihilation – would be substituted with forms of resistance to outrage, to perversity. This way, submission-faith toward a destiny that would reflect God's will makes way for a spurring faith of loving rebelliousness. In this process, there is an understanding of the body – for those who have evolved in their faith – as the dwelling of sin turns into an intelligence of the body as the temple of God. (1997, p. 103)

Freire is cautious about those who use their faith in situating themselves above the interests of those who lack it. He writes:

> I cannot see how those who so live their faith could negate those who do not live it, and vice versa. If our Utopia is the constant changing of the world and the overcoming of injustice, I cannot refuse the contribution of progressives who have no faith, nor can I be rejected for having it. What must not be accepted in those who proclaim their faith is that they use it at the service of the popular classes' uncriticalness. This is how I have always understood God – a presence in history that does not preclude me from making history, but rather pushes me toward world transformation, which makes it possible to restore the humanity of those who exploit and of the weak. (1997, pp. 103–104)

For Freire, there is an urgency to confront the "pornography of our lives" by denouncing injustice which simultaneously awakens in ourselves and in others, the need and taste for hope. Freire is worth quoting at length on this issue:

> Once more, in Brazilian history, it is urgent for purity to manifest itself against two-faced moralism, and for translucent seriousness to shine through against the audacity of shamelessness. In order to preserve hope, it is necessary to identify also as examples of deterioration the disrespect for popular classes, the indecent salaries paid to teachers in basic education, the lack of respect for public property, the excesses of government, unemployment, destitution, and hunger. These truly constitute the pornography of our lives. And so does discrimination, be it against blacks, women, homosexuals, the indigenous, the fat, the old. It is imperative that we maintain hope even when the harshness of reality may suggest the opposite. On this level, the struggle for hope means the denunciation, in no uncertain terms, of all abuses, schemes, and omissions. As we denounce them, we awaken in others and ourselves the need, and also the taste, for hope. (1997, p. 106)

What, then, is the "pornography of our lives" that we, as critical educators, need to confront on a daily basis? For me, living in the US, it is the struggle against fascism. Throughout history, fascism has often been the default response of those capitalist politicians who fear the economic universe in which they rule is facing an interminable crisis. Or when their sponsorship of the evangelical community – one that normally keeps their base ecstatically compliant and speaking in tongues by promises of a Mar-a-Lago Club afterlife – provokes enough citizens to raise ethical questions surrounding the legitimacy of the prosperity gospel. Dancing with the Stars is one thing, but how about Golfing with the Saints in Neverland, where the golf caddies look like Tinkerbell trussed up in Stormy Daniels dominatrix-style apparel. When politics and religion begins to go this far south, which it has in the U.S., then it's time to have a military parade and a photo of yourself taken cuddling an American flag. Which Trump has done.

Those whom we categorize as filthy rich, who loathe the parasitical poor whom they complain are grubbingly panhandling outside big-box retail stores and CVS pharmacies, frightening the children of the affluent with their blackened teeth and muddy opioid eyes, are especially ripe for fascism because they lack empathy for others' suffering and have no understanding – and no wish to understand – the role that the contradictions of austerity capitalism play in the creation not of trickle down affluence but rather of structured hierarchies of power and privilege.

What could be more pornographic than the Jesus industry being taken over by big-dollar evangelicalism? Or suffering a president whose corrupt business ethics have permeated the entire logic of his presidency? What could be more pornographic than listening to William Consovoy, an attorney for President

Donald Trump, in a hearing before the Second Circuit Court of Appeals in Manhattan, argue that President Donald Trump is immune from prosecution if he literally shoots someone on Fifth Avenue? We live in a pornographic universe where captains of the nation's industry still profess admiration for Ayn Rand, who modelled her capitalist will-to-power hero on a real life serial killer, where Education Secretary Betsy DeVos has said states can decide whether school districts can use federal funds to arm teachers, where the Trump administration's environmental reviews stubbornly acknowledge the extent of today's environmental devastation but minimize the connection between that damage and human-caused emissions, wording policies so as to protect fossil fuel interests, where neo-Nazi and white supremacist organizations are proliferating throughout the country (the far right accounted for 73% of extremist murders in the U.S. between 2009 and 2018, according to information taken from the Anti-Defamation League's Center on Extremism, compared with 23% by Islamic extremists – the result, in part, of a lack of appropriate domestic terror laws that would criminalize being a member of domestic terrorist organizations such as Atomwaffen or Feuerkrieg Division), and where the prosperity gospel of Christian evangelicals led by Franklin Graham, Paula White and Jerry Falwell Jr. have aligned themselves politically with the hate-filled anti-immigrant policies of Donald Trump. When, under such circumstances, we ask ourselves if critical pedagogy has become so dehydrated that it can no longer function as a serious counterpoint to the rise of fascism in the U.S. and worldwide we have to side with Freire, who writes that there can be no critical pedagogy without hope:

> Whatever the perspective through which we appreciate authentic educational practice – gnoseologic, aesthetic, ethical, political – its process implies hope. Unhopeful educators contradict their practice. They are men and women without address, and without a destination. They are lost in history. In an effort to maintain hope alive, since it is indispensable for happiness in school life, educators should always analyze the comings and goings of social reality. These are the movements that make a higher reason for hope possible. (1997, p. 107)

And where we find history being made by us, rather than for us, there is hope.

Critical pedagogy will remain a vital force in shaping the future of our collective commons when teachers assume the role of public intellectuals, of social activists, of political protagonists who are able to work with the insight that what happens inside the classroom cannot be disconnected from what is happening in the local community, the school district, and the wider precincts of democracy, including state and federal levels of governance – all the way to transnational movements for change. In this manner we can include as active, protagonistic agents those 43 teachers in training from Raúl Isidro Burgos Rural Teachers' College, that overlooks the village of Ayotzinapa in the poverty-stricken southern state of Guerrero, Mexico, who were forcibly abducted and then disappeared in Iguala, Guerrero, Mexico, and who have been missing since the night of 26 September 2014. As a critical educator, I admire and support the post-revolutionary educational movement known as the Rural Normal Schools, through which schoolteachers are introduced to critical pedagogy and trained in political organizing in some of Mexico's most impoverished communities. In the 1950s and 1960s, Lucio Cabañas, who founded the Party of the Poor in 1967, studied at Raúl Isidro Burgos Rural Teachers' College. The teacher and guerrilla fighter, Genaro Vázquez, was also a graduate from Ayotzinapa. Misael Núñez Acosta was a graduate of the Rural Normal School in Tenería and in 1979 he founded the Coordinadora Nacional de Trabajadores de la Educación teachers union and was killed two years later. Graduates of the rural schools are trained to educate poor "campesinos" or peasant farmers through a tradition of socialist education. Attacks on students are far from a rare occurrence in Mexico. We cannot forget the hundreds of brave students who were beaten by police and massacred on 2 October 1968, in Tlatelolco square in Mexico City. Or the struggle for land of the Manoba peoples in the Philippines. Or Brazil's landless peasants movement, the Movimento dos Trabalhadores Rurais Sem Terra, or the Abahlali baseMjondolo, or shack-dwellers' movement in South Africa. Or Idle No More, or Black Lives Matter. And there are more, so many more movements.

What is the future of critical pedagogy? The answer can be seen on the streets, on the picket lines, among young and old alike working to save communities assaulted by corruption and neglect and striving amidst great odds to create sanctuary cities for immigrants under assault by the Trump administration's group of fanatical and ruthless aides-de-camp and adjutants, and his Freikorps group of U.S. Immigration and Customs Enforcement agents. And lest we forget, the future of critical pedagogy can also be found in cramped university offices jammed with metal desks and cheap Office Depot swivel chairs, where lecturers, sometimes working as adjuncts and forced to survive on food stamps, write their articles and books and heat up the conversations in seminar rooms, which in turn get reinvented, reappropriated and repurposed by teacher educators, and then teachers, in classrooms across the country and this helps to fuel the process of *conscientização* (conscientization) among students. They are the educators who teach about the 1921 Tulsa Massacre in Tulsa, Oklahoma, when Tulsa's "Black Wall Street" in the Greenwood District, home to black millionaires, was burned down and some estimates put the slaughter of black people – men, woman and children – that day at 300. They teach about the intersectionality of race, class, gender and sexuality without reducing difference to identity. And in so doing they will continue to make history. Young people today are more readily able to distinguish the dangerous cost of choosing a humanizing capitalism over a socialist alternative, and are willing to participate in the mobilization of the working-class rather than to remain content with participating in a reciprocal and balanced relationship between business, labor and the state, with creating better policies rather than an oppositional politics. The future is open for the creation of national working-class parties and critical pedagogy needs to be at the ground level of this revolutionary struggle if it is to remain vital and relevant for the future of humanity. They teach about the Greensboro Massacre, which occurred after the Ku Klux Klan made common cause with the American Nazi Party in North Carolina. On 3 November 1979, the Nazis and Klansmen confronted a group of communist protesters at a rally, brought out pistols, rifles and shotguns from the back trunk of a car, and shot to death five members of the Workers Viewpoint Organization and injured ten others. They teach about movements in the global south, such as the struggle to create popular baccalaureate schools in Argentina. The struggle to create popular baccalaureates – such as the Workers University at IMPA (Industrias Metalúrgicas y Plásticas Argentina) and the Maderera Córdoba, which are housed in factories recovered by the workers (*fábricas recuperadas*) – is no easy task, especially in the current era of neoliberal urbanization. Such a challenge is of vital importance in the ongoing fight for a radical democratic and socialist alternative to the enduring crime of capitalist exploitation that has divided the world between the transnational capitalist class and those who depend upon wage slavery to survive. The creation of popular baccalaureates in Argentina must be seen in the context of unleashing the emancipatory potential of the larger struggle for workers' rights. This struggle cannot and must not make invisible the major contradictions that define today's austerity capitalism–the systematic transfer of wealth from labor to capital which has had a devastating effect on housing, food, health care and education in poor, marginalized communities. In addition, this struggle must necessarily involve a diverse alliance of political and cultural actors that include the workers from the recovered factories, students, teachers, professors, artists, lawyers, government legislators and unionists–all who agree to a politics of "unity in difference" in supporting and strengthening the workers' cooperatives, in creating expropriation laws in favor of workers, in reforming the Bankruptcy Law, in assisting workers in their acquisition of state subsidies to purchase necessary factory equipment and in supporting new innovations in modes of production. Popular baccalaureates that have been born out of the struggle to recover the factories, especially those driven by revolutionary critical pedagogy, make explicit their resistance to capitalist exploitation and foster a strong link between learning and praxis. It is a emancipatory praxis that employs theater, music, cultural activities, community-building, and critical literacy – as well as an emphasis on science and mathematics taught under an ethical stipulation that all learning be dedicated to improving the lives of the population in a world threatened by planetary extinction. This work could not be accomplished without the valiant efforts of groups of teachers, workers, community members and other supporters in forging an alliance that gives both the youth and their families the opportunity to exercise their creative capacities in becoming critical citizens who can dream beyond the limits imposed on them by the neoliberal state.

So far critical pedagogy has shown itself to be durable and enduring. It will survive and continue to develop in the coming years, as the struggle for a democratic socialism becomes more fierce and fraught with danger. In this, one of the darkest hours of our national life, critical educators take no pleasure in censuring the most desperate and loathsome designs of neoliberal administrations, designs fueled by the political bloodlust of a bourgeoisie in crisis, designs that can only be described as a tryst with the devil. What defeats we have experienced recently are not irremediable, are not inevitable. Critical educators have come to recognize that only by sheltering the persecuted, and only by creating the conditions of possibility for new and emancipatory forms of praxis in all spaces of human sociability can we obtain as a people a new birth of freedom.

Acknowledgment

This chapter originally appeared as P. McLaren, The future of critical pedagogy, *Education Philosophy and Theory*, 52(12) (2019), 1243–1248. Reprinted here, with minor edits, with permission from the publisher.

References

Bolsonaro to erase Paulo Freire and feminism from textbooks. (2019, February 19). *TeleSur*. https://www.telesurenglish.net/news/Bolsonaro-To-Erase-Paulo-Freire-and-Feminism-From-Textbooks-20190212-0018.html

Freire, P. (1997). *Pedagogy of the heart* (D. Macedo & A. Oliveira, Trans.). Continuum.

McLaren, P., & Jandric, P. (in press). *Postdigital dialogues on critical pedagogy, liberation theology and information technology*. Bloomsbury Publishing, Inc.

Peter McLaren in Orange, California, 2020 (photograph by Wang Yan)

Printed in the United States
by Baker & Taylor Publisher Services